Secul

Also available from Continuum

Consuming Religion, Vincent J. Miller

The Continuum Companion to Religion and Film, Edited by William L. Blizek

Graven Images, edited by Christine Hoff Kraemer and A. David Lewis

Pop Cult, Rupert Till

The Springfield Reformation, Jamey Heit

Secular Steeples

Popular Culture and the Religious Imagination

2nd edition

by
Conrad Ostwalt

BLOOMSBURY
LONDON • NEW DELHI • NEW YORK • SYDNEY

Bloomsbury Academic
An imprint of Bloomsbury Publishing Plc

50 Bedford Square	175 Fifth Avenue
London	New York
WC1B 3DP	NY 10010
UK	USA

www.bloomsbury.com

First published 2012

British Library Cataloguing-in-Publication Data
A catalogue record for this book is available from the British Library.

ISBN: HB: 978-1-4411-5617-4
        PB: 978-1-4411-7286-0

Library of Congress Cataloging-in-Publication Data
Ostwalt, Conrad Eugene, 1959-
Secular steeples : popular culture and the religious imagination / Conrad Ostwalt. -- 2nd edition.
pages cm
Includes bibliographical references and index.
ISBN 978-1-4411-5617-4 (hardcover) -- ISBN 978-1-4411-7286-0 (pbk.) -- ISBN 978-1-4411-8341-5
(ebook (epub)) -- ISBN 978-1-4411-2314-5 (ebook (pdf))
1. Popular culture--Religious aspects. 2. Religion and culture. 3. Secularism. I. Title.

BL65.C8O88 2012
201'.7--dc23

2012005875

Typeset by Fakenham Prepress Solutions, Fakenham, Norfolk, NR21 8NN
Printed and bound in India

to
Mary and Heather
for
everything

Contents

Acknowledgments

American secular culture is saturated with religion and religious messages. I am not sure if I arrived at this conclusion through my academic reflection or because my youth was dominated by religious and moral teachings and primed me to view the world in this way. Nevertheless, I believe the unique history of America has encouraged a culture that is at once thoroughly secular in its organization while essentially religious in its orientation. I began years ago to explore this dual character of culture through my teaching and writing. This book continues that investigation.

I began formal research for this book during the autumn of 1996. I thank Appalachian State University for a semester off at that time to pursue my initial research. This work eventually led to the publication of *Secular Steeples* in 2003, and I thank all those who have read the manuscript and used it in courses since then. In particular, I thank the students from Warner Pacific College for their thoughtful use of the First Edition through the years. Further, the editors at Continuum have contributed significantly to the Second Edition—in particular, Lalle Pursglove has seen this work to completion after Kirsty Schaper first envisioned and commissioned the Second Edition—Rachel Eisenhauer and Kim Storry have provided guidance throughout. As the Second Edition evolved, several people acted as inquisitors and helped shape some of the new work: Garrett Draper and John Michael Cord pushed me on Whitehead; David Smith challenged me to think about the emerging tradition and utopian cultures; the Pathways Sunday School Class allowed me to play provocateur; Mike Vines helped me formulate some of my ideas and provided feedback and correction; Brad and Sue provided inspiration and information on sacred space; Boots and Red provided insight to motorcycle culture; Oldie Goldie helped me think in new ways about time and space; Wiggles helped me clear my head.

My teachers and colleagues continue to shape my work in ways that I do not even fully realize. Drs. Grant Wacker, Wesley Kort, Christy Lohr Sapp, Peter Kaufman, Joel Martin, and Carolyn J. Medine have helped me through the years. More recently, Dean Anthony Calamai has provided support for my work at Appalachian State University and moral support as a friend. The faculty members in the Department of Philosophy and Religion have been instrumental in my work in one way or another through the years.

I am grateful to my previous publishers for permission to use or to reprint previously published work. Some of this work is reprinted in edited or altered form. Appropriate acknowledgement is given in notes.

These works include "After Eden: The Secularization of American Space in the Fiction of Willa Cather and Theodore Dreiser (Bucknell University Press, 1989); "Screening the Sacred: Religion, Myth, and Ideology in Popular American Film, ed. Joel Martin and Conrad Ostwalt (Westview Press, 1995); and "Love Valley: An American Utopia" (Popular Press, 1998), reprinted by permission of the University of Wisconsin Press. In addition to drawing in general upon these sources, some material is reproduced by permission. "North Carolina Humanities," "The Southern Literary Journal," "The Journal of Religion and Film," and "Currents" have all granted permission to use previously published material and work.

As always, Mary and Heather give me joy and hope; love and care; happiness and inspiration; beauty and grace. Through them, I have come to see the world differently, and it is a much brighter place because of their presence in my life. They have taught me what is important and what is not; they have modeled tenacity and strength and purpose of being. I owe them everything, and I dedicate this work and my life to them.

Conrad Ostwalt
Appalachian State University
December 21, 2011

1

Popular culture, the religious imagination, and the evolution of God: A new metaphysics

During the first two decades of the twentieth century, a group of ingenious young physicists were remaking the way scientists and philosophers would understand reality. Niels Bohr, Werner Heisenberg, and others were pressing ahead with "quantum" thinking, building on the revolutionary work of Albert Einstein. Their work questioned the old certainties of Sir Isaac Newton's mechanistic world where causation and determination ruled science and theology. The new thinking had little room for certitude and, in its place, physicists began to think in terms of probabilities and uncertainty. At the same time, a mathematician-turned-logician-turned-metaphysician was trying to establish a philosophical foundation for this new physics. Alfred North Whitehead wrote to create a metaphysical basis for the new reality of the quantum world. New ways of thinking emerged as part of the postmodern agenda of the late twentieth century, and the result was, at one and the same time, a world where God could be declared dead yet also could be freed from the shackles of old thinking. If God were to exist in the quantum world, it could no longer be a God of causation or even an ultimate ground of being. Rather, God must be thought of as "becoming" and reality as "novelty."[1] God had been liberated by the quantum theorists, not buried, and process theologians began to press the question of God given the new metaphysical limitations.

Of course, theological orthodoxies die harder deaths than do scientific ones. And, as Newton's laws still describe the workings of the world quite well for most purposes, so does traditional theology cling to a Sovereign God to explain metaphysical questions. But process theory began to nag at the traditionalists because for some it seemed that an evolving God best fit what we now think about the workings of reality. In any event, a new metaphysics crept toward the twenty-first century with ways of thinking that accepted blurred distinctions between previously separate and delineated worlds. The sacred realms melded into the profane in ways they had not since the Enlightenment. The metaphysical and physical realms were sometimes joined at the theoretical level, making scientists and philosophers alike uncomfortable. Meanwhile, popular culture began to reclaim metaphysical categories, which the Enlightenment had pushed into the realm of the irrational. Physical and metaphysical, sacred and profane, spiritual and material realms began once again to comingle, and the boundaries between them began to blur. It is this blurring of boundaries that this book explores in the realm of popular culture. The blurred intersections of the sacred and the secular come together and inform one another in ways that are not always apparent and in ways that break down the separation of subject and object.

If we accept the blurring of sacred and secular realms, as I argue popular culture has already done, and if we strike a blow to determinism as the new physics has already done, then we are left with a metaphysical world that not only does not determine the physical world but is affected by its interaction with the physical. Causation either does not exist, or if it does, exists in two directions, with the sacred affecting the secular and vice versa. In popular culture we have already accepted the notion that God is affected by the profane rather than being an uninfluenced cause. To the extent that sacred and secular culture have been intertwined and correlated in the twentieth and twenty-first centuries, God is in dialectical relationship with the world and is expressed omnipresently in the culture. Secular culture reveals sacred reality, and sacred reality adopts the profane world.

This postmodern, blurred landscape, where all the old verities are anachronistic or are at least doubted, did not arise overnight (as it seems the new physics did) but has resulted from a long history of secularization in Western culture that I outline in chapter 2. For now, suffice it to say that the new physics, which threatened to abolish the distinction between subject and object, has given us a physical basis for metaphysical distinction where subject and object as distinct from one another no longer makes sense. As such, the concept of a God distinct from creatures or a sacred realm distinct from a secular one also embraces anachronistic principles that fail to recognize the dynamic center of twenty-first-century views of reality. In order to understand the dynamic principle of culture upon which this book is built, one must first accept a dynamic and dialectical view of the sacred principle—one must view God as becoming.

God as becoming

When Whitehead established the notion of God as becoming, he gave theology the impetus to liberate God from outdated metaphysical constructions of reality and perhaps save God from irrelevance in a scientific age. The main point of many of the new atheists is that the traditional concept of God is small and unnecessary given contemporary advances in science. If science has not already answered all the questions religion at one time attempted to answer, then it will in a matter of time. Perhaps this critique points to a truth—not that there is no God, but that God understood primarily in a Newtonian sense is too small for a quantum world. Many critics, and many believers for that matter, understand God to be an unchanged and unchangeable first Cause whose existence must be proven like Newton's laws of motion can be demonstrated. But this necessity of proof misses the mark, whether it comes from skeptics or believers, because thinking about God in this way does not give us the necessary language or images to understand God in a quantum world. Causal, mechanistic, literal language is not wide or deep enough to give adequate representation or understanding of God. In order to understand a dynamic God of becoming rather than a static God of being, we must employ language that itself is more flexible and malleable rather than literal and scientific. We must reach back behind the scientific revolution and reclaim a religious language of vitality that has been lost since the Enlightenment. We must reclaim metaphorical language as real, vital, and "truthful." Metaphor is the key to understanding the sacred in a secular age.

The God metaphor: the process of becoming God

Joseph Campbell taught us the power of metaphor and demonstrated that much of what religion oversees is a "concretization of … the metaphoric perspective."[2] When concretization occurs, religion loses it mystery. Campbell challenges us to recapture the metaphoric perspective. Campbell's point is important, and it is the perspective that I have adopted for coming to recognize the sacred. The way to come to know God is a process actualized through metaphorical thinking. Likewise, God, in metaphorical process, is coming into being through our heightened language. The sacred becomes real when actualized through metaphor, through story, and through the metaphorical products of our culture. This is where the sacred and secular intersect, precisely because most of those metaphorical products come couched as secular culture: books, movies, music, and the like. This is how the sacred, the ineffable, is made known through metaphor. If metaphor is "an implicit comparison, something presented as if it were something else, for what that substitution can reveal about the original"[3] as Richard Gollin defines it, then metaphor becomes, by default, the language of the ineffable. How can scientific or literal language express that which is inexpressible and beyond categorization or description? Metaphorical language occurs whenever one thing represents another thing in order to illustrate it in figurative fashion or when one thing represents another thing that either cannot be understood using literal language or can be understood more richly with figurative.

The key, it seems to me, to reading and understanding what the Bible says about God is to understand the Bible largely as metaphor. When the Bible talks about God, the ineffable, the Bible speaks through metaphor. Metaphor is the flame of the burning bush, the heart of God's self-identifying "I am," the substance of Jesus's parables ("I am the true vine . . ."). When we understand this, we free God from the literal prison that defines him so narrowly as to make him irrelevant. This is the sepulcher that traditionalists and atheists alike have constructed for God.

Much of science, both the hard sciences and the social sciences, understands God in the latter, narrow, literal sense—so does Christian fundamentalism and anyone who insists on a literal reading of the Bible. Thus, science claims to uncover the nonexistence of God (skeptics like Richard Dawkins) and fundamentalism simply makes God a relic. But the god that science makes nonexistent and the god that fundamentalism makes into a museum piece come alive with relevance as the God of metaphor. I can agree with the atheists who say: Science has made the traditional concept of God seem small and unnecessary and has proven that this God does not exist. But perhaps the God they presume from much of traditional theology was never meant to exist, or, if so, existed in a particular time and context. It is the mechanistic God whose oversight has been downsized by scientific theory. The beauty of seeing God through the eyes of metaphor is that it allows God to "change," to evolve, and to expand. It allows God to be understood through poetry rather than through Newton's equations. In the movie *Contact*, Dr. Arroway, a scientist and skeptic played by Jodie Foster, had no words when she was sent into space and saw the grandeur and beauty of the universe. Arroway comments that, instead of a scientist, they should have sent a poet. A poet, the master of metaphor, provides us the key to understanding God as metaphor so that God is never fully known and thus never fossilized but rather is becoming known and being revealed.

Metaphor is not an inferior way of knowing something—in fact it is stronger and superior to other forms of figurative language and even literal language. For example, if I say to my son-in-law, "You are like a son to me," I pay him a great compliment. But if I say to him, "You are a son to me," I accept him into the family, a much greater act of grace. The first is a simile, the second metaphor— one can sense the greater power of the metaphorical in this example. Or, if I say, "The sky is blue," I have constructed a simple descriptive sentence that is valuable to someone wanting to know the color of the sky. But if I say, "The sky is a cerulean canopy," I have added to the basic description an attempt to provide meaning that is illusive without figurative language. Of course this statement is factually false but attempts to describe the transcendent appearance of the sky above. To be factually correct, I might try saying "the sky appears blue because gases in the atmosphere absorb and scatter light the wavelength of blue." The factual account provides a certain type of information, but metaphor is powerful in its inexactness, in its heightened language, in its desire to express the ineffable. Metaphor exists in the gap between the ineffable and literal description, and it is in that gap that meaning resides.

Relational knowing (or coming to know)

What does it mean to say that metaphor exists in the gap wherein meaning resides, and what are the consequences to cultural theology of such an understanding? Metaphor is comparison and, as such, it is defined through relationship: of objects; of concepts; of images; of people. In metaphorical language, we experience a linguistic relationship that understands one thing or being in a relationship in light of the other thing or being in a relationship. The metaphorical thus involves a dynamic understanding. Likewise, dialogue involves communication that is based on dynamic and relational under- standing. True dialogue exists only in a relationship where one is willing and open to being changed by the dialogue partner. This contrasts to debate where words are meant to affect a change in the debate antagonist or to defeat the debate opponent. True dialogue, then, is based on relational knowing that forges a dynamic and evolving "coming to know" between dialogue partners. We see this dynamic in virtually every successful human relationship. For example, children are not only formed and forged through interaction with parents, but parents likewise are affected and changed through interaction with children. If one extends this notion of relational knowing to God, then we can see that relationship with God (something that many believers claim and is understood here as true dialogue) means not only that the believer will be changed by God but that God is changed through relationship with the individual. If it were otherwise, God would be static, unyielding, approaching irrelevance through increasing distance from an evolving creation. Rather, through this understanding of relational knowing, of metaphoric dialogue, God the ineffable can be made known, but this knowing must be in terms of a process of being understood through intimate relationship that changes both parties. When we arrive at this dialogical model, then we can begin to construct a metaphysics that can undergird the visions of reality being suggested by theoretical physics. If we maintain the vision of a static God based on literal language and debate-style orthodoxies, then we will run the risk of maintaining a theology of irrelevance in a quantum world.

This view of relational or processional knowing based on metaphorical language and dialogue frees God from the literal and mechanistic standards of the past—this view allows God the luxury of novelty and creativity and to enter into true dialogical relationship with creation. This gives God over to serendipity and sacrifices the old standards of certainty, but uncertainty is the price of relationship, and uncertainty seems to be a given of the new understanding of reality anyway. So relational knowing simply gives theology a way of describing and understanding the ineffable that allows God to retain metaphysical standing in a quantum world. Whatever we understand about relationship with God, whether we are moving toward God or God moves toward creation, or both, such movement in time or space means that God changes (relatively) in relation to humanity or to creation. Such a shift in understanding God does not mean that God simply becomes relative in the sense that relativity means unnecessary. Rather, God is moving toward us (God changes in relation to us) and in this sense exists and relates relative to our lives and our struggles. Neither does this mean that God is untrustworthy or unpredictable—rather, it means that God trusts us (gave us free will) and asks for our trust in return. In all these ways, God exists in relation to our changing selves and thus God changes in relation to our changing selves. God evolves, and we can come to know God through relation, dialogue, and metaphor. As a result, we know God though time in a variety of ways.

We can illustrate knowing God through dialogue rather than debate through a pair of metaphors. I would suggest that, throughout most of Christian history, we have been taught to know God through debate. Traditional theology, orthodoxy, preaching, and teaching tend to use the debate model to convince non-believers of the one Truth. Imagine that God and the non-believer are marble pillars, strong in their inflexibility, immoveable in their position, ready to debate and defend their position. If force is applied to the two pillars in order to move them toward one another, they will crumble and fall before yielding ground. Now imagine that God and the non-believer are bamboo poles, strong in their flexibility, bending toward one another as dialogue partners rather than debate opponents. The two bamboo poles will bend but not break. If we can imagine God in dialogue with individuals, perhaps also we can imagine God in dialogue with culture, bending toward it, speaking to and through it, revealing divine truth in relation to culture, and coming into being through culture's language and metaphors.

Towards a theology of culture

Theos and logos—the study of God; the word of God; the reason of God; "Words" about God. Given these definitions, theology is an abstraction. We need to change the perspective, or, in this case, change the preposition. Rather than theology being "words about God" (human abstractions), or even "word of God" (static abstractions), why not understand it as "words from God" or "reasons from God" or even "matters of importance or matters for discussion from God." Change perspective from abstract to active. When theology is understood as "words from God," we allow God to speak to the world into an ongoing creative process, we allow God to be in the process of becoming and moving to us (in John, chapter 1), we move theology away from abstraction and toward action, and we move theology away from the abstract and toward praxis. God speaks to humanity in relation to culture and in dialogue with culture, opening up to and moving toward creation and evolving with humanity. If theology is understood primarily in terms of praxis, then relational knowing must not only occur between God and the individual, developing individual spirituality, but also between the Church and culture, creating a type of cultural spirituality as well. Theology as praxis demands that the Church interact with popular culture, to change and be changed through this interaction.

Is this book then a theology?—certainly not in the sense that the book promotes right belief about God (orthodoxy or orthodox dogma as theology). Nor does this book claim to provide any enlightening new insights about God that have not already been offered. This book simply asks questions about God in relation to culture. This is an extrapolation, an exercise in "What if …" thinking about God. In this sense, this book provides a theology that suggests not only "matters for discussion from or to God" but also accepts "uncertainties from God" as an appropriate theological exercise. Even if I write in the declarative, I do so to uncover questions, not provide answers. So I am engaging the reader and even God in a dialogue in the best sense of the meaning of that word—a dialogue that seeks to be relational.[4] I hope that readers and all those engaged in dialogue with God will do so in the spirit of bending toward the other in mutual understanding.

Some components of a theology of culture that depart from traditional theology

Creation, theodicy, omnipotence, redemption, unchanging God

Debates between Darwinian scientists and Creationists or Intelligent Designers have shown us that theologians and scientists debating is a contrived exercise, going nowhere. I suggest giving up the debate with science. Give science its due—Darwinian evolutionary theory really is the best empirical explanation for understanding the diversity and complexity of life on the planet. If we stop long enough to think about the argument, I think we'll discover the following:

The reason some scientists celebrate and many Christians fear that Darwin removes the necessity for God (for some this leads to atheism; for some Christians, evidence of Darwin's atheism!) is the concept of random variation—randomness is the linchpin. Both the atheist and the most strident proponent of Intelligent Design are actually in agreement: belief in God demands belief in supernatural design for natural phenomena, but the atheist sees no evidence of this and proponents of Intelligent Design cannot imagine a reality based on *contingency* rather than *necessity*.

But what happens if we jettison the notion of a *necessary* God, an unchanging God, a static God—what if, in other words, we accept the notion of a *contingent* God, that is a God whose existence is contingent upon his interactions with a creation in the process of being realized—such a God exists only in relation to creation and is open to becoming what is good in response to an evolving and changing creation. Such a God is allowed freedom and creativity to respond to a constantly evolving and developing creation with love and possibility. Such a God is contingent upon the random changes that take place every day when a new creature inhabits a changing creation. Such a God responds one way because a random set of events changes the process and nature of history, and such a free God would respond yet another way had another set of events resulted in another historical process.

What a radical notion—set God free—release God from the shackles of creeds and dogmas that demand God act a certain way or cease to be God. What arrogance we exhibit when we suggest that God be such and such a way or else— what is this, if not the creation of God in our own image?

But the free God, the God who can respond randomly to a randomly changing evolutionary creative process, constitutes a God who is the God of serendipity and grace, a God of metaphor, a God who cannot be pinned down by our limited human need to quantify and verify and prove. Does God really need for us to prove divine existence? Fundamentalists and scientists are alike in their need for verification and proof—the first deriving proof from exercises of reason (however flawed) based upon certain presuppositions (however narrow); the latter deriving proof from observations (however imperfect and subjective) to test hypotheses (however unlikely). BUT both need proof and discard all other competing visions that challenge that truth unless reason or observation creates another acceptable truth. While these approaches to understanding reality work, they are limited ways of thinking and living in the world—limited in that only Fact can be conceived of as Truth.

Darwin disproves God only if God is literal, historical, and imprisoned by our inabilities to see beyond what we are and what we imagine truth to be. Allow God to escape this prison through the liberating principle found in metaphor; embrace the peripatetic nature of God, who is open to and operates through serendipity; grow with a God who embraces growth and change; consider the notion that God changes randomly through relation to his creation to be a comforting, sensible, and real way of conceiving God. If God is truly free, and if humanity is free, and if creation is in the process of coming into being, then God, freely responding and relating to a free creation, must be contingent upon the random and free choices of creation just as creatures are contingent upon the serendipitous and peripatetic nature of God. Such contingency, rather than a necessary God of history, frees not only God but creation to evolve and become. God, thus, is Becoming rather than Being; and creation is evolving rather than evolved.

Traditional theology usually is predicated on the notion of God's omnipotence and sovereignty (two different notions that are sometimes collapsed into the same category). It is hard to imagine Christian theology without God's ultimate power and control at its base, yet it is equally hard to imagine ultimate power in light of twentieth- and twenty-first-century physics. Could it be that we need to rethink what theology has to say about power and sovereignty in light of more recent theories about reality? Could it be that the ideas of omnipotence and sovereignty are human projections placed upon God that have imprisoned God to our notions about divine role and function?

Throughout the history of Christian theology, and indeed in much popular theology, God's power seems to come down to a case of "all or nothing"—either God is all powerful (omnipotent) or God does not exist, at least not as God (God would not be God if God were not all-powerful). Is there a need to rescue God from this label of omnipotence? What does omnipotence mean in a world (as it is defined by science) that lacks absolute answers or laws that govern reality—is this a divine characteristic that has lost its relevance?

It seems that there should be a way of talking about power (even divine power) given a relative scale rather than an absolute one. Relative to humanity, for all practical purposes, God is ultimately powerful, seemingly infinitely more so than human beings. Relative to all of creation, perhaps, God is powerful beyond imagination, many multitudes of power beyond anything else imaginable. Relative to evil, God is vastly more powerful and will eventually exert dominance over the evil powers that torment creation now. But is this the same thing as omnipotence, and can we talk about God being powerful without the traps omnipotence lays upon theology?

Surely God cannot be contrary to rationality, thus, God cannot create free beings yet exert Sovereignty over them, nor can he give created beings power over choice while remaining omnipotent. So for practical purposes, the ideas of sovereignty and omnipotence can never be more than "Ideals" if theology insists on human free will, and, of course, not all theologies insist on human free will. But, if we accept that God gives human beings and creation free will, then we have already denied God's omnipotence and sovereignty: If God has limited sovereignty over creation for the sake of free will, unchallenged sovereignty cannot exist. Also, omnipotence cannot exist since God cannot at one and the same time reign supreme and unlimited yet yield to human free will and the right (or gift) of self-determination. Yet, if we allow God to wield power to ultimately reign over the Kingdom of God, or to defeat evil, hate, and injustice with goodness, love, and justice, then we can speak of God's power in such a way that inspires awe and wonder but that does not require the theological trap of omnipotence.

In a universe marked by relative states of being, random events, and uncertainty, the infusion of an ultimate Ideal perhaps needs to be restated in a way that corresponds more to our current understanding of reality. Can we say that God is the most powerful entity in creation and over creation but that even God is not omnipotent? Does this make God any less God? And might we understand that God's power and grandeur, relative to human weakness and frailty, is on such an unimaginable scale that God appears omnipotent, and for all practical purposes is ultimately powerful; however, pure omnipotence is neither conceivable nor consistent with a theology of human free will.[5]

What would be the purpose of this? For one, it solves the dilemma that is theodicy. If God is not omnipotent, the dilemma disappears, for, since God is not all-powerful, God cannot guarantee a creation that is perfect and just. Evil is a powerful force as well, and Christians believe that God will ultimately triumph over evil. But to give God the attribute of omnipotence and then to face the reality of evil in the world simply invites some unsettling conclusions for theology. The dilemma raised by theodicy is a challenge to omnipotence that cannot simply be dismissed by hiding behind the notion of "divine mystery" every time a dilemma raises its head. It usually turns out that we raise the notion of "mystery" to explain why our logic cannot support our presuppositions. Rather than rethink our presuppositions or practice better logic, we hide behind the veil of the ineffable.

There is yet another advantage to trying to understand God's power on a relative scale. If God's power is so vastly greater than human power as to approach infinity, then, by scale, difference among human beings approaches such an infinitely small scale as to become meaningless. Thus, what we perceive to be great injustice among us and among the world's population pales in a divine perspective. It is therefore left to humans to accept the responsibility to solve this world's problems rather than wondering why God is not bringing about a just world. It is the responsibility of human beings to build a social structure that is just and good, so we should work unceasingly for such a society rather than appeal for supernatural intervention or apocalypse or any other type of transcendent solution to cover our failure.

If we apply this same reasoning of relative scale to the concept of righteousness or goodness, then we have another theological dilemma solved. It is difficult to reconcile God's grace with God's justice. All sorts of spiritual accountings have been employed to explain salvation in a way that makes God's grace absolute while not upsetting God's sense of judgment. But these dilemmas come about only if we see God's judgment and grace as absolute. Let's say, for the sake of argument, that God's sense of justice is relatively so much greater than human sense of justice and that God's grace is relatively so much more expansive than human grace that they appear absolute and infinite to the human perspective. If, however, the relative difference between divine and human grace is the driving force, then God's grace is relatively so much greater than ours that the differences in individuals when it comes to justice, goodness, and grace are inconsequential from a divine perspective. In this scenario, there are no infinite chasms to overcome, only relative difference. In such a system, we should not be outraged by the notion that God would save all of creation, including all human beings, since this would not outrage God's sense of justice (from the divine perspective, the difference among creatures is infinitesimally small although such difference might seem of great significance to us). By the same token, it would be equally reasonable for all creatures to be lost since differences in grace and goodness would also be infinitesimally small from a divine perspective. This is why we have a theology of grace and hope—so that our hope in God's grace and goodness leads to salvation and redemption rather than condemnation. By any measure, we place that hope squarely on divine grace.

It is important to at least consider these challenges to traditional theology if a theology of culture is to work. For at heart, a theology of culture must take seriously how the world, worldviews, intellectual achievement, technology, and human advance make the contemporary world vastly different from the ancient. It follows that the creatures that inhabit this different planet must be different themselves, in fundamental ways of relating to reality and understanding reality.

And if we understand God to be in relationship to the creatures of this world, then God, too, must be different, changing, and evolving.

Freeing God

By the end of the eighteenth century, Newtonian physics had explained the universe in mechanistic fashion. The beauty of planetary motion lay bare in Newton's mathematics, and the universe was predictable, precise, and certain. Is it any surprise then, that God was also understood in this fashion? For traditionalists, God was predictable, precise, and certain. For deists, God was predictable, even calculable, through divine calculus and equation. God had become a superb machinist, devising a mechanical model for the universe run through universal and unimpeachable laws. Was it Newton or God who authored the Third Law of motion? Newtonian physics gave us a worldview that suited traditional theology very well: God authored the universe and eternal laws that cannot be violated. Physics had God cornered, imprisoned by divine laws that we could isolate, manipulate, and immortalize. And once the physical laws were established, it was an easy step to make the same claims concerning moral law, natural law, and ethical precept. If God's physical laws are predictable and immortal, so too must be moral and religious law—immutable truths are part of God's plan in Newton's universe, and those truths can be deduced from the highly mechanized and intricately planned nature of the universe.

Thus, it should really be no surprise that Darwin's bombshell so drastically threatened the prevailing Christian theological worldview. Not only did Darwin remove humanity from the lofty position of the "created favorite" (humanity becomes a part of creation, not the pinnacle of the created order), but Darwin also popularized the notion of random variation. Darwin's theories put forth naturalistic explanations such as "random variation," which seem to have removed from the process of creation any element of design. Thus, random variation became a challenge to Christian theology which depended not on chance but on planned and supernatural creative processes. According to Darwin, the created order as we know it exists because of "randomness," not a design, intelligent or otherwise. How could this be? Newton's universe obviously points to a design and a designer; Newton's physics presupposes predictability, not random variables; traditional theology and even deist theology depended upon immutable laws and truths, not mutable variations in nature. Darwin, according to traditional theology, just did not make sense, and theological presuppositions about the nature of God were not big enough to include this notion of random variation.

For a while, theology responded either by surrendering to science, rebutting and rejecting science, or by rejecting faith. The challenge to theology continued through the twentieth century as Darwinism became accepted in public education although often challenged in the courts. By the late twentieth century, Darwinism versus creationism became one of the battles of the ongoing "Culture Wars" between "Christian fundamentalism" and "secularism." As fundamentalists pressed the cause and tried to have creationism accepted as alternate science in public schools, science struck back, first in the courts and then through critics such as Richard Dawkins. From the faith perspective, writers such as Francis Collins have tried to find a common ground where science and religion do not have to be at odds in an either–or confrontation. The biology challenge joined with the physics of the twentieth century and demanded that theology reevaluate. Perhaps theology must accept that randomness helps us to understand how the universe comes into being, and that randomness points to creativity on God's part. Randomness does, however, force theologians to rethink what is meant by "created order." It forces a change of worldview that must have implications for theology if theology wishes to remain relevant. Rather than "created order" (past tense, complete, and immutable), theology needs to think in terms of "creative disorder" (ongoing, incomplete, and mutable). Then perhaps theologians and biologists can talk productively.

However, as much as nineteenth-century biology challenged Christian theology, there exists a more significant challenge that has not been fully realized in theological, or at least ecclesiastical, circles. Twentieth-century physics challenges much of Newtonian certainty and precision. Relativity and quantum mechanics shatter Newtonian mechanistic certainty. We still appreciate Newton every time we fly in a jet or ride a roller coaster; however, we now live in a world where we must think in terms of relativity rather than absolutes; uncertainty rather than certainty; statistical probabilities rather than proven necessities. We live in a world that is connected at levels we cannot see or feel. We live in a world where actions and events are affected by eventualities in extreme portions of the universe. We live in a strange world, a superluminal world, and our theology must respond to the challenges of the new physics. This new world is one constructed on relational relativity, and this is the model I have suggested for understanding God. God exists in relative relation to humanity; God reveals through relative relation to culture; God creates in relative relation to creation; God rules in relative relation to the divine kingdom; God's love is experienced in relative relation to a beloved universe; God's grace is becoming in relative relation to the redeemed order.

By relativity in this sense, I do not mean simply a collection of relative moral precepts that many critics of postmodernism want to claim as part of the postmodernist structure. Rather I mean that God exists and works relative to creation, not in absolute disconnection from it (radical transcendence). By relation I do not mean the popular "Jesus is my friend" proclamation but rather the deep relational connection that exists in the interconnectedness of the reality structure. God becomes God through responding to creation, bending toward it, rather than through some Cartesian division of the transcendent realm from the imminent.

A theology of culture can be modeled after the physics controversies of the early twentieth century. As physicists attempted to deal with the quantum world, Einstein and Bohr staked out two positions. Bohr was the pragmatist who admitted that, even though we may never be able to understand the quantum world, quantum theory could be used for prediction of reality on a quantum level. Einstein objected and offered a realist alternative. Einstein argued that it is possible to understand the underlying truth of the universe but that we would need to change accepted paradigms and categories to arrive at better ways to envision and understand truth.[6] Likewise, in a theology of culture, one can proceed with a pragmatic or realist position. The pragmatist would suggest that one can never understand God but that culture and theology can help us approximate paradigms for expressing God. The realist would insist that God's truth can be appropriated; however, one must be willing to change the paradigms in order to grasp truth as our understanding improves and evolves. Either way, a theology of culture provides the laboratory for testing these paradigms and advancing knowledge.

A theology of culture

Culture might be understood as a dynamic collection of human artifacts, products, creative endeavors, and ways of relating in socially dynamic settings. Literature, art, music, yes, but also human relationships make up culture. Culture is dynamic and is a way of communicating those ideals and virtues and values that motivate us to strive and to live and to love. Culture is high and culture is low; it is elitist and it is popular. And in all things, it is at the center of what defines our context, our particular situation and time and place. And right at the center of culture lies religion, a contextual human construction bound by time and place that seeks to understand our most cherished value traditions in the context of a frame of reference that we consider "ultimate" or "transcendent" or "pure." Since theology is a product of human culture and is context-bound as well, it makes sense to allow theology to develop in dynamic interaction with the current cultural matrix. This does not mean that theology needs to bow to culture or to surrender theological values to cultural ones, and this does not mean theology needs to surrender its prophetic voice. On the contrary, placing theology in dynamic tension with culture ensures a lively prophetic role for the theologian who is in dialogue with cultural mores.

"Understanding culture through the concept of otherness": the holy and un-holy—two sides of the same coin

Otherness describes a philosophical concept, sometimes called the "constitutive Other," which describes an entity or concept that opposes some different entity or concept. The idea of the other is traced to Georg Wilhelm Friedrich Hegel,[7] and, as a philosophical category, otherness helps define what culture believes about a person, a category, a group, or a concept. For example, one person's idea of someone as "other" tells us how one defines oneself. Likewise, if one sees another culture as "other," then those attributes of the culture that are identified as other tell us what that person perceives to be "not other" about his or her own culture. So when we designate something as "different," we are really defining self and attributes of the culture we recognize as our own.

When we designate something or someone as "other," we set it apart, often with the intent (conscious or not) of subjugating, subordinating, or condemning—this is called othering. After all, from a psychological or sociological view, it would be against self-interest to identify something as other and then recognize it as superior. So, more often than not, othering is also accompanied by value statements about the relative worth of the other in relation to the self. This process provides positive self-identity through the negative judgment of the other. I will refer to it as "negative othering," the act of designating something as other with accompanying negative value judgment in order to allow positive judgment of the self.

We can also talk about positive othering—the act of designating something as other with accompanying positive value judgment of the other in relation to the self. When we designate "the other" as superior to the self, we are essentially defining something that is "extra-human," divine, or God. This process I will refer to as "positive othering," the act of designating a reality as superior in relation to the self. This line of thought can be traced philosophically to Emmanuel Levinas, who defined the other as radically other and transcendent (such as symbolic order and language). Furthermore, this line of thought has been applied to traditional religion by Rudolf Otto. Otto talked about the spiritual experience as the "numinous," that which is outside the self, unknowable, "ineffable" (William James), mysterious, beyond rational explanation, wholly other, and transcendent.[8] This "other" is greater than the self and is manifested in world religions in different ways.

The irony is that both positive and negative othering are processes that define self and culture by defining other reality—holy and unholy. These processes define the inferior and the superior realities in relation to self and thus help legitimize the place of self and culture in the reality matrix. I will borrow some concepts from Peter L. Berger to illustrate this. Berger is writing as a sociologist of religion, so the processes he describes are related to a macro level. However, we can use reference to these processes to help us understand how otherness in relation to self helps us define self and God in relation to one another.

Berger argues, in his classic "The Sacred Canopy," that religion helps to create a meaningful world through world construction and reality maintenance. For

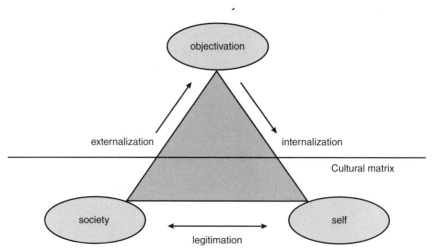

Figure 1.1 Peter L. Berger's social construction of reality.

Berger, society and culture are founded upon the human acts of "externalization, that is, as a product of human activity …," "objectivation," whereby "the humanly produced world attains the character of objective reality …," and "internalization …, the reabsorption into consciousness of the objectivated world in such a way that the structures of this world come to determine the subjective structures of consciousness itself."[9] This process of objectivation, externalization, and internalization creates ideas and products that act back upon their producers as objective reality. This process, in Berger's terms, provides "legitimations"[10] that reinforce the place of self in society and culture in reality. An illustration of this dynamic would look something like Figure 1.1.

This process sets up a triadic interaction where cultural beliefs create and are acted upon by objectified and internalized belief systems. Culture externalizes, objectifies, and internalizes at social and individual levels. Objectified truths then reenter the triad to further influence externalizations. Truths are thus recycled, reinvented, processed, and evolved through interactions over time. Individuals and societies both create and are created by the beliefs that give them meaning.

If we replace Berger's terms with beliefs, we can see how this process reinforces and legitimizes beliefs and thus those who hold them against other beliefs in a way that grants legitimacy to the internalized set of beliefs. For example, Figure 1.2 demonstrates positive othering of a religious belief.

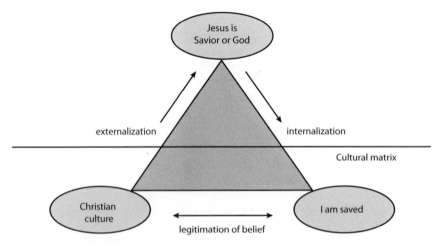

Figure 1.2 Positive othering example for religion.

Likewise, one can illustrate negative othering of a religious belief (Figure 1.3).

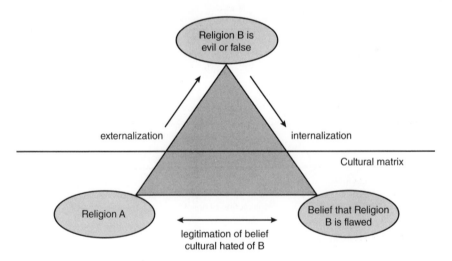

Figure 1.3 Negative othering example for religion.

Other sorts of beliefs work in the same way, as can be seen by Figures 1.4 and 1.5.

Figure 1.4 Positive othering example for politics.

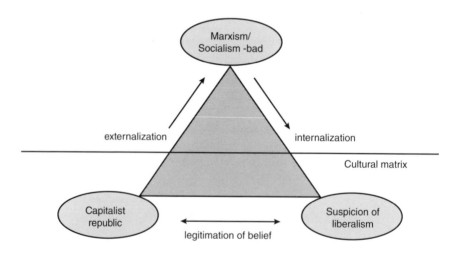

Figure 1.5 Negative othering example for politics.

As these diagrams illustrate, othering works as an externalization of values. Let's say we externalize a conscious belief that people of *x* race or *y* gender are inferior to people of *a* race or *b* gender. Perhaps this belief comes from individual or societal insecurity or is part of the cultural matrix, but externalizing the belief allows it to gain an objective semblance that can then be internalized as a facticity or truth that then legitimates one's own superiority claim in relation to x and y. Likewise, if one externalizes a belief that God is father, perhaps using Freud's notion of origin of divine paternalism, that belief can become objectified and in turn internalized as objective fact or truth. This then legitimates one's position in relation to or a religion's claim of relevance concerning the notion or understanding of God the Father. In each case, negative and positive othering, we build our own reality schemes and then believe them as if they are objectively true apart from us. This is how we maintain illusions about national, cultural, racial, and religious superiority.

This process lends the self a measure of control. When we objectify (designate) a reality construct (for example, God), we control it. If we define God in the effort to define ourselves and deny that God can be different from that definition because God is objective truth, then we have not only created God but also control the notion of God. When we objectify, we control, we define, and we imprison that which is objectified (God, others), and we also limit ourselves within the socially constructed reality order. So, we define, we control, we objectify, and we internalize to both create and accept truth and to legitimate our reality in the world. In this way, we give our lives and beliefs ultimate meaning through "othering."

Othering also allows us to see secularization from a different perspective, as an interaction between secular and sacred perspectives rather than as a competition between them. Again, the diagram demonstrates how secular beliefs can be objectified and sacralized and then internalized as a recycled part of the cultural matrix (Figure 1.6). Sacred and secular thus interact in dialogue within the triadic relationship of legitimation to create beliefs and to be created by beliefs.

What we often fail to recognize is the subjectivity that underlies the objectification. This is what Berger implies and Alfred North Whitehead helps us understand. When Whitehead establishes his metaphysics of perception, he underscores that our perceptions, based on sensory observation, produce data that we objectify but that contain the subjective novelty and creativity of perception.[11]

This triadic relationship illustrates how cultures and cultural beliefs are created and perpetuated as universal truths. It helps us to construct an understanding of culture that is dynamic and evolutionary. It helps us to understand the dialectic in society between the sacred and secular. It helps us see how myths are created and operate in culture. These are the processes I want to uncover in the rest of this book. In addition, this dialectic between the sacred and secular can allow us to see that the artificial differences that are generated and ordered through "othering" could dissolve into an acceptance of humanness at a fundamental and experiential level. This is what I hope can happen with increased understanding, of how "other" religions and "other" people understand "otherness." By reflecting on the philosophical concept of "otherness," the process of "othering," and the

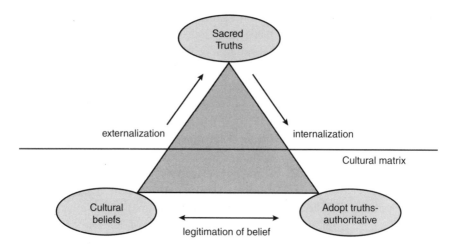

Figure 1.6 Sacred othering—religious truth.

objectified claims about the "other" as produced and believed culturally, perhaps we can rediscover our shared and common humanity.

The triadic process of "truthing" might just allow us to maintain the integrity and relevance of religion in an increasingly secular world. For example, let us return for a moment to the concept of metaphor and use it to understand how we perceive the Bible given this cultural process. The Bible was a product of cultural and historical context. Because of this, we shortchange the scripture if we insist on a "literal" reading of the text. Such a reading imprisons the text in its historical context and, in the extreme case, does not allow it to speak to contemporary situations. This is why it is important to recapture the metaphorical sense of scripture (as argued elsewhere) and to try to understand the context of the text. Only by contextualizing the text can we begin to see the cultural dynamic taking place that gave rise to the dialogue between religion and the rest of culture at the time of writing and recording.

We can see this dynamic clearly when we consider the nature of Jesus's message as recorded in the gospels. At least one part of Jesus's message was prophetic and aimed at the self-righteousness of the religious structures of his day. Jesus entered into direct dialogue with religious insensitivity and bigotry of his day and thus with a culture that created, allowed, and promulgated a society of inequity and poverty. The prophetic teachings of Jesus were aimed at a particular cultural and religious context, and we lose the impact and force of those teachings without a proper grounding in the cultural forces that gave rise to them. If we think of Jesus's teachings as a type of theology (word of God, words about God) then we can see the development of abstract theology (for example, the Sermon on the Mount) and praxis (for example, healing lepers and the absolution of the woman caught in adultery). Both these examples of theology take place in the context of culture: the antitheses in the Sermon on the Mount engage the religious teaching of orthodox Judaism of the day, while healing lepers and overturning a death sentence of stoning are statements made for particular problems of first-century Palestine but not so much in contemporary society.

So, while it is important to establish the context, we must also be willing to allow scripture to break free from that context and engage readers and hearers of the Word. Like scripture engaged ancient believers in their context, scripture also can work developmentally in dynamic relationship with any culture—this allows theology to bolster cultural virtue while hoping to communicate redemption through dynamic interaction with culture. Theology needs to engage culture in dialogical fashion, opening itself to culture, willing to bend toward culture while recognizing that culture is constantly engaging theology. It is this intersection and dialogue that this book explores. Culture is engaging religion and theology often in meaningful ways. Popular culture, music, film, and literature make use of religious themes and symbolism, engage value structures and orthodoxies, and question morals and ethics. Theologians must return the favor and engage culture, not in superficial ways or through judgment and censorship, but through honest and open engagement with the products of our culture. In some ways, religion has forfeited some of its function to popular culture by refusing to acknowledge that the cultural arena is where values and beliefs live and are nourished. When theology fails to engage culture in meaningful dialogue, culture moves on and defines values and beliefs on its own terms. The last chapter explores the implications of the dialogical relationship between the sacred and the secular. Between here and there, this book seeks to understand the dissolving boundaries between the sacred and secular through a reexamination of the secularization question and through analysis of various products of contemporary culture.

Study guide

Important words and concepts

Contingency
Creationism
Intelligent Design
Metaphorical understanding of God

> Omnipotence
> Otherness and othering
> Peter L. Berger's terms: externalization, objectivation, internalization, legitimation
> Process understanding of God
> Random variation
> Relational knowing
> Relativity
> Triadic relationship of religion and culture

Study questions

(1) How does quantum physics challenge traditional Christian theology?
(2) How does Darwinian evolutionary theory challenge traditional Christian concepts of God?
(3) Describe the difference between understanding God as "being" as opposed to understanding God as "becoming."
(4) Delineate between reading scripture literally or as metaphor.
(5) How are religion and culture related in triads?
(6) Describe the relative relationship of God to creation as outlined in this chapter.
(7) Describe the process of othering in everyday life.

Guided readings

(1) Read the first creation story in Genesis (Genesis, chapter 1) twice. On the first reading, attempt a strict literal reading of the text. On the second reading, attempt a metaphorical reading of the account. In what ways does the metaphorical reading change the perspective of the reader? Does the metaphorical reading change the way one would talk about creation with a scientist? How?
(2) Read the Eleventh Teaching in the Hindu classic, *The Bhagavad-Gita*. How does the revelation of Krishna's form illustrate or challenge what science and religion tell us about time and space.

2

Secularization[1]: The evolution of Western religion

Imagine an old monk, bent and nearly blind from years of hunching over ancient manuscripts by candlelight. His fingers are deformed and stained from his careful grip on pen or quill. He stays at his task for a lifetime because his call to preserve a sacred object provides divinely inspired determination and energy. Compare this image to that conjured by a contemporary monastery with its electronic scriptorium. Computer screens emit a mysterious blue glow that replaces the dim, yellow light of candles. Monks hunch over keyboards instead of over manuscripts, and rather than faithfully reproducing sacred words, they design web pages for worldly corporations and provide information about their order through their own website.[2] The sacred task has changed, the tools include the most sophisticated and worldly technology, and the once isolated monastic life has been linked to the outside world via the World-Wide Web.

Now, imagine any number of medieval cathedrals, their splendid architectural details rising to the heavens to extol the glories and greatness of an almighty God. Imagine the mystery and awe surrounding the sacred spaces of those cathedrals, the Dome of the Rock, the Wailing Wall, a Buddhist shrine. Compare this to the image of a family of four retreating to the vestibule of a large suburban church to eat lunch in a fast-food restaurant located just outside the sanctuary. Or imagine the re-creation of sacred space in what was once PTL's Christian theme park,

Heritage, U.S.A., where sacred space was defined by a reconstructed American town based upon a conservative Christian ideology. In the first contemporary image, a fast-food culture invades our sacred spaces; in the second, the sacred space was Main Street, U.S.A., not the church or the mosque or the synagogue. Sacred space has changed, in function and in organization, just as the tasks of our monks have changed.

Finally, imagine a family singing the Seder service, gathered around the dining room table, or the Primitive Baptist preacher's singing-style sermon[3] or the Hallelujah Chorus of George Frederick Handel's *Messiah*. These very traditional and orthodox invocations use auditory manipulation and musical forms to tell the divine story. Compare these images to a seductive young woman asking musical questions about God to MTV viewers or to a scantily clad singer resurrecting a Christian saint through song and dance.[4] Music as a medium for information about the divine has remained constant—the content of the message and the origin of its production have changed. And in the MTV image, the performer acts independently of a religious institution or tradition to raise the question of God's nature.

In contemporary American society, there is no doubt that religion has changed; that an intimate relationship exists between religion and popular cultural forms. This change and the accompanying involvement of religion with culture make it difficult to know where religion stops and the secular world begins. Was PTL's Heritage, U.S.A. a sacralization of secular America or a secularization of the Christian message? These questions, these images, and the relationship between contemporary culture, religion, and ethics have prompted a debate of at least five decades in duration, perhaps one that has extended for five centuries or more. The debate is about secularization—what is it, is it occurring, and what are the implications for religious faith?

This debate has produced several common assumptions about secularization and its effect on religion. Since the 1960s, the predominant thesis comes from sociologists of religion and has been known as the secularization thesis. The early assumptions of this thesis suggested that secularization is a process that will eventually free humanity from religious manipulation and control, that enlightenment, science, or other social institutions will replace religion or make religion irrelevant or at least less relevant.[5] This predominantly sociological view of religion is one that many contemporary religious organizations have taken to heart in their attempts to be more relevant to their constituents. Nevertheless, some contemporary sociologists challenge the view and now seem convinced that religion is not destined to disappear. Peter L. Berger, who contributed much to the secularization debate in the 1960s himself, questions the major premises of the secularization thesis. Berger writes that the "core premise" of the theory, "modernization necessarily leads to a decline of religion," is wrong and needs revision.[6] Berger goes on to say the notion of "counter-secularization" is of prime importance and religions that really succeed in the contemporary situation are those that do not accommodate to the secular world.[7] Mark Chaves argues that secularization should not be understood as "declining religion" but rather "as the declining scope of religious authority."[8] Still other writers attack the secularization thesis more aggressively. Andrew Greeley takes the secularization paradigm to task,[9] while sociologists like Rodney Stark, William Sims Bainbridge, Daniel Bell, and others look for other models or for more helpful ways to view secular culture's relationship to religion.[10]

The upshot of the current thinking on secularization is that religion is not simply going to capitulate to the advance of secularism—but religion is still viewed as precarious or as a less-than-legitimate way of understanding reality. Once again, a predominant scholarly, particularly sociological perspective suggests that in a secular society, which is how we understand contemporary Western society, rational people should not take religion seriously.[11] This assumption is based on the notion that the importance of religion will decrease as society becomes more secularized. Both of these assumptions posit an antagonistic relationship between secular culture and religion. This might be true if by religion one means traditional religious faiths and institutions.[12] However, most religious studies scholars define religion in much broader terms and some sociologists have recognized the necessity to broaden our understanding of the sacred. N. J. Demerath suggests that, rather than focusing on religion, sociology should be looking at the sacred and at various possible sources for the sacred. Sometimes this will be religion and sometimes it might be something else, possibly some aspect of secular culture.[13] All of this suggests that there need not be an all-or-nothing dichotomization of religion and the secular and that in some ways, our oppositional presuppositions concerning religion and the secular are misguided and misleading. One of the assumptions to be tested and challenged in this volume is the presupposition that religion and secular society exist in a necessarily antagonistic relationship to one another. Certainly this can be the case, especially with traditional religious institutions, but the evidence simply does not support the notion that religious and secular worldviews cannot exist side by side. In fact, in most cases if not all, as with Christianity since at least Constantine, religion and secular culture exist in a tandem co-dependency.

While my current work recognizes its genesis in my reaction to the secularization thesis, and while I am influenced by recent attempts to revise, rescue, or debunk the old thesis, this book should not be considered a sociology of religion. I am not trying to enter the debate on paradigms here, nor am I trying to advance new theoretical positions on the future of religion. Rather, I am more interested in how religion functions in relation to secular society, and conversely, how secular society reacts to or recognizes religious organizations. One of the major arguments of this book hinges on the idea that the secular and the religious worlds can and do coexist. In fact, they have always coexisted. If they do not feed off one another, certainly they affect one another. The whole secular–sacred polarization needs to be reconsidered in the light of the relationship of religion and culture. For, whatever else it is, religion must take up secularity as a necessity. Even if the subject matter of religion is another world, religion's task is to exist as relevant in this world; thus, by definition, religion is a part of the secular world just as religious institutions are by nature secular institutions (they reside in and operate in this world, not in a transcendent one).

For years, sociologists have viewed religion as Peter L. Berger's "sacred canopy,"[14] a worldview human beings have constructed to give reality meaning.[15] This view assumes that, since religion deals with ultimate meaning, it covers all aspects of life and leads to religious authoritarianism; and that religion, being other-worldly directed, is a derived reality construction and is suspect if not deceptive.[16] In more recent studies, such secularization thought is undergoing revision. Perhaps it is time to think of society in terms of a "secular canopy" rather than a sacred one. Religion, as a cultural form that operates in this world, falls under a secular umbrella with all other cultural forms. All cultural products, including religion, are affected by and must conform to the exigencies of secular life, although religion's content or subject matter includes speculation about the transcendent, the sacred. Because of this secular umbrella, we should not be surprised when we witness intimate connections between religion and other cultural forms. In fact, religion should be understood as a secular cultural form. That its object is transcendence or the ethical ideal or an otherworldliness no more invalidates this than the goal of an aesthetic ideal denies that art is a secular cultural form, not to mention that other secular forms can deal with the sacred.[17]

Of course, many will say that considering religion as a secular cultural form is a condition of contemporary, secular society and proves the secularization thesis. That argument rests on the assumption there was once a sacred society, generally thought of in the Western tradition to be medieval sacred society. If medieval Christendom seems to run counter to understanding religion as a secular cultural form, this is not evidence that religion is other than a secular cultural product, because the medieval church, as the self-proclaimed gatekeeper to the afterlife, was the most secular institution of its time. Real sacrality would be better found in the folk religions and superstitions of the peasants—that is, in the popular religious practices of the time.[18]

This work attempts to move away from the idea that religion as a sacred ideal must be at odds with secular society and that religion will diminish as secularization continues. I hope to shift the discussion away from paradigms and, following Mark Chaves[19] and others, focus on the functional authority of religion in society. For example, secularization might not destroy religion, but it might shift the authority away from religious institutions to other elements of society. The religious impulse will not disappear with secularization if, as many believe, humans have a fundamental religious consciousness.[20] However, where we find religion and how religion operates in society might change as authority structures within society shift. For example, if it is true that the institutional church is losing authority in contemporary society, as Chaves suggests,[21] we should not be surprised to find religion expressed with new vitality outside the institutional church, in new religious movements,[22] or in "secular" cultural forms like literature, film, or art. So even if religious institutions lose authority, the power of religion does not diminish in scope—the location of that power might, however, shift in focus.

If the first major theme of this book is that secularization does not destroy religion, that religion will persist across cultural forms, the second theme, and a corollary to the first, is that secularization occasions a shift in the locus of authority to express religious ideals. Authority might shift from traditional religions to new religions or from institutional religion to some other cultural form: governmental institutions (secular state), the entertainment industry, the media, or the publishing industry. This work assumes this shift in authority to be an ongoing result of secularization in the West, so much so that religion in the postmodern West has become reactionary. Religion in a secular world has in some cases lost the power to reify a culture and has found itself in the position of reacting to a culture that occasionally assumes the tasks previously reserved for religion.

A third major theme addresses another commonly held assumption about religiosity in contemporary society. Many commentators believe that European society is more thoroughly secularized than American society. This assumption is based on statistics that measure church membership and attendance, as well as on less official anecdotes concerning public religion in American culture. This work argues that secularization is a reality both in America and in Europe—not necessarily to varying degrees, but in different ways. This in part is a result of the history of organized religion in America, in particular as it relates to disestablishment of the churches. Because of disestablishment in America, religious institutions since the American Revolution have been unable to ascend to the level of elite power institutions as they did in Europe. Since the process of secularization as understood in this study depends on shifting loci of power, secularization would necessarily proceed differently in America than in Europe. Because in America religious institutions have been excluded from the elite power structure of government, religion in America has always tended toward popular culture and thus is dispersed more thoroughly through secular components of society. This might help to explain in part why American intellectuals seem more anxious to investigate popular culture and religion than their European counterparts.

In *Selling God: American Religion in the Marketplace of Culture*, R. Laurence Moore argues that, because of disestablishment, religion in America became popularized in order to compete in a free market.[23] The open market theory is found elsewhere in sociology (for example R. Stephen Warner) and religious studies (for example Nathan Hatch) to explain the evolution of religious traditions in America.[24] Religion operating in a free-market environment finds itself competing with entertainment for attention and often adopts the stance of entertainment in order to thrive. As a result, religion in America is more worldly and secular than religion in Europe, where historically religion has not had to compete. Secularization has proceeded differently, and in America we witness religion that is more attuned to the secular environment and a popular culture that is more infused with religious images. In a sense, then, America is more thoroughly secularized than Europe in that religion appears in secular, popular culture and the church has become more like the secular world. This is perhaps one reason church attendance is higher in the United States—because America, including American religion, is more secularized than Europe, not less so.

The comparison of the European and American situations brings up the fourth and final major theme to run throughout this work. This chapter began with a series of images that asked the reader to imagine the confused boundaries between religion and the secular in contemporary society. As Paul Nathanson suggests, increasingly we witness not confused boundaries but "flexible" ones between "religion and secularity."[25] From Nathanson's "flexible boundaries," we see secularization taking place in two directions in contemporary society. First, there is a tendency for religious institutions to employ secular and popular cultural forms like television and the movies to make religious teachings relevant for a modern audience.[26] In this instance, we see contemporary religion making concessions to secular cultural forms and becoming more like society in general in the struggle to stave off obsolescence. As Bernard Meland pointed out, theological works such as John A. T. Robinson's *Honest to God*, Paul Van Buren's *The Secular Meaning of the Gospel*, and Harvey Cox's *The Secular City* demonstrated this dynamic some 30 years ago.[27] The end of the nineteenth century and early part of the twentieth witnessed this dynamic in the Social Gospel's attempt to build super churches, and contemporary society sees this development in the creation of "megachurches." This first direction of secularization across boundaries makes religion reactionary to secular culture and comes as a result of religion's perceived loss of authority or relevance in society.

The second way secularization is proceeding is by the dispersion of the religious sensibility through a variety of cultural forms. When religious institutions no longer dominate culture, they lose their grip on what might otherwise be their prerogative—the religious sensibility and striving of humanity toward the sacred. With this loss of prerogative, religious concerns find expression in other cultural forms, so that cultural products perceived to be secular can carry authentic and meaningful religious content and deal with sacred concerns. In fact, I would argue, much in the vein of theomusicologist Jon Michael Spencer,[28] that secular and popular culture might contain more authentic belief than official religious theologies, because it is in the popular culture that one can encounter belief and values apart from and freed from paternalistic religious doctrine and dogma.

Both ways secularization takes place in contemporary society originate with the loss or perceived loss of authority or relevance by religious institutions. This supports the contention that secularization has more to do with shifting structures of power in society than it does with the disappearance of religion. The second way secularization occurs will receive the most attention in this study by focusing on how religious sensibilities are spread out through the cultural spectrum. To use N. J. Demerath's phrasing, this might be referred to as the "sacralization" of society.[29]

The remainder of this chapter will focus on developing these four themes and contextualizing a more thorough study of the second way secularization occurs in contemporary society—through the dissemination of the religious impulse in a variety of cultural forms external to traditional religious institutions and expressions. The underlying assumption is that human beings are religious and will express themselves religiously in a variety of cultural forms that have relevance and meaning to them. If institutional religious traditions are among those forms, we will find vital religious institutions; if they are not relevant and meaningful (and even if they are), the religious impulse will find expression elsewhere. In any event, we should not be surprised to find interaction between religion and other cultural forms. Just as Western civilization nurtured state Christianity, just as Christianity co-opted pagan practices, we should expect to see a fusion of the religious and the secular. So monks using computers, Christian singers employing rock rhythms, and coffee in the vestibule should not surprise us, nor should the suggestion that religious images, messages, and content can be found at the movie house, in the pages of popular novels, and in the lyrics of pop music. This work on secularization is about the relationship between culture and religion.

The secularization paradigm and its revision

The predominant paradigm for understanding secularization as a process comes to religious studies via sociology and has defined the discussion to one degree or another since the 1960s. This paradigm has several features, chief among them the assumption (shared by religious studies) that religion views sacred reality as a wholly different order from the secular world and that the two worldviews are necessarily mutually exclusive and antithetical. In the following pages, I attempt to reconstruct the main features of this model as it developed from the sociological study of religion, suggest additional recent revisionist ideas to the paradigm, examine the sources or causes of the secularization process, and posit a different way of thinking about secularization that does not require a polarization of secular and sacred but allows a commingling of the two.

For the most part, the term secularization is used in two ways: to describe the process of making religion more worldly, which is how religious leaders often use the term, and to describe the process of a contemporary growing irrelevance of religion.[30] In either usage, the term is ideologically charged. In the first instance, secularization is often attacked from religious circles as a compromise to those parts of culture and society that are antithetical to religion. In the second, the term is often employed by those anti-religion idealists who view religion as an outdated and repressive cultural system.[32] Secular ideologies suggest certain ways of viewing the world, just like religions sponsor worldviews, and these secular worldviews often compete directly with religious ways of understanding reality.[33] Religion apologists counter the secular worldviews by claiming such views abandon humanity to alienation[34] and are responsible for a modern crisis of faith, a situation that leaves postmodern society in limbo concerning order—a situation where postmoderns might no longer be able to understand reality or gain meaning from their world.[35]

In this book, I will be less concerned about secularism as an ideology and more interested in secularization as a process that offers the key to understanding the relationship between the secular and the sacred and even the relationship between religion and culture. As a process, secularization does more than simply signal surface changes in habit or custom: it is a cultural process akin to "religionization" that helps define how human beings make sense of their world.[36] Thus, whatever else it might be, secularization involves and helps direct how we relate to the cultural forms in society, including religion. The predominant sociological secularization model is summarized by Paul Nathanson and others as a process that 1) is essentially modern in scope, 2) will lead to the demise of religion or its power, and 3) is an irreversible and chronological societal and historical process of Western civilization.[37]

This model stems from the Enlightenment notion that, in the words of Andrew Greeley, "the progress of science, technology, education, and ... modernization"[38] will eventually make religion unnecessary. In the earlier years of secularization theory, Peter L. Berger took this so far as to posit a "secularization of consciousness" leading to a worldview in which "an increasing number of individuals ... look upon the world and their own lives without the benefit of religious interpretations."[39] If this model is correct, if indeed the Enlightenment and the scientific revolution will answer all the questions for humanity that religion at one time tried to answer, if there is a secularization of consciousness going on, then we can expect a shift in the structure of belief: religious beliefs will be adequate for fewer and fewer people as a meaningful explanation of reality.[40] As Stephen Carter points out, we can expect to see a society where the culture rejects the idea of the supernatural, ridicules religious devotees, trivializes religion, and replaces supernatural explanations with supreme reason.[41] Although certain of these characteristics show up in contemporary U.S. and European society, there is still no consensus that the secularization model does indeed explain postmodern society. In fact, as we shall see, there is much evidence to counter that assumption.

If the secularization model described above is correct, we should be able to see religion losing social significance at the institutional level. Religious institutions would not only lose their power to enforce belief and behavior with individual constituents of religious communities, they would also lose power over other institutions such as government.[42] In short, religion, as institution and as individual belief, would become marginal to the point of irrelevance in a technological civilization.[43] Furthermore, if the secularization model is accurate, according to Bryan Wilson, secularization will lead to a "transfer of property, power, activities, and both manifest and latent functions, from institutions with a supernaturalist frame of reference to (often new) institutions operating according to empirical, rational, pragmatic criteria."[44] According to Steve Bruce and Roy Wallis, this process might include differentiation (where other institutions will take on the roles religion once handled) as well as individualization and fragmentation of religion into increasingly less powerful and smaller units.[45] In *The Sacred Canopy*, Peter L. Berger argued this would eventually leave a society with cultural artifacts displaying a lack of religious content.[46] Bernard Meland even suggests the process could be a conscious one that leads to an effort to build a secular state where pluralism and toleration replace religious hegemony and bigotry and where separation of church and state allows for greater "justice to an entire citizenry of a culture."[47]

This secularization model, which predicts the inevitable and irreversible decline of religion as a condition of social processes initiated in modern Western culture, is now being revisited, questioned, and revised, at least in part because the data do not support that religion is becoming increasingly irrelevant. Poll after poll, study after study, suggest that religious observance in America is as strong as ever. At the beginning of the 1990s, 90 percent of Americans claimed to be religious,[48] evidence indicates that church adherence increased in the nineteenth century and remained steady during the twentieth, and contributions to religious organizations continue to increase steadily even when adjusting for inflation.[49] These figures are based largely on a traditional definition of religion. If a focus on popular religious practice were measurable, one might find an even greater level of religiosity in American life.[50] Thus advocates of the secularization theory are forced to make concessions about the American situation and put forth revisions to some of its premises. And even in Europe, where the numbers suggest a much less impressive religiosity and where public religion is less visible, the secularization paradigm is not necessarily supported. For the European situation to support the model, there must have at one time been a Europe that was not secular, that was defined by a sacred worldview. The popular image of a sacred medieval European society is the product of history written from the perspective of medieval elite society, which was controlled by the church. Therefore, we have no reliable evidence that religious life in Europe has declined since the Middle Ages.[51] We can, however, rest assured that there was never a Western civilization that was "not secular"[52] and that the secular did not simply arise in Europe in the fifteenth to seventeenth centuries.

If we cannot demonstrate that religion is declining, what do we do with our secularization paradigm? Must we abandon it as a way of understanding the relationship between religion and culture in the contemporary world? Certainly not. However, it does seem that certain of its major tenets need revision. The major problems with the dominant theories about secularization lie in their intransigence. For many, such as Jeffrey K. Hadden, secularization has become as much a doctrine as a theory and represents a cultural elitist attitude that expects religion to vanish.[53] Andrew Greeley echoes this sentiment when he says, "'secularization' ... is the religious faith of the secularized."[54] Greeley goes so far as to say adamantly that secularization is not occurring, that religion is just as important individually and institutionally as it ever has been in the past, and that declining religious affiliation is not proof that religiosity is in a state of decline.[55] Greeley and Hadden are joined by others such as Laurence Iannaccone, Rodney Stark, William Sims Bainbridge, Mark Chaves, and Peter L. Berger, who all challenge the secularization paradigm to one degree or another and call for its revision.[56]

It seems that we must question the notion, at least for the time being, that religion is becoming less viable or less important in contemporary society. We will talk about the mode of expression of religion later. It also seems that the notion that secularization is a modern phenomenon must also be discarded. Surely, Christianity in Constantine's empire experienced as much secularization (becoming more worldly) as do contemporary religious expressions. We might also conjecture that religion is a characteristic of humanity and is fundamental to a way of being, and that human beings have always been religiously oriented and always will be.[57] Thus, we can consider religious striving a constant, but that does not mean religion is unchanging. And it might be that what we often think of as the decline of religiosity is nothing more than a natural evolution of religious being.

The idea of religious evolution is not new. As W. Warren Wagar points out, theologians and religious studies scholars as diverse as Martin Marty, Harvey Cox, Rudolf Bultmann, and even Dietrich Bonhoeffer have suggested that a decline in belief in the supernatural and of the institutional expression of religion does not mean that religious faith might not arise anew "in some reconceived but still authentic form."[58] These theologians challenge us to think differently about secularization and about religion so that we might view religion in broader terms, as individual faith rather than as institutional expression, as a more basic way of thinking about the sacred in general.[59]

In this context, where we can think about religious evolution without theorizing the extinction of religion, we can look at secularization as an agent for change, as do Stark and Bainbridge in their enlightening study, *The Future of Religion: Secularization, Revival and Cult Formation*. Stark and Bainbridge argue that secularization happens constantly in religious communities, sometimes leading to the collapse or weakening of some religious traditions, even the dominant ones. Nevertheless, religion does not disappear or become irrelevant, nor does religion forfeit all its functions to secular institutions; new religions surface, sects become churches, cults form, the religious landscape shifts and evolves, and secularization becomes a "harbinger of religious change," not of its demise.[60] They identify a pattern wherein secularization is always happening, religious communities are supplanted by other new religions when they become too worldly, and secularization leads to either revival or religious innovation, in other words, religious change.[61] We might add to their pattern that other cultural forms can and do participate in the communication of religious meaning when traditional religions wane and even when they do not. We need to broaden our categories so that religious institutions are not the only cultural forms seen as participating in the religious enterprise.[62] So, in the context of religious evolution as a result of the secularization process, we can think about literature, film, music, art, and other cultural products as vehicles, along with traditional religious structures and new religious groups, which carry and transport our religious longings, rituals, and beliefs.

So we can think in new ways about secularization. It need not destroy religion, nor is it necessarily antagonistic to religion. It might be a catalyst for change, but secularity can also be a partner with traditional religions and religious institutions in the process of making known the sacred. Secularization and religious devotion are not necessarily inversely related, that is, the one does not have to suffer for the other to prosper.[63] We can think about religion and secularity, indeed religion and culture, as maintaining Nathanson's "flexible boundaries" where secularity and religion are on the same continuum rather than antitheses of one another.[64] Finally, we can recognize that much of the debate over secularization has been misdirected. Secularization theory might hold for institutional expressions of religion, but even then not universally. This should come as no surprise, because religion has always found expression through secular institutions like the Christian Church. The religious impulse remains constant—that religious nature of humanity that, through its quest for the sacred, results in the creation of religions and religious institutions. Humanity's religious impulse also finds expression through many secular, cultural forms, including but not limited to the church and other religious institutions.

As we look at the evolutionary nature of religious development, one element of change stands out as the type of secularization taking place in Western religions in particular. This element has to do with religious authority relative to other cultural institutions[65] and is where the secularization paradigm is most instructive. It seems that, even though religious devotion is as strong as ever, or at least not measurably weaker, and that religious bodies are not disappearing, there is a sense in which religious institutions do not exercise the degree of control and authority over society they once did in Western culture. This can be seen, for example, in the secularization of American education from a situation where Christianity once enjoyed a privileged position in higher education to its current state as a peripheral or excluded philosophical component of secular education.[66] This shift should not be conceived as a loss of religious efficacy, however, but as a loss of worldly authority, because usually when a religious institution exercises control it is because that institution acts as a secular institution, controlling law, government, and even education.

Mark Chaves has argued persuasively that secularization results in a decline in religious authority when religious authority is defined as "a social structure that attempts to enforce its order and reach its ends by controlling the access of individuals to some desired goods, where the legitimation of that control includes some supernatural component."[67] Therefore, for Chaves, "secularization is most productively understood not as declining religion, but as the declining scope of religious authority."[68] This view has validity when we consider that antagonism between secular institutions and religious ones usually centers on the locus of power. Thus we can look at the contemporary American situation, for example, and see a tug-of-war of sorts between religious institutions and political institutions, because the separation of religion and state made that power struggle inevitable. If at one time religious institutions had the power not only to direct secular matters but also to nourish spiritual needs, then we can say that secularization has occurred to the extent that religious institutions seem to have lost some of their ability to direct secular matters, although certainly not all of it. However, we must not equate this loss with the disappearance of religion from public life, because we still see the evidence of the religious quest in our art, music, literature, civil religion, and other cultural forms.

This brings us to our rethinking of the dominant secularization paradigm. We certainly do not want to discard it, because there is evidence that secularization is taking place, in that religious institutions are becoming more like the rest of secular society, less "other," and we do note a decline in the ability of religious institutions to authoritatively affect secular matters even if we do not witness a decline in religiosity itself. What we are left with is a model of secularization that views religion, secularity, and other cultural forms on the same interactive continuum. We see shifts in functions of these forms and a shift in the location of authority in culture in such a way that secularization entails and perhaps initiates transition in the culture and evolution of religion without its necessary extinction. This evolution has resulted in changes in the ways humans are religious and often in the ways humans express themselves religiously, so we get a constant infusion of new religious expressions, new religions, revivals of religions, and new vehicles for the expression of the religious imagination. Oftentimes these new vehicles for expression come from outside the traditional religious institutions and draw upon other cultural forms that may or may not be formally related to religious institutions. As a result, we often find popular cultural forms taking on some of the tasks of traditional religions in this constantly evolving, shifting secular landscape. In later chapters, this book explores some of those popular cultural forms to see if and how religious longings and questions arise outside traditional religious institutions in what we normally consider "secular" forms of culture. It might be that in our postmodern context, with its shifting authority structures, popular cultural expression of religiosity is more important, more available, and more powerful than traditional expressions of religious truth.

The origins of secularization

However we perceive secularization in Western civilization, there is little doubt it is occurring and affecting religion and other cultural forms. We can understand those effects better if we try to locate the source of the secularization process. As I mentioned above, in the Western tradition religious institutions have always been secular or have evolved into secular institutions. The history of Christianity, its antagonism to and then acceptance by the Roman Empire, the Orthodox tradition's state church, the Catholic Church's involvement in secular matters throughout the Middle Ages, Protestantism's various experiments with state–church relations, and modern developments that have changed the face of Christianity, all testify to the evolution of religion in light of secularization. So in some sense it will profit little to search for the origins of secularization in the Western tradition—the impulse to secularize has been there from the beginning, and secularization's beginnings correspond with the beginnings of Western religions.

Peter L. Berger suggests the seeds of secularization are to be found in the nature of Western religion, in the oppositional relationship Western religion draws between itself and the rest of society—and particularly in the idea of transcendence, which polarizes the transcendent and profane realms. Berger argues that the biblical concept of a transcendent God leads to "disenchantment of the world" and the separation of the world from the sacred realm.[69] As this transcendent philosophy developed into the Christian tradition, the tendency to create an oppositional relationship between religion and society was heightened by the institutionalization of the church. Berger argues that, when the church separated itself from the rest of reality by locating all "religious activities and symbols in one institutional sphere," it defined the rest of the world as separate, profane, and secular.[70] Nevertheless, as David Martin points out, European religious patterns evolved from the Roman model of a partnership between Caesar and God, an idea that led to the commingling of the sacred sphere the church defined and the secular sphere the church set apart.[71] So when looking for the roots of secularization in Western traditions, one need look no further than Western religion itself. Indeed, Western religion sponsors the divided worldview that allows for reality to be divided into secular and sacred realms in the first place.

Nevertheless, in addition to this general origin of secularization, we might argue that Western religions are in a specific phase of secularization, particularly if we look at secularization as involved in the ongoing evolution of religion. This view generally points to the Enlightenment as the genesis of the current phase of secularization that is changing the way religiosity is communicated and understood in society and changing the role and function of traditional religious institutions. Based on the work of John Sommerville, Vernon Pratt, Olivier Tschannen, and others, this phase of secularization can be generally characterized by societal and institutional differentiation, pluralism of belief and disbelief, confusion of boundaries between secular and sacred, and the transfer of activities between cultural forms.[72] The following pages will outline the major events, institutions, activities, or ideologies flowing out of the massive transitions in European society during the fifteenth through the seventeenth centuries that seem to exert continued influence on the contemporary evolution of Western religion.

If we look beyond the nature of Western religious experience as the origin of the secularization impulse, we can look at the specific historical phase of secularization that confronts contemporary Western religions. In particular, as the power of the Catholic Church began to wane in the fourteenth century, we might argue that the modern phase of secularization began as the Middle Ages came to a close. The Catholic Church, which during much of the Middle Ages defined and controlled social order, power, and thought, entered into a period of decline marked by the Avignon papacy and the Great Schism. This weakened church never regained its far-reaching ability to control society; nevertheless, it attempted through futile measures to maintain a tight control over society and religion. When the Protestant

Reformation movements succeeded, the Catholic Church realized its privileged position as a power broker in Western Europe had been seriously compromised.

This period, from approximately 1300 to 1550, can be understood as a transition period for the Catholic Church and for Western Christendom in general. With the loss of ecclesiastical prerogative came the dismantling of the feudal system (which favored the church with its vast land holdings), the rise of nationalism, the flourishing of a middle class, the growth of self-governing towns, and a revolutionary spirit that was in many cases directed at the church and its power structure. As broad, sweeping changes flooded Europe, the power structures of the Middle Ages fell apart. The institution that best defined that structure, the church, did not emerge unscathed. The ties between church and state began to unravel, and religion in the West was forced into a new role.[73] According to W. Warren Wagar, at the end of the Middle Ages, out of the rubble left by these movements, "the foundations of modern Europe were laid ...," and this foundation supported the weight of a new secular edifice.[74]

The edifice that emerged from the general social, economic, and religious upheaval of 1300–1550 included the Catholic Church, an institution that was less powerful than before, but it also gave new legitimacy to secular institutions and to secular thought. Secularism defined the mood of the day, as the rush of revolution provided excitement for burgeoning new governments. The church was often intransigent in its reaction, and moved into a posture of reaction. No longer occupying a position that allowed it to define and control life in Western Europe as it once did, the church's reactionary stance helped establish the process of secularization we recognize at present. As loyalties were transferred from ecclesiastical power brokers to nationalistic ones, the church suffered in power and prestige and feared the fate of irrelevancy. The Catholic Church has since sought ways to define itself in relation to the "world" rather than defining the world. In the Catholic Reformation, the First Vatican Council, the modernist movement, and the Second Vatican Council, the Catholic Church struggled to understand itself over against the secular world. Long gone was the powerful, all-encompassing institution of the Middle Ages that had the power to define the secular world over against the church.

We might say the sources of Western secularization included the sweeping socio-economic changes in Europe between 1300 and 1550 and the reactionary stance the Catholic Church assumed in response to these changes. However, it is perhaps unfair to characterize the Catholic Church as an unyielding institution that heightened the secularization of Europe by refusing to acknowledge the great transitions affecting European life. Something much greater and more broadly conceived was happening to Western Europe that changed the worldviews of Europeans. The European Enlightenment provided a philosophical basis for a new secular worldview that not only succeeded in secularizing the Continent but also provided the free-thought tradition that led to English secularism[75] and ultimately to the Enlightenment traditions and religions that characterized the American Revolutionary period. The modern prejudice against religion, if such exists as a characteristic of a secular society, might have begun, according to Stephen Carter, with "... the Enlightenment, when the Western tradition sought to sever the link between religion and authority."[76] The Enlightenment's emphasis and reliance on reason made Christianity seem unreasonable, based as reason is on revealed truth. Thus we could argue that one of the results of secularization, mistrust of religion in general, stems from the Enlightenment emphasis on reason.[77]

Beyond the mere emphasis on the rational as opposed to the revelatory experience, the Enlightenment was accompanied by an epistemological revolution sponsored by the seventeenth-century scientific revolution. The scientific revolution, particularly the rise of natural science championed by Newtonian physics, changed the way the West perceived the world. Natural science ushered in a new paradigm, a new worldview, that disrupted, if not in some cases destroyed, what Bernard Meland called the "mythos of the West."[78] Natural science introduced and legitimized a worldview that had no need to resort to supernatural phenomena or explanations to explain reality.[79] This whole movement put the church in an awkward stance: either Christianity would accept naturalistic explanations for the workings of the universe and thus invalidate the basis of revealed religion and some of its long-accepted precepts, or the church would retreat into a defensive stance, reject naturalist explanations, and, thereby, render itself irrelevant in the modern world. In many ways, this has been the dilemma of the Christian Church since the scientific revolution, and either choice on the part of the church results in secularization: either the church becomes more secular by accepting scientific ways of thinking, or the church heightens the sacred–secular antagonism by entrenching itself against science. The church has employed both strategies at certain times during its history.

Newton's "mechanization of nature" made the divine, as the divine had been previously perceived, somewhat obsolete. Many scholars claim this led to a decline in religious belief as science began to assume some of the roles previously reserved for God—what Vernon Pratt calls the "naturalization of the supernatural"[80] made religion a less reasonable pursuit for Enlightenment-minded Europeans. As God became less a reality, human beings suddenly found themselves alone in the universe, and what Meland called the "idealization" of humanity resulted.[81] However, this created another existential dilemma for human beings. On the one hand, with the supernatural out of the way, human beings were supreme, yet on the other hand, the scientific revolution changed the way human beings could think of themselves. The scientific revolution pushed humanity to the periphery—no longer could humanity think of itself as the focus of God's created order. Rather, the Copernican revolution removed the Earth from the center of creation to the periphery, and the Darwinian revolution heightened this anxiety when it came to the biological sciences. Humanity found itself in the precarious position of no longer being the favored of God's creation but instead the result of random and natural events[82]—without God's providential care, humans were alone in the universe. This is why religion did not crumble and has not disappeared in the wake of advancing science; even though science created a crisis for revealed religion, it failed to answer fundamental existential problems of humanity and even heightened human anxiety about contingency.[83]

The scientific revolution made religion seem unreasonable, and since European intellectuals were in an Enlightenment frame of mind, science certainly created problems for Western religions as natural explanations impinged on the territory of the supernatural. The boundaries were malleable, and they were shifting. This is one way religion became more secularized. Stark and Bainbridge claim that, as it became increasingly more difficult to defend supernatural explanations, theologians began to make fewer and fewer claims for the supernatural in order to avoid conflict with science.[84] We see concessions grudgingly made by the church in such situations as the Darwinian challenge. We also see religion reacting against this trend with such movements as Christian fundamentalism. In any event, the scientific revolution forced secularization by placing the church in a dilemma: either become more secular or become less relevant. As we shall see, this dilemma still faces many contemporary Christians.

Yet another likely source of secularization in Western society can be found in the French Revolution, as well as in the American Revolution and other revolutionary movements of the late eighteenth century.[85] The French Revolution helped nationalism to materialize in Europe by replacing the old monarchy model (undergirded by divine right) with a new democratic model fueled by the middle class. The democratic ideals of the resulting Republic not only undercut the divine rights of kings and thus helped sever church and state, but it also led to greater toleration of religion and eventually to a greater pluralism of belief in Western society, one of the characteristics of secularism.[86] One can see a parallel phenomenon in the American Revolution and the separation of church and state in the United States. The French example perhaps resulted in the greatest degree of secularizing tendencies, because there was a purposeful move to secularize life in the French Republic. Since the Catholic Church opposed the Revolution, the church quickly became a symbol of the Old Regime, and the newly formed Republic tended to view the church as an impediment to progress. So there were active efforts in the Republic to replace religious ethics with secular ones and to oppose the church as a social institution.[87] With the French Revolution, we see the increasing marginalization of religious thought in everyday life as secular concerns dominated during the revolution itself, and we see the increase of religious pluralism as democratic principles took hold. Both of these elements are characteristic of the modern phase of secularization in Western society.

Earlier we saw how Catholicism probably contributed to secularization in the late Middle Ages and during the Enlightenment period. However, Protestantism is probably an even greater culprit in the secular enterprise than the Catholic Church, so much so that William Lloyd Newell dubbed "modernity ... the secular child of Protestantism ..."[88] A quick look at the central tenets of Luther's reform demonstrates how Protestantism participated in and served as a source of secularization in Western Christianity. As Paul Nathanson points out, when Luther claimed that God is known through Scripture alone, he effectively "desacralized" the church[89] by making the revelatory experience less necessary. As Timothy B. Husband and Jane Hayward remind us, when Luther attacked good works as a means of salvation, he "separated ... earthly endeavors from ... eternal life"[90] and heightened the tension between the secular and sacred realms; and when Luther declared the existence of a priesthood of believers, the democratization, and thus the secularization, of religion was complete—with the priesthood of believers there need be no sacred hierarchy. The democratizing effects of Luther's reform and of Protestantism in general paralleled some of the social upheaval in European society at the time and contributed to the secularization of European life.

These are a few of the possible sources of the modern phase of secularization of Western society. Many more possibilities exist. For example, David Martin argues that secularization is a Christian phenomenon and then discusses various types of secularizing tendencies based on revolutionary events and patterns,[91] leading us to a multitude of revolutionary movements that could serve as sources of secularization. Others point to the nineteenth-century Industrial Revolution as one of the harbingers of modern secularization.[92] We have neither the time nor the space to pursue these directions here, but the above examples should suffice to illustrate where some of the characteristics of the modern phase of secularization in Western religion originated. From the nature of Western religion itself to the revolutionary political and economic changes in Europe to the epistemological transition accompanying the scientific revolution to the basic tenets of Protestantism, these and other changes have produced a process of secularization that results in institutional differentiation, pluralism of belief, permeable boundaries between the sacred and the secular, and the transfer of religiosity to other cultural forms, to politics, science, literature, and more. Following this general orientation to the secularization process, I will continue to examine the relationship between religion, culture, and secularization in the European and American settings and discuss the two dominant directions secularization is taking in contemporary society.

One of the major extensions of the secularization thesis is that Britain and Europe are more thoroughly secularized than the United States. Why is this?

The main assumption of the paradigm is that, as secularization occurs, religion will become irrelevant and will eventually diminish. Thus, a measure of the degree of secularization is the level of religious observance in a society. Many observers of European and American religion make the claim that America is a much more religious society than Britain or Europe. And indeed, if the political influence, membership, and public expressions of religiosity measure the degree of secularization, then America does seem to be less secularized than Europe. Many commentators note the degree to which intellectual life in Britain, Scotland, and France had become secularized by the eighteenth century.[93] Others warn against generalizing about secularization in Europe and suggest that the degree of secularization in Europe differs drastically from country to country. For example, cites Andrew Greeley, Ireland and Poland have a very high degree of religious participation.[94] Still others warn about making judgments concerning religiosity based on measures such as membership rolls and the appearance of religion in the public realm. For example, Stephen Carter suggests that Americans have mixed feelings about religion. Whereas there is an abundance of public religion in America, Americans do not take religion seriously and treat it as "a hobby."[95] If Carter is right, then we cannot be sure that statistics demonstrate anything about the religiosity of the United States as compared to Europe.

Nevertheless, the numbers seem to support at least a superficial acceptance and practice of religion as part of American culture that outpaces religious life in most parts of Europe. Although American intellectual life demonstrated some of the same secularizing tendencies in the eighteenth century as European intellectual life, the twentieth century seems to suggest that religion in America is more vital than ever and perhaps an even more important component in American society than secular aspects like politics.[96] Since Alexis de Tocqueville noted the level of religious observance in the United States and its role in maintaining a thriving democracy,[97] American religious studies scholars have been theorizing about the abundance of religion in American life. Over half of Americans claim to attend church regularly, some 85 percent believe the Bible is divinely inspired, public ritual is filled with religious rhetoric, and even popular music contains religious images.[98] The ever-present American civil religion suggests that U.S. society is godly and moral,[99] making it difficult to be irreligious in the United States. Sociologists like Peter L. Berger recognize the level of apparent religiosity in America. Berger writes, "[T]he majority of Americans are as furiously religious as ever—and very probably more religious than they were when de Tocqueville marveled at this quality of American life."[100] How can we account for this apparent disparity, and what does it mean for the current study?

A major argument accounting for the seeming vital religiosity in America focuses on the disestablishment of religion in America as the key to its religious vitality. According to R. Laurence Moore, state religion, as it was practiced in Europe for much of the modern era, relieves religion from the necessities of the marketplace.[101] The flipside of the coin is that, when religion loses its privileged position in society through disestablishment, as was the case in America, then religion is forced to compete not only against other religions but also against other cultural forms.[102] So, in American society, religion has found itself in the position of wooing its clients for allegiance, often against rival suitors as diverse as Friday night dates and Sunday afternoon football games. Many scholars, like Moore, believe this competition increases religious participation in America.[103] If this is true, then disestablishment helps us to understand the high level of religiosity in America; however, it does not help us understand, as Greeley points out, the high levels of religious participation in countries where religion is established.[104]

At least partly because of disestablishment in America, religion has never occupied the position of an elite power establishment in post-revolutionary America as it did in Europe. Since religion had to compete against secular institutions and secular forms of entertainment, the church in America has tended to favor popular culture and has been more closely tied to secular concerns than in Europe. In Europe, the church occupied a privileged position as part of the cultural elite and maintained a position aloof from popular cultural forms. As an institution, the church came under attack or at least under suspicion during the French Revolution, and since then has become an institution falling out of favor in the popular culture. This indicates that there have been two different trends in secularization in America and in Europe. In America, secularization is expressed through the church aligning itself with popular, secular cultural forms and becoming more like them; in Europe, secularization is expressed through the rejection of an elite institution by the populace, thus attendance and religious fidelity are apparently lower than in America. Secularization is taking place in opposite directions: the church is moving toward popular culture in America; popular culture is moving away from the church in Europe. With this scenario, one could even argue that America is the more thoroughly secularized society as its church becomes increasingly akin to popular and secular cultural forms. According to R. Laurence Moore, this helps account for the vitality of American religion.[105]

Thus, to mount a study of secularization in the context of religion and culture, one area of investigation must be how religion surfaces in and is reflected by popular cultural forms as well as by elite institutions. This book seeks to do just that, and the following pages contain reflections on how religion and culture relate in society and how secularization in postmodern American society takes place in two directions: 1) traditional religion becomes more like secular cultural forms; and 2) religious concepts find expression in popular cultural forms beyond the traditional institutions.

Religion and culture

This work assumes that religion is a crucial part of a larger cultural system and exists in relation to other cultural forms within a society. Borrowing from Clifford Geertz's famous "web" analogy, religion is one strand among many cultural strands that are interrelated in society.[106] As Robert Booth Fowler points out, religion is a cultural form that is integrated into life, society, and culture, and from thinkers as diverse as Max Weber, Emile Durkheim, de Tocqueville, and H. Richard Niebuhr, we see that religion shapes, undergirds, reflects, challenges, and critiques the social order and other cultural forms.[107] Of course, other cultural forms also shape, undergird, reflect, challenge, and critique religion, so Geertz's web is a dialectical one.

Religion's relationship to culture raises questions about the function or uniqueness of religion as a cultural form, that is, is religion any different than other cultural forms? As a cultural form, religion resembles other cultural products; however, religion's subject matter[108] directs its attention to otherworld-liness, and it functions, according to James Moseley, to "express ... culture's relation to a primordial, fundamental order or ground of reality, often imagined as a divine being." Religion functions as "an anchor of meaning" that often regulates behavior and morality.[109] When it does this institutionally, religion is expressed through traditions that relate to the world through secular organizations like the church. Of course, other cultural forms can function similarly and thus function religiously without being categorized as religion. Religion, therefore, should be considered a cultural form that is directed toward the sacred and that exists in dialectical relationship with other cultural forms that sometimes explore religious content. This is not a reductionist definition that allows everything in culture to be classified as religion. Rather, it recognizes that cultural forms can act religiously just as religion can be expressed through a secular institution like the church.

Religion is necessarily entangled with secular culture, and attempts to dichotomize secular and sacred realms in society blur this crucial relationship. Religion, according to Greeley, is intimately connected to culture because it emerges as a "story" within a culture, a type of cultural story that operates communally[110] but does not discount the possibility of private religious expression. Religion evolves as a culture evolves and changes in respect to cultural changes—sometimes religion changes the culture, but religion must always relate to the rest of the culture if it is to remain vital.[111] If religious expression runs too counter to other cultural trends, it runs the risk of being rejected by the rest of the cultural system as fundamentalism was culturally rejected in America in the 1920s because of its intransigent stance against modernism.[112]

Because religion and culture are indelibly connected, we must be careful to study religion and culture, as Jon Butler reminds us, in relation to "particular historical settings among real people in real places across real centuries."[113] Too often religious leaders and religious studies investigators place religion in cultural contexts other than its own, perhaps because religion is perceived to be the repository of eternal truth and thus immune from the vagaries of historical process and change. Religion has always been connected to, part of, and affected by the culture of which it is a part. If religious traditions attempt to remain aloof from contemporary culture, they will cease to be dynamic and relevant. When religious institutions absolutize beliefs and values, often in opposition to other aspects of the culture, they run the risk of stagnating the culture or of stagnating the tradition and becoming culturally irrelevant.[114] Thus, religion finds itself in the awkward position of competing in the cultural marketplace and aligning itself with a society's popular cultural forms.[115]

R. Laurence Moore's *Selling God: American Religion in the Marketplace of Culture* demonstrates very effectively how religion must compete with other cultural forms if it is to remain viable in a culture. According to Moore, religion becomes entangled with popular culture in various ways, often by first opposing it, but it almost always seems to find a way to embrace cultural trends in the competitive quest to remain relevant. When religion is popularized, it becomes closely aligned with entertainment and is sometimes virtually indistinguishable from secular amusements. Our consumption of culture includes our consumption of religion, and religion must be made palatable to remain current.[116] One of the most effective ways religion can compete for popular consumption is through mass media. The mass media offer both a challenge and a great potential for religion, threatening to lure away the interests of potential religious adherents and at the same time offering a means of reaching more people more effectively.[117] It is easy to see from the era of televangelism how the latter occurs, and author Quentin Schultze warns how the former can become problematic. According to Schultze, contemporary families do not communicate enough and depend too heavily on media information. Schultze believes that the media have invaded life and have impinged upon the ability of families to communicate meaningfully, and he advocates using popular media as a stimulus for communication rather than as a detriment to it.[118]

This trend in the popularization of religion as a cultural product signals a new era of secularization that differs from that described as the modern era of secularization. If the modern era of secularization promised the disappearance of religion, the new era, the postmodern era of secularization, promises the increasing relevance of religion expressed through popular cultural forms. In this way, perhaps Langdon Gilkey's premonition that the latter part of the twentieth century might witness "the beginning of the decline of the Enlightenment"[119] might come to fruition in the changing forecast for the future of religiosity.

Reflecting on postmodernism as a method and as a description of contemporary society can help us better understand this new era of secularization marked by the popularization of religion.

Postmodern culture and the popularization of religion

The Enlightenment and the modern era focused knowledge toward the empirical. Thanks to the scientific revolution, life and nature became explainable, understandable, and mundane. As with secularization in the modern age, we witnessed a loss of mystery, a loss of awe, a loss of the sacred myth that infused life with transcendent possibilities. The result is a Western society that has been demystified, and this has changed religion. For example, traditional religion has seen the rise of fundamentalism in the twentieth century, and fundamentalism, at least in the Christian tradition, focuses on the empirical. When fundamentalist Christianity demands an inerrant Bible, for example, it wants a standard of truth that allows no ambiguity, no mystery, no myth. In other words, it demands a faith based on empirical proof, on fact, and on historical evidence.

The postmodern world no longer needs a scientific revolution to drive its premises: rather its premises are the result of that revolution. Postmodernism is driven by the technological revolution, pluralism, and new threats to Western life. Whereas the scientific revolution demystified life by offering objective standards of truth, postmodern culture threatens to depersonalize life by championing diversity over conformity; heterogeneity over community. The call to diversity threatens to polarize society into insular camps and identities based on race, gender, affiliations, and ideologies. Technology, from air-conditioning to e-mail, makes this separation possible, threatens to insulate us from personal contact, and frees us from the necessity of community building. This depersonalization threatens to cut us off from familiar ways of considering the mysteries and myths formerly housed in religious traditions and institutionalized religious rituals.

Yet, even when this secularization and the loss of mystery occur, the religious sensibility does not disappear, and the need for mystery is dispersed through areas of life besides traditional religions. As religious beings, we desperately search for myths in other places, in art, literature, film, and a variety of other cultural forms. If secularization has demythologized our religion, then it has also remythologized our culture, and we find ourselves needing mystery, needing to think in some other way than empirically, needing to visualize in some other way than literally—we need and nurture this remythologization. This volume represents an exploration of our ability to nurture such abilities to think and visualize in some other ways than literally. This volume explores the reinvigoration of metaphor in religion. Contrary to realist and fundamentalistic assumptions, we want to continue to believe things are not always as we see them and hear them. If institutional religions no longer allow that belief, the religious sensibility will search for it elsewhere, and our postmodern world might find itself with a secular religiosity that has co-opted some of the functions formerly reserved for religious institutions.

The result is a postmodern society "defined by paradox"—a society that is "uncomfortable with religion" and the sacred, but one that is confronted with religious categories and images through various modes of popular culture. As the secularization of society continues, so does the dissipation of functions formerly reserved for religious institutions. We find popular culture functioning in some of the same ways as institutionalized religious ritual, so that popular culture is the entity that provides the context for understanding values, belief systems, and myths.[120]

Postmodernism describes a perceived condition of our contemporary society, particularly as it relates to popular culture. John Storey's *An Introductory Guide to Cultural Theory and Popular Culture* traces the development of postmodernism through various theoretical thinkers such as Jean-François Lyotard, Jean Baudrillard, and Frederic Jameson. According to Storey, a new pluralism is supposed to be one of the characteristics of our contemporary society following the collapse of modernism. Modernism was marked by the distinction between high culture and popular culture, including a suspicion of popular culture, which became associated with anarchy, and high culture, which reflected the ruling and bourgeois classes. Modernism became associated with "Truth" and standardized hermeneutics, while popular culture was associated with democracy and anarchy.[121] Postmodernism as a theory and method tends toward popular culture as the material for investigation. Postmodernism thus makes the study of popular culture more accessible and legitimate.

According to Storey, a landmark study that emphasizes this change is Jean-François Lyotard's *The Postmodern Condition*. Lyotard distinguishes between metanarrative and narrative in his assessment of the collapse of modernism and the rise of postmodernism. He asserts that metanarratives are universalist stories that focus on and provide an overarching meaning and order to produce a type of homogeneity of culture. Metanarrative characterized the modernist era with its standardization of culture, taste, and belief. However, in postmodernist culture, metanarratives are collapsing and being replaced by narratives, the voices of the periphery, the voices of difference and plurality. Postmodernism thus produces a culture of heterogeneity and diversity, where truth is no longer recognizable with a capital "T." Postmodernism signals the end of objective truth and replaces it with a culture without truth standards.[122]

Storey views the work of Jean Baudrillard as a continuation of the work of Lyotard and has investigated the possible consequences of the collapse of objective Truth. Baudrillard argues that postmodern culture operates in the realm of the "hyperreal" through "simulation," the blurring and merging of the imaginary and reality. With the collapse of objective Truth, claims Baudrillard, postmodern society has difficulty distinguishing simulation from reality, so that postmodern society experiences a crisis of belief as objective sources of authority and certainty lose efficacy. When this happens, the hyperreal can become more real than the real and postmoderns might have a difficult time separating depictions of reality from the real thing. If the film *JFK* comes to represent a new myth for the assassination of President John F. Kennedy, then the hyperreal has merged into the real; if we confuse movie violence with the real thing, then simulation has taken on primary meaning; if Disneyland becomes Americans' primary experience of their country and its history, then Baudrillard's point demonstrates the postmodern tendency to blur the lines and to confuse the distinctions between reality and simulation.[123] It is easy to imagine how traditional religious authority structures, science, or other systems making truth claims can collapse and be replaced by "simulated" realities. When this happens, not only does the concept of Truth or reality suffer, but story also loses its power as we transfer our illusions of objective truth onto cultural forms that should operate mythically. Nevertheless, when we turn to these simulations, we turn toward popular cultural forms for truth.

Finally, according to Storey, Frederic Jameson adds to the discussion by defining postmodern culture as a culture of "pastiche"—a culture that finds truth and value only in a nostalgic representation of the past. Postmodern culture suffers from "historical amnesia" and cannot distinguish real history from a nostalgic representation of stereotypes about an imagined past. This postmodern tendency creates false representations about truth that we have difficulty processing.[124] Examples of this "historical amnesia" abound in contemporary films like *Dances With Wolves* where nostalgic representations of history are paraded as real history and accepted as such by the culture.[125] What Jameson and others demonstrate is that popular cultural forms have the power to construct realities and myths—art becomes life, representation becomes reality.

If these assumptions about postmodern culture are accurate, then such a culture will value popular cultural forms as its main source of cultural meaning, myth, and legitimization. In the examinations that follow, one item for consideration will be the differing attitudes toward the study of popular culture in America and Europe. It seems that European intellectuals are less open to the value of studying popular culture as a source of meaning. Does their attitude mean that Europe as a society is less characterized by postmodern elements than the U.S.? Perhaps it suggests that European scholars accept what many of the postmodern theorists hypothesize: namely that postmodernism represents a decay of culture and a demise of society. This demise is expressed not only in how a culture views history but also in the way a culture views ultimate reality. In such a culture, it is as easy to receive truth from the movie house as from the synagogue or church. When this happens, we witness what David Jasper has referred to as the "absorption of the sacred into the profane," which might be, as Jasper has suggested, "a kenotic move."[126] Certainly, if postmodern society infuses the profane or the secular with sacred significance, the kenosis is complete and the response of the religious institutions in such a society is to embrace the sacred by embracing the profane. This leads us to the two ways secularization occurs in postmodern society.

The two directions of secularization

If the modern era promised the disappearance of religion through secularization, the postmodern era promises the increased visibility of religion, although not necessarily in traditional packages. Contemporary American culture witnesses secularization occurring in two directions: 1) the churches and religious organizations are becoming increasingly more attuned to the secular environment, particularly to popular culture, and are in some cases trying to emulate it in the effort to remain relevant; 2) popular cultural forms, including literature, film, and music, are becoming increasingly more visible vehicles of religious images, symbols, and categories. These two directions of secularization demonstrate the blurred or malleable boundaries between religion and culture, the sacred and the secular, that define the relationship of religion and culture in the postmodern era.[127]

First, if we focus on the American Christian community in particular, it is clear that some segments of the population are drawn by church traditions that are closely aligned to secular and worldly culture. R. Laurence Moore suggests this occurs because religion in America has had to sell itself to compete and defines secularization according to religion's "commodification," not its disappearance.[128] Others understand this alignment with the secular in light of Christianity's perceived obligation to act in the world.[129] Regardless of the motivations behind the trend, it seems this pattern puts religion in a reactive stance, where religions that work best are the most effective in dealing with the crises or trends of a society.[130] Religion tends to do this through revival and innovation, according to Rodney Stark and William Sims Bainbridge in *The Future of Religion: Secularization, Revival and Cult Formation.*[131] As R. Laurence Moore makes clear, in *American Christianity*, this spirit of innovation is clearly seen throughout its history, from George Whitefield's ability to make sermons entertaining, to Charles G. Finney's guidelines for mounting a successful revival, to the hedonistic air of some nineteenth-century camp meetings, to twentieth-century televangelists, to Heritage, U.S.A.-type theme parks.[132] In every case, these religious innovations were designed to allow Christianity to compete for popularity and remain relevant, and they led to the church taking on aspects of worldliness. Perhaps the most conscious efforts of ecclesiastical innovation to remain relevant came from the Social Gospel movement in the late nineteenth and early twentieth centuries. The Social Gospel movement wanted to reform all aspects of life (work, education, entertainment, etc.) in order to protect Christianity's relevance in the modern world.[133]

In the attempt to remain relevant in contemporary society, more and more churches are employing popular cultural forms from the media and technology to raise religious questions in a way that parishioners will embrace.[134] This seems to be particularly effective in attracting young people to church. Jacqulyn Weekley puts it this way: "Archaic terminology doesn't resonate with the younger genera-tions because they've been brought up with technology. If the church doesn't use the language they're familiar with, then we're perceived as having no relevance in their lives."[135] And in an article in *Christianity Today*, Timothy C. Morgan demonstrated the extent of this perceived need for using technology in the church. The title of the article itself suggests the church's way of thinking when it comes to keeping up with the times: "Cyber Shock: New Ways of Thinking Must be Developed for the Church to Keep Pace in the Coming Information Age."[136]

The emphasis on media and technology is probably nowhere more clear than in the "megachurch" movement that increased in popularity during the 1990s in the United States and even in Europe. Megachurches are huge suburban churches with membership rolls in the thousands that seek to be relevant by sponsoring elements of secular life, including technology and media-produced presenta-tions and entertainments, within the walls of a church. In any particular week, a member of a megachurch might go bowling, attend an aerobics class, play basketball, seek family counseling, and attend a multimedia presentation, all within the church's confines.[137] American church historian Bill Leonard calls the megachurch movement the "Wal-Martization of American religion"[138] by noting that the megachurch philosophy is to provide for every need of the potential consumer. Finally, the megachurch worship service tends to be high-energy and includes entertainment forms such as contemporary music, plays, and skits, while youth programs might include church-made music videos, arcade games, and laser light shows—the emphasis seems to be on entertainment to keep a high level of interest.[139] The megachurch movement is an international trend. The movement's model church, Willow Creek Community Church in suburban Chicago, boasts some 27,000 worshipers on Easter morning.[140] But even in smaller communities in traditional Bible-Belt settings, the megachurch influence is alive and well with community churches modeled on Willow Creek using secular entertainment like popular movies or business tools like PowerPoint to preach the gospel.[141]

These examples suggest that many contemporary religious traditions have adopted a reactionary stance toward technology, popular culture and the secular world, employing elements of popular culture in an "if you can't beat 'em, join 'em" mentality in order to remain competitive and relevant in contemporary society. Perhaps no better illustration is needed than the one that introduces this chapter: the monks of the Monastery of Christ in the Desert in Chama River Canyon, New Mexico, who stay connected to the world via the World-Wide Web. On the one hand, like ancient monasteries, this one is no different in providing the monks retreat from the secular world and materialism. On the other hand, the monks are not afraid to use secular technology as a tool to remain relevant and to prosper.[142] As we see more and more examples of religions becoming more like secular culture, we witness the first direction secularization is taking in postmodern culture. This phase of secularization seeks to regain what was lost in the modern phase of secularization—relevance and power.

The second direction of secularization involves the spreading of religious messages, symbols, and concerns in other cultural forms besides the traditionally religious. When traditional religious institutions lose their power, and even when they do not, religiosity will express itself in other parts of the culture, oftentimes in popular cultural forms. So, in the contemporary secularization movement, not only do we see religious institutions becoming more like the secular world, we also see secular forms of entertainment and culture carrying religious messages. If this is true, then secularization in the postmodern age could result in a wider dissemination of religious messages than ever through a broader base of cultural vehicles. Rather than witnessing religion diminish, we might witness a culture of religious saturation where religious symbolism and questions are dispersed throughout the cultural landscape.[143] Many religious elements are expressed through secular forms characteristic of culture and time period. This does not mean that everything can be religion but that many different aspects of culture can provide a forum for religious discussion.[144] Thus, in our cultural studies, which include the study of literature, art, film, music, and so on, we expect to find a religious dimension beyond the traditional that extends to the popular level,[145] because myth and ritual can be expressed through story and aesthetic expression as well as through doctrine.

Often, religious leaders adopt certain popular forms of culture to express religious truth when they recognize that those forms can command the attention of the public. Thus, even though some such forms might be initially suspect (for example, Hollywood and popular novels), they can also provide an excellent vehicle for carrying religious messages.[146] In these cases, the "sacralization" of secular forms is purposeful and direct. In other cases, the sacralization of secular cultural forms might be simply a product of the dialectical relationship between religion and other cultural forms, because they have the ability to express a cultural worldview as well as the personal attitudes and beliefs of the artists and creators of cultural products.[147] This is why, as R. Laurence Moore suggests, Mark Twain could declare that religion came more from the "despised novel" than from the "drowsy pulpit."[148] But this is also why many secular products of culture can carry sacred significance—from civil religion to modern fiction with apocalyptic messages.[149] One thing is certain: with the constant pressure to censure popular cultural forms, the public perceives these forms to have the power to shape and define morality, attitudes, and ethics. In this sense at least, they carry religious significance and aspirations.

Looking ahead: secular/sacred portals

This chapter began with an image of twentieth-century monks slaving away at keyboards that connect them to the outside world through cyberspace and the World-Wide Web. Technology has provided them with a way to connect with the world without involving themselves in the world. This real-life image reminds me of a series of commercials for a photocopy machine years ago: a monk produced perfect copies of an ancient manuscript in record time by using a photocopy machine, and his fellow monks thought it was a miracle. This real-life example and the humorous commercial message tell us something about our culture. They demonstrate on a fundamental level how the secular has intruded upon the sacred realm or how the sacred has been subsumed into the profane. The examples also suggest that how we receive the truth has changed—if secularization has not changed the fundamental religious need of humanity to ask ultimate questions, perhaps it has altered the way we seek answers to those questions. Rather than relying solely on revelation, the inbreaking of the sacred, we rely on reification, the secular manufacturing of truth. The chapters that follow examine how secularization has occurred in two directions in contemporary American culture, helping the reader understand his or her own religious sensibilities, cultural involvement, and perhaps even future trends and possibilities for religion and culture.

Without trying to be exhaustive, I have chosen to limit the investigation to four areas (windows or portals to truth) that have been constant in Western culture and, more precisely, in American culture. Thus, the examination will focus on American popular culture and the American religious imagination, but is based on Western ways of searching for meaning. Throughout the history of Western religion, there have appeared human windows to the transcendent—attempts to see beyond and experience truth, wholeness, holiness, God. Four of these portals—space/place, text, image, and community—arise time and again in the attempt to conceptualize the transcendent. The portals also provide avenues for secular stories as well. Places, texts, images, and communities tell stories both sacred and secular, and, regardless of whether the place, text, image, or community is sacred or secular, we often find these portals attempting to establish some truth. The temple and the secular monument, Scripture or state constitution, art, both sacred and secular, church groups and civic organizations—all of these participate in telling stories, myths, and foundational truths about humanity's relationship to the divine and to society. These portals, sacred and secular, establish an interconnectedness, a dialogue, a constant interchange about reality. Perhaps the definition of truth will differ, but these sacred and secular windows function similarly—to provide a sense of meaning and order to life.

In ancient, medieval, and pre-modern Western societies, space, its organization and humanization, allowed a sense of place to grant meaning. In cultures where literacy was largely absent or limited, places (such as the magnificent cathedrals of Europe) allowed a portal to truth, to the transcendent, for those without the written word. As such, space constitutes a type of pre-text to meaning in the West, replaced during the modern era by text as narrative meaning, which replaced spatial meaning as a primary portal of truth. As literacy rose in the modern era, text became the primary medium for humanity's deepest yearnings. We see this most clearly expressed religiously in Luther's reliance on "Scripture alone" for authority and expressed generally with the technology offered by the printing press. Now our postmodern era witnesses the decline of textual supremacy as images, television, movies, virtual reality, and image-rich web pages compete with and, some believe, supplant text as the primary conveyance of meaning in our culture—supported, of course, by the advent and popularization of new technologies. In one sense, we have reached back beyond text to the pre-textual situation, coming full circle so that our post-textual reliance on images mirrors our pre-textual dependence on spatial orientation.[150] And with our reliance on image, where our identities are defined by Facebook, we seek more than ever that fourth portal, community—real and virtual.

This does not suggest mutual exclusiveness during historical periods. Quite the contrary. The human quest for meaning takes place through all four portals, sometimes in concert. For example, images such as Christian art were an integral part of spatial orientations in a pre-textual situation, just as text is a critical part of a post-textual, postmodern film. And art is both defined by and experienced by a community. Nor does it suggest that other components of culture are absent in the quest for meaning. Rather, I am suggesting that sense of place, text, image, and community have and do contribute to the process of building and perpetuating myth, which seems to lie at the heart of humanity's search for meaning. Sense of place, text, image, and community participate in a culture's storytelling and represent four and only four of the various ways humans seek and express truths.

At some times and in some places, one or the other may tend to dominate, but all four are present in the cultural sacred and secular myths that help define what cultures hold to be true.

In the following pages, I look at each portal and examine the secular–sacred dialogue taking place in contemporary America. The dialogue illustrates the claim in this chapter that secularization should be seen as taking place in two directions: secularization equals secularizing the sacred as well as sacralizing the secular. This secularization of space, text, image, and community, regardless of its orientation or direction, constitutes the relationship between religion and culture that steers our search for meaning.

Study guide

Important words and concepts

Enlightenment
Fundamentalism
Institutional religion
Megachurch
Myth
Popular religion
Rationalism
Sacralization
Sacred
Secular
Secularization
Two directions of secularization as outlined in this chapter
Western worldviews

Study questions

(1) How does this chapter redefine the process of secularization as it is normally understood in sociological theory?
(2) Why do religions in American have to compete for adherents or relevance?
(3) How might popular culture function as religion in contemporary society?
(4) Describe the process of shifting power and authority structures in society. How does this affect religion?
(5) Describe the concept of permeable boundaries as used in this chapter.
(6) How does a literal understanding of scripture damage religious myth/truth?

Guided reading

Read the following:

(1) The First Amendment to the U.S. Constitution

(2) Thomas Jefferson's Letter to the Danbury Baptist Association of 1802

(3) Supreme Court Case Lee v. Weisman (1992)

(4) How do the First Amendment stance against establishment, Jefferson's "wall of separation," and the opinion rendered in Lee v. Weisman illustrate the way that secularization is proceeding in America?

Part One
Pre-text

3

Space/Place/Pre-text

In what is probably the most famous presidential speech in American history, Abraham Lincoln concisely and eloquently spoke words that describe the consecration of sacred ground through great and heroic deeds. Speaking at the dedication of the cemetery at Gettysburg, President Lincoln declared, "… we can not dedicate, we can not consecrate, we can not hallow this ground. The brave men, living and dead, who struggled here, have consecrated it …"[1] With this short declaration, President Lincoln defined the sacralization of secular space: heroic struggle and supreme effort transform ordinary space into transcendent place and create a sacred site, a portal to the divine. We see this most clearly on battlefields like Gettysburg where the supreme sacrifice of warriors consecrate the soil. We also see the sacralization of space in the creation of monuments to great people and historic events. Washington, DC, for example, is awash with sacred spaces, monuments built to commemorate the struggles that have consecrated American history. Monuments to Washington, Jefferson, Lincoln, and King sacralize the great deeds of our canonized leaders; monuments to soldiers and tombs of warriors sacralize the sacrifice of the fallen; sacred cathedrals preserve founding documents and American history. All of these sites are secular in intent but sacred in function, serving to provide sanctuaries for worship in the great American civil religion.

In the same way, lesser-known individuals and events can hold sacred meaning and create sacred spaces for individuals. My grandfather's 1966 farm truck sits in my driveway. The sweat of his and my father's work and efforts has consecrated that truck for me. As I sit in it or drive it, it becomes a portal for transcendence, a means of connection with those spirits from beyond. A spot in China, where I first held my daughter, provided a transcendent experience upon my pilgrimage back to that sacred place. Family land, old homesteads, familiar churches, places of importance in the individual and collective lives of people can transport us beyond ourselves because they have been consecrated by important moments or great deeds or collective experiences. In American culture, one of the most recognizable and accessible collective sacred places is the field of athletic contest. The court, the diamond, the field, the pitch, the course: these are places where Americans compete and seek collective transcendence, to be transformed beyond themselves to an elevated place of being, meaning, and ecstasy—to experience "the thrill of victory …." as the "Wide World of Sports" introduction went, "and the agony of defeat."[2]

Since Michael Novak published his *The Joy of Sports* in 1976, I have been acutely aware of the spiritual underpinnings of sports in our culture. Novak brilliantly made his case that "sports belong in the category of religion."[3] His portrait of the rituals and ceremonies accompanying sports helps to define the permeable boundaries of religion and culture in America. Novak also treated sacred space in his book and talked about how the sports field defined sacred and profane boundaries. The field as sacred space demarked an area for the priests (the athletes) to perform the sacred rituals. Novak says sports fields "are consecrated places"[4] and arenas are "our cathedrals."[5] The sacred field, writes Novak, establishes sports as "religions of place" where great deeds consecrate the ground like Gettysburg or some hallowed battlefield.[6] But the field also can function as sacred space for the non-clerical or non-priestly participant. The fan also has a stake in the field, and, just as the boundaries of stadia mark off the space for the sacred ritual, so do the confines of stadia provide a cathedral for the believer. As an illustration of the power of sports fields to function as sacred space, I will focus on two iconic American football stadia—Lambeau Field in Green Bay, Wisconsin, and Cowboys Stadium in Arlington, Texas. These two sports fields/complexes could not be more different in history, tradition, and character. Nevertheless, they both function as sacred space where the collective devotion of thousands of fans is focused on the sacred character for what otherwise is a very secular activity—football.

It is difficult for a non-fan to appreciate the fanaticism and devotion of Green Bay Packers fans to their team and their stadium. Lambeau Field, home of the Packers' games for more than a half-century, is one of the most tradition-laden sports arenas in the country. That the team is the only publically owned team in the National Football League adds to the sense of ownership fans have for the stadium and increase the sense of collectivity and kinship felt by the Packers' faithful. Lambeau has the longest history of any football stadium in the NFL, and fans revel in its tradition. Even though upgrades have necessarily been made through the years, the original site remains, and great care has been taken to maintain original features and an authentic retro feel. Effort has also been made to communicate the sense of awe that surrounds this sports team and its spiritual home. When you log on to the official website for Lambeau Field and go to the heading for History, the section begins with the words, "Hallowed Ground."[7] The website description of the stadium includes words and phrases such as "hallowed," "awe-inspiring," "mystique," "revered," and "majesty." These are not words one would normally associate with the ultra-masculine sport of football, but they are words one associates with religion. Lambeau Field is not just a space for athletic events; it is a place consecrated by great and heroic deeds and dedicated for future moments of transcendence. All Packer fans, for example, know of the infamous Ice Bowl, the NFL Championship held on December 31, 1967 in temperatures of –13 to –15 degrees (–46 wind chill). The Packers quarterback, Bart Starr, directed a drive that ended with a quarterback sneak into the end zone in the last minute of play to defeat the Dallas Cowboys, 21–17. One of the most famous games in history, made more so by the extreme conditions, this moment made heroes of players who are permanently etched into the collective memories of Packers fans. And their great achievement that day consecrated the field—it gave the field mythic status as hallowed ground, which it otherwise might not have attained.

For any Packers fan, a journey to Lambeau is a pilgrimage; attendance at a game, a sacred rite; presence at a championship game, a transcendent moment. I dare say that the feelings involved rival the deep-seated religious emotions engendered when a devout believer takes a pilgrimage to a religious site of meaning. Devout believers often recreate sacred spaces while away from pilgrimage sites. A Catholic might have a shrine in the home; the Protestant might seek out a prayer chapel; a Muslim uses a prayer rug to ensure ritual cleanliness for prayer; a Buddhist finds a meditation spot convenient for daily practice. In these examples, believers create sacred places away from major sacred sites in a way that connects them to a sacred place and a transcendent reality. Shrines abound so that veneration may take place. It is no different for the sports fan. I have a friend who has created just such a shrine—for the outsider, it may seem a bit of cultural shtick, but for the initiate, my friend's shrine pays homage to the Packer heritage in a small, recreated space that stands in for the Lambeau experience. My friend has a Packer room in his house. Filled with Packer memorabilia, turf wainscoting, framed Packers stock certificates, and a life-size cutout of Brett Favre (whose head and number have been covered over by those of Aaron Rodgers—what can I say, heroes and saints can fall from grace), this space serves as a portal, as all sacred spaces do, to something larger than self; something transcendent in space and time; even something redemptive in intent. Quotes from perhaps the greatest Packer patron saint, Vince Lombardi, line the walls and provide inspirational (scriptural) truths; autographs from Bart Starr and Ray Nitschke (Packer legends) become saintly relics, like bits of fabric or splinters of wood from the lives of Christian saints; a spiritual journal detailing a 1998 pilgrimage to the Superbowl with all its trials and tribulations records for future generations the long trek to a holy event. And perhaps the most meaningful display in the space, which truly makes this a shrine, is a small bit of grass and turf, from Lambeau Field itself, taken from the field after the 1997 playoff victory against the 49ers. This is sacred earth, hallowed ground, and it consecrates my friend's shrine, promising connection to the place where great deeds have occurred and great myths have been born.

On the opposite end of the spectrum in the National Football collection of stadia stands a modern marvel of engineering and glitz: Cowboys Stadium. Cowboys Stadium was completed in May of 2009, replacing Texas Stadium where the Cowboys had played since the 1970s, so it stands in stark contrast to the historical Lambeau Field. And while Lambeau Field has attempted to retain a retro feel, Cowboys stadium is postmodern in feel and appearance. Standing before its huge glass wall with steel retaining buttresses, one gets the feeling of standing before a postmodern Notre Dame or a secular version of Robert Schuller's Crystal Cathedral in California. It is impressive, and its amenities, which make the mind boggle, are designed to enhance the experience of the attendee. The domed stadium includes a retractable roof, which mimics the distinctive open-roof design of the former Texas Stadium, and suspended from that roof is a huge high-definition television so the fan can revel in the collective, ritual experience without missing the replays or highlights. Cowboys Stadium lacks the history and tradition of Lambeau, but it pays homage to sports and creates a sacred space through its awe-inspiring architecture and overwhelming ambience. And that it is new, the storied Cowboys team has the opportunity to write a new myth with new heroes in the space where the gods compete.

The spaces we inhabit become the places we construct, the places in which we move and live and love and worship. Human beings project meaning into the spaces they inhabit. Spaces tell stories, but they do so as pre-text, apart from text, and sometimes supplementary to text. In the Christian tradition, no space is more obviously enriched with metaphorical meaning than a church. From the grand cathedrals of Europe, to plain Puritan structures of the New World, to megachurch sports arenas in Los Angeles, these worship spaces enfold symbolic religious meaning and express fundamental values, beliefs, and desires. But specifically religious buildings are not the only spaces that express values and beliefs. Secular spaces such as patriotic monuments, memorials, and commercial icons sometimes become "holy" ground with deep meaning for a culture or society. Thus with spaces we have a pre-text that enfolds metaphorical and symbolic meaning, and we have places that demonstrate the flexible and malleable boundaries that exist between the sacred and secular—our sacred places sometimes mimic our secular ones while our secular spaces often take on sacred functions. I examine the two directions of secularization through spatial arrangement by considering contemporary changes in church structures and functions and by examining a secular political institution that functions with sacred intent. Megachurches and Love Valley demonstrate the secularization and sacralization of American space.

The secularization of tradition: megachurches and the marketing of Christianity

Zurich, Switzerland: heart of the sixteenth-century Swiss Reformation. Huldrych Zwingli led the reform with a brand of zealous Christianity designed in part to drive worldly and Catholic characteristics out of Christian worship. In Zwingli's church, if the Bible did not prescribe a certain act or ritual, such an act was disallowed. Thus, there would be no organ music in worship or icons to adorn the ritual space. These were fine for the Catholic Church but too worldly for Zwingli. His complaint centered on the secularity issue. For Zwingli, both the Catholic Church and many of his Protestant allies were too embroiled in worldly cares and practices. Yet Zwingli allied himself with civil authorities in order to carry out his reforms. Thus, we see the problematic nature of dealing with the relationship of religion and secularity.[8]

Contemporary Zurich is marked by wealth and by the high living that accompanies being the banking capital of the world. The city is characterized by a vibrant youth culture that stands in stark contrast to Zwingli's austere religion. Old Town Zurich teems with swarms of young people streaming in and out of bars, cabarets, sex shops, and X-rated movie theaters. On centuries-old streets, where Zwingli walked and preached a faith of austerity, the ambience is now high-energy to appeal to youth, to members of Generation X in search of entertainment and immediate gratification. If Zwingli were alive in Zurich today, his fiery sermons would likely take on a new zeal and fervency.

This scene plays itself out in the narrow streets of the medieval Old Town to create a strange setting for what some hope to be a new kind of church reformation. In stark contrast to Zwingli's attempt to drive out worldly and secular elements from the church, the International Christian Fellowship (ICF) is promoting a reformation for the twenty-first century—the megachurch movement. Some three and a half centuries after Zwingli, Zurich has once again become a center for church reform, and this time, rather than leading a Swiss reform movement, the ICF is attempting to use Zurich as a European spearhead for the megachurch movement. Rather than battle worldly characteristics that make their way into the church, the ICF embraces secular ways that capture the attention of what they see as a restless 20-something generation that is largely unchurched but in search of spiritual peace. The ICF uses secular enticements to attract these young people to church by filling their services with a Christianized version of high-energy, entertainment-oriented activities in worship that tend to mimic what one might find on the streets of the Old Town. Visiting an ICF worship service, one gets the impression that the church is in competition with the secular attractions in this thriving city and that it is using or borrowing secular activities from popular youth culture to compete with those elements attracting Generation Xers.[9]

A service that employs movie clips, MTV-style entertainment, and pop music with Christian lyrics in order to draw the unchurched to worship seems strangely out of place anywhere in Europe, let alone in Zurich. But it seems to be working as the church continues to experience success and growth. With a heavy emphasis on outreach and evangelism, the goal is to recapture a lost generation. The strategy is to use the culture of that generation to shape a liturgy and, to some extent, a theology. The church is very forthright and conscious concerning its target audience, Generation Xers; its motivation, outreach; and its strategy, use of popular culture.[10]

The first Sunday of each month at the ICF is set aside for special services to attract new young people to the church. It is during these services that the megachurch philosophy is most visible. In particular, the philosophy embraces using elements of popular culture that will make going to church relevant and attractive and necessarily adopts secular culture as its baseline standard. In contrast to Zwingli's sixteenth-century reform to drive secular elements out of the church, the megachurches' and the ICF's contemporary reformation embrace parts of popular and secular culture to make Christianity relevant for a generation searching for some meaningful, guiding philosophical or ethical perspective. Will this movement, which became popular first in the United States, prosper in Europe? A strong history of state religion makes the scenario improbable. But in Switzerland, a country historically proud of its independence, the movement seems to be gathering steam. A decade after I first encountered the ICF movement in Zurich, the church has grown, spread, and seems to be experiencing success. Certainly, Switzerland would be the logical place for any such movement to begin and take root in Europe, if in fact it does. The outcome of the Zurich experiment will tell us much about the state of American and European society and the extent to which each has secularized in the contemporary world.

Christianity and secularization

Many theologians critique the megachurch movement and decry the state of the contemporary church for allowing itself to become secularized. Much of what critics term secularization arises from a comparison of current practices to what religion used to be: a debate between innovation and tradition. But the suggestion that the secularization of Christianity is a contemporary or Protestant phenomenon ignores the history and development of the church from its inception. When we witness the concessions religion makes to secular science, no matter how delayed, such as Pope John Paul II's recognition of the theory of evolution or the Catholic Church's 1992 reversal of its condemnation of Galileo's theories about a heliocentric solar system,[11] it is easy to forget that the Christian tradition has been secularizing since its beginning. Many of the prescriptions outlined by Paul, and other early Christian writings, arise from the complexities stemming from the church's contact with secular society. One might even argue that one of the church's early defining moments, the Council of Jerusalem, occurred in response to secularization. In the first century, the struggling new religion was still as much a Jewish sect as it was a separate religion. The tradition's first crisis came when Paul and others began to make "concessions" to Hellenistic culture in order to spread the religion and to make the religion relevant on a larger scale. These concessions to secular culture allowed Christianity to survive and spread, but the tradition was changed by these secularizing trends.

Alongside these secularizing trends in early Christianity, a pattern of anti-secularism developed during times of crisis and hardship in the Christian community. The Book of John's Revelation urges the persecuted faithful to remain steadfast in light of the dawning apocalypse. According to John's vision, the final judgment would separate the faithful from the worldly, the sacred from the secular; for these reasons, Christians were urged to abstain from secular ways (Roman ways) even if it meant death. This same anti-secular attitude was echoed by Montanus, a second-century prophet who warned of doom and urged the church to return to its pure state, or to the way things were in the early days before the church had been tainted by worldly concessions. Prophets and reformers invariably take up the call to reform the church by returning it to its pristine and primitive condition. Whether Paul, Montanus, St. Francis, Zwingli, or Alexander Campbell and Barton Stone, the message represents a reaction to the same enduring secularizing tendencies that have been part of Christian history from the beginning.

So a pattern established itself early on: the tradition institutionalized and necessarily made concessions to secular society, and some leaders/prophets spoke out against such concessions in favor of a pure, untainted religion. But not all reaction was disposed against secularizing tendencies. Some in and outside of the church were able to use secularization to great political and ecclesiastical advantage. For example, Christianity experienced a wholesale period of secularization when the Emperor Constantine recognized Christianity as a legitimate religion. Until this point in its history, the Christian story often had been told through martyrs' blood as the sect struggled in a hostile culture. Worship was simple, if not secret. Worship places, if they existed as such, were more often than not someone's home or the catacombs. Hierarchy was at a minimum. Then suddenly, in one swift move in the early fourth century, Constantine revolutionized Christianity. He recognized the persecuted religion, granted it tolerance, and perhaps even adopted it. For the first time in history, Christians were free to worship with imperial sanction. The church changed rapidly: rituals were formalized and became more elaborate as befitting an imperial religion; creeds took on a greater and more political role; rich and impressive worship houses were constructed; artwork flooded churches as an aid to worship; clergy took on greater prestige in society. In short, the church became more institutionalized, more political, wealthier, and took on a more prestigious and culturally central role in society. Christianity became more secular and worldly than ever before, but once again secularization allowed the church to thrive. With its newfound wealth and respect, the costs of being Christian were greatly diminished.

Because of these changes, one would expect a protest against such secularization, and of course it happened. The Donatists believed the church had been corrupted, and they created a noisy schism. Some priests viewed imperial sanction as a worldly apostasy and protested quietly by retreating into seclusion where they could escape the worldly entrapments of the new church. The monastic movement began to organize seriously and gain momentum in a rejection of Constantine's new Christianity, in which membership was easy and fashionable. "Too worldly" was the complaint of the first Christian hermits, and they sought seclusion away from the secularized aspects of their church. But the protest was small, and the church entered a new era of its history.

Constantine's legitimization of Christianity led to a new and energized church, a church that would grow to enjoy power and prestige in the secular realm. In the East, the Byzantine Church quickly became the imperial church and was intimately involved with the imperial dynasty. In the West, Augustine wrote about the relationship of the Christian to the secular powers. In his classic work, *City of God*, he asserted that Christians, who must for a time live in the secular world, were ultimately citizens of the heavenly city, a higher authority. While Augustine's treatise was meant to direct the Christian's ultimate allegiance, later interpreters read him as establishing a hierarchy of sorts that justified their assertions of ecclesiastical authority in secular matters. And by the collapse of the Roman Empire in the fifth century, the church in Rome was poised and ready to step into the power vacuum created by a crumbling secular governing structure. Armed by later interpretations of Augustine's *City of God*, and led by opportunistic and able popes like Gregory the Great, secular power was virtually thrust upon and readily accepted by the medieval sacred institution. The church of the Middle Ages became the power broker in medieval Europe, manipulating secular rulers and secular events and culminating with the symbolic coronation of Charlemagne as Holy Roman Emperor in 800. With this event, the Holy Roman Empire, an intimate marriage of church and state in medieval Europe, was formalized, and the secular involvement of Western Christendom was actual as well as expedient.

The Middle Ages saw the rise and fall of a succession of popes, some of whom used their secular powers very effectively to build an empire for the Christian church. Incredible wealth and extensive political clout transformed the papacy into an administrative and governmental quagmire requiring skilled and able leadership and diplomacy. The secular powers of the church were never greater, and state Christianity became the norm throughout Europe. Popes manipulated rulers and controlled events. Their power is perhaps best illustrated by the well-known and famed story of Hildebrand (Pope Gregory VII) and the German King Henry IV. During the eleventh century, the two found themselves at odds over the issue of lay investiture. Hildebrand, a reforming pope, sought to discontinue the practice of lay investiture as a means of centralizing authority and maintaining stricter control. The temptation of secular princes to settle favors and debts by handing out attractive bishoprics as a means of political expediency was simply too great in Hildebrand's eyes. Henry, however, balked at this restriction of his power and made an appointment in direct disobedience of papal decree. The crisis came to a head when Hildebrand excommunicated Henry, and the German nobles pressured their leader to make amends with Rome. The two sides scheduled a summit at Augsburg to settle the issue. While Hildebrand made his way north to embarrass Henry on his own turf, Henry headed south in hopes of spoiling Hildebrand's staging. Hildebrand fortified himself in a castle at Canossa in northern Italy because he feared Henry came to meet him with the sword. But Henry appeared before the pope at Canossa barefoot, dressed as a penitent, eventually able to wring a reluctant absolution from Hildebrand. This clash between sacred and secular forces represents the degree to which ecclesiastical and secular authority had become intermeshed and interwoven. The church, a sacred institution, had secularized to a tremendous degree during the height of the Middle Ages. Likewise, secular authority in this case was undergirded, if only symbolically, by sacred sponsorship.

Medieval Catholicism was not alone in its ecclesiastical involvement with secular and worldly authority. The Protestant reform movements of the sixteenth century were as much interested in ecclesiastical/institutional reform as they were in theological reform. Luther's protest started as disgust over clerical abuse, and he sparked a revolution against ecclesiastical authority structures. But Luther's reform did little to undo the extent to which secularization had affected the institutional church. Luther found himself an ally of civil authorities when he was appalled by the peasant revolt. And neither Luther nor Calvin would hear of dismantling the church–state partnership that medieval Catholicism had so meticulously constructed. In fact, Calvin's Geneva experiment in theocracy represents the claim of a church with unquestioned secular reach. Henry VIII's state church in England did nothing to challenge a secularized ecclesia. Of the Protestant reform movements, only the radical wing of reformers, the Anabaptists and their offshoots, tried to sever the church–state tie and undo the effects of a secularized ecclesia. Even today, the descendants of these reformers hold staunchly to the principle of separation and normally maintain strict provisions against worldly involvement. Perhaps in contemporary America, the Amish groups in Ohio and Pennsylvania best represent this protest movement against a secularized religion.

While secularization of Christianity is best expressed in Europe through its history of state religion, this is not the case in the United States, which has attempted through civil law to keep church and state separate. Does this mean that the United States is less secularized than Europe? Although many scholars claim it is so, it is not necessarily the case. The church in North America since the Revolutionary period has not enjoyed state support as in Europe, so the sacred–secular entanglement is not established as the rule. Nevertheless, Christianity in the United States has secularized in different ways, including voluntarily adopting and competing with popular culture and secular models of entertainment.[12] In the absence of compulsion, the church had to attract, and in many cases it attracted by conforming to popular trends. As noted earlier in this book, traditions such as the Social Gospel movement of the nineteenth century provide an excellent example. Unable to compete with popular culture with a radically different worldview, the Social Gospel proponents attempted to compete by adopting and revising the popular, secular worldview and thus competing with secular culture bolstered by sacred foundations.

Religion in the United States has always operated on a voluntary basis; however, this concept is relatively new and developing in Europe. Therefore, in Europe, with church participation no longer compulsory or even expedient, it often appears that European society is more secular (less religious) because European churches have not operated on the basis of competition. Although church attendance is not an adequate indicator of religiosity by itself, the statistics are telling. According to Ronald Inglehart of the Institute for Social Research, the United States boasts 30–32 percent of the population attending church on any one Sunday, while countries in northern Europe only cite a 5–15 percent church attendance.[13]

More than church attendance, however, we can look at the history of the entanglement of the sacred and secular in Europe and America to assess the extent of secularization. Whereas, in medieval Europe, secularization appears to have occurred under what Peter L. Berger termed a "sacred canopy,"[14] where the church's sacred authority included secular society, in modern America the opposite appears to be occurring. The church in the United States appears to be operating under a "secular canopy," where secular and popular trends often dictate ecclesiastical strategy. The level of authority for religion in these two paradigms is drastically different, but in both models, secular involvement is a given and secularization is a foregone conclusion. If secularization means that a religious tradition loses authority to control society's ways, then perhaps Europe is more secular; however, if secularization means entanglement with secular and popular culture, then the church in the United States seems to be more defined by secular society. We should not make this an either/or definition of secularization but adopt a definition broad enough to include both trends of secularization.

This brief survey of Christian secularization is neither exhaustive nor representative in intent or effect. It is meant simply to point out that, from its inception, the Christian religion began institutionalizing and interacting with the secular world. This interaction led to secularization—the church in Western society has never been a purely sacred entity. And despite the title Holy Roman Empire, Western society has never been a completely sacred culture. The process of secularization has differed in its extent and effect at various points in the church's history, but the process has been a consistent and on-going part of the Christian institution. Secularization is different in Europe than in America, not as much in degree as in kind. It is probably fruitless to argue that one culture is more secularized than another, as many do in the case of Europe or in comparing the great diversity of cultures that make up Europe and the United States.

In addition, this survey sets the stage for a discussion about the megachurch movement. This movement is a purposeful attempt to incorporate secular and popular culture in the life of the church; therefore, it presents in concentrated form trends that take place anyway. A description of this movement will reveal much not only about how Christianity might be secularizing but also about how American and European communities will respond to such a movement. Will American Christians respond more readily to the megachurches because they are already more in tune to popular and secular culture? This seems to be the case at least initially, as we will explore later. At least in part, the ready acceptance of the megachurch movement in the United States has developed as an American trend during the last 20 to 40 years.

The megachurch movement in some ways grew out of the rise of media evangelism in the 1970s and 1980s, a movement that enjoyed much more momentum in the United States than in Europe. Fundamentalist Christian leaders discovered a mass market for their evangelical form of Christianity through various forms of mass media. After pioneering efforts in radio and television, evangelists wholeheartedly embraced these worldly media as a way of spreading the gospel. Their entanglement with secular culture is symbolized perhaps most clearly by Jim and Tammy Bakker's Heritage U.S.A. theme park. The Bakkers managed to market Christianity by nostalgically depicting secular America through a sacred lens, or was it sacred religion through a secular lens?

At its height of popularity, Heritage featured Main Street, U.S.A., a mock street of yesteryear depicting small-town America and values associated with an ideal and nostalgic appropriation of the past. Social and religious conservatives rely upon such a view of America to resurrect a vision of a lost golden age of America—an age that can and must be recaptured through revival and return to God. The message of Main Street was clear: America was blessed by God, but it was the America of the past that had been so blessed. Contemporary America had lost its spiritual moorings, and, short of a return to the nostalgically-centered values of yesterday, America would be doomed. Just when this golden age was supposed to have occurred is unclear, but it was definitely before the dramatic social changes that marked the 1960s and 1970s. Vestiges of this and of the social agenda of the conservative Right appeared on the Main Street of Heritage's mock village. Toy stores sold "pro-life" dolls and Christian story books. Main Street advocated nothing less than John Winthrop's "city upon a hill," where America was envisioned as a sacred society blessed by God and Americans were considered God's people. This civil religion was not so much the vision of a sacred society as it was a secularized religion, because the main vehicle of its expression (Main Street), was an American and contemporary secular icon.

These secularized themes and a gospel based on cultural and material prosperity were marketed and communicated using technology and media, a method evangelicals have been experimenting with throughout the twentieth century. Even before twentieth-century advances in technology, as Mark Noll demonstrates, evangelicals had long since effectively learned to communicate and evangelize by shaping their message to appeal to their audience. Thus, we see in George Whitefield's preaching to "plain people in plain language"[15] the nascent philosophy that would spark later attempts to catch people where they are in life. And in nineteenth-century evangelical tract societies, we see evangelicals using the technology of the day to evangelize beyond the evangelical community.[16] These two tendencies, to identify with the audience and to use technology to communicate, form the backbone of the secularization of the evangelical message in the twentieth century.

Evangelicals learned early on to use mass media in the attempt to reach a large audience beyond the evangelical community.[17] Realizing that periodicals, magazines, and printed material in general might galvanize a community within the evangelical culture but were largely unsuccessful as evangelizing tools,[18] evangelicals turned to new technologies as a way of overcoming the cultural and sometimes geographical space between them and their targeted audience. At first, the telephone seemed to be a promising tool for reaching large numbers of people easily and was often used to start new churches.[19] Creative churchmen recognized radio to be a medium for reaching the masses and began to use radio ministries to overcome geographical barriers.[20] Radio evangelism experienced remarkable growth during the 1970s and 1980s in the United States in terms of the number of broadcasts, but there is little evidence that actual audiences increased dramatically.[21] Thus, evangelicals went in search of a more effective medium for spreading the Christian message. They found it in television, which gave evangelical preachers "access to millions of living rooms"[22] and to mainstream America.

Claims by televangelists about audience size via television vary and stretch as high as 40 million during the height of televangelism in the mid-1980s. However, many question these estimates and the effectiveness of television when it came to actually gaining new converts, the goal of the evangelical ministry.[23] Others question whether television really closes the cultural gap between evangelicalism and broader American culture.[24] Nevertheless, it is certain that the use of media, particularly television, connected evangelical culture to secular, popular culture in a way that was new and novel, and this experience provided evangelicalism and evangelicals a sense of relevance and power through participation in a popular, secular medium.[25] This sense of relevance and inclusion in the mainstream culture eventually became one of the cornerstones to the megachurch movement and provides the best example yet of the secularization of the evangelical message.

In the end, televangelism reached its peak and declined not because it was a failed method but because bad press and scandal affected the ministries of the Bakkers and Jimmy Swaggert. While the methods seemed to be effective, regardless of whether they were proper, the managers and messengers of the movement transgressed and televangelism lost its momentum. Nevertheless, the acceptance of secular values to market religion did not disappear and has re-emerged with a vengeance in the megachurch movement.

At the same time as evangelicals were experimenting with technology, they also discovered the power of large churches. The 1970s witnessed the rise of super churches in America that developed alongside of, in conjunction with, and sometimes in competition with radio and television. As Joel Gregory points out, these churches often exert tremendous "religious and secular power"[26] and attempt to influence popular culture, political processes, media, education, and other secular institutions. By involving themselves in secular matters and institutions, these churches are perhaps the best example in America of the secularization of the traditional Christian institution.[27] For example, First Baptist Church in Dallas, Texas, called by Gregory the "mother church of all the super churches,"[28] operates radio and television outlets, a newspaper, and a college.[29] The church has attempted to create a society within its doors and to control the flow of knowledge by creating its own institutions that function in competition with secular institutions. However, in doing so, it has adopted secular models and methods and has become secularized in the process. Coral Ridge Presbyterian Church, according to Scott Thumma, offered a concert series including country music stars and the music of Andrew Lloyd Webber.[30] A final example includes Robert Schuller's Crystal Cathedral, which operated with the philosophy of marketing that mimics secular marketing and advertising. In the attempt to meet the modern needs of his constituency, Schuller attempted "to throw the kind of bait out that they would like."[31] Critics suggest this baiting allows the concerns of the secular world to determine the agenda of the church.

Study guide

Important words and concepts

City of God
Civil religion
Donatists
Huldrych Zwingli
International Christian Fellowship
Jim Bakker
Megachurch
Robert Schuller
Sacred space

Study questions

1) What types of activities, associations, or myths sacralize space?
2) How can sports function religiously?
3) Think of a personal space that you consider sacred, and define what makes it so.
4) What are the implications of Robert Schuller's direction "to throw the kind of bait out" that would attract people to church?

Guided reading

1) Read John Winthrop's "A Modell of Christian Charity" (1630). In what ways did the early colonists in the New World consider American sacred?
2) Next, read Chief Seattle's letter of 1854. How does this document provide a different narrative for America as sacred space?

Megachurches

They are known by several aliases: megachurches, super churches, the next church, "full service churches, seven-day-a-week churches, shopping-mall churches and pastoral churches."[1] Some are huge, while others have visions of grandeur and growth. However, what binds these "megachurches" together is not so much their size but their philosophy of evangelism: a way of conceiving church that focuses not on the churched but on the unchurched, that ministers not so much to the believer as it pitches to the non-believer. The megachurches bring the unchurched into the sacred walls with a seven-day-a-week approach to the needs and worries of contemporary life. The philosophy has worked well in America, not so well in Europe. At a time when mainline denominations are hurting and small churches are failing, some boast the megachurches are the fastest growing segment of the religious population in the United States.[2] Others claim that the megachurch movement represents the future of the church in America and will lead to a major reform of American Christianity. At the same time, the movement is carving out a shaky foothold in Western Europe.

The megachurches represent the secularization of traditional religion—not its failure, disappearance, or loss of authority but its conformity to secular life and to popular culture. These churches are thriving, growing, spreading, and exerting influence over the lives of their parishioners. Traditional theories that view secularization in terms of loss of authority or the gradual disappearance of religion do not stand up in light of this contemporary church phenomenon. However, these churches are secularized because they represent a molding of tradition to the exigencies of secular culture. In these "next churches," Christian tradition has been altered by mass media, geographical mobility, democratization, and the rapid social change characterizing contemporary life.[3] These secular developments in the twentieth century have provided challenges to the Christian community; in the case of the megachurches, they have provided opportunities and an avenue for reform.

Except for fundamentalist groups or groups that define themselves over against popular culture, the contemporary church in America is a solid part of the popular culture mainstream. As R. Laurence Moore has persuasively argued, the church in America competes in the marketplace for loyalty and attention, and as a result has had to market its product in order to compete.[4] The church in Europe, with its history of state support, might not be required to adopt the same market mentality, but it shares an intimate history with secular power structures. Thus, even though the church's connection to secular society traces a different history in America than in Europe, in both places Christianity has secularized to the extent that it has taken on the characteristics of secular culture, either to compete or to satisfy its secular benefactors. In this way, Christianity in the contemporary world is reactionary to secular culture,[5] and the megachurches, wanting to compete not only with other churches but with secular enticements as well, are perhaps the most reactionary of all. Particularly in America, if these churches are to compete with secular entertainment and enticements, they must create and offer an attractive lure.[6]

How do the megachurches produce a lure that will entice contemporary, restless, overstimulated non-believers to attend their services? How do the megachurches convince their parishioners that they would be better served attending church than pursuing other activities on Sunday morning and during the week? They compete by giving their parishioners the same product, by providing and peddling popular culture in sacred clothing. These churches use television, drama, movies, games, technology, and other brands of secular entertainment to explore the supernatural,[7] to attract those who might otherwise not attend church. Some of this entertainment might be purely secular, such as aerobics classes, counseling centers, and church-sanctioned dependency groups,[8] but they contain a Christian prefix, such as "Christian aerobics."[9]

Many scholars have produced important work on the megachurch movement. I am indebted to Scott Thumma's work on megachurches in general and to a full-length study by G. A. Pritchard on the megachurch history and philosophy.[10] The megachurch movement embraces communities across the world, but one church stands out as the unquestioned leader in this reform movement: Willow Creek Community Church in the suburbs of Chicago. Willow Creek is huge—it has attracted 27,000 people for special Easter services[11] and recently boasted a weekend attendance of 20,000. In the year 2000, regular weekend attendance was around 17,000, representing a 20 percent increase during the previous five years. This average has increased to 23,400 in 2011.[12] Willow Creek has taken a philosophy of church growth and developed it more than any other contemporary church community; the church is leading a worldwide movement under the leadership of Bill Hybels, a huge staff, and the Willow Creek Association, the organization that oversees the vast network of churches modelled after the Willow Creek philosophy. The more than one million people who attend Willow

Creek functions annually represent only a fraction of those who are influenced by the church through the association, books, and tapes.[13] This phenomenal church began as a youth group that Hybels helped lead called "Son City." Hybels and the other leaders of the group stumbled onto the discovery that young people responded to their ministry when they used youth culture, popular music, and "hip" language to communicate. The successful strategy provided the prototype for the method employed at Willow Creek and its associated churches—using the language of the unchurched, a language that is necessarily secular, to attract them to church.[14]

At least one proponent refers to Willow Creek's approach as "the 'apostolic' church" because it models the early church as the church spread into the Hellenistic world.[15] The "apostolic" designation implies that acculturation and secularization have characterized the church from the beginning and even account for much of its evangelical success. The strategy of acculturation or adaptation shows the strong influence of Robert Schuller on Hybels. Schuller's ministry in California, symbolized famously in his Crystal Cathedral, played an important role in forming Hybels's own approach to church growth and outreach. Hybels was influenced by Schuller's book, *Your Church Has Real Possibilities*, and in 1975, before the birth of Willow Creek, Hybels attended the Robert Schuller Institute for Successful Church Leadership. What Hybels learned from Schuller was how to respond to the needs of the unchurched, epitomized by Schuller's famous "drive-in" church.[16]

Schuller inspired the dominant and key concept in the megachurch movement, "relevance." Relevance is the key, and relevance is voiced over and over again by ministers of megachurches as the one goal they seek to attain—the most crucial characteristic that separates their churches from the traditional, denominational churches. In the attempt to be relevant to their targeted audience, one minister boasts, "We give them what they want, and we give them what they didn't know they wanted—a life change."[17] Another describes relevance in commercial terms: the new way of doing church is "one-stop shopping for your social, educational and spiritual needs ..." By contrast, "... some churches are stuck. They're still doing church the way it was done in the 50s. It's boring, and people will not attend."[18] The "one-stop shopping" metaphor for relevance recalls Bill Leonard's phrase for the megachurch movement, the "Wal-Martization of American religion."[19] Bishop Charles Blake, the leader of the 18,000-member West Angeles Church of God and Christ, likened his church to a "shopping center" in an interview with NPR's Duncan Moon. Blake said, "I feel that a large church should be something like a shopping center, so that individuals in the community can come to a church institution for whatever need or whatever goal or objective they may have at that given moment."[20] Bishop Blake's assessment demonstrates the megachurch need to be everything to everybody, or at least to meet the needs of the church's targeted audience. In Bishop Blake's church, the congregation in the community of South Central Los Angeles is African American, and the church supports some 80 ministries, many with a focus on social and urban renewal.[21] Another minister connects relevance with technology: "Archaic terminology doesn't resonate with the younger generation because they've been brought up with technology. If the church doesn't use the language they're familiar with, then we're perceived as having no relevance in their lives."[22] Some church leaders adopt the language of business, of corporate America;[23] others use the language of youth culture or popular culture. The message from these ministers is clear: in order to survive, in order to grow, in order to reach a lost world, they must address the existential concerns of a secular society by adopting its language and customs to appear relevant to such a society.[24]

Most of these churches adopt secular standards in subtle ways, perhaps by organizing themselves around secular, cultural holidays rather than around the liturgical calendar.[25] Others deliberately and publicly abandon "centuries of European tradition and Christian habit,"[26] as if habit is synonymous with irrelevance. Regardless, as Pritchard reveals, the desire to be relevant moves the ministries and methods of these churches "toward the language and priorities of popular culture ... [and] affirms the surrounding culture."[27] The concern of some critics is that if its goal is to affirm society, such a church compromises its ability to speak prophetically to society. The desire of these churches to be relevant replaces denominational loyalty and erodes theological and creedal importance.[28] Without the standards of creedal guidance, secular culture threatens to provide the creeds and beliefs governing these congregations. If there is such a secular creed, it is the creed of relevance.

Obviously, the megachurches' purposeful abandonment of "European tradition" would not work as well in a society that is heavily traditional in its religious institutions. In America, religion has always been innovative and mutable, changing to meet competitive demands in a society where the success of religion depends on its ability to attract adherents.[29] As one might imagine, the megachurch philosophy seems to work best in this free-church environment. On the other hand, in Europe, where tradition rather than innovation has defined the Church in the modern era, the megachurch movement is catching on very slowly, despite a concentrated effort by Willow Creek Association. Willow Creek Association staff attribute this slow growth to Europe's history of state religion and a cultural suspicion of large institutions with popular appeal.[30] This points out some interesting differences between the European and American situations when it comes to the secularization of tradition. Europe, a much more traditional society than the United States in religious matters, is less prone to secularize its religious traditions when secularization is defined as it is here.

In the subsequent pages, I will be drawing upon information and trends gleaned from two megachurches in particular: The Willow Creek Church (the paradigmatic megachurch in America) and a pioneering and relatively successful megachurch venture in Zurich, Switzerland (the International Christian Fellowship or ICF). The ICF is one of the most successful megachurches in Europe. In 1996, it boasted 600–1,000 in attendance at its larger services and held a variety of services, some targeting the unchurched in the best Willow Creek fashion and others, charismatic-style services, geared to believers.[31] The ICF targets young adults, the Generation Xers, and incorporates plenty of music and video technology into its services.[32] The service is certainly unconventional and seems out of place in a European city like Zurich. In addition, it is very different from the Willow Creek service and will provide some interesting contrast in the pages that follow.

How megachurches secularize tradition

Christianity has witnessed and participated in secularization since its inception, but the megachurches represent an exaggerated example of this dynamic in the contemporary church scene. In the next few pages, I will briefly examine ways that megachurches secularize Christian tradition, focusing on what Bryan Wilson and others call "internal secularization," a process that leads to the "evacuation" of sacred orientations within the church.[33] Internal secularization occurs when churches purposefully use "elements of the broader culture" to eliminate a perceived cultural gap between the Christian message and the unchurched.[34] Churches might employ many strategies to bridge the gap, but in the final analysis the results are the introduction of secular elements, categories, and standards into Christian worship and theology. With this introduction of secular culture, the process of secularization is initiated or continued. My understanding of how megachurches secularize tradition has been profoundly shaped by the descriptive and interpretive work of two authors in particular. The writings of G. A. Pritchard and Scott Thumma provide invaluable information on the megachurches' unique philosophy, methods, and characteristics. From their work and from my own exposure to the megachurch movement, I have isolated at least six areas that demonstrate the secularization of Christianity in the megachurch movement.

(1) Packaging: The megachurches "package" and market Christianity to a secular audience through a secular lens. They use market research and secular marketing methods to determine how to present their product to the public in a nonthreatening and attractive package. This consumerism approach works well in the United States because of the free market

mentality when it comes to religion. The result of this marketing scheme is a secularized package.

(2) Organization: Since many of these megachurches are huge, organization and structure can be a nightmare. In the attempt to manage the sheer magnitude of the undertakings of these churches, secular models of organization are borrowed from the business world.

(3) Programming: The megachurches place a premium on interesting and engaging programming, and the predominant model comes from the secular entertainment world.

(4) Ideology: For the most part, the megachurches have incorporated a secularized theology into their sermons and evangelization in order to make their message more palatable. This secularized theology is based in large part on insights from secular psychology as well as biblical and systematic teachings.

(5) Function: The megachurches have in practice taken over the roles generally associated with the secular sphere. Self-help groups, exercise groups, education, childcare, and other "secular" functions can be found within the walls of the church as a means of attempting to meet the needs and fulfill the desires of parishioners.

(6) Space: The megachurch movement represents a secularization of sacred space where meetings might take place in or mimic the space of secular institutions.

Packaging

When megachurch ministers talk about evangelism, it is difficult to distinguish between their discussion and a presentation on effective advertising. Phrases like "product loyalty," "target audience," "consumer orientation," "client needs" and the like dominate the discussion. This marketing phraseology has replaced theological terms like sin, the lost, and even repentance. The megachurches bring in tons of people because they have developed an effective method to reach the unreached and to convince them they should come to church. When Bill Hybels talks about marketing strategy, he speaks about Christianity as if it were a product and about those he evangelizes as clients or consumers. "The 45-and-under generation has a consumer-oriented mindset. They patronize the restaurants and stores they like, and they'll attend a church for the same reason."[35] Ministers who have modelled their churches after Willow Creek echo the same sentiment.[36]

Armed with this understanding of the lost as consumers, ministers strike out on aggressive church-growth campaigns using market research to understand the needs of the unchurched and to meet them by understanding their culture and mimicking it in the worship setting. In order to accomplish this, they often rely on secular models for marketing.[37] When Pastor James Emery White started a Willow

Creek-style church in Charlotte, North Carolina, he first commissioned a survey of unchurched people in the area, tallied the results of the survey about their needs and wants, and set out to build a church designed to meet those needs.[38] The results? The successful Mecklenburg Community Church in Charlotte, and White's book on church growth, *Opening the Front Door: Worship and Church Growth.* This marketing approach is typical of Willow Creek-type churches, and, according to David Luecke, represents the "most important innovation" of the megachurch movement.[39]

Once the survey is done, ministers then develop a strategy for meeting the needs that are highlighted by the needs analysis. In general, these churches develop "seeker services" designed exclusively to attract the unchurched. They are not designed to meet the needs of believers but to ensure that visitors, who are primarily unchurched, return. Seeker services are designed to "identify" with the unbeliever by being relevant and by responding to the needs expressed through the survey and market analyses.[40] In order to better identify with their target audience, staff members and ministers at Willow Creek are encouraged to maintain active lives "in a totally secular realm," and market research teams might attend secular plays and rock and roll concerts to get a better understanding of popular culture.[41] Early on, Willow Creek developed a seven-step strategy for reaching the unchurched individual: 1) church members and leaders befriend the unchurched; 2) church members and leaders invite the unchurched to attend services; 3) unchurched individuals then visit services designed specifically for them; 4) unchurched individuals begin attending; 5) they join a small group; 6) they become involved in a service role; and 7) they become good stewards.[42] This and similar strategies characterize the megachurch philosophy of evangelism and church growth.[43]

Who are these folks targeted by megachurch evangelists? They are baby boomers[44] and, to some extent, the Generation Xers as the first-generation participants in the movement begin to age out. The megachurches are trying to tap into that very large group of people who are also very affluent. According to Pritchard, Willow Creek is very clear about whom they are trying to attract to their church. The target audience is made up of unchurched baby boomers, especially the male heads of households with a typical client profile being a professional who is 25–45 years old, college educated, white-collar employed, and married with children.[45] With this kind of strategy, it should be no surprise that these churches produce homogenous congregations[46] and that they are located in affluent suburbs. But there are exceptions to this typical profile, one being the ICF in Zurich. Zurich has targeted a different client, the Xer generation, the baby busters rather than the boomers. Early market surveys indicated that the urban environment in Zurich lent itself better to reaching that audience, a group less likely to be tied to traditional religious groups, so the Zurich congregation set out to reach a different target audience. As a result, their worship patterns are different and are designed to appeal to a younger, single, and more restless crowd. In fact, the music resembles "MTV-style" music, accompanied by multimedia presentations, and crosses over to embrace popular, contemporary Christian music.[47]

The marketing approach works, at least for targeting groups and designing programs for them. However, as some critics point out, it is not necessarily a good trend for the church. For some, megachurch growth strategy is too market oriented[48]—a secularized and marketed kingdom of God.

Organization

As you might imagine, these large churches with growing numbers, huge staffs, fluctuating budgets, and fluid and ever changing attendees provide special challenges for church leaders. Since these churches represent a secularized institutional form, one would expect them to adopt secularized methods for organizational structure. This seems to be the case. Bryan Wilson notes that secularization in general leads to the ecclesiastical tendency to organize along the lines of business corporations.[49] This tendency can clearly be seen in the comments of leaders in megachurches in the Los Angeles area who emphasize the commercial and business nature of the religious mission of these huge churches.[50] The tendency is modelled in Robert Schuller's writings and refined in the practices of Willow Creek Community Church. In addition, churches in the Willow Creek Association learn and often adopt this secular management style to run growing institutions.

As Pritchard details, the Schullerian approach can best be seen in Schuller's influential book, *Your Church has Real Possibilities* (1975). In the chapter, "Principles of Successful Retailing," Schuller outlines several principles of management and planning that help to direct church growth. The reader is initially surprised to see "surplus parking" as one of the priorities for ensuring church growth. However, when you consider the target audience, affluent corporate heads of households in the suburbs, the parking requirement and the need for general "accessibility" make perfect sense. Schuller also writes about the necessity for "inventory," a retailing phrase that for Schuller means understanding what the target audience wants and making it available. Third, Schuller outlines "service" as a requirement for success. Like any good pep talk from a CEO of a corporation, satisfying the customer becomes the cornerstone of a growing church. It is not surprising that critics point to this ideology as destructive to Christianity. After all, how can a church maintain a prophetic role in society if its priority is to satisfy the client? Schuller also describes the importance of "visibility" through advertising, and finally, the importance of positive "cash flow." The language, if not the priorities, are those of the corporate world and represent the marketing of Christianity in a consumer-oriented world.[51]

Willow Creek has adopted this management approach and implements it very effectively. From the supervision of staff and volunteers to the managing of budgets, the language and methods of corporate America predominate. In fact, according to Pritchard, staff members at Willow Creek early on began to read and model the concepts from Kenneth Blanchard's *Leadership and the One Minute Manager*,[52] a secular business bible for corporate executives. This management style creates very efficient and well-managed organizations and seems to work well in the megachurch setting, at least in terms of organization.

The secular, corporate style of managing churches is particularly well suited for the megachurch movement in the United States, because of the strong free-market economic machine driven by corporate America. The management style appeals to the target audience of these megachurches as well, since the client will likely as not be a corporate manager of some sort. The style resonates well with the audience. Whether or not this corporate management style catches on in Europe is yet to be seen, as the megachurch movement in Europe has not really emerged as a recognizable entity. The Zurich ICF has adopted some of the Schullerian techniques described above. For example, the ICF does a particularly good job of advertising using eye-catching flyers, a slick German–English newsletter to promote church activities,[53] and a professionally-constructed website.[54] Yet, other corporate techniques are understated at the ICF, which might be a reflection of the different target audience as much as anything. In any case, the European megachurch movement has not yet demonstrated the commitment to corporate-style management that has worked so well in the United States.

Programming

Bryan Wilson has noted that the secular entertainment industry makes traditional church services appear bland and uninteresting, and that this is one of the motivations behind revivalism, that is, to revive interest as much as anything.[55] In fact, as R. Laurence Moore points out, from the preaching of George Whitefield during the Great Awakening and the camp meeting revivals of the nineteenth century, interest and entertainment have always been a part of the revivalism movement. According to some, this has shaped American religion in a society that promotes competition of religions.[56] So, American religion, at least, has a built-in entertainment quotient that in the minds of many is related to the successful luring of congregants. Willow Creek Community Church and megachurches in general take this observation to heart. Although insisting that they do not entertain as much as teach in an engaging manner, the programming or entertainment component in seeker-style services is perhaps the most important part of the service. Scores of hours from dozens of volunteers go into each week's programming. The result is a worship service that resembles secular entertainment in form with the use of contemporary-style music, video clips, and other visual aids to engage the worshipers.[57]

The Willow Creek philosophy hinges on the assumption that affluent baby boomers, its target audience, were weaned on television and, therefore, cannot respond to an argument without visual and auditory stimulation. So in order to capture the short attention spans of contemporary church goers molded by sound bites, commercials, and half-hour TV spots, megachurches use the arts and contemporary programming and entertainment styles to reach the seeker.[58] There is some evidence that Willow Creek assumptions about auditory and visual stimulation are accurate;[59] although mainly anecdotal evidence supports the effectiveness of this programming on religious education, it does at least seem to pique the interest of churchgoers and keep them engaged for a short period of time.

The megachurches are careful to offer professional quality, and they expend energy and money to ensure quality equipment and performers. They are also concerned that the entertainment be interesting. The death knell for a weekend service seems to be boredom, and the megachurch philosophy tries to stamp out uninteresting programs. Multimedia drama is a main component of these services and includes 12-foot-tall video screens and computer-generated graphics. One service even included a rappelling Rambo character to illustrate a Father's Day lesson.[60] While some megachurches often incorporate Hollywood images, the focus in the ICF church in Zurich seems to be music, popular music. The ICF even creates its own CDs with worship music.[61] This focus on music probably reflects the interest of the ICF's Xer target audience. One church mounted an "anti-boring" advertising campaign to attract the disinterested–unchurched crowd. The church's flyers confidently proclaimed, "Lots of people are coming because they're fed up with boring sermons, ritual that doesn't mean anything … and music that nobody likes."[62] A church newsletter printed the headline, "Dull, Boring, Dead on Arrival: Sound like the last church service you went to?" The newsletter then continued to describe how "to create a definitely fun and totally non-boring service."[63]

The programming of the megachurches focuses on keeping seekers engaged and keeping them from being bored, and the methods they employ seem to work.[64] But church ministers insist that the focus is not on entertaining but on communicating the gospel message.[65] So the entertainment value of the programming energies in megachurches is of secondary importance to the theology communicated through them. And it is to this theology, to a secularized theology, that I now turn.

Ideology

One of the ecclesiastical tendencies that accompanies secularization is ecumenicalism, the attempt to break down differences between groups and to remove boundaries for greater cooperation. This was a practice early on in the church's history and remains a predominant strategy in the mission field,[66] resulting in greater acceptance of church teaching by a wider audience because the sharp edges of theology are muted. However, ecumenicalism also results in an erosion of theology or a watering down of the theological standards that make groups distinctive. So it is not surprising that many, if not most, megachurches are non-denominational.[67] Even more importantly, this loss of distinctiveness seems to promote the emergence of a secular theology purposefully designed to attract those who are immersed in secular culture. The ideology becomes secular, as does the language. This has happened with much of the theology in many of the megachurches, representing a danger to some critics because success depends on a large degree of accommodation to the secular.[68]

This secularization of theology is unavoidable once megachurches target their audience and then adopt methods to "identify" with that audience. Rather than trying to mold their audience to a "foreign" way of viewing reality, these churches adopt the worldview of their target audience. According to G. A. Pritchard, historian of the Willow Creek Church, the worldview adopted by and promulgated by megachurches is none other than "the psychological worldview of the American culture"[69] and represents a secular measuring stick for the church's theology.

Pritchard argues persuasively that the origin of this secularized theology is Robert Schuller's "self esteem" approach to theology, in which a theocentric approach is replaced by a "human needs approach."[70] When theocentric theology is replaced by anthropocentric ideology, the secularization of theology has taken place and the theology has become anthropology. The result is theology based on secular psychology that replaces God's will with personal fulfillment and that uses psychological principles to exegete Scripture and communicate theological principles.[71]

According to Pritchard, this emphasis on personal fulfillment can be seen quite clearly in the content of weekend messages at Willow Creek. Psychological categories and topics such as self-esteem, addiction, conflict resolution, self-identity, self-awareness, and family history tend to direct, if not dominate, the preaching and teaching of the seeker services. In addition, secular psychology books are recommended, referred to, and sold in the church bookstore.[72] This pop-psychology approach is predictable given the megachurch philosophy of relevance and identification. In its most menial form it panders to the needs of baby boomer angst over personal fulfillment. Of course, not everyone agrees. For example, George Hunter calls the movement apostolic because it mimics the early church in its techniques for reaching converts. He suggests it is the method and not the message that sets megachurches apart.[73]

Function

Bryan Wilson has pointed out that, with secularization, religious content in church is reduced; therefore churches must take on other functions in order to remain relevant. Wilson writes, "With its reduced religious content, the act of church-going in the United States may fulfill other functions ..."[74] This is a predictable development with the megachurches—they have taken on the functions of everyday life, attempting to fulfill the mandate the earlier Social Gospel movement failed to complete. The irony is that at the same time the churches are taking on secular roles of everyday life, trained professionals are taking on some of the traditional roles of the priest and clergy (for example, secular marriage counseling).[75] The result is that the boundaries between sacred and secular functions are disappearing, and this seems particularly true with the megachurches' purposeful openness to secular society.

The same strategy that allows the megachurches to grow, as Trueheart suggests, also threatens to turn these churches into "the Welcome Wagon, the USO, the Rotary, the quilting bee, the book club, the coffee shop ..."[76] or any number of other secular clubs and organizations. The ever-present and unmistakable presence at the megachurches of secular-style and sometimes secular-sponsored groups demonstrates the ever increasing secular functioning of the megachurches. Trueheart describes the programs at one church, but this generic scene could easily be transferred to any number of megachurches. At one megachurch there is "a seminar on effective single parenting; 12-step recovery meetings by category (alcohol, drugs, abuse) ... a parents-of-adolescents meeting ... and a women in the workplace brunch ..."[77] The secularization of function begins with the megachurch philosophy of relevance. Because the churches allow the client to set the agenda, it becomes necessarily a secular agenda.

As these churches grow and expand into suburban areas, they often do so with considerable controversy, in part because their existence as religious bodies offers them some protection in development issues. In large part, religious institutions do not have to abide by the same zoning restrictions as private business. Therefore, these "meet-all-your-needs" institutions can sponsor any number of services and conveniences in areas where private enterprise cannot compete.[78] There will certainly be legal wrangling on the rights of megachurches to set up shop in ways that otherwise might be forbidden by local zoning, and this comes as a direct result of the purposeful function of these churches.

Space

Finally, a more recognizable but less definable characteristic of the church that is subject to secularization through the megachurch movement is the secularization of space. The contemporary church has responded to secularization by trying to lessen the physical and psychological distance between the clergy and the laity. This has resulted in a shift away from formalism in all parts of worship, including the appearance and structure of buildings.[79] The great cathedrals that at one time were designed to instill awe, to demonstrate the magnificence of the Almighty, and to strike worshipers with a sense of otherness, have been replaced in many instances by nondescript buildings that seek to make people comfortable. The megachurches do not want to confront their clients with a sense of otherness. Rather, they want the seeker to feel at home.

This change in worship space philosophy is reflected in the meeting places of the megachurches. Many of them are corporate and hotel-like with atriums, food courts, and fountains.[80] Willow Creek's grounds resemble and are modelled after a four-star hotel or corporate headquarters.[81] Other churches begin by meeting in large urban hotels (e.g. the ICF in Zurich) or in school buildings. Regardless of whether the megachurch meets in a church building that looks like a secular building or in a secular building that houses the church, the space philosophy is the same—meet in a place that is informal, familiar, nonthreatening, casual, and immediate. Oftentimes, spaces that enhance or make possible multimedia events are necessary for the contemporary-style worship that is so characteristic of megachurches.

Sometimes this philosophy of space creates strange scenes that bring elements of the amusement park or ballpark into the confines of the church. One Los Angeles megachurch, the Faithful Central Bible Church, meets in Great Western Forum, where the L.A. Lakers at one time played basketball.[82] Fast-food stands, coffee stands, and, in Trueheart's phraseology, "a cappuccino cart with parasol … dispensing the secular sacrament"[83] conspire to secularize religious and holy space. Sacred ground is modelled on the profane; transcendent space on the mundane—all done to remain relevant to the unchurched rather than to provide contact with the sacred. This physical transition once again produces an irony. Whereas in the past secular buildings (banks and colleges) used architecture to remind their clients of great cathedrals, now the sacred institutions are adopting architectural styles to resemble secular institutions.[84]

Results and conclusions of the secularization of tradition

My focus in this chapter on the megachurch movement should not be taken as a suggestion that the megachurches are the only contemporary churches to be secularized or secularizing. Christianity is experiencing secularization and has done since its inception. In fact, the whole Christian continuum could be viewed in terms of relative position on a secular scale, with some traditions more accommodating to secular culture than others and none static on the scale but changing in relation to acculturation and other factors. My focus on the megachurch phenomenon is to highlight some of the more obvious effects of secularization in concentrated form. The characteristics discussed above could be used to describe any number of Christian traditions to some extent—some more, some less.

Secularization is definitely taking place in the Christian community, but it will not result in the disappearance of Christianity or in the complete absorption of the church into the social context. There will always be sects in the tradition that define themselves against the establishment and against culture. Even if these sects secularize and accommodate, others will take their place.[85] Nor will secularization necessarily result in a loss of power for religion because groups exist which so identify with secular culture that they draw vibrancy from it. Rather, secularization is a measure of the degree to which traditions accommodate themselves to popular culture, which in turn results in subtle changes to the tradition. While secularization certainly changes the face of Christianity, it does not necessarily spell its decline. In fact, secularization, by popularizing the religion, might make Christianity more viable, more resistant to decline, more widespread throughout the culture even if it is less recognizable as a counter-culture movement.

Those who caution against secularization in megachurches are not so much worried about the disappearance of Christianity as they are about the wholesale changes that occur when involvement with popular culture becomes the standard. Many are concerned about the "gimmicky" approach to attracting parishioners or about the dilution or distortion of the Christian message to make it palatable for a wide audience.[86] Certainly, when the tradition acculturates, it risks its prophetic voice, because it can no longer speak out against the culture it has adopted.

This accommodation and compromise with society and culture, which they see as a compromise of eternal truths for relative cultural standards, is what worries most critics.[87] Marketing makes the audience sovereign, rather than God, according to these critics, and the gospel message becomes simply relative to time, place, and opinion.[88] Church leaders insist they never compromise the truth but simply make it relevant. Certainly there is a fine line that leaders and critics alike must balance.

The concern of critics that megachurches will capitulate to cultural standards rather than stand as a theological standard against which culture is measured is borne out by the theological foundations that this movement has evolved from. Much like the Emerging Church, which this book examines in chapter 12, the megachurch theology is at least partially influenced by postliberalism and its related theological positions that embed theology in culture, language, and contemporary context. Postliberalism abandons many of the liberal theological presuppositions, such as basing biblical interpretation on the historical and textual context, and challenges the notion of objective standards and truths. Thus, postliberal theologies are always responsive to interpretive influences from the predominant culture. The readers, the worshipers, the potential converts, and the religious "clients" shape postliberal thought as much as church traditions. As a result, when the megachurches target unchurched people as potential clients, they construct a whole religious edifice based on the presumed needs of that target group. Of course, at the heart of this postliberal commitment is the attempt to deal with postmodernism and the presupposition of change and evolution in religion. In the case of postliberalism, evolution is assumed, and one must presume that this not only includes culture but also truth commitments as well.

Proponents insist that this is a natural process, and chapter 1 of this book has suggested how Process thought could represent one example of this postmodern theological experiment. Critics, however, complain that postliberal thought is one more example of religion succumbing to cultural relativism and that such disintegration of theological integrity will eventually result in a descent to moral relativism or even amorality.

Regardless of whether or not Christianity is capitulating to relative cultural standards, it is certain that secularization is changing an evolving tradition. Whether or not this is a positive or a heretical move often depends on the individual making the value judgment. I make no such attempt to judge but rather recognize that secularization is changing the tradition in significant ways and that secularization is a powerful force, perhaps a strengthening force that will allow Christianity to grow and thrive, or perhaps a weakening force that will destroy Christianity as a distinctive voice in the cultural landscape. One could also draw parallels with other religious traditions and their relationships to culture. However, by focusing on the Christian tradition, and one part of that tradition, we can see how the interaction between religion and culture involves an on-going, evolving relationship that can change either culture or religion, or both.

Secularization involves a disappearing, or at least a malleable boundary, between religion and culture, a boundary that can either make religion more relevant (as the megachurches seek to do) or completely irrelevant (by becoming indistinguishable from the rest of the culture).[89] When churches secularize and accommodate for whatever reason, they not only evangelize the unchurched to Christianity, but, as Pritchard articulates, they are "also evangelizing Christians toward the world."[90] This is the dialectical relationship that secularization brings to the religion and culture question—the dialectic is as old as the tradition and will continue to both strengthen and corrupt the church, to shape the tradition in significant ways. Whether the megachurch movement will continue to participate in this dialectic perhaps hinges on how well it continues to uphold the tension between religion and culture. If the accommodation to secular culture becomes complete, then the dialectic will disappear, and the megachurch movement will become an inconsequential footnote in the annals of church history. If, on the other hand, the movement can maintain a creative tension with popular and secular culture without capitulating, then the megachurch movement might realize its goal of leading a significant church reform movement. Perhaps even Willow Creek and its association of churches will define the American church for the near future, as proponents suggest.[91]

The ability of the movement to adapt to Europe might determine its future. If the megachurch movement can make significant inroads into European Christianity, then it stands a chance of creating significant reform. If, on the other hand, it remains tied to American Christianity as it is now, the Zurich congregation and a few others notwithstanding, then the movement is likely to become simply one of many in the diverse and freely evolving landscape of American religion.

Already by the early twenty-first century we see new trends evolving in relation to these movements. The Emerging Church reemphasizes some of the megachurch movement's commitments without the attendant value of size and the "awe" factor of large and impressive campuses. On what is perhaps a cautionary note, Robert Schuller's Crystal Cathedral, what some consider the granddaddy of the megachurches, filed for bankruptcy in October 2010. The Crystal Cathedral was sold to the Roman Catholic Diocese of Orange County in November of 2011. The glass and steel cathedral, which was a symbol of affluence and innovation, changed hands in bankruptcy to the Catholic Church, steeped in history and tradition. The irony is not lost, and perhaps this move will prove to be prophetic if church trends move more toward tradition and away from the innovation so prominent in the later twentieth and early twenty-first centuries. Will the churches' adoption of secular culture's values lead to greater growth and a new "reformation" period as some hope, or will the church, perhaps yearning for the security of tradition, downsize, weary of the weight that cultural baggage brings?

Study guide

Important words and concepts

Bill Hybels
Megachurch
Megachurch characteristics
Megachurch philosophy
Postliberalism
Robert Schuller
Willow Creek

Discussion questions

(1) What types of accommodation have megachurches made to contemporary culture?
(2) What challenges does the megachurch philosophy present to the traditional church?
(3) Describe how churches might balance "relevance" with a "prophetic stance" in culture.

(4) Why has the American context been more conducive to the developing megachurch ethos?

Guided reading

(1) Read 1 Corinthians in the New Testament. In this letter, Paul is attempting to deal with many issues that have arisen in the Corinthian church. He is trying to negotiate an accommodation to Hellenistic culture and observance of established law and custom in the church. How well does he balance accommodation and observance? Does he demonstrate a philosophy in accordance with megachurch philosophy or not?

Love Valley: The sacralization of secular space

As the megachurch movement results in the secularization of sacred space, function, and intent, other cultural movements attempt to sacralize what would normally be considered secular or profane. They try to locate transcendent possibility in the mundane—to allow sacred import and sanction of some secular means to perfect society—to allow the kingdom of God to exist in and through human social organization. This spreading out of sacred possibility through secular forms represents the second direction of secularization. We see it in religious utopian movements, whose attempts to organize social and natural space to perfect secular society provides the basis of sacred experiments—where the "city upon a hill"[1] is rooted in secular soil but is given life by sacred water.

Creating a sense of place is a human tendency done to grant legitimacy to the places we inhabit and to places where something special has happened or happens. We see the sacralization of place everywhere, in our civil religious monuments, in our utopian spaces, in our veneration of pilgrimage sites such as Graceland or the Grand Canyon, in our sports "cathedrals." I hope to demonstrate how we sacralize space by positing a template of sorts—a categorization of spatial attributes that characterize sacred space. The template can be superimposed on a place to gauge its intentions toward the sacred and arises out of the following portrait of a unique, eccentric experiment in the sacralization of American space—the North Carolina utopian town, Love Valley. By bringing this town to light in the following pages, I hope to understand how to recognize the sacralization of space when it occurs.

Love Valley and sacred place[2]

Like the Congo in Joseph Conrad's *Heart of Darkness*, the Mid-Western landscapes of Willa Cather's fiction, and the confining cityscapes of Theodore Dreiser, Love Valley represents the way humans (authors, readers, film makers, architects, and others) have shaped their spaces to create a "spirit of place." Whether these spaces come alive on the page, the screen, or the town main street, organizing spaces into meaningful places is a sacred, creative act much akin to the Genesis act of organizing chaos. The creative act of organizing sacred place describes the sacralization of secular spaces like the town of Love Valley.

To demonstrate this meaningful attempt to create sacred place, I will discuss the spirit of place as containing both sacred space and time, and suggest some elements that give places sacred qualities. Second, I will describe Love Valley as a contemporary utopian experiment built upon the notion of sacred place wherein the "spirit of place," including both sacred space and time, functions at both the physical and ideological levels as a utopian text for the town. In the process, I am suggesting that a "community text" exists in Love Valley. This community text is made up of oral history, the character of the town and its inhabitants, and the story of the town as reported in newspapers and promotional material. The crucial element in this community text is how the town and community are perceived by its founders and inhabitants. The community text may differ and probably does differ significantly from how others perceive the town; it may even differ from an objective history of the town. But the community text tells us how Love Valleyites understand their town, its history, and its utopian impulse.[3] The community text validates the idealism upon which the town was built in part by defining the town of Love Valley as sacred place.

In talking about Love Valley as a sacred site, I am using a definition of sacred place that is clearly recognizable in religious studies and could be used to describe traditional types of sacred spaces such as buildings erected for worship or natural areas where rituals take place. However, it is my feeling that places can constitute sacred space through their function, not just through their proposed or planned purpose. Therefore, I define sacred place functionally and have isolated a few characteristics I will discuss before continuing with the community text of Love Valley.

First, definition:

> Sacred Place includes notions of "space" and "time," geography, and temporality—sacred places can be located on a map and on a timeline or temporal circle.

> A Sacred Place must be "uncrowded," if not empty, in order to allow for projection of fantasy and the evolution of myth. A Sacred Place acts as a void into which myth comes into being.[4]

So, for the purpose of this discussion, a sacred place is located in space and time and functions religiously to bring about a crucial myth. This definition suggests seven characteristics of sacred places that allow them to function religiously and mythically.

(1) Pre-modern Western worldviews, for example a biblical worldview, defined sacred place as a site that mediated the divine Other and allowed otherness, God, access into profane reality. However, a postmodern Western worldview no longer places God in opposition to humanity; rather, place itself works in opposition to human being and thus becomes otherness itself. So, rather than mediating the divine Other, sacred places are the "other"—holiness is not contained within a sacred place, holiness is the otherness of place—powerful, seductive, and challenging to human being.

(2) This otherness of place comes about in part when place is dangerous and provocative.[5] These characteristics of spaces and times carry the ability to inspire awe and fear. It is not fear of the Lord that makes a place sacred as much as it is the fear produced by the implied threat of place—the dense forests of Appalachia, the sheer height of the Alps, the shrouded depths of oceans. And, while not necessarily inducing fear, even medieval cathedrals continue to create awe and wonder based on an illustration of power. The awe produced from threat can elevate place to otherness.

(3) Sacred places carry a utopian element. Be it a temporal utopia or a spatial one, sacred places tend to attract like-minded individuals who to varying degrees imbue a place with a sense of utopian perfection, social reformation, or individual transformation. For this reason, one's sacred place might be another's mundane world. A utopian element—function, purpose, or agenda—can make a place sacred: examples include Eden, Jerusalem, Mecca, Puritan New England, Love Valley.

(4) Sacred place is foundational—it provides the place (space and time) wherein enlightenment takes place. Sacred places not only construct paradigmatic space but also set the space in an era beyond time, a time other than the present. The Eucharist altar transports one to the first-century upper room; the Buddhist temple offers transcendental possibility that lifts one beyond location and time; Jerusalem provides spatial as well as temporal connection to sacred events in Jewish, Christian, and Islamic history; U.S. civil religious shrines in and around Washington, DC, transport us to the times and places important to our nation's founding and early years—Mount Vernon, the Lincoln and Jefferson Memorials, the Washington Monument. In every instance, sacred time and sacred space are invoked in sacred places.

(5) Sacred places assume and promote a participatory element, as Robin Sylvan points out in his work with the Burning Man Ceremony[6]—in other

words, tourists do not sacralize a cathedral, communicants do. Sometimes pilgrimage functions as a sacralizing act, but so too does dance, music, and other ritualistic acts of faith that are integral to the character of the space. Furthermore the act must be an appropriate participation. For example, a priestly sacrifice constituted a sacred participatory act in the Jerusalem Temple; Antiochus IV's sacrifice to Zeus was a desecration.

(6) As in other areas of contemporary American life, secularization affects how we define and treat sacred places. An understanding of sacred space is shifting dramatically in the Western world. We no longer need saints, relics, or the association with sacramental grace for a space to appear as sacred, although these things are often present. Secularization in the West witnesses the continuing disintegration of boundaries between sacred and profane—we have no problem sacralizing the formerly secular or desacralizing the sacred. Thus, our civil religion declares the Tomb of the Unknown Soldier sacred while our popular religion does the same with Graceland, the Grand Ole Opry, or, in this case, Love Valley. At the same time, we can turn religious buildings into art museums or homeless shelters—we can desacralize.

(7) Finally, I think we are obsessed in America with sacralizing natural or wild space. Whereas medieval Europe built its sacred places, its grand cathedrals, Americans humanize their wild places. This has been part of the American appropriation of sacred place and part of the American religious psyche since the founding and colonization of a vast continent that yielded a country stretching from sea to sea. Sacralizing natural space was a new idea for Western Christianity, not European at all, and it is characteristically American. We see it in our reverence for our national parks; for our once real and now romantic obsession with the West, an untamed frontier beckoning a nation to it; with Thoreau's sojourn in the woods; with John Muir's rhapsodies about Yosemite Valley;[7] with the environmentalist's sermons about preservation and conservation.

Love Valley and the sacred spirit of place as utopian, community text

With these seven elements defining sacred place, I would like to introduce to you Love Valley, a utopian community that functions as sacred place through community text and metaphor, which were established by the founder and by the inhabitants of the town. In short, Love Valley is an intentional community established as a sacralized secular space (an incorporated town), which is expressed primarily through metaphor based on rural agrarianism and Western myth.[8]

A lone cowboy reined in his Chickasaw stallion and clipped slowly down the dusty street. Once outside the general store, Dakota hopped off his mount, threw his reins over the hitching post, dusted off his long riding coat, and started toward the store. He stopped long enough to consider cooling his parched throat before buying supplies and decided against the saloon. The café sounded good, though, and he decided to stop in there before returning to the trail. As he sauntered toward the store, the old planks of the boardwalk creaked under the weight of his boots. He shouted a greeting and tipped his hat to a couple of friends who had just returned from hunting game in the surrounding mountain passes, and the sight of their rifles brought a smile to his face as he remembered and patted the six-shooter at his side. Once inside the store, the cowboy bought a few camping supplies. As he browsed among the leather goods, he remembered he must stop at the saddle shop before leaving town. The cowboy cast a long glance down Main Street, looking for the mayor of the town: he had some business with the mayor, but that could wait until later. Dakota decided against the café, mounted his horse, and through the dust of an early fall afternoon, they cantered out of town and returned to the trail.[9]

Dakota and his mount do not constitute the opening scene of a Western movie. Rather, this is a fictionalized account of what you might encounter on the dusty streets of Love Valley, North Carolina. Andy Barker, the founder and long-time patriarch of Love Valley, harbored a childhood dream not so different from that of many of his playmates—he dreamed of horses, cowboys, and the West he saw immortalized in classic Westerns. His religious conversion on a French battle-field during World War II was added to this vision of playing cowboy. From a foxhole promise made to God, Barker fashioned a plan for his return home and outlined his idea to his mother in a letter: "My part of the bargain (with the Lord) is to build a town, a Christian Community with clean recreation and strive to help people know more about God and His outdoors. I know I'd never make a preacher, but can build a church and help out personally in many ways. We can keep young boys occupied and out of trouble by letting them help run the place."[10]

Nine years later, Barker bought a large parcel of land in a rural section of northern Iredell County in the hills of the Brushy Mountains, quit his lucrative contracting business, moved out of an elegant Charlotte, North Carolina home, and moved into a tent on his newly acquired land. From makeshift headquarters, he began building, by himself, a cabin and a "cowboy town." His wife and children eventually joined him in the cabin, and they began to gather a community of eccentric individuals attracted to living in an intentional community that looked like the set of a Western movie, complete with dirt streets where no cars are allowed, hitching posts for the only approved form of transportation, wooden sidewalks, a saloon, a dance hall, a jail, and a general store, all conforming to the principle (and later law) that all buildings look at least one hundred years old and mimic simple clapboard buildings.

Why? Barker harbored goals of transforming and reforming society. He wanted to restore what he perceived to be a lost sense of morality and sanity. He harbored a romantic vision of an American golden age based on Western nobility. The myth of the West which Barker wanted to reconstruct in Love Valley was the West of the silver screen, where ambiguity concerning right and wrong did not exist; where independence, courage, and chivalry were regarded as primary virtues; where young people mastered the art of outdoor living to counter other, less savory teenage activities; where "'wholesome' activities" corresponded to Godly living and advanced the cause of Christianity.[11] A Christian, cowboy town—this was the community text of Love Valley that has been written and revised through five decades of struggle and turmoil. But the town still exists, the cowboy persona still prevails, Country and Western music provides the anthem, and Love Valley still functions, at least in the minds of the founders and some old timers, as a paradigmatic place—a sacred place that offers an antidote to some of the problems of society. And this antidote comes in the form of a reconstructed place and time—the American West of the nineteenth century—the American West symbolized by Gene Autry and Roy Rogers.

According to my functional definition of sacred place as a time and place that allows the production of a crucial myth, Love Valley qualifies. Love Valley's history reflects a community text based on strong oral traditions and consistent community self-understanding. This utopian text includes the functioning of the town as a sacred place that reflects the seven characteristics listed above.

First, Love Valley constructs a place that functions as otherness itself—Love Valley is the thing—it does not mediate otherness; in other words, it is not a church or synagogue. Rather it is key itself. A visit to Love Valley, according to early promoters of the village, could produce escape from the demands of everyday life and lead to spiritual and moral renewal and regeneration. To live there would help create a holy community that would in time lead to the regeneration of the larger society. That Love Valley has generated tremendous controversy, suspicion, and even hatred during its history hints at the power generated by its alien status.

In part, the otherness of Love Valley establishes the utopian village as a sacred place because the town itself is tinged with danger and menace. This is the Wild West, after all, and Love Valley's community text is filled with stories mimicking the best of the untamed Western myth. The text includes stories of lawbreakers, fights on Main Street, rodeo heroics, and the martial imposition of law by the justice of the peace and his deputies (Barker served as justice of the peace as well as mayor for much of the town's history). A municipal law requires that, if visitors and residents of Love Valley carry guns (guns were commonplace at one time and are not uncommon at present), the guns must be loaded. So if you walk the streets of Love Valley and see a cowboy with a six-shooter strapped to his hip or a rifle on his horse, you can be assured that the weapon is loaded. A tinge of menace fills the community text of Love Valley, as it must to fulfill its character as sacred place.

Love Valley as otherness also gives us a clue to Barker's vision of the utopian element of Love Valley. Part of what set Love Valley apart was his promise that to live in Love Valley was to separate from the larger society, if only to establish a smaller society that would be reforming in nature. Love Valley was begun as an intentional community and was meant to maintain a transformative relationship with the larger society. Love Valley was not conceived to be merely a weekend retreat. In fact, Barker spent much energy in the early years discounting the characterization of his community as a dude ranch. Rather, Love Valley was designed to be a self-supporting permanent community that would aid in the spiritual renewal of its inhabitants to equip them to spread reform to the larger community. This utopian purpose is most clearly expressed through Barker's attempts to use the town as a base for social reform projects (including at various times providing low-income housing, job training, and relocation; rehabilitative camps for troubled youth; educational reform proposals designed to help rural and impoverished school districts; activities and programs designed to promote racial tolerance; and other similar socially progressive initiatives). Barker sponsored some of the projects; the town sponsored more. Barker also envisioned using Love Valley as a political base to spread his vision of social reform to a statewide level. He launched state senate campaigns and ran for governor of North Carolina twice on a strong populist platform. Alas, he was elected to nothing but the mayoral post of Love Valley, a position he held for most of the town's history. Still, in its intentional character to reform not only its inhabitants but also larger society, Love Valley exists as a utopian town. Not surprisingly, the community text of Love Valley thrives on stories extolling the acts of altruism and self-sacrifice by Love Valley's leaders and its citizens. These range from extraordinary kindness to strangers and opponents to self-sacrificing behavior for animals. In every case the community defines itself by a community creed based on the Golden Rule, and the community text, its collection of stories and tales, tie back into the magnanimous character of the town's leaders.

Love Valley promotes enlightenment for participants and for the larger society by recreating a sacred time and space—the Western, pre-industrial, rural-agrarian town—and by suggesting at least implicitly that many societal ills can be traced to industrialization, urbanization, and the breakdown of families. For Barker and Love Valley, the "Old West" is the golden age, paradigmatic, and Love Valley functions to transcend time and space to give its idealistic inhabitants access to this sacred place. The West carries mythic weight—undoubtedly, the West that Barker has recreated resembles the real West little, but it does recreate the West of our popular culture—the mythic West of "B" movies. It is a myth based on tough-minded independence, unambiguous morality, and peaceful coexistence with nature.

In this West, Love Valley requires—or at least encourages—a participatory element. The Western theme is pervasive—virtually everyone rides horses and dresses in Western garb; the music of Nashville is preferred everywhere except for the Barker household, where strains of classical music from the Barker radio are heard during the day. The rodeo persists as the principal entertainment. The cowboy persona is ubiquitous and infectious—it even attracted and affected a counter-cultural element that settled in Love Valley in the early 1970s. In 1970, Love Valley and Barker hosted a music festival that attracted over 70,000 hippies and counter-culture drifters to hear the Allman Brothers Band. The festival was a public relations and logistical nightmare for Barker and the townspeople of Love Valley, because of the huge crowds, drugs, nudity, and the countless problems any town of 70 would encounter if its population surged to 70,000 in a weekend. After the festival, a few of the hippies stayed on in the town to clean up the place or because they had nowhere else to go. Soon, they were riding horses and playing cowboy right along with the most clean-cut and conservative cowboy Christians of Love Valley. Even some of the Allman Brothers themselves used Love Valley as a base for a short time.[12]

Love Valley blurs the distinction between sacred and secular at every point in its history: its political reform agenda is wrapped in Christian language; its genesis as a cowboy town is confused with Barker's desire to seal a deal with God; rough and tumble association with guns, outlaws, and motorcycle gangs is balanced by the unofficial creed of the town, the Golden Rule (a rule Barker stated publicly on more than one occasion). Love Valley's one time association with popular, rock and roll, and Country and Western musicians inspired two songs about Love Valley that are filled with religious language. The first by Loonis McGlohon pictures Love Valley as a valley of peace and hope between mountains of hate, a place absent of intolerance.[13] The second was written by Don Berg and recorded by the rock group, Flood; it tells the story of a young man who finds "the promised land" in Love Valley.[14] A world-famous strongman, Joe Ponder, who lived in Love Valley and holds a couple of Guinness world records, prepared for his strength feats (such as pulling tractor–trailer rigs with his teeth, a stunt he advertised with business cards that read, "Pulling for Jesus Christ") in his sauna chapel, which is enclosed with stained glass representations of religious scenes.[15] The first permanent building Barker erected is the little church that stands on a hill overlooking town, arising from Barker's belief that any community should be built on the church. Here you have a cowboy town with a reputation as a hard living, rough kind of place, overseen by the church of the gentle Savior. The sacred–secular distinction in Love Valley is blurred.

Finally, Love Valley, as a self-styled representative of Americana, tends to elevate the natural world to sacred status. Barker's initial venture was predicated on the belief that communion with nature produces communion with the divine, that rural life produces this sort of closeness, and that natural space, or at least rural space, is somehow superior to urban space. It is simplicity, the type of simplicity lauded by the Transcendentalists of the nineteenth century rather than promulgated by the best-selling books of the twentieth, that Barker and the Love Valley residents were trying to produce through communion with nature. While building Love Valley, Andy and Ellenora Barker and their two children lived for two years in a cabin with no running water, not even an outhouse, while cooking meals over an open fire. Perhaps a cowboy named Arizona, a long-time resident of Love Valley, said it best: "The simple life is better … Why, even plumbing gives problems. I sometimes think we were better off before we had indoor plumbing and running water."[16]

Love Valley is an intentional community built on utopian idealism. Its history has produced a community text that defines the experiment for those who know the story well. The setting of this story is a sacred place, a setting that transports one beyond space and time to a paradigmatic place, a place where the necessities of secular life give way spatially to sacred place.

On Sunday, August 14, 2011, a crowd gathered in the Silver Spur Salon on Main Street in Love Valley. Covered dishes lined several tables, and the hundreds of attendees at the celebration crowded into the large dance hall and spilled out into the rainy weather and muddy streets. They were dressed in cowboy attire, jeans, boots, motorcycle vests, and work clothes. They were of all ages and many walks of life. As on many occasions in the past in Love Valley, the mood was festive and hinted at a very large family reunion. Friends and family greeted one another, hugged, shook hands, and mingled through the crowd. But unlike those many past reunions, this one was marked by sadness because the crowd had gathered to pay last respects to Jetter Andrew Barker, Jr., who had died three days earlier. Andy, the founder of Love Valley, the longest-tenured mayor in North Carolina, a celebrity in his own right, and the patriarch of the little Western town, had passed away. The celebration of his life included a gun salute, speakers, lots and lots of barbeque, and a shared, communal respect for the man who had dared dream an unconventional and controversial vision of a utopian community. As the official speakers gave way to informal speakers and the attendees made their way through the food line, a full, double rainbow filled the sky, arching over the community designed with utopian ideals in mind. The rainbow sign recalled the utopian call to build a sacred space, a place where the secular gives way to the transcendent, be it cowboy dreams or godly virtues. Where this community goes from here is unknown, but Andy's spirit lives on in his survivors, his friends, and his community, a place built on the hope of love—Love Valley.

Study guide

Important words and concepts

Andy Barker
Love Valley
Sacred "place"—definition
Sacred "place"—characteristics
Utopianism

Discussion questions

(1) How does Love Valley illustrate a concept of sacred "place"?
(2) Describe sacred "place" as containing both space and time.
(3) Describe a sacred "place" in your own life, and tell how that place constitutes both space and time. How does that place "function" religiously?
(4) Is there a utopian element in most/all religious movements? Why, or why not? How are utopian myths in religions generally promoted?

Guided reading

(1) Read Thomas More's *Utopia*, B. F. Skinner's *Walden Two*, or any other example of utopian literature. Focus only on elements of space and time. How do these examples of utopian literature establish a sense of sacred place?

Part Two
Text

6
Narrative/Text

An Anglican priest kisses the text after the morning's reading; an observant Jew touches the mezuzah, a repository for sacred words; a grandmother gently, or not so gently, scolds a youngster for mistreating the family's King James Version of the Bible; the U.S. Constitution and the Declaration of Independence are preserved in the National Archives building; Mao's Little Red Book was once treated with devotional intensity. Texts carry sacred import, contain within their pages sacred power. We know this about religious texts, but it is also true, or can be, about secular texts. Any text that has the power to change lives or to open the portals of truth possesses sacred possibility so that the phrase "religion and literature" is a given and self-logical turn of phrase—at least in Western culture since the Enlightenment, as the written word rose to supremacy as the truth-bearing entity within society and culture.

However, in our postmodern, contemporary context, we see a demystifying of text, a secularization that, like the trend affecting other parts of our culture, is proceeding in two directions: the secularization of sacred texts and the sacralization of secular texts. In order to see what is happening with the secularization of sacred texts, we need only focus on the treatment of the Bible in our culture during the last 150 years or so. I will do so only briefly in order to focus on the second direction of secularization within literature—the sacralization of secular texts. In the case of the sacralization of secular texts, the disciplinary approach to religious studies known as "religion and literature" gives us the best systematic approach to understanding secularization. In that context, I will consider what popular prose and classical literature have to offer a culture in search of religious landmarks.

The secularization of sacred texts

The Kama Sutra is the one ancient book from a spiritual tradition that college students usually recognize by name. That is not because they are proficient readers of ancient Hindu texts but because the Kama Sutra has been stripped of its spirituality, stripped of its religious import, and sold to the American public in the pages of *Cosmopolitan* and on the shelves of bookstores in the "relationships" or "sexuality" section. While there is certainly advice on sexuality in the Kama Sutra, the text contains more than just technical descriptions of various sexual positions. The Kama Sutra contains advice on many aspects of aesthetic and sensual pleasure and the role of pleasure as a goal of living. The Kama Sutra is a single text that describes a small part of an overall spiritual approach to living embodied in Hindu spirituality and devotion. Most people who find it in the "relationships" section of the bookstore are not interested in Hindu spirituality but are drawn to its secularized and denuded (pardon the pun) versions that highlight the titillating parts as a sex manual. American culture is drawn not only to erotica but also to religious esoterica. When Madonna became involved with Kabbalah in the late 1990s, fans scrambled to find out what Jewish mysticism and Kabbalistic teachings entailed. When the Beatles demonstrated an interest in transcendental meditation, large numbers of fans were attracted to Eastern teachings and texts on meditation. There seems to be a general interest in sacred practices and sacred texts that are representative of the esoteric; however, this interest is often of a secularized nature—as if our culture is looking for the sex and ecstasy without the attendant spirituality.

But American culture not only secularizes unfamiliar sacred texts in the hopes of gleaning wisdom and practical advice—there is also a tendency to do the same with America's most familiar sacred text, the Bible. American culture is at once intimately familiar with the Bible and also grossly ignorant of its contents. Stephen Prothero's work on religious literacy suggests that not only are American students largely uninformed about world religions but also failing in their knowledge of the Bible, arguably the most influential book in the English-speaking world.[1] So, if we are so uninformed about a text that most in our culture recognize as a sacred text, how do we explain the disconnection between our cultural beliefs and our cultural knowledge? Or perhaps, despite what most would say, our cultural beliefs no longer include perception of the Bible as a sacred text.

What makes a text like the Bible sacred? If the mythic structure of story gives revelation validity, then we can issue the following postmodern dictum: the Bible is no longer a sacred text—at least not functionally so—at least not for the majority of readers. Contemporary Christians and biblical scholars have virtually rendered the Bible devoid of sacred function, as a text that can open up transcendent truths through the mythological task. I have no statistics to prove this—I am simply reflecting on my own efforts at Bible reading and study, on my interactions with sincere Christians of all denominations, on my familiarity with serious and accomplished biblical scholars and exegesis methods, and on my teaching experience with undergraduate students of religion. The postmodern Bible has been thoroughly secularized—and the project came from two sources: the scholarly community whose approach was adopted by the left and the fundamentalist community in reaction to the intelligentsia. Both sides secularized the sacred in different ways, and the result is a barren Bible, stripped of its mythological power to reveal truth.

When Julius Wellhausen popularized the documentary hypothesis for explaining authorship of the Hebrew Bible, the result was a revolution in biblical reading. Wellhausen convincingly demonstrated that the religion of the Hebrews evolved through historical periods and this evolution could be seen in the various historical and cultural patterns reflected in his progressive dating of the Pentateuch. Literary methods and historical and cultural considerations entered the conversation when readers attempted to understand biblical meaning. Wellhausen helped transform biblical scholarship, and from at least his time through much of the twentieth century, the attempt to employ literary, historical-critical, and cultural studies to understand the Bible has been motivated by the desire to add empirical validity to the textual study.[2] Others followed Wellhausen: many attempted to write biographies of Jesus in their "search" for the "historical Jesus"; others sought ways to use historical-critical methods to make the Bible more meaningful for contemporary Christians. Almost all ended with portraits of Jesus or the Bible that differed greatly from the sacred text because the approach tended to sidestep myth while still giving credence to the importance of myth.

Rudolf Bultmann, a German Form critic of the New Testament, proposed a program of demythologization of the New Testament so it would be more relevant and understandable for contemporary Christians. Bultmann's working thesis was that the culture and worldview of the New Testament period was so alien to the contemporary scientific worldview that mythological components in the Gospels needed to be excised or reworked so the message of the gospel could become preeminent. To his great credit, Bultmann reminded us that myth is a powerful religious element that is rightly understood metaphorically, not literally. Nevertheless, Bultmann has often been misunderstood and misused, and his program of demythologization has sometimes been used to strip away mythic elements in the New Testament rather than to bring them into symbolic focus. In the end, Bultmann's demythologizing stance submits mythological meaning to historical and cultural analysis, and once again myth becomes subordinate to history and science, in method if not in hermeneutics. As myth props up historical interpretation, the sacred becomes secularized.

From Wellhausen to the most hardened Bultmannian demythologizer to the ardent Christians in search of the "historical Jesus," from Form critics to redaction critics to source-critical historians, the past 150 years or so of biblical scholarship have given us fresh insights into biblical texts. Historical perspectives and literary criticism have provided a wealth of information for understanding biblical texts and traditions. Yet, for all the indebtedness the Jewish and Christian worlds owe literary-critical methods for understanding biblical texts, what has this methodology cost?

When such methods are used exclusively to study biblical texts, the result may be a "demythologized" text that has been also desacralized. While historical criticism promises to provide insight into the text by giving historical and cultural grounding and literary criticism promises to reinvigorate the study of metaphor, these methods do not always deliver on their promises. Often the biblical text's meaning becomes secondary to reconstructing the historical circumstances or the literary structures so that the hermeneutical task becomes less crucial or falls away entirely. Or liturgical and doctrinal demands locate meaning in history or literary structure and cement it in place—freeze it in the past or in the text, so to speak, so that meaning becomes static, frozen to the intent of the author (as if we can know that), imbedded in the structure, unable to escape and transmute or evolve, and thus unable to become alive and meaningful for contemporary readers. In the effort to enliven the text, modern criticism, if taken alone, makes the Bible a sterile and barren literary landscape. If the biblical text stands for nothing more than any historical tome or poetic text, then the Bible has been secularized—the authority of historicism supersedes truth; the mandate of empiricism supersedes the yearning for revelation. When only historical and literary methods are used in the study of the Bible, the metaphorical power of myth is lost. Such approaches may be mandated in state universities to avoid separation issues; they may be required in seminaries in order to exegete texts effectively; but it must be remembered that these marvelous tools arose to provide scientific validity to biblical studies. The need to make the process scientifically verifiable provides us evidence of the secularizing process in the tools and methods of biblical scholarship.

However, the academic Left of biblical scholarship is not the only culprit when it comes to secularizing the Bible. Responses from the Right to scientific and historical criticism of the Bible also desacralize the Bible, perhaps unintentionally and even unwittingly. Christian fundamentalism, arising in the early part of the twentieth century partially in response to new critical methods that questioned some long-held truths of biblical narrative, equally destroys the metaphorical power of the Bible by insistence on an inerrant text. Requiring an inerrant text is another way of submitting the Bible to empirical mandate. The desire for an unambiguous Bible with a straightforward truth is not only misguided but exposes the need for "hard facts" rather than the more "substantive truths" of metaphor and myth. Fundamentalism desacralizes the Bible as much or perhaps more than historical-critical methodology because it submits the text to the test of empiricism, and in doing so destroys the mythic element that makes a text sacred.

Christian fundamentalism simply cannot handle a sacred text because fundamentalism confuses truth with fact, myth with history, metaphor with literalism. And in such confusion, fundamentalism destroys the integrity of the sacred text and renders it a secularized instruction manual, barren and frightening in the wrong hands. Both historical-critical methods and fundamentalist demands destroy the metaphorical use of the Bible through empirical readings—one relying on historicism, the other on the assumption of divine perfectionism. But both destroy the metaphorical authority of Scripture if misused and thus strip the Bible of its sacred import. What both approaches must uphold, a task easier for historical and literary methods than for fundamentalism, is that the sacred text's power lies in metaphor and myth. Both approaches need to rediscover what Tim O'Brien describes as the power of "story-truth," which can be "truer sometimes than happening truth."[3]

A personal example highlights the levels of textual power and myth. As an undergraduate religion major, I remember being undisturbed by my first exposure to historical and literary methods for studying religious texts because they were applied to non-biblical ancient texts—the myths I studied historically were not myths crucial to or related to my faith or beliefs. But when my teachers first asked me to use those same tools on biblical literature, I took it as a challenge to my ingrained notion of an inspired text. Likewise, I also distinctly remember having a very difficult time the first time I was exposed to an alternative myth or metaphor that challenged the one I had inherited from my biblical tutelage in conservative Christian churches. When I read and studied the gnostic myths, I experienced a crisis of sorts because the challenge of Gnosticism was at the mythic level, not at the literary or historical level. I worked through this challenge of an alternative myth based on the same text, but it required me to strip away the immature faith I had inherited from others and claim a faith of my own. This was the first time I began to understand the power of metaphor and myth in religious faith, the first time that I discovered personally that developed faith requires the epistemological step of examining honestly, and sometimes jettisoning, your presuppositions. Sacred metaphor demands this philosophical step—doctrinalized religious story forbids it.

A last reference will give another example of how the biblical text has been secularized in recent time. The phenomenally successful *Left Behind* series by Tim LaHaye and Jerry B. Jenkins demonstrates how the religious right might secularize the Bible. In the attempt to make the apocalyptic message more relevant to contemporary readers, Tim LaHaye conceptualized the series and Jenkins fictionalized Christian and Hebrew apocalyptic texts in a brilliant bit of extrapolation. Asking the famous "What if" question of science fiction, LaHaye and Jenkins explore how a premillennial conception of the apocalypse might play itself out in contemporary society. The interesting thing about this series is not the literature but the concept. This evangelical experiment is based on the notion that a fictionalized account is necessary to get the message across. So, using a secular medium to impart a sacred message, LaHaye and Jenkins fictionalize, literalize, and secularize. If these Christian bestsellers and thrillers adopt the medium, the structure, the tone, and the method of secular literature, can the sacred stories be retold without destroying the metaphorical import of the original? Christian fiction, like *Left Behind*, witnesses another attempt at historicization (based on the belief that relevance is contingent upon contemporary location) and literalization (transferring biblical metaphor to actualized fact).

Left Behind, or any Christian fiction for that matter, represents contemporary secularization of sacred literature by adopting the forms and structures of secular literature to transmit an evangelical message. Like the megachurches, these fictions adopt secular cultural forms and infuse within them a Christian message. From outward appearances they are successful—it is hard to argue with the huge numbers flocking to megachurches or the millions of books bought and read. Nevertheless, the numbers do not prove effectiveness. They do not even prove relevance. The question becomes: Will the success of Christian literature and institutions like the megachurches lead to relevance through the secular media or to irrelevance by sameness?

The really instructive element of the *Left Behind* novels is their perspective of a post-rapture situation. In the first novel, the book opens with the moral ruminations of a 747 pilot at about the time of the rapture, which in premillennialist lore includes the fantastic disappearance of true Christians. So the plot of the story takes place entirely in a post-rapture world as the main characters, the pilot, a newspaper reporter, an airline attendant, and the pilot's daughter, try to make sense of the chaos and fear following the disappearance of loved ones and a goodly portion of the world's population (including all children). The perspective is post-rapture, and the thinly veiled theological enterprise of the book is to prove biblical prophecy by placing it in the historical setting (prophecy, which is often seen as predictive, becomes past and thus verifiable). The perspective is subtle—by historicizing prophecy in the past, the authors lay claim to Truth and make their evangelical plea to those left behind. The urgency is palpable, energized by prophetic texts that have come true in the book. But this perspective changes the prophetic texts—it transfers the metaphorical to the literal—it takes the visionary experience of the author of John's Revelation and other prophetic texts and cements it in historical concrete, and it sterilizes the potential richness and meaning of the apocalyptic myths by trying to literalize them in historical perspective. And all this is done through the secular medium of the novel. The secularization of the sacred apocalyptic myths has been completed in *Left*

Behind. That these books are wildly popular gives us some clue to the extent that evangelical culture has adopted secular standards as the receptacle for the Christian message.

Just as the scholarly community has fixed the sacred texts in history, culture, and literary structure, conservative religion has hitched the Bible to doctrinal presuppositions. In both cases, the metaphorical power of the Bible has been lost, and with the loss of metaphor we lose religion.[4] The rejection of the metaphorical stance is the destruction of the sacred, the secularization of the sacred, and the exchange of truth for fact. And this secularization comes not from secular powers nor from popular culture nor from enlightenment forces but from the religious community itself. If religious texts have been so chained to liturgy and doctrine, if the sacred myths have been historicized so that symbolic meaning is lost, where does one turn to regain metaphor or myth? One must look to fiction that is not tied to or guided by religious doctrinal perspective or historical methodology: that is one must turn to "secular" literature in the attempt to recover the sacred, and it is to the sacralization of the secular in literature that I now turn.

The sacralization of the secular: the religion and literature movement

The infamous megalomaniac of Herman Melville's *Moby Dick* finally appears in the novel some 28 chapters into the narrative. Ahab's dramatic entrance provides a clue to how literature can participate in the secularization of religion through the sacralization of the secular. Ahab's presence not only demonstrates how Ishmael could experience the extraordinary, the Other, in the context of mundane experience, but it also suggests the power of literature to mediate an experience of the Other for the reader. As much as Ishmael had wondered about the mysterious Ahab, as much as he had anticipated meeting the man, when he does finally appear the apparition is a revelation for Ishmael: "Reality outran apprehension," writes Melville.[5]

Reality does outrun apprehension—mundane experience outstrips the imaginings of even the most creative visionaries.[6] Our mundane experiences can lead to wondrous occasions, filled with transcendent possibilities. For the reader, it can happen in the pages of a book;[7] for the character Ishmael, it happened on the deck of the Pequod. Many individuals claim it happens outside the confines of sacred institutions or rituals. When this happens, secularization of religious experience occurs because religious experience takes place outside the auspices of sacred organizations or sacred spaces. In such a case, the secular becomes sacralized.

The tendency in religious studies has been to dichotomize the concepts of sacred and secular based upon the significant work of Rudolf Otto and Mircea Eliade in establishing the polarized concepts of sacred and profane. Thus, Eliade elaborates on Otto's terminology by suggesting that something becomes sacred when our mundane, profane world becomes a receptacle for "something of a wholly different order."[8] Too often Eliade's work is used to polarize different kinds of objects or different states, so that the contemporary world is often seen as emphasizing the secular or the profane rather than the sacred, in Lynn Ross Bryant's words, the "human rather than the transcendent."[9] But this polarization into types is not necessarily the logical conclusion to Eliade's categories. In fact, Eliade speaks of a confusion of types through the interaction of the mundane world and sacred reality. Thus, as Giles Gunn suggests, sacred and secular do not delineate "different kinds of objects" but "different ways of perceiving and then relating."[10] Perhaps we can step back from the polarization of sacred and secular and see them as part of a continuum rather than as different sorts of realities. This allows interdisciplinary approaches to religious studies, such as religion and literature, to flourish and to be effective. If sacred and secular are partners in a continuum of experience in approaching otherness, it certainly makes sense that religious experience can be expressed in either sacred or secular form; therefore, the study of sacred and secular culture and their intersections is appropriate.[11]

In the study of religion and culture, particularly when that study focuses on secular expressions of religious questions, the interdisciplinary field of religion and literature is perhaps the most developed subfield of its type in religious studies. In a sense, the modern study of Western religions, until recently at least, has been a project in religion and literature because these traditions are so heavily dependent on texts for their ritual and even for their institutional life. In addition, religious traditions often spawn devotional texts, such as The Bhagavad-Gita, as a natural outgrowth and expression of religious feeling. Often these devotional texts tell us more about the practice of religion at a particular time than do official sacred texts of a religious tradition. Literature has and can provide an outlet for religious yearning just as it provides a medium for the expression of love, passion, horror, awe, and beauty. David Jasper has suggested that religion and art can teach truth in ways that overcome or outflank theological and doctrinal tyranny.[12] Thus, as a cultural form, literature will certainly overlap religion and religious expression because all cultural forms participate together in building meaning.

Nevertheless, in a broader sense, the study of religion and literature has grown into an interdisciplinary subfield that touches religious studies, literary theory, and cultural studies in general. This fact itself provides a good demonstration of the secularization of religion as the definitions of "religion," "the Other," and other sacred terminology have been broadened to function meaningfully in other secular forms of intellectual pursuit. Linking religion and literature in formal intellectual contexts has had a greater effect than simply recognizing the overlapping of two cultural forms. This linking has formalized within academia a secularization of religious studies, because, at its heart, it seeks to find "the Other" not in the sacred sphere but in the secular realm of the literary imagination.

The study of religion and literature as a formal discipline has had a checkered history and development; its current vitality as a recognized, independent field of study has lagged in the past few years, particularly in America. One will find few formalized programs of study in religion and literature either in the United States or in Europe. Nevertheless, this interdisciplinary pursuit still exists in departments of English, theology, religious studies, interdisciplinary studies, and American studies. Theology courses are taught in seminaries using only "secular" literature. Literature courses are taught in universities using only "sacred" literature. And cultural studies courses are being taught everywhere that recognize the power of literature to carry and to communicate religious longing and belief. The religion and literature movement continues to build on a century of work by scholars from various disciplines. For a history of development of this interdisciplinary pursuit, one could hardly do better than chapter 1 of Giles Gunn's seminal work, *The Interpretation of Otherness: Literature, Religion, and the American Imagination.* Here, Gunn traces the movement through three phases beginning in the early twentieth century, helping us to understand how the discipline has attempted to define itself. Eric Ziolkowski's more recent essay, "History of Religions and the Study of Religion and Literature: Grounds for Alliance," provides a type of history of the movement as well placing it in the context of the development of the history of religions movement in religious studies.[13]

If religion and literature studies seem to be floundering at present, it is not because of lack of interest or participation. Rather, the field is undergoing redefinition as its initial momentum slowed after a "golden era." A generation of scholars built the discipline of religion and literature (Nathan Scott, Giles Gunn, Robert Detweiler, Wesley Kort, and others), and the one-time premier program in the field, at the University of Chicago, constructed a rich and expansive approach to religious studies. Nevertheless, instead of producing a field of study with a unified goal and direction, religion and literature studies carry with them a variety of objectives and presuppositions, including testing the validity of formalism and New Criticism that dominated literary critical circles earlier in the twentieth century.[14] If the initial movement was reactionary, it ran its course without a unified vision of religion and literature. Now, a younger generation of scholars, some of them students of the above pioneers, are redefining the field, molding it in various ways to be even broader and more inclusive. Scholars like David Jasper, Carolyn Jones, Irena Makarushka, Mark Ledbetter, David Arnold, and Eric Ziolkowski have taken the study of religion and literature in various directions with equal lucidity and insight. Thus, the field's lack of a center or unifying force appears to be a weakness. This does not mean, however, that the field is faltering. Rather, it might be argued that the study of religion and literature is stronger than ever, more vital than ever—stronger and more vital through its presence and greater diversity across curricula and across scholarly interests than ever before. Whether the field will survive in recognizable form may depend on the emergence of strong leadership to focus its great diversity.

In the final analysis, the fact that religion and literature exists as a field at all demonstrates the secularization of religion because it rests on the assumption that religious longing is expressed through secular cultural forms and that religious meaning can be gleaned through the study of secular writings. This is particularly true in the United States where the field developed in the context of New Criticism and tended to move away from theological reflection in the study of religion and literature.[15] Yet, even in European circles, which seem to be much more open to religion and literature as a theological pursuit (indeed, David Jasper even calls for a "rediscovery of theology" in religion and culture pursuits),[16] the study of literature and religion, when undertaken outside the confines of sacred literature, represents essentially a secularization of religion. With this in mind, I will discuss some issues basic to the study of religion and literature before examining the work of writers as a way of demonstrating how religion and literature as a field might incorporate various emphases.

As noted previously, the current state of the study of religion and literature is multi-directional, broad, and inclusive. It thereby embraces many different approaches, attitudes, assumptions, and methodologies. Yet, with all the diversity in the field, work in religion and literature comes from two basic groups—religious studies scholars, or literary theorists. For the most part, the work being done in this field comes not from "religion and literature" scholars *per se* but, as Giles Gunn has pointed out, from religion scholars with an interest in literature or literature scholars with an interest in religion or theology.[17] These two groups more often than not demonstrate vastly different approaches. Great diversity in terms of motivation and methodology is found even within the religious studies group. To demonstrate this diversity, I will discuss three different approaches to the study of religion and literature, recognizing that these general approaches do not exhaust the current complexity of the field.

The study of religion and literature proceeds as a literary pursuit, as a theological method, or as a religious studies tool. I will mostly avoid considering religion and literature as it relates to "sacred" or devotional texts such as the Bible, the Qu'ran, or the Bhagavad-Gita. Rather, I will focus and limit my attention to religion and literature as it occurs in relation to "secular" texts and authors: D. H. Lawrence, Toni Morrison, Willa Cather, James Agee, William Faulkner, Clyde Edgerton, and Amy Tan for example.

Religion and literature scholars operating predominantly from a religious studies perspective generally fall into two broad and fluctuating categories: theological studies and religious studies. Although the distinction between these two categories might not be readily apparent, often the motivations and presuppositions of these scholars are vastly different. Those who proceed theologically sometimes begin with a set of assumptions, theological precepts, truth constructs, or accepted beliefs, and use or search literature to demonstrate or legitimize them. Literature becomes an extended metaphor that illustrates a belief already in hand. Carried to the extreme, of course, this approach destroys the integrity of literature as literary works become little more than the handmaidens of preconceived truth constructs. In Noel Rowe's words, when this happens, "art is the servant of theology ..."[18]

In many ways, the field started with this approach of subverting literature to a theological perspective. The writer considered by many to be the father of religion and literature, T. S. Eliot, suggested that religion should dictate a standard for literature. In his famous essay, "Religion and Literature," Eliot begins by asserting that "literary criticism" proceeds "from a definite ethical and theological standpoint."[19] While some would dispute that Eliot is making literature subservient to theology in his essay and instead creates ambiguity and uncertainty,[20] it seems to me that Eliot opens the possibility for a Christian moral standard that will judge literature suitable for Christian readers. This relationship between religion and literature exists for those who make religion, in this case Christianity, the authority that judges aesthetic value from a particular theological stance.

Eliot's influence struck hard during the early and developing years of the religion and literature movement and produced scholars who were Christian apologists, such as Gabriel Vahanian in *Wait Without Idols*.[21] G. B. Tennyson suggests that literature found its origin in religion but was quickly divorced from it, becoming secular with no concern for religion. The implication is that literature arose to serve religious ends but later became deviant.[22] Making literature subservient to religious or orthodox standards may have found no greater expression than in Randall Stewart's *American Literature and Christian Doctrine*. As Giles Gunn and R. W. B. Lewis point out, Stewart reduces American religion to the concept of original sin and judges American literature by this single standard, effectively reducing literary criticism to a narrow doctrinal orthodoxy.[23]

Perhaps the most influential writer who falls into this apologetic category is Nathan Scott, a prolific and important scholar in the history of religion and literature who employs a muted and understated theological approach. Scott assumes that, to have an adequate knowledge of Christian faith, one must study literature because literature informs theology. Scott's writing is lucid, moving, and persuasive, giving apologetics an effective spokesperson for the literature and religion movement.[24]

Religious studies scholars, as opposed to theological apologists, might also fall in the trap of using literature to support or bolster a particular position, but, at least in theory, they should approach literature as a product that might display the multitude of ways human beings have of expressing religious imagination. Religious studies scholars broaden the definition of religion so that it represents not one theological agenda but a host of religious problems that are common and basic to human beings as religious beings rather than to individuals committed to a particular religious sect or denominational affiliation. Thus, a religious studies approach to religion and literature might focus on issues of race and gender because they encompass the religious categories of liberation, equality, and humanness that extend beyond orthodox conceptions and prescriptions.

Beyond the numerous scholars who study religion and literature from a religious perspective, there are a whole host of scholars who pursue the study from a literary theorist's perspective. Just as a theologian might make literature a tool for religion, critics whose work in religion and literature is informed primarily by work in literary theory often make religion subservient to literature. David Jasper claims that theology became subservient to literature, making "the poet ... a kind of priest."[25] One example of this tendency to exalt the literary side of religion and literature can be seen in the critics who were heir to the New Criticism of the 1930s. These theorists tended to hail literary texts as supreme cultural forms unaffected by cultural settings, authors' beliefs, or audience sensibilities. Therefore, if religion is related to literature, it is only in the sense and to the extent that literature creates it. Literary texts and the critic's work must be unaffected by cultural forms such as religion and, in a sense, replace religion as cultural standard bearers. In its most extreme forms, art and literature as aesthetic forms function religiously and replace religion.[26] Religion is thus completely secularized as it is subsumed and swallowed up by art.

In previous descriptions of religion and literature studies, I have employed extremes in order to point out inherent dangers to this interdisciplinary pursuit, namely that one discipline will overwhelm the other and that the legitimacy of religious studies, theology, or literary studies will be compromised. The dialogical nature of the religion and literature field has flowered into various approaches and emphases on author, text, or reader as methodological foci for study. Often defenders of one or the other position have argued for their approach as a way of politicizing the field. These arguments, while helpful perhaps for defining method, oversimplify the nature of literature by reducing it to either authorial intent, objective text, or reader interaction. Likewise, scholars tend to oversimplify religion by reducing it to historical context, to objective truth or inerrant text, or to believer response. Literature and religion encompass at least these three corresponding movements, and, when working between disciplines in the field, it is crucial to employ flexible methods to handle the complex nature of literature and religion.

Peter L. Berger's sociological view of religion is helpful in imagining the complex ways religion and literature might interact. In his classic text, *The Sacred Canopy*, Berger pictures religion and other cultural forms arising in three stages. The first is "externalization," the "outpouring" of human spirit and hopes in creative expression. The second is "objectivation," in which such outpouring results in a product that takes on an objective status of its own. The third is "internalization," the "reappropriation" of these cultural forms by human beings in meaningful ways, usually done in social contexts. For Berger, this is how society produces its cultural structures such as religion.[27]

Berger's paradigm is instructive for religion and literature because the three stages of development coincide with the three focal points of religion and literature. If these forces operate on the individual level as well as on the social level, then the literary process can be described using Berger's terminology. Externalization is the author's expression and outpouring of hopes, beliefs, and the creative spirit. Objectivation occurs when the author's creation becomes a "thing," a reified work that has objective status—a text. Internalization allows the text to be appropriated meaningfully by the reader. These stages are not independent occurrences, but are interrelated and interdependent. A reader cannot appropriate meaning (internalize) from a nonexistent text or in the absence of any creative activity to produce such a text. Likewise, as David Jasper notes, the literary process is complete when assimilated "by the reader."[28] The reader is also sometimes influenced in this internalization process by a community. As obvious as this seems, we often proceed methodologically as if readers read in isolation and as if writers create without an audience. We need a hermeneutical approach that focuses not solely on one or the other but that is large enough to consider all three moments in the life of the literary experience.

The field of religion and literature, if it is to survive as a viable and fruitful discipline, must be truly interdisciplinary in nature without allowing the agenda of one field to overwhelm the other or without allowing one methodology to run roughshod over contributions from cognate fields. Because it is an interdisciplinary pursuit, religion and literature work is difficult, especially at the methodological level. However, looking at and recognizing these extreme methods also give us some idea of the great diversity of the field precisely because it exists across disciplines. As examples, theologians might be more willing than others to be apologetic in their analyses, literary critics might be more interested in myth analysis, and feminist critics might be more inclined to find interest in the potential ideological components of literature. What is needed at the present is more constructive and less competitive dialogue—the field must be large enough and complex enough for all these approaches.

Religion and literature criticism must be done between the religious studies and the literary studies disciplines, with literature and religion interacting as implied long ago by R. W. B. Lewis.[29] Yet Lewis does not define the "between," and for years critics have been trying to pinpoint what has proven to be a shifting and flexible middle ground. Is the "between" Giles Gunn's "humanistic" and "hermeneutical" orientation to the common ground of culture and its symbols?[30] Or does the middle ground lie with Wesley Kort's narrative elements?[31] Or maybe the "between" lies in something more difficult to define, the ability of both religion and literature to challenge or critique culture.[32] Regardless, great variety of approaches and procedures exist in the field of religion and literature, and we would be wise to practice what Giles Gunn long ago named "principled eclecticism."[33] In any event, we would do well to keep foremost in our minds the possibility of a dialectic existing between religion and literature—a dialogue where, according to David Jasper, each part of the dialectic protects against ideological intransigence.[34]

Methodological questions aside, if we embark on a study of religion and literature in the manner it has been practiced over the past 50 years, then we participate in the secularization process. A study of religion and secular literature assumes either that religious longing can be and is communicated through secular cultural forms or that secular cultural forms can be a prop for religion or theology. In either case, religion is found elsewhere besides sacred literature and sacred spaces. This should not be seen as a demise of or threat to traditional religion. Rather, this kind of secularizing tendency witnesses to the strength, vitality, and resourcefulness of human beings and their religious longings.

Study guide

Important words and concepts

Documentary hypothesis
Hermeneutics
Historical Jesus
Historicization
Literalization
Literary critical methods
Myth
Premillennialism
Religion and literature movement

Discussion questions

(1) How have literary-critical methods improved the study of texts? How have they obscured the meaning of texts?

(2) Describe the contribution of the religion and literature movement to the study of religion.

Guided reading

(1) Read an annotated version of T. S. Eliot's "The Waste Land" (1922). Notice how many religious and mythic allusions and references are in the poem. How does knowledge of these annotations and references help in the hermeneutical process?

7

Religion and secular text

In the pages that follow, I will consider the works of several writers to demonstrate various emphases within the religion and literature field. I have chosen three Southern U.S. writers to suggest that religion and culture are not monolithic entities even within regions that are often considered to lack diversity in religion and ideology. I have chosen an Asian-American female and an African-American male to demonstrate that the same diversity and the same "sameness" exist across ethnicities and gender, across cultural lines and tradition. And I have chosen the remarkable work of British author J. K. Rowling to suggest that the human need for the transcendent is universal. A look at Clyde Edgerton's *Raney* suggests the power of secular literature to critique a culture's ideologies, religious institutions, and moral codes. Randall Kenan's *A Visitation of Spirits* shows us how a theology can grow out of the pages of secular literature and the cultural experience of Southern African-Americans. Amy Tan's *The Hundred Secret Senses* shows us how comfortable popular literature and culture can be with the dissolving boundaries between the sacred and secular. Lee Smith's work demonstrates how secular fiction can operate as myth to offer insight into women's spiritual issues. J. K. Rowling's fantasy world crosses boundaries between the ordinary and phenomenal. While limiting my evaluations of Edgerton, Kenan, Tan, and Rowling, I have chosen to provide a more comprehensive examination of Smith's body of work by way of contrast. By looking at these diverse works, I hope to show that these novelists, in various ways, provide fruitful subjects for religion and literature work because each deals with the tension existing between the sacred and the secular world.

I have chosen these writers for other reasons besides their demonstrating a religious and secular diversity within regional, ethnic, and fantasy literature. If we do live in a secular age, as many religious commentators suggest, then we can understand why our time is so characterized by various fundamentalisms. As I suggested previously, a society marked by the empirical quest for certainty, as a secular society ruled by rationalism might be, should not be surprised to witness the rise and flourishing of fundamentalisms in its religion, politics, and other cultural institutions. If fundamentalism is a characteristic of secular, postmodern society, Edgerton, Smith, and Kenan offer stinging critiques of the fundamentalist quest for Truth. Rather than providing certainty, Christian fundamentalism in the works of these authors stifles and limits characters, sometimes with tragic results. Thus, they provide a critique of one of their culture's most enduring symbols: conservative, Southern religion. While Tan deals less with fundamentalism of the twentieth century, her novel pictures missionary religion of the nineteenth century in its conflict with foreign cultural traditions. Although not directly critical of missionary religion, the portrait of Christian missionaries exposes the shortcomings of the evangelical approach to Christianity. Rowling's novels hardly mention religion if at all, yet they are infused with the magical, the sacred, and the transcendent. With Rowling, the sacred is enduring but without needing traditional religion at all for a catalyst. This literature challenges cultural and religious symbols and presuppositions, deconstructs and reconstructs cultural truths, shares with religion the ability to make and grant meaning.

Finally, I have chosen these "regional" and "ethnic" writers in order to challenge preconceptions some readers bring to regional and ethnic literature. Regional and ethnic work is often seen to be exclusive, irrelevant for the large majority of readers outside the group. Nevertheless, it is my contention that such writing is as universal as any type of literature and can provide a particular kind of focus for the postmodernist context of religion and literature work. According to Wesley Kort, one of the problems of postmodern literature and criticism is its devaluation of a sense of space and place. Kort argues for religion and literature work that always includes narrative analysis of place and space.[1] Regional literature has always claimed a sense of place as its lifeblood and can provide a particular focus for literary work in a postmodern context. And the ethnic literature included here also focuses our attention on place in interesting ways: Kenan on the black community and Tan on China. In this way, literature is not simply about a particular place but about a sense of place—a sense of human beings struggling with universal problems in the context of the places where they live and function. So Kenan's and Tan's works demonstrate not only that universality can come from particularity but that universal concerns can exist across cultural divides. And like Flannery O'Connor suggested years ago, regional writing—I would include ethnic writing as well—provides us the "possibility of reading a small history in a universal light,"[2] thus binding readers together through their shared humanness. Finally, even Rowling is a type of regional writer, setting her novels in England. But Rowling goes beyond regional—the sense of place established by Rowling is magical and universal. From the insular halls of Hogwarts, Rowling's youthful characters expand the possibilities of space and time.

Therefore, I have chosen these writers in order to view how diverse voices can critique sacred symbols in a way that speaks universally beyond the particularity of region, race, age or gender. In this way, literature can establish a sense of place beyond the boundaries that create difference and separation and help us overcome our postmodern sense of dislocation in a challenging and secularizing world.

Clyde Edgerton, *Raney*

Clyde Edgerton's delightfully funny first novel appears to be a harmless story about the inhabitants of a small Southern town and the strong sense of place and community we like to imagine existing in such towns. The story follows the first year of marriage of Raney Bell, a sheltered and innocent Primitive Baptist from Listre, North Carolina, and Charles Shepherd, a more experienced and worldly city dweller from Atlanta. The story has predictable conflicts that provide much of the humor and promise to keep the reader entertained, if not laughing, throughout the entire novel. But beneath the charming story, beneath the hilarious antics of Edgerton's characters, lies a darker humor—a satirical look at the South, its beliefs, and its practices. Edgerton's satire critiques stereotypical views of religion, morality, and race in this book, and it is this power of his story to challenge and overturn dominant ideologies that highlight the role of place and community in the crises that define life. It is also this power of story that so frightened the administration of the Baptist college where Edgerton taught that it cost him his job. Edgerton's assessment of the episode is that the organization did not understand the satire and thus responded in fear to his novel.[3]

Edgerton's critique of Southern, evangelical religion begins with but does not stop with *Raney*. The same theme arises as a central problem in his second novel, *Walking Across Egypt*, as the 86-year old Mattie Rigsbee, one of the main characters of the novel, struggles with her Southern Baptist religious heritage throughout the story in her quest to do what is right and moral.[4] Mattie's religion permeates every aspect of her life and motivates her Christian benevolence and service;[5] it is because she takes her religion seriously that moral conflict arises. This conflict between religion and morality takes on an even more biting tone in *Killer Diller*, a story that continues with the characters from *Walking Across Egypt* and introduces the element of a Baptist university with a very strong need to control.[6] But *Raney* is where the most moving and soul-searching conflicts take place.

The novel represents an extended story-telling session for Edgerton, and the story-telling tradition in his art is an integral part of his work.[7] Like a good story-teller, Edgerton creates a sense of place that not only delineates the action of the story, but grants possibilities for complex interactions between characters.[8] For example, even though the story is set in the 1970s in Listre, a small Southern town, the setting is complicated by the introduction of Charles (from Atlanta) with his progressive ideas on race relations. The resulting interactions between Charles and native inhabitants of Listre suggest that race relations in Listre are more rooted in a pre-Civil Rights era than in a post-1960s setting. So the simple 1970s small Southern town setting is made more complex by the introduction of alien elements that set the stage for change in the story. In many ways, the novel is about change and conflict in the South—conflict between old ideas and new, between rural and urban, between conservative fundamentalism and social progressivism, between bigotry and civil rights. These grand social challenges are played out in microcosm in the lives of Edgerton's characters, Raney, Charles, and their families, and it is with the development of these characters that Edgerton's storytelling and skills as a novelist emerge.

An examination of the novel's structure reveals the basic themes in Edgerton's satire. The story comes in three parts. In part one, "Blood Kin," the basic conflicts and issues of the story are presented through the introduction of the two families of Charles and Raney. With these two families, the reader learns that the central conflicts are cultural ones that embrace major items such as religion, morality, and racism but that even include smaller parts of life such as eating habits. In part two, "A Civil War," the tension between the newlyweds and their vastly different worldviews grows against the backdrop of the lingering remembrances of the Civil War, a conflict that set family against family, countryman against countryman. In this section, these cultural conflicts lead to the breakup and then partial reconciliation of Charles and Raney. Finally, in part three, "The Feed Room," the beginnings of resolution and reconciliation surface when the couple begins to compromise on some of the hard-line positions they hold concerning family and morality.[9]

The issues that provide the tension and then the occasion for reconciliation are cultural and nearly always revolve around religion in some way. Part one introduces the basic conflicts of the story. From the beginning, it is clear that Raney and Charles will have a hard time of it in their new marriage because of the vast differences in their background and upbringing. Raney is an uneducated, conservative Baptist who is narrow minded in her acceptance and tolerance of difference. Despite her often acerbic nature, she is a likeable character because of her charming innocence. She is childlike and confuses words like "consummate" and "consumed" or "psychiatrist" and "psychiatric." Her childlike innocence is part of what attracts Charles and the reader but is also a source of tension in her marriage. By contrast, Charles is a college-educated, socially liberal, Episcopalian with ideas that run directly counter to the conservative values Raney and her family hold so dear. These differences lay the groundwork for a battle of values deeply rooted in the respective families and backgrounds of the newly-married couple.

Conflict surfaces in several areas of family and personal life for Charles and Raney. For example, while Raney and her conservative family abhor alcohol, Charles and his family view alcohol as an acceptable and necessary part of social life. Raney condemns drinking as less than Christian behavior on the part of some progressive Christians (p. 15). But drinking is not something good Christians do—alcohol is of the devil and drinking is a sin, and her alcoholic Uncle Nate symbolizes the disastrous effects of drinking for Raney's family. Imbibing is a litmus test of sincere Christianity for Raney, and it leads to conflict early on in the couple's relationship. When it becomes clear to Raney that Charles's father and Charles and his buddy have been drinking at the wedding rehearsal, she is outraged. Later, Raney and Charles experience a disastrous wedding night, Raney being repulsed by Charles's actions. She blames his offensive behavior on the champagne he was sipping (p. 21). So for Raney and Charles (representing diverse cultural attitudes in the South), alcohol consumption is a source of conflict and negotiation.

Their attitudes toward alcohol highlight a deeper source of friction for the couple that comes to light in a delightfully funny passage describing the couple's wedding night from Raney's point of view (p. 20). The honeymoon encounter is a disaster, and sexuality becomes a threat to the couple's happiness. Raney is repressed sexually, very innocent, and filled with notions (mainly gleaned from her mother) about how sexual encounters are to proceed. Raney views sex as her womanly duty, something to be endured grudgingly. Charles is more liberated and curious about sexuality.

The second night proceeded more smoothly when Raney discussed with Charles how his part in consummating the relationship should proceed (pp. 21–2). Nevertheless, the problem with sex does not vanish on the second night of the couple's marriage and continues to plague the relationship through the middle part of the novel. Raney associates sex with prostitution (pp. 85–6), sees it as dirty (pp. 174ff.), and exposes her ambivalent attitudes toward sex when she discovers men's magazines for sale behind the counter of her daddy's country store (pp. 205–7, 212). She abhors the magazines but is curiously drawn to them and to images in her mind of naked men. When she discovers Charles is buying the magazines, her contempt for them overcomes her temporary curiosity. Raney's attitude toward sex becomes clear: desire is the problem. As long as sex is approached as a duty, a biblical duty, it is acceptable. But once desire enters and sex becomes something you want to do, it becomes a sin. Raney's repression of sexual desire remains a sore spot in the relationship until a wonderful scene in part three.

Charles and Raney begin to overcome some of the turbulence in their relationship toward the end of the novel. The couple stops by Raney's daddy's store after closing and after Raney has had wine with dinner. Raney finds herself in the feed room, inundated by feelings of desire she cannot explain. She reasons that marriage legitimizes a couple's actions (p. 226), and she and Charles end up sipping Southern Comfort and making love on the feed bags in the back of her daddy's store. Raney allows herself to feel sexual desire for the first time, she overcomes some of her inhibitions about alcohol and sexuality, and she begins to understand that sex can be more than a duty. While her maturation is occurring, Charles reciprocates with compromise of his own, and the two seem to be on the road to strengthening their turbulent relationship.

Other issues find at least partial resolution by the end of the story. For example, in the beginning of the novel, Raney maintains a very conservative view about the relationship of husband and wife. However, by the end of the novel, Raney has taken a job and has begun to question the preacher on some of the traditional attitudes about the subservient role of women in marriage. In addition, racial attitudes become a prime component of the couple's tense relationship. Charles's best friend is Johnny Dobbs, an African-American army buddy. Charles's friendship with Johnny leads to ugly confrontations with Raney's family because of their racist attitudes. Raney eventually begins to mellow in her prejudices, and she consents to naming Johnny as the godfather of their baby; however, her openness to more liberal social attitudes is not complete. In a symbolic move, Johnny stays at a hotel rather than at the family's home when he visits. Nonetheless, by the end of the novel and the first year of the couple's marriage, the reader sees both Raney and Charles making concessions, compromises, and changes that bridge the cultural gap that separates them.

Finally, the friction points that make Raney's and Charles's first year of marriage difficult find clear expression in their differing allegiances to religion. Raney grew up Free Will Baptist and represents fundamentalist religion in the South, one of the South's enduring cultural symbols. Charles grew up Episcopalian, a tradition that symbolically represents a type of secularized and worldly religion for Southerners. Fundamentalism is presented in this story as being narrowly focused on conversion, a personal relationship with Jesus, and a literal interpretation of the Bible while it ignores some of the pressing problems of contemporary life, such as mental illness and alcoholism. On the other hand, Charles's Episcopalianism seems overly rational, formal, socially oriented, and insensitive to individual need. While his social orientation might tackle society's problems on the grand level, Charles is often blind to human need on the individual level, and he remains egotistical and aloof through much of the story.

For Edgerton, both types of religion are inadequate. Thus, Edgerton is able to critique religion in the South, a region that is known for its religiosity, in a sensitive and nondiscriminating way. Edgerton's novel addresses and critiques many moral, ethical, and social issues and traces them to roots in religious belief. In this way, he delves to the core of some of the South's most cherished notions, questions them by raising religious issues, and mounts this religious and value-laden critique not through religious literature but through a secular novel. This, of course, demonstrates the power of the secular medium of literature to raise religious questions and issues. Edgerton himself notes the connection between the religious and the mundane when questioned about religion and his writing. He claims that "the religious spirit" is reflected by "everyday life."[10] Edgerton's articulation of the relationship perfectly demonstrates how literature can represent a secularization of religion, where theology is constructed in secular writings not about God but about human beings.[11]

Lee Smith, "Witches and Jesus"[12]

Rather than focusing on one of Lee Smith's works, I will consider several of her novels and short stories. The larger body of her work reflects a consistent concern for issues that are ethical and religious by nature if not by subject. Like Clyde Edgerton, Lee Smith is critical of Southern religion, in particular the conservative, fundamentalist variety, one of the South's most enduring cultural symbols. Unlike Edgerton, Smith's fiction goes further to construct a competing religious mythology based in women's spirituality. Like Edgerton, Smith's fiction relies on a strong sense of place and in-depth character creations. Unlike Edgerton, Smith's place is the southern Appalachian mountains and her characters are the people of the southern highlands. Both Smith and Edgerton write about changes in the South in the last half of the twentieth century and point out the shifting boundaries between the sacred and secular in contemporary American and Southern society.[13]

Spirits roam through the deep hollows of Sugar Fork; the rural country around Black Rock teems with the haunts of ghosts; witches glide through the forests across the hill boundaries of Hoot Owl Holler; the Holy Spirit descends with unexpected swiftness. At the same time, the revival preacher's drone rises from the tent into the night in the shadow of Black Mountain, calling poor sinners home; a young girl emerges from the baptismal waters of a plastic swimming pool; a man ponders the differences that split the Missionary Baptists from the Primitives; a preacher falls to his knees to seek cleansing after lovemaking. Two sets of images permeate Lee Smith's Appalachian fiction to portray a dual religious consciousness: the first is characterized by an elemental, supernatural power bound up by nature and the mountains themselves; the second appears in the form of traditional religions that attempt to transcend the mountain peaks and valley floors.

Both sets of images abound in Lee Smith's Appalachian settings and are entangled in the rich stories about her mountain characters and communities. These stories reveal a complex religious consciousness that at once is bound up in nature yet transcends nature; that focuses on the mountain setting as sacred yet often denies that sacredness in favor of a heavenly home beyond the Appalachian sky. This dual consciousness more often than not depicts traditional religion as restrictive and often portrays its adherents, particularly its leaders, as hypocritical or repressed. Yet there is in Smith's fiction a spirituality that is available and empowering to her characters—a spirituality that is often found outside traditional religious institutions. This religious consciousness provides order and chaos for the lives of Smith's characters (for Crystal Spangler, for Richard Burlage, for Moses and Ezekiel Bailey, for Grace Shepherd), yet for all the importance of spirituality in Smith's fiction, in the end traditional religion appears as mostly irrelevant and ineffectual in an Appalachia in the midst of change, modernization, and secularization.

Smith's fictional depiction of Appalachian religions relies heavily on generalizations and stereotypes. Even *Saving Grace*, which is the most religious of her works in terms of content, depends upon stereotypical images of poor mountain preachers and people to portray the religious worldview of her characters. However, this in itself does not demean Appalachian religious traditions as long as the reader does not make the mistake of taking Smith's vignettes and generalizing them to all Appalachian religious traditions and faiths. These depictions do help to set the context for her stories; her generalized representations determine what is possible and dictates the actions and feelings of her characters. Thus, while other types of writings are more helpful for understanding the intricacies and varieties within the Appalachian region, Smith's fiction gives insight into the religious condition in general and provides counterpoint to the study of Appalachian religious history and tradition.[14]

Smith's fiction represents the secularization of religion in two ways. Her depiction of traditional religion provides a kind of secular critique of religious faith by making value judgments concerning the relevance of religion to culture. Her portrayal of traditional religions symbolizes the extent of secularization of sacred institutions through the construction of sacred stereotypes. The second set of religious images in Smith focuses on an elemental religion divorced from sacred institutions, and here we see secularization occurring differently. With these images we see a sacralization of the secular as her mountain stereotypes and traditions rise to the level of myth.

Traditional religion in Lee Smith's fiction

Of the two images of religion and spirituality in Lee Smith's Appalachian fiction, those images surrounding traditional Appalachian religious movements are the most easily recognizable. Smith's work contains scenes and descriptions from the Free Will Baptists, the Primitive Baptists, the Missionary Baptists, the Holiness tradition, the tent revival, snake-handling evangelists, and Appalachian Methodists and Baptists. Most of these groups are barely represented outside Appalachia, some are dying out even in the high country, and Smith represents them in such a way as to reinforce notions that Appalachia has a sense of otherness about it, an exotic element in all facets of its culture including religion. In her descriptions of these "exotic" faiths, it is clear that they are different from the mainstream churches outside Appalachia. Indeed, Smith's fiction provides a social hierarchy of churches that "primitivizes" some of these traditional churches.[15] Karen, the narrator in Smith's short story "Tongues of Fire," describes this exotic sense with her social scale for congregations where the congregations lower on the social ladder acted in wild and unsophisticated ways (pp. 64, 57).

In Karen's world, and in Lee Smith's fiction, the more traditionally Appalachian the religion, the wilder and more uninhibited it appears and a greater sense of otherness accompanies it. Smith faithfully portrays some unusual worship practices of these Appalachian religious traditions such as the peculiar preaching style found in some Appalachian Baptist denominations where the preacher punctuates his phrases with a characteristic "ah."[16] Sam Russell Sage uses this technique in *Fair and Tender Ladies* (p. 93) as does the preacher, Mr. Looney, in "Tongues of Fire" (p. 80). Smith also refers to the Primitive Baptist practice of "churching" its members in *The Devil's Dream* and in *Fair and Tender Ladies*. "Churching," according to Appalachian religion scholar Howard Dorgan, is an act of discipline where "an errant member is literally expelled from fellowship."[17] Reminiscent of frontier religions and revivals, in *Fair and Tender Ladies* Preacher Sage lines out hymns (p. 93), and Oakley, Ivy's husband, dislikes Mister Blue because he has ministerial education rather than a simple "call" to the ministry (pp. 264). This sense of otherness accompanying Appalachian religion is most obvious in *Saving Grace*, Smith's story of the daughter of a snake-handling evangelist who travels through North Carolina and Tennessee preaching in brush arbors and little independent Holiness churches. This novel depicts the bizarre rituals of handling snakes, drinking poison, fire handling, and raising the dead.

Smith's portrayal of these unusual practices from traditional Appalachian religions highlights the differences between them and mainstream faiths. In *Oral History*, Richard Burlage, a socialite from Richmond, makes this observation when he takes a pilgrimage to the wilds of Appalachia to teach school and refresh his soul. He draws a comparison between his own restrained Episcopal tradition

(p. 135) and the free abandon in worship with the Freewill Followers at Grassy Creek. The Freewill Followers resemble the members of Karen's little Appalachian churches, have questionable social status, are uninhibited in church, speak in tongues, handle snakes, and rush the altar in a frenzy of emotion and fear for their eternal soul (pp 138–9, 152–4). More often than not, when Smith portrays traditional Appalachian churches, they appear exotic, unrestrained, and oddly peculiar in terms of their relationship to other more socially acceptable religious faiths. Smith portrays these traditional religions as being less secularized (or at least less acculturated) and, thus, less relevant and more vulnerable than mainstream religious traditions.

Beyond this presentation of Appalachian religions as otherness, Lee Smith's fiction creates a type of generic Appalachian fundamentalism that is common in these traditional religions. Differences between the various groups and sects are present, and Smith's readers recognize an ongoing theological battle between groups concerning the role of grace, behavior, and the Holy Spirit. However, there is much more commonality between these various groups organized within one traditional religious worldview. This worldview is characterized by narrow and constrictive thinking, by the all-important conversion experience, by an overarching concern with the afterlife, and by an individualistic and self-centered religious concern.

For the most part, Smith's traditional religions are defined by a narrow and restrictive worldview that reduces religion to obsession with the afterlife. The traditional religious attitudes in *Saving Grace* are so restrictive they prevent Holiness women from wearing jewelry and Travis Word from going to college on a basketball scholarship. Such restrictions are meant to keep adherents of the faith separate from the world because of the belief that a heavenly home is their true world. This insular posturing promotes a method of dealing with secularization in a changing and modernizing Appalachia. In *Saving Grace*, Virgil Shepherd's proclamation that his children may not have material possessions but that they will be in heaven (p. 9) demonstrates the belief that the saints should remain separate from this world in order to inherit the world to come.

This restrictive attitude toward the secular world and its accompanying focus on the afterlife is found and reinforced throughout Smith's fiction.[18] For example, in *Devil's Dream* Moses Bailey believes fiddle music belongs to the Devil and tries to keep his son from becoming interested in music (p. 27) because it would lead to Satan instead of to heaven. In *Black Mountain Breakdown*, the main representative of religion in the book is the Reverend Garnett Sykes, Crystal Spangler's uncle. Garnett's main concern throughout the first portion of the novel is the eternal state of the souls of his family. Garnett expresses frustration that he cannot save Grant (p. 49), and Crystal avoids Garnett because she knows he will try to save her (p. 63). Later in the book, a tent revival works up participants' emotions over fear for their eternal souls, and the whole purpose of the revival meeting is to bring people to a state of contrition based on fear. As the hard sale affects Crystal during the revival, it is fear more than anything that moves her (p. 121). It is this fear that the revival preacher orchestrates, and it is this concern for the afterlife that drives traditional religions in Smith's work.

Fear for the eternal state of the soul is so strong in the presentation of these religious faiths that it eclipses the role religion plays in determining behavior. In other words, behaving morally is less a concern than getting saved, and all energy goes into salvation rather than morality. For example, Sam Russell Sage, the evangelist in *Fair and Tender Ladies*, cares only for saving souls and is known to sleep around when he is not preaching, and, in *Saving Grace*, the charismatic Virgil Shepherd keeps mistresses in various locations and believes you can sin and then ask for forgiveness as many times as necessary (pp. 164–5). In *Oral History*, Richard's journal describes this characteristic of traditional Appalachian religious faith when he notes the disconnectedness between morality and salvation (p. 139). Richard later demonstrates this observation when he walks the aisle on the fourth night of a revival meeting to receive salvation only to rush out of the church moments later to make love to Dory, the mountain girl who is the object of his obsession, even though he admits that to do so would go against everything that he knows to be right (pp 152–4). The same loose connection between religious conviction and morality appears in *The Devil's Dream* as well. As Fred Chappell remarks, the Bailey family members have only three things in mind, "religion, music, and sexual love," and are quite willing to suspend their religion for sexual love.[19]

The most glaring example of Richard's observations about mountain religion's concept of salvation comes with the life and behavior of Crystal in *Black Mountain Breakdown*. Crystal experiences conversion at a tent meeting revival with such intensity that even her preacher uncle Garnett is envious. Crystal's mother's reaction is one of relief that Crystal has been saved, and, for a time, Crystal becomes a religious dynamo, reveling in the intensity of her experience, reading and studying the Bible daily, singing hymns around the house, and helping her mother more than usual (pp. 129–30). However, Crystal's religious intensity fades quickly—she discontinues her daily Bible reading within a week of the end of the revival and shortly thereafter she considers, with some degree of concern, her illicit love affair with Mack Stiltner. She quickly concludes, however, that even though her sexual relationship with Mack was a sin, it had very little to do with the state of her soul (p. 136). Crystal decides that morality has nothing to do with salvation, that behavior is incidental to the Christian life, and proceeds to fill her life with a series of illicit and adulterous relationships. In Crystal's life, as with others in Smith's fiction, religion has little to do with how one acts in this life and everything to do with where one goes in the next, assuming a discontinuity between sacred and secular worlds.

The one obvious exception to this general depiction is Travis Word, Grace's preacher husband in *Saving Grace*. According to Grace's narration, Travis alone emphasized "works above grace" (p. 164). Grace contrasts this to her father who holds that believers can live life however they wish and receive forgiveness for their sins. Nevertheless, even though Travis emphasizes behavior, the goal is still the same—heaven. For Travis, the connection between morality and salvation is so strong that it drives him to his knees after he makes love to his wife, Grace. His long prayers seek cleansing, and his obsession with purity leads to a depressed and repressed life that eventually enslaves Grace and drives her away. But once again, with Travis, Crystal, and many of Smith's characters who get caught up in religion, the goal is otherworldly, the obsession is heaven. These traditional religions reject the secular world and its concerns in favor of the promise of heavenly paradise in contrast to religions that accommodate to the secular, a form of secularization. The danger, of course, is if sacred institutions do not secularize and acculturate, they will become so otherworld-obsessed as to be irrelevant, anachronistic, and tragically comical.

Because this is the predominant religious attitude in Smith's traditional religions, it makes sense that the premier religious event be a radical and exemplary conversion experience. There are ample scenes scattered throughout Lee Smith's writing that chronicle this conversion experience: Richard Burlage's trip to the altar, the emotional experiences of those Richard is observing, the adolescent conversion of Karen in "Tongues of Fire," and the electrifying and sensuous crisis of Crystal herself. Crystal's conversion is the most detailed and will serve to illustrate the rest. Not long after the death of her father, Crystal becomes interested in religion and makes her way to a tent revival on the invitation of her childhood friend, Jubal Thacker, who eventually becomes a television evangelist. Crystal is a teenager with average adolescent anxieties at the time she visits the tent revival; however, she is burdened with extraordinary circumstances as well. She is trying to recover from the death of her father, and she has repressed the memory of being raped by her Uncle Devere. Thus, in addition to the normal adolescent uncertainties that often make individuals susceptible to extreme emotion, Crystal is emotionally more fragile because of her particular circumstances. The reader is not surprised, then, when she experiences powerful emotions during the revival service.

Crystal's conversion is a crucial scene in *Black Mountain Breakdown*. Crystal attends the big tent revival mostly out of a sense of loyalty to Jubal, but once she is there, she quickly is taken in by the emotional impact of the service. The service begins with the local Pentecostal preacher exhorting the crowd (p. 121). There is singing, prayer, testimony, and the revival proceeds with a carnival-like atmosphere complete with a karate champion who uses his skill to demonstrate how God breaks the barriers between God and humanity. The main event is the sermon delivered by a visiting evangelist, Fred Lee Sampson. His sermon is traditional enough, emphasizing the impossibility of entering heaven by good works and the necessity of accepting Jesus (p. 126). All of this has a peculiar effect on Crystal, and she slowly but powerfully responds to the emotional and persuasive techniques of the evangelist.

As the service continues, Crystal feels something akin to electricity run through her (p. 126). Fred Lee Sampson brings the service to a close by asking the congregation to sing "Just As I Am" as the congregation bows in prayer (p. 126). Veterans of old-time revivals immediately recognize the ritual, the hymn, and the technique as Sampson continues to plead over the soft chords of the organ. The words, the hymn, the persuasion have the desired effect—people begin to walk to the altar. And, of course, Crystal walks the aisle, gives herself to Jesus Christ, is baptized in a plastic swimming pool, and emerges saved (p. 128).

This conversion scene is a typical one for Smith. A similar event plays itself out in "Tongues of Fire," Richard's conversion in *Oral History* shares some of these elements, and when Grace, in *Saving Grace*, finally experiences the Spirit, it is accompanied by a physical sensation "like lightning" (p. 271). This general experience is reminiscent of the nineteenth-century camp meeting revivals and represents a generic Appalachian revival service for Smith's fiction. The implication is clear—Lee Smith chronicles an Appalachia where the old-time religious traditions have been preserved, at least until fairly recently, but are giving way to intrusions of modernity and the secular world, such as the plastic swimming pool and Jubal Thacker's television ministry. And in this old-time generic religion, conversion (getting saved) is much more crucial than good works for salvation and ultimately outweighs even moral action in terms of importance. The thoroughly anti-secular stance of such religion leads one inward and upward, not outward. Smith's fiction portrays Appalachian religion as individualistic and self-centered—it is all about what the individual gets out of the experience and not what the person gives. And what one gets is no less than the promise of eternal life. Lee Smith's stories depict these traditional religions as making little difference except to pacify the individual who has the experience.

This suggests an additional characteristic of Smith's generic traditional Appalachian religion—it arises from insecurity, if not psychosis, and afflicts mostly those who are marginal in some way. Ivy Rowe, in *Fair and Tender Ladies*, comments that difficulty in life makes people religious (p. 157); Crystal gets religion shortly after her tragic rape and after her father dies; "Tongues of Fire" begins with the adolescent Karen "speaking in tongues" amidst family tragedies and during emotionally charged times (p. 56); Richard Burlage's religious experience comes at a time when he is struggling with his own sexual passions; *Saving Grace* depicts the exotic practice of snake handling that seems, in this book, to be the affliction and ritual of the perpetually poor. In almost every case, religion erupts during times of emotional distress or during times when religion provides some sort of release from difficult situations. Likewise, when times are good, when characters prosper, religion may be present, but it has little force in a person's life.

Elemental religion in Lee Smith's fiction

If Smith's depiction of traditional Appalachian religions represents the negative impact of sacred traditions resisting secularization, her portrait of a more elemental religious orientation suggests that authentic religion can arise outside so-called religious institutions, especially if those institutions are irrelevant. With her presentation of elemental religion, we see the sacralization of the profane, that which is extra-ecclesiastical.

Alongside traditional Appalachian religion, which erupts at various places in Lee Smith's narratives, there is a second type of religious consciousness that pervades Smith's Appalachian fiction. This second form of religion is elemental, primal, closely associated with the landscape and nature, and often invokes a secret power that is disclosed to or available through female characters—a power that is sometimes revealed and symbolized through Smith's use of witches and her portrayal of women who are mystically connected to spirituality or nature.[20] This second type of religious consciousness is not as easily identifiable as the first because it is not as obviously intrusive into the narrative. Nevertheless, it is perhaps more pervasive and ever present, and perhaps that, too, is why it is not as easily recognizable.

This elemental religious consciousness is first recognized in the strong sense of otherness in the profane world, often in connection to the natural environment.[21] The landscape has a mystical quality about it, and the setting takes on sacred characteristics in much of Smith's fiction. This is particularly true in *Oral History*, which is concerned with the land and physical changes brought to the mountains.[22] The novel is set in and around Hoot Owl Holler (p. 22) and traces the history of the Cantrell family in order to explain the Cantrell curse. The first significant Cantrell figure is Almarine, a man who enjoys a special relationship with the land and with nature. Indeed, in this story, as Rosalind Reilly has noted, the mountains themselves initiate longings that "propel the novel forward."[23] The mountains themselves cast spells because they constitute a sacred space where "supernatural enchantment"[24] sways the actions of characters. Almarine brings the curse upon the family by getting involved with the witch Red Emmy, and the curse is passed along through successive generations to visit tragedy on the family. This family myth operates as all myth does, to provide sacred explanations, and it takes place, as all myth does, in a sacred setting. This sacred sense of setting is particularly strong in the first section of *Oral History* where settings are mystical, often associated with circle imagery that gives them sacred power, as Reilly suggests, and where action sometimes takes place in "froze-time" (p. 40), a sacred time where time is suspended and events become surreal.[25]

This image of the mountains as sacred place is reinforced at the beginning of section two of the novel when the reader is introduced to Richard Burlage, who is a foreigner to the area and whose response to the mountainous terrain is "Dear God!" (p. 93). Richard, in his awe-stricken state, means for his sojourn in the mountains to be "a pilgrimage" (p. 93). Richard's pilgrimage is to a sacred place and time rooted in the mystical bends and crevices of the mountains and valley floors.

The elemental and primal sacred setting of Lee Smith's fiction is reinforced by the role of ghosts, witches, and superstition in the mountains. The belief in spirits ranges from Crystal Spangler's naive belief in Ghost King Clarence B. Oliver, who would protect her from all the other ghosts who sometimes threatened her at night, to Granny Younger's insistence that Red Emmy belonged to the Devil, was a witch, and was responsible for the Cantrell curse. Perhaps this traditional connection to superstition and its part in an Appalachian religious consciousness can best be seen in Granny Younger's role as healer and, therefore, life force in her traditional community. Granny Younger typifies the confusion of superstition with traditional Christianity by reciting a magical formula to stop bleeding. The formula is based on Ezekiel 16.6: "And when I passed by you, and saw you weltering in your blood, I said to you in your blood, 'Live ...'"[26] but in Lee Smith's mystical, sacred Appalachian setting, it takes on magical and supernatural qualities (p. 20). Granny Younger also suggests a magical incantation that includes the mark of the cross, ashes, and the recitation of the name of the Father, Son, and Holy Ghost in order to break the witch's spell (p. 46). With Granny Younger, the traditionally Christian is fused with the primal, and the mystical element of Appalachian religion becomes clear. And with Granny Younger, one can see in Smith's female characters a mystical ability to harness a bewitching connection with the elemental powers of nature.

This connection between Smith's female characters and the elemental powers is sometimes evident in the context of traditional religious forms. If female characters in Smith's fiction are connected to and empowered by ghosts and the elemental spirits, this connection is extended to the relationship with the Holy Spirit in *Saving Grace*. There is an authentic, empowering experience of the Spirit in this novel, yet it seems to elude Grace's father, who handles snakes for show without anointing, and it is unavailable to Travis Word, whose restrictive religion makes him melancholy and sad. Rather, it is discovered by Grace's mother, who plunges her hands into hot coals without harm, because she was empowered by the Spirit (p. 26). And later, near the end of the novel, Grace discovers this secret place in the soul through the Spirit and she presumably handles the burning coals as well (p. 271), just like her mother.[27]

This elemental religion affords wholeness and connection, according to Rosalind Reilly, by "providing meaningful myths to empower the lives" of Smith's characters.[28] Personal, family, and communal myths provide meaning for the characters in Smith's narratives. This is seen most powerfully in Crystal Spangler's life. Crystal's breakdown occurs because she loses herself through the loss of her own story (she represses the memory of the rape by Devere and dissociates herself from that event) and through the loss of her father, whose relationship with his daughter was based on storytelling.[29] When Crystal loses her source of story and myth and forgets her own story through repression, she breaks her link to wholeness; she disengages herself from the elemental religious consciousness that provides connection; she loses herself through the loss of her mythic past. Crystal tries in vain recapture that link to wholeness through her radical conversion experience at the revival, but the traditional Christian experience fails to make up for the loss—only the recovery of myth can do that; only the recovery of the elemental, mystical connection to sacredness can empower Crystal.

The importance of story, the power of myth, is also strong in the novel *Fair and Tender Ladies*, a story told entirely through a lifetime of letters written by Ivy Rowe. Ivy's letters, the most intimate to a dead sister, Silvaney, allow Ivy to remember and tell her story. At one point in the narrative, Ivy slips into depression (p. 193) when her oldest child leaves home, and she tries to recapture her past through the stories that provide connection to her father and to the eccentric Cline sisters who used to come to Ivy's house on Old Christmas Eve and tell stories. Ivy's depression also comes at a time when she discontinues her reading, her letter writing, and, thus, her connection to her own story. The cumulative effect is that Ivy loses her connection to the past through the loss of stories, and she loses herself in the process. Ivy is lifted from her depression when she once again connects to her past through story. Ivy leaves her family and home for a short time with Honey Breeding. The pair started on what was to be a short hike up the mountain. During the walk, Ivy feels so comfortable that she begins to tell Honey all about herself. She surprises herself by talking so openly to a stranger, but it feels like the first time she has really talked in a long time (p. 223). They spend the afternoon telling stories and making love; Ivy is reminded of the stories she heard from her father during her childhood; they spend days in a cave; her depression is lifted—she feels young again.[30]

Nevertheless, Smith's characters learn that the past is not fully recoverable or knowable and that connection to the past, no matter how fulfilling, carries a price.[31] Ivy returns to her family to find her daughter dead and is faced with the ordeal of being forgiven by her husband and of forgiving herself. And Crystal slips into paralysis after the memory of her rape comes flooding back. So, there is a paradox with Smith's depiction of recovering the past. On the one hand, it is, or should be, a source of strength. On the other hand, the past fails to fully integrate characters like Ivy and Crystal. The key to recovery is the *myth* of the past, perhaps what Lee Smith calls "the central mystery of the past."[32] Ivy recovers from her ordeal because she reconnects to her past through the stories of Honey Breeding and through the recovery of her own story. This recovery of myth is empowering and is a sacred act that takes place in a sacred setting, for Ivy near a mountain bald that she had never seen and in a mountain cave that provides shelter and nurture. Crystal does not recover because she loses the "mystery," the myth, when the past comes to her in all its reality.

Thus, Smith's Appalachian fiction is often characterized by the recovery of an elemental religious consciousness. And in Lee Smith's contemporary Appalachian settings, the connection to the elemental and the sacred, which depends on the connection to nature, the land, the spiritual, and the mythic past, becomes tenuous as the unspoiled, wild beauty of the land that captivated such characters as Almarine Cantrell and Richard Burlage slowly yields to strip mines, shopping malls, and towns and villages—to secularization and modernization. As concrete and pavement fills the mountain hollows, the witches disappear, superstition is replaced by religion, and Smith's female characters, who had enjoyed a mystical connection with the primal, search with fewer results for that secret power available through nature and spirit. Yet Smith's characters find ways to access that elemental spirit in a contemporary setting. Sometimes they attempt to reach the primal through traditional religions, yet the presence of the traditional impinges on the empowering capabilities of the primal.[33] Discovery of the primal through traditional religious experience can be seen in what Virginia Smith calls the "sexualizing of the spiritual"[34] (or the spiritualization of sexuality) and in Smith's depiction of women's connection to a primal force in nature.[35] The former can be seen in *Black Mountain Breakdown*, *Oral History*, and *Fair and Tender Ladies*, while the latter is best exemplified by "Tongues of Fire."

The spiritualization of sexuality (sacralization of the sexual), the connection of powerful religious experience with sexual desire and feeling, is a strong theme in much of Smith's fiction. In *Saving Grace*, Grace attends a homecoming revival, gets swept away by the emotionally charged event, and finds herself in the backseat of her father's car with Lamar, transferring the "butterflies" (p. 102) in her stomach and excitement of the service (p. 106) into sexual passion. After making love, Grace finds herself prophesying while in "the Spirit" (p. 107), and she discovers her spiritual gift of discernment. The connection between spiritual and sexual energy is clear.[36] Even a more mature Grace discovers this same connection after an afternoon of passionate love with Randy Newhouse. Energized rather than exhausted, "on fire" and "sizzling," Grace sings hymns all the way home and shouts, "Glory hallelujah!" She felt as though she "had been born again" (p. 225).

The connection is even more pronounced elsewhere in Smith's fiction. In *Oral History*, Richard Burlage confuses his religious longings with his feelings for Dory. Richard attends a revival faithfully with the intention of meeting Dory there and is surprised to find that he is moved during the "invitational" on the fourth night of the revival. However, it is not clear whether his religious reaction is authentic or is instigated by his feelings for Dory (p. 153). During his conversion experience, when he walks the aisle to the front of the church, Dory bursts into the back of the meeting house. Richard immediately leaves with Dory and they make love for the first time. The two lovers end up spending a passionate six weeks together. This period constitutes an epiphany for Richard, a period he describes as "a state of grace" (p. 158). Richard's confusion of religious emotion with sexual desire ends with his finding grace in the latter rather than the former.

A similar confusion of feelings occurs in *Fair and Tender Ladies*. When Ivy Rowe, in Linda J. Byrd's description "the novel's sacred-sexual-maternal protagonist,"[37] attends a revival meeting, she is caught up in the emotionalism and is on the verge of responding to the preacher's pleas to respond. She feels "the firey hand …" and is ready to respond to the altar call when her companion, Miss Torrington, encourages her to leave (p. 94). The feeling is significant, and later Ivy associates her religious experience with her sexual desire. The "firey hand" she associates with God returns when Ivy feels sexual desire (pp. 97–8, 113).

The connection that Ivy makes between religious feeling and sexual desire is even more explicit in the experience of Crystal Spangler in *Black Mountain Breakdown*. As Anne Goodwyn Jones has suggested, Crystal "feels 'real' only when a man has shown sexual interest in her to which she responds, or when God enters her."[38] The sources of empowerment for Crystal are spirituality and sensuality. When Crystal visits the tent revival meeting and experiences intense religious feeling, she feels "electrified," as if she were "on fire, flaming …" (p. 127), and she associates this feeling with her sexual relationship with Mack Stiltner. The intense religious feelings Crystal experiences are similar to the physical feelings she has with Mack (p. 126). According to Jones, "Crystal trusts the sensual and spiritual voices inside her,"[39] and because she confuses these voices, she cannot unite them, and neither spirituality nor sensuality alone can empower Crystal—both are dead ends and neither can prevent Crystal's breakdown.

Smith's spiritualization of sexuality often happens in the lives of her women characters who are desperately seeking to unite body and spirit, as in "Tongues of Fire."[40] In this story, the adolescent Karen also confuses the spiritual with the sensual when young Johnny Rock Malone preaches (p. 65). Later, she experiences the physical feeling familiar to Smith's characters that is "like the hand of God" (p. 84). But Karen goes a step further in her spiritual empowerment—she speaks in tongues. This is an exotic ritual that captivates Karen the first time she hears of it (p. 72). The first time Karen hears glossolalia, she knows she has discovered a source of power[41] when she goes to a Holiness church with her friend, Tammy, and discovers "a language" she "knew intimately" (p. 81).

Virginia Smith suggests the description of Karen's experience demonstrates how "Smith confronts seriously women's need for a passionate language, an original voice that merges body and spirit."[42] Karen's finding that voice contrasts sharply with Crystal's paralysis and inability to speak at the end of *Black Mountain Breakdown*—Karen is empowered while Crystal is immobilized. This immobilization, in Smith's assessment, represents the "cautionary" element of the story concerning Southern women's tendency toward passivity.[43] In any event, it is clear that this very sensuous, religious experience has the effect of reaching a primal, elemental source of strength and freedom. Oddly enough, Karen discovers this liberation through a traditional Appalachian religion. It is here, through the empowering possibilities of religious feeling and through the spiritualization of sexuality, that the two types of religious consciousness in Smith's fiction, the traditional and the elemental, sometimes come together. Yet, despite the occasional intersection of the two types of Appalachian religious consciousness, the two rarely work in concert. The traditional religious categories can intrude upon and upset the primal and vice versa because the former focuses on transcendence and the afterlife while the latter is firmly anchored in nature and the mountain settings, the mythic past, and in a spirituality expressed through physical, bodily experience. The two types of religious consciousness create a paradox—a conflict between the transcendent and imminent, the sacred and secular—a paradox that rarely allows Smith's characters to fully overcome their marginalization.

At least two sets of images surrounding spirituality give the reader a glimpse of Lee Smith's vision of an Appalachian religious consciousness. Religion appears in all its traditional denominational and ritual constraints and as a more primal and universal spirituality based on the natural world, the mythic past, and sensuality. Sometimes these types of religious expression collide, but when they do come together, it rarely leads to wholeness or empowerment. Instead, the sensual element leads the experience beyond social convention, the encounter is censored, and individuals lose any meaning because they suppress the experience rather than allowing it to free them. Richard returns to Richmond without Dory, Karen is jerked back into line and becomes socially acceptable again, and Crystal suffers a paralyzing emotional breakdown. The elemental experience of sensuality and spirituality is suppressed by social convention or by traditional religion, and results, according to Anne Goodwyn Jones, in a group of characters "who fail, who prefer intellectualizing to feeling, moralizing to sensuality, religiosity to spirituality."[44] As a result, in Smith's fiction, traditional religiosity becomes largely irrelevant.

This theme of change is consistent throughout Lee Smith's Appalachian fiction, and change affects religion as much as any other cultural attribute of Appalachian society. In Smith's Appalachian fiction, she most often chronicles an Appalachia that is losing its pristine and traditional past and that is rapidly losing its Appalachian distinctiveness.[45] Part of the reason for this dominant picture of change is that many of Smith's novels trace stories through generational changes—sometimes beginning in the late nineteenth or early twentieth century and following a family or story to the present or near present. The effect of these narratives is dramatic. *The Devil's Dream* follows a family legend through 150 years from 1833 in a little cabin on Cold Spring Holler to the glitz and glamour of the lobby of the Opryland Hotel at Christmas. *Oral History* chronicles a 100-year family history, and the dramatic change, modernization, and commercialization of Appalachia surfaces when the old family home place becomes an attraction in the middle of a theme park, Ghostland.[46] In *Fair and Tender Ladies*, the nostalgic scene of the eccentric Cline sisters trudging through snow on Old Christmas Eve to share stories with their neighbors is replaced at the end of the novel by retrieving toys from layaway at a department store on December 23. Old Christmas is a thing of the past, and Ivy laments the changes and the old ways (p. 251). In *Saving Grace*, a food store with "drive-thru pick-up" replaces the old Duty's Grocery, a community, crossroads store that used to sell homemade cakes (p. 254). Finally, economic prosperity changes everything in *Black Mountain Breakdown* and even affects religious representatives in the book. In the space of a few short years, religion moves out from the dusty floors of a tent revival to the electronic, televised, healing evangelism of Jubal Thacker. These changes result in the transition of a sacred, mystical Appalachia to a modernized world stripped of its sacred power in part because traditional religions reject change and secularization. In other words, the result is a secular Appalachia stripped of the sacred rather than a mythic one.

Religion is pervasive in Lee Smith's Appalachian fiction—sometimes in the traditional settings of Primitive Baptist or Holiness congregations; sometimes in the mists of the hollows and hills of her settings; sometimes in the spiritual and sensual intersections experienced by her characters. But it is always present, always disruptive, sometimes empowering, sometimes deceptive, and sometimes devastating. Religious feeling and spirituality are rarely neutral; rather, her portrayal of an Appalachian religious consciousness is as passionate and alive as the characters themselves.

In Lee Smith's fiction, as in Edgerton's, the Southern setting allows the critique of Southern religion, an enduring cultural symbol. However, Smith's fiction goes further in positing an alternative religious vision based on women's spirituality and on other strong cultural symbols peculiar to the Appalachian region. And, finally, Smith mounts this critique and constructs an alternative spirituality in the context of a secularizing and changing society, relying upon an ongoing dialectic between sacred and secular categories—between elemental spirits and shopping malls, between the myths of a region and the gradual disappearance of its distinctiveness. Once again, reading and interpreting Lee Smith's fiction chronicles the secularization of religious longing, myth, and experience and demonstrates the spreading out of religion through secular cultural forms and media, in this case the novel.

What we see in Smith's fiction is a double meditation on secularization. The fact that sacred impulse arises through her secular art is representative of the second direction of secularization: the sacralization of the secular. In addition, there seems to be a form of critique in Smith's fiction: religious institutions that refuse to secularize become irrelevant, and, when sacred bodies no longer allow authentic religious experience, such sacred impulse will arise elsewhere through secular or non-religious elements of the culture.

Amy Tan, *The Hundred Secret Senses*

Lee Smith explores the complex relations between men and women; modernity and tradition; the existential and the spiritual. While many describe her as a regional writer, it is mistaken to limit her in such a way because her fiction carries much more universal significance than is implied by the designation of regionalist. In like manner, Amy Tan's fiction has often been described as ethnic because of Tan's own ethnicity and the topics and characters of her stories. Victoria Chen talks about Tan's female characters and their "dual cultural enmeshment" as if they represent Asian–American women.[47] Some have even implied that Tan's novels can become a source for understanding Asian religion because of the focus in works like *The Kitchen God's Wife* on ancestors, deities, luck, rituals and the like. In *Asian Religions in America: A Documentary History*, Thomas Tweed and Stephen Prothero refer to *The Kitchen God's Wife* as a text where Tan most clearly explores the religious landscape of Asia through her depiction of a Buddhist funeral.[48] And although Tan does give readers a glimpse of Asian traditions, especially as they have been appropriated in America, it would be a mistake to limit Tan's fiction to its helpfulness in understanding Asian–Americans' struggles with a foreign culture. Tan's fiction far exceeds the parameters of Asian culture and embraces such universal concerns and topics as death and rebirth and the relativity of time. My interest in Tan's fiction concerns not what she represents or reveals about Asian religion or culture. Rather, Tan is important to this book because her fiction develops characters who live and function in a secular world while easily moving between this world and the spirit world. Tan's characters often negotiate an easy intrusion of the sacred, the supernatural, into the secular world. Like Smith's fiction, Tan's is populated with ghosts and spirits, and, because it works, Tan and Smith demonstrate the extent of sacralization of the secular in American popular culture. So Tan's fiction represents not so much cultural conflict as the sacred–secular tension in our society. What appears to be traditional Chinese culture in Tan's fiction is often little more than a sacred approach to the world—the conflict arises from the sacred encroaching on the secular, not from the East encroaching on the West.

This intrusion of the sacred into the secular is most clearly seen in *The Hundred Secret Senses*. Tan spoke in an interview about her emphasis on the spirit world and her fear that this emphasis would be seen as simply "Chinese superstition." Her perspective in the book comes through Kwan's (a main character) "Yin eyes"—the unusual vision that allows her to communicate with spirit people in the world of yin, people who have died and whose presence can be sensed all around us.[49] This is not a ghost story but a story that takes place between worlds, drawing heavily upon the spirit world. That she can write so convincingly about the world between worlds gives us some clue to the extent that our secular society is open to the sacred. Through Tan's creation and use of "Yin eyes" and "the World of Yin," her fiction opens the postmodern reader to a premodern concept—an "other" world accessible through the agencies of this-world senses.[50]

Kwan's ability to see with yin eyes transports the reader across time and geography to nineteenth-century China, and part of the plot revolves around Christian missionaries in a Chinese village. The Christian message of the missionaries is ineffectual and the efforts of the godly are farcical. At the same time we see the failure of this traditional religious mission, the power of the spirit world is affirmed through non-religious avenues. The reality of the yin world in this story brings the power of myth to play in a highly secularized San Francisco setting. So, while traditional Christian missionary efforts are seen as misguided, the sacred through the power of myth receives new power and life.

In her full-length critical work on Amy Tan's fiction, E. D. Huntley devotes a chapter to *The Hundred Secret Senses* and a portion of that chapter to a Jungian archetypal reading of the novel.[51] This perspective is appropriate and helpful because it highlights the mythic component and structure of the novel to reveal the universal elements ascribed to Jungian theory, allowing the reader to negotiate the spirit world, the dream world, and the shift in plot perspective across two centuries. The story's setting also shifts from modern, secular, multicultural California to a "Yin world" based in China, and this jarring transition allows the intrusion of the sacred into the secular. It allows the spirit world to enter this world through memory and the senses, an intrusion that is related to spiritual and psychological wholeness in Tan's fiction. This spiritual perspective stands in stark contrast to the element of the supernatural in Lee Smith's fiction, which is anachronistic and superstitious, and the supernatural in Randall Kenan's fiction (to be examined next), which is related to pathology. Tan's perspective, seen through the Jungian lens, demands that the spiritual reside within the natural for human wholeness to occur.

Perhaps even more importantly, such a Jungian approach allows the easy transition from the world of yin to this world without having to sacrifice credibility.

Tan allows us to reconnect with the world of myth and gives us an example of how secular literature can do what sacred literature once did and perhaps can no longer do in the age of religious literalism. When we can learn from secular literature what once was the purview of sacred texts, the secularization process advances.

Randall Kenan, *A Visitation of Spirits*

Randall Kenan published *A Visitation of Spirits* when he was 26 years old, a young age to be able to produce such a dark vision of a world populated by ghosts and spirits and to expose the tormented feelings of a young African–American boy. In Kenan's vision, we learn the story of Horace, a black teenager who struggles with his homosexuality in a conservative religious community unequipped to help him deal with his feelings. The inability of Horace to seek and find appropriate guidance in a world where everybody and everything tells him he is a freak, ultimately leads him to suicide. Trapped in a world where his community fails him, Horace leads the reader on an adventure that explores the prospects of being gay, black, and Southern.[52]

Kenan's story, like Edgerton's and Smith's works, highlights and critiques the ability of fundamentalist religion to deal adequately with the complexity of the contemporary world. But with Kenan's work, the reader is introduced to a different South. Whereas Edgerton's work provides glimpses of rural and urban white middle-class existence and Smith's work portrays Appalachian life, which is mostly white, Kenan's novel takes us into the world of black Southerners and reflects the community values and religious beliefs dominant in a Southern African–American community. Like the aforementioned authors, Kenan uses his story to reflect on the values and morals promoted in the community through cultural religion and beliefs. Yet, unlike Edgerton and Smith, Kenan's work demonstrates a conflict of cultural values within the black community.

There are two dominant worldviews that inform Kenan's novel: that of conservative, Calvinistic traditions, which Kenan likens to existentialist philosophy,[53] and a metaphysical vision based on an African–American cultural history steeped in a belief in demons and spirits. Here again, the sacred and the secular collide in fiction, and Kenan uses these two worldviews to create the crisis that Horace faces. Horace gets no help from his preacher cousin Jimmy, no understanding from the staunch Christians among his elders, and nothing but censure from a religious ethic that condemns him as a sinner. Rejected by his family and by his religion, Horace ends his life after being tormented by a demon during a hellish night battling the spiritual underworld.

Horace enters his hell when he attempts a transformation, a conjure common in the shamanistic practices of African traditions. Unable to live with himself the way he is, unable to deal with the rejection and pain caused by his homosexuality, Horace attempts to change his essence with the conjure. However, the experiment goes awry, and Horace finds himself trapped in the spiritual world and goes insane. Horace's insanity and his subsequent suicide raise important questions about the relationship between religion and insanity, homosexuality and spirituality, and the ability of traditional religious responses to deal with the complexities of contemporary problems.

Kenan's novel represents a secular theology at work. Matthew Guinn argues convincingly that Kenan's literature is a literature of revision that rejects "the dominant ideology." Drawing upon Henry Louis Gates, Jr.'s concept of "signifyin(g)," Guinn points out that Kenan's rejection comes from his double marginalization as black and gay. Not only is he marginalized as a black man but he is also marginalized within the black community as a homosexual.[54] Kenan's signifyin(g) ideology points out that not all enemies of black culture are external, that the black church has in some sense failed the African–American community.[55] Religion has failed Horace, not because it is unable to deal with his secular challenges but because it is not large and expansive enough to deal with his spirit, his internal torment, his vision of beyond. Thus, religion fails him on a sacred level because legalism has replaced grace.

This cynicism about the church is reflected in Kenan's own agnosticism, which he openly discusses and which he claims has evolved from influences that shaped his religious worldview. An early experience, the death of a close uncle, led him to a fear of ghosts and spirits and to a worldview where visitations were possible. This African metaphysical worldview dovetailed with his early Calvinistic upbringing and with what he describes as an existential enlightenment during his college years. Kenan asserts that "existentialism actually dovetails with Calvinism—how bleak the world is."[56] What emerges is a dark world defined by sin and depravity, as well as helplessness, overseen and populated by spirits and ghosts. In *A Visitation of Spirits*, the result is a frightening and upsetting vision that provides the backdrop for Horace's struggle with his tortured thoughts and insanity. Such a setting and background provide the stage for intense scrutiny of the human situation, of sin and forgiveness, producing a theology worked out in an arena that is expanded beyond the boundaries of orthodoxy—a philosophy that is secular, but not necessarily atheistic.

Kenan's book is tragic and moving and represents a secular expression of religious themes perhaps exceeding those of Edgerton, Smith, or Tan. Because of his controversial subject matter that includes both race and sexual preference, Kenan finds no outlet in his traditional religion or in his community—the subjects, at least homosexuality, are taboo or condemned. Therefore, he addresses homosexuality and spirituality through a secular medium, the novel, since traditional religion avoids a meaningful discussion of the status of homosexuals in the church. Kenan's explorations of race and sexuality are beyond the reaches of the traditional conservative church in the black community; finding no other outlet, Kenan raises these issues in secular literature. But because this literature is certainly dealing with important moral and value-laden issues, as well as with a spiritual world beyond the mundane, it carries a certain religious import.

J. K. Rowling and *Harry Potter*

Like Smith, Tan, and Kenan, J. K. Rowling has created a world filled with awe, spirits, and ghosts. Unlike these other authors, Rowling's work takes place in a world that moves easily from the recognizable (secular) to the magical (sacred). It is hard to imagine that only a decade and a half have passed since Rowling introduced the world to Harry Potter, the unassuming hero who dared face down the embodiment and personification of evil.[57] The first Harry Potter novel began in a reserved manner, not at all hinting at the phenomenal success that lay in store for Rowling and her hero. While the story begins in a recognizable setting of average life,[58] the reader quickly learns that Rowling's tale, which eventually evolves into seven novels, challenges and redefines what one might consider to be normal, acceptable, or real. After initially experiencing difficulty with publishing her first manuscript, and after dealing with title issues (the U.K. edition title was "Harry Potter and the Philosopher's Stone," and "Philosopher's" was changed to "Sorcerer's" for the U.S. publication), Harry Potter finally got a reading, and the publishing world—and, one might argue, the reading world—has never been the same. Rowling has become the most successful (financially) and probably the most famous and recognizable author in the world, while Harry Potter has evolved into one of the most recognizable characters in all of literary history—all this in a few short years.

One has a hard time accounting for the phenomenal success of Rowling and her Potter novels. Yes, they are highly entertaining, but rarely can one boast of an audience that defies age and gender boundaries like Rowling's audience seems to do. While the Harry Potter novels are probably most accurately described as magic or fantasy stories, they also are coming-of-age stories in that they follow the adolescent years of Harry and his friends. Nevertheless, Rowling claims legions of adult fans as well as adolescents. And, yes, Rowling is a talented writer. While her critical reviews have been mixed, it is hard not to be drawn to her descriptive, imaginative prose, which in my mind is her greatest strength. Rowling is able to bring the magical world of Hogwarts to life in a way that makes it not only accessible but believable as well. Rowling's work is masterful, and I believe her novels will rank among the best of the classics, but even this does not account for the popularity she has achieved. Perhaps her appeal lies in the adolescent struggles of her protagonist and his friends—does this connect with the audience strongly enough to account for the broad cultural impact her stories have exerted? It seems unlikely. While Rowling's success would not have been possible had she not been a writer of extraordinary talent and imagination, this alone cannot account for the phenomenon that she and Harry Potter have become. I believe the key to answering this question lies in Rowling's ability to tap into a cultural and societal hunger for the supernatural and transcendent; a hunger for the sacred in life; a hunger for the ancient myths retold in a modern world; a hunger not for escape from but immersion in the existential crises that bring us face to face with our own mortality and the prospect of immortality. Rowling's novels are not religious—one would be hard pressed to find even the scantest reference to religion in the pages of the Harry Potter novels. But Rowling does present us with a world that is spiritual, supernatural, and transcendent, and this, I believe, is where the appeal lies. J. K. Rowling, more than any other contemporary writer, has demonstrated for the world how the sacred and profane boundaries of reality meld and dissolve into one another.

Because her works demonstrate the permeable boundaries between the secular, Muggle world and the sacred, magical world, Rowling has introduced countless readers who live in a techno-scientific and, perhaps, imaginatively sterile world to the possibilities of transcendence embedded in the world of myth—for that is really what Rowling's work brings us: myth. I doubt that more than a few readers take the magical world of the Potter novels literally. But, just the same, it is a mistake to think that her created world exists simply to provide an escape from reality. Rather, Rowling's world is a mythical world in the same way that Homer's is or in the same way that religious literature creates mythic settings. Rowling's world allows immersion in reality, not escape from it, by allowing her readers to cross boundaries and return. As Harry moves from the Muggle world into the magical, Rowling's reader travels from the literal, immanent world to the mythic, transcendent one. This is the true magic of Rowling's work and what makes it classical in its intent—the novels allow the reader permission to do what is not allowed in most everyday circumstance and even not allowed by much formal religion, to think in some other way than literally and scientifically. Rowling challenges her reader to enter a pre-rationalistic world where the mythic world defines reality and births truth. Rowling's work is postmodern in the sense that it challenges modern assumptions about truth and reality and yet ancient in the sense that she reinvigorates the sense of mystery and myth and beauty of a world not completely understood and of truths not fully gleaned. This is Rowling's genius and Harry Potter's humility.

Much has been written about the Harry Potter phenomenon, and much is yet to be written about it. It is not my intention here to fully explore Rowling's work or the Potter corpus. Rather, I am interested in commenting on how the Harry Potter novels operate to cross the sacred–secular boundaries that our contemporary world has helped produce. Transcendent reality, not religion, is the key, and in that vein this commentary on Harry Potter will touch upon the magical elements of the stories and their abilities to capture our spiritual imagination. It is also worth noting that, while the Harry Potter novels do not contain religion *per se*, they have created quite a stir over religion in the cultural reaction. On the one hand, many conservative religious voices have objected to the Harry Potter stories on the grounds that they promote magic and witchcraft. On the other hand, some have ventured to find within the Harry Potter novels religious and Christian messages and symbols. Perhaps there are Christian allegorical symbols and implied Christian motifs (Christmas celebration and Harry has a godfather, for example), but one has to look long and hard to find a formal mention of religion or the Church. Certainly, there are symbols throughout that might have religious or spiritual significance (see www.harrypotterforseekers.com). There are also commentators who use the Harry Potter series as an allegory for Christian teaching. Connie Neal has produced *The Gospel According to Harry Potter*, in which she finds scriptural parallels and Christian allegories throughout the Harry Potter corpus.[59] Her intent is to allay the concerns of those who are threatened by the witchcraft and magic in the book. Neal's subtitle (*Spirituality in the Stories of the World's Most Famous Seeker*) cleverly plays off Harry's role as Quidditch seeker and the Christian contemporary concept of seekers—those who are seeking Christ. However, to say that the novels are primarily about Christianity or even religion, either pro or con, is misconstruing the nature of the work. The novels use a fantasy, magical world to explore the transcendent realm—magic has nothing to do with evil *per se* but rather an exploration of transcendent reality and the metaphysical realm, a reality and place not confined to the physical and material.

Of course the magical world of Harry Potter, a parallel world to the one we know, is the basic setting of the novel, so to try to analyze the use of magic is a difficult task. One can open any of the books at random, point to a passage with closed eyes, and stand a pretty good chance of running into some magic. Rowling's imagination must be boundless as, throughout the series, she introduces new and creative ways to dazzle her reader. To give just a quick example of Rowling's mastery at this type of writing, one can look at the remarkable chapter 7, "The Sorting Hat", in the first book, *Harry Potter and the Sorcerer's Stone*. In 17 phantasmal pages, Rowling gives the reader the first glimpse inside Hogwarts Academy. The reader is introduced to ghosts, floating candles, an enchanted ceiling that appears to be a night sky full of stars, a banquet table that magically fills serving plates and cleans up after the meal, floating song lyrics, portraits of people who move in and out of the scene, a portrait that acts as gatekeeper, and a battered old hat that reads one's thoughts, sings, and sorts the students into their houses based on their character and traits. The Sorting Hat lies at the center of the Sorting Ceremony, one of the most important ceremonies at Hogwarts. Not only does the Sorting act as an initiation for the first-year students, but is also establishes the houses at Hogwarts, the sacred groups based on tradition and history that symbolize human traits such as courage, loyalty, rationality, and cunning. The Sorting and the establishment of houses and character profiles not only introduces the basis for the conflicts that will come to dominate the action of the series, but it also gives the reader an introduction to the type of Jungian archetypes that become part of the character development and symbol usage throughout the series. The magic allows the transcendence, and it is transcendence that provides access to the mythological archetypes that abound in the Potter series.

Carl Jung believed that universal archetypes reside in the collective consciousness of humanity and are represented through literary characters. Some famous archetypes are the hero, the shadow, the anima/animus, and the persona.[60] So much has been written on the archetypes in Harry Potter novels that an analysis here is unwarranted. However, it might be worth noting that the Sorting Hat's song outlines the basic qualities of the houses of Hogwarts in a way that roughly corresponds to the heroic stature of Gryffindor (important for Harry's journey to self-individuation), the animus rationality of Ravenclaw, the anima loyalty of Hufflepuff, and the shadow cunning of Slytherin. One could argue that the novels are organized around the hero's journey made famous by Joseph Campbell[61] and that this journey is part and parcel of Harry's development to overcome ego and to experience wholeness of self. In this journey and process, Harry's arch-nemesis is, of course, Voldemort. And while Voldemort is the villain, it is overly simplistic to view him simply as a personification of evil. Rather, Voldemort embodies the shadow archetype and represents what the self can become if the self capitulates to ego. Voldemort is the dark side or the shadow of the hero, Harry. Voldemort is what Harry can become and signifies what will destroy Harry if he fails in his quest. We are clued to this when Harry purchases his first wand from Mr. Ollivander. The phoenix that gave the feather for Harry's wand also gave the feather for Voldemort's wand. Ollivander knows that the two wands, Harry's and Voldemort's, are vitally linked;[62] Harry and Voldemort are linked, too, as hero and shadow. In myth, the hero must meet the shadow and recognize the shadow and its danger in order to overcome it. Proceeding on this assumption, then, Harry's struggle against Voldemort is a war against evil, but it is also a struggle toward wholeness and individuation of the self against the destructive dangers of ego. This is the mythological element of Harry Potter as understood through a Jungian lens.

If Voldemort represents the archetype of the shadow, then surely Albus Dumbledore represents the archetype of the Wise Old Man, a fatherly mentor figure who is often eccentric but always wise, dispensing philosophical wisdom to Harry and thus aiding him on his journey throughout the series. In each novel,

Harry and Dumbledore find themselves alone and Dumbledore speaks to Harry, dispensing wisdom in the form of a moral or a lesson, or he provides necessary information so Harry can understand the events that are happening. It is here that the powerful lessons Harry needs to overcome ego are articulated. In the first novel, Harry is nearly killed in his struggle with Professor Quirrell (who was possessed by Voldemort) in an effort to keep the Stone from falling into the wrong hands. When Harry awakes, Dumbledore is there, and he answers Harry's questions. In the process, Dumbledore dispenses wisdom: sacrificial love defeats evil; the things we desire are sometimes the things that are worst for us (this is the ego problem); the quest for immortality and riches will destroy us; hatred can overtake us.[63] The mythological echoes of Jungian archetypes ring throughout Dumbledore's wisdom, and the archetypical merges with the transcendental to set Harry on the hero's journey beyond the self, beyond this world, beyond the limits of the real. In book two, Dumbledore commends Harry on his loyalty and tells him that it is not one's abilities but rather one's choices that define a person's character.[64] In book three, Dumbledore highlights truth and nobility in Harry's actions and reminds Harry that consequences of one's actions are convoluted and difficult to discern.[65] In books four, five, and six, Rowling returns to previous themes in Dumbledore's speeches to reiterate some of the most important developmental aspects of Harry's journey: Harry and Voldemort, their fates and their lives, are mortally connected; love is a powerful force and contains a self-sacrificial element; the search for power leads to evil; one's noble actions and pure motives make one whole.[66] Finally, in book seven, Dumbledore's speech takes place after Dumbledore's death and after Voldemort has been rendered helpless. Voldemort exists and Harry lives, but Voldemort has been rendered powerless because Harry was willing to accept death in order to defeat Voldemort[67]—Harry has met his shadow, wrestled with it, and internalized it. The shadow continues on, but it can no longer hurt Harry because he has completed his journey and returned home a whole person, a heroic individual. Taken together, the speeches of Dumbledore highlight the most important themes of the series. And while some may be Christian in nature (the self-sacrificial nature of love), they do not constitute a Christian theology. Also present are Buddhist themes (karma, based on action, is unpredictable but certain), Jungian archetypal themes (the shadow must be acknowledged if one is to overcome ego), and other more general spiritual themes that may or may not be related to specific religions. In general, Dumbledore's speeches highlight a spiritual philosophy based on personal responsibility, noble action, pure motive, and the ego debasement that comes from love directed to others.

But Dumbledore is not the only character in the series who helps to highlight these themes. By far the most complex of the Harry Potter characters, and thereby the most subtle and contradictory in terms of Jungian archetypes and spiritual themes, is Professor Severus Snape. Snape seems to be Harry's arch-nemesis at

Hogwarts, a competition engendered by generational hatred beginning with Snape and Harry's father. Nevertheless, by the end of the series, Harry recognizes Snape as a courageous and honorable man[68] and names his son Albus Severus after his mentor, Dumbledore, and Professor Snape. At the very least, Snape acts both as Dumbledore's ally and as counterpoint to his moralistic lessons. During his first meeting with Harry and his comrades, Snape introduces his class on potions with eloquence and creepy intimacy, promising his students knowledge that could bring them exaltation and even immortality.[69] Power and immortality—these are the attractions of magical or spiritual knowledge. Yet these are also the very goals that Dumbledore warns against in his advice to Harry. Power, and the promises it holds, must be overcome, and this is the problem of ego in the process of becoming a whole person. If one is to become whole, fulfilled, then one must let go of egocentric lust for power over others, over wealth, over life, over ego. And if Dumbledore was important in leading Harry away from the false allure of power, Snape was the key to Harry's final victory over ego. Harry needed Snape as much as he relied upon Dumbledore, and it was only in Snape's death that Harry comes to understand this.

While there are many moralistic lessons throughout Harry's story, battles over good and evil, the self-sacrificial nature of love, and others, surely this Jungian warning about the ego stands apart as one of the predominant themes of the series. Harry is on the hero's journey that Joseph Campbell writes so eloquently about, yet, more importantly, the masterful mythmaker Rowling taps into these archetypal images so subtly and seamlessly that, without knowing it, the reader embarks as well upon a hero's journey beyond the self, beyond this world, beyond the limits of the real. The Harry Potter saga, told by one of our best storytellers, demonstrates better than most fiction the permeable boundaries between the secular and the sacred, the immanent and the transcendent, and as such can serve as a mythological world apart, where Harry struggles to find himself.

Summary

The idea that religious longings and beliefs can be expressed through secular literature is nothing new. In fact, the idea establishes a well-accepted basis for many studies and classes in universities and colleges. The acknowledgment that religious meaning can be gleaned from this secular cultural form indicates that secularization of religion is occurring in the second direction, the sacralization of the secular. This is not secularization in the sense that religion is disappearing or that it is becoming unimportant in contemporary society. On the contrary, this is secularization in the sense that the religious imagination has a persistence about it that allows it to spread out into society and to be expressed in secular cultural forms. When formal religious organizations become too narrowly focused, religious questioning, moral instruction, and discussions of values find their way into the cultural landscape in secular forms like literature. Academicians acknowledge this secularization. When we are willing to study religion through a secular lens, then secularization is fairly well advanced.

We have seen how some authors fall back on their art to raise existential and religious questions, to seek religious answers, and to pose religious solutions. They are theologians in their own right, posing many of the same questions theologians have posed throughout history. At the same time, these writers contextualize such questions in a dialectic that juxtaposes sacred and secular characteristics in an ambiguous world. And this religious process takes place not in sacred literature or in writing located within a religious tradition. Rather, it takes place through cultural products other than religion, through the secular form of literature. The study of religion and literature represents more than an overlapping of separate disciplines and categories; rather, the intersection of religion and literature represents the extent to which secular forms can supplement, or even replace, religious structures as vehicles for religious longings and conversations.

Study guide

Important words and concepts

Agnosticism
Ethnic literature
Fantasy literature
Jungian theory
Marginalization
Regional literature
Spirituality versus religiosity
Traditional religion/non-traditional religion

Discussion questions

(1) How can secular literature function religiously or serve as a conduit for spirituality?
(2) How does Clyde Edgerton use comedy to function religiously?
(3) How does Lee Smith's elemental religion compare to Amy Tan's "yin world?"

(4) Describe the role of marginalization in Randall Kenan's novel, *A Visitation of Spirits*. Can marginalization be thought of as a religious category?

(5) How does the magical context of the Harry Potter novels allow the supernatural to break into the profane world?

Guided reading

(1) Choose and read any secular novel or short story. Write an essay on the story, and make sure you answer the following questions:
- How does the narrative function religiously or spiritually?
- What is the worldview of the narrative?
- Are there symbols in the story that function religiously?
- How does the author use characterization to include transcendent themes?
- Does the setting indicate a sense of otherness or sacred place?

Part Three
Post-text

8

Image/Post-text

On weekend nights across America, young people and old flock to movie theaters or rent DVDs to participate in one of popular culture's most pervasive sources of entertainment. The variety of available films is mind-boggling: from classic to experimental, adult to children's, suspense to comedy, emotionally draining to cheerful and light-hearted. Communal or solitary film watching has become a staple of modern American culture, and it reflects how substantially we contemporary Westerners are drawn to audio-visual presentations that take us beyond textual storytelling. Images are everywhere in our new technologies: television, movie theaters, DVD players, Internet pages, and so on have inundated us with an image-rich culture. Certainly, the movie industry is a leader in this postmodern, image-rich, post-textual society. Because it is so omnipresent, it behooves us to consider seriously how this medium shapes, reflects, and otherwise dialogues with our cultural attitudes and beliefs. The American film industry is huge and influences the distribution of popular films and viewing habits in both America and Europe. Popular films constitute a significant portion of the fabric of popular culture and potentially exert powerful influence in society because of the mass market they reach. Popular films have the power to shape attitudes and to reflect beliefs. Film as a shaper of and reflection of our collective ideologies has sparked a contemporary interest in the intersection of religion and film.

As we have seen secularization marking our spaces and our texts in postmodern America, we see films marking a secularization of images and their accompanying sensations. Just as we see secularization proceeding in two directions with other cultural components of society, we also see this process happening at the intersection of religion and film. Films reflect the secularization of sacred image through movies devoted to presenting religious topics through a secular medium and the sacralization of secular image through films seemingly unrelated to religious topics yet religious or spiritual in their nature or functioning. The dual-direction of secularization seen elsewhere in our culture arises in the film medium with such strong force and in such ubiquitous fashion that we may need to consider our culture post-textual in the sense that images have begun to supersede text,[1] thus reversing the effects of the rise of texts to supremacy since the Enlightenment.

Are we gathering at movie theaters for worship? Hardly. But some find in the experience uplift, community, sensation, value definition, and so forth, many of the things we search for in religion. So, as the lights dim and sound comes up; as our minds are inundated with the sensations of light, color, and sound; as we hold hands, flinch, cry, and laugh, we return to a primal place, an elemental place, a place where the gods are defined and die—a sacred landscape of the soul molded by the secular screen of the movie theater.

Religion and film[2]

That images are replacing texts as a primary vehicle for entertainment, if not instruction, is obvious to anyone who has struggled to get students to read seriously as opposed to watching a film. Religion and film classes have become wildly popular in religion programs, not because they are easy or perceived as such, but because many students relate more readily, more enthusiastically, more intuitively, and more meaningfully to films than to books. I have experienced this in my undergraduate religion classes and through intensive discussions with colleagues who use film to teach religion. The power of image is manifested in today's youth, who have been reared with a steady dose of manufactured image on television, the silver screen, and the computer monitor.

Yet students are not the only ones embracing the power of image in myth-making. Religion and film classes are being taught by professors from a variety of perspectives, and religion and film books are produced from a rich collection of methodological approaches, including religious studies, myth studies, psychological studies, film studies, and the like. Scholarly approaches to religion and film range from exploring the ability of film to dialogue with and in some cases rewrite scripture,[3] to studies of the importance of film in theological dialogue and to procedures for and reasons for watching films from a theological perspective,[4] to studies that focus more on values and film's power to reform society,[5] to studies that focus on religious aspects of movies that are not defined by traditional texts, theologies, or moralities.[6] The recent list goes on and the titles themselves often reveal the perspective: *Explorations in Theology and Film: Movies and Meaning,*[7] *New Image of Religious Film,*[8] *The Word Became Flesh: Catholicism and Conflict in the Films of Martin Scorsese.*[9] The great diversity of religion and film studies demonstrates how seriously scholars take the idea that images can be powerful purveyors of sacred reality, theology, and ideology.

This realization about the power of film extends beyond the walls of the college classroom. Christians of all persuasions have had a long-running debate with Hollywood concerning the possible harmful influences of films. Robert Johnston has written about this relationship in his exceptional book, *Reel Spirituality.* By focusing on the relationship between church and theater, Johnston demonstrates the growing sense in which religion has attempted to act as conscience for the movie industry. This demonstrates both the cultural connection between the movies and the church and acknowledgment by the church the potential efficacy of the theater in affecting ideologies and morality.[10] Beyond the ethical debate, there is even ongoing political concern, particularly in America, about the negative impact films might exert on societal values. That prominent public figures have used film in social commentary suggests at least the perception that movies can play an important role in shaping or influencing behavior and morals. For example, 1996 U.S. presidential candidate Bob Dole reflected publicly about the destructive potential of Hollywood morals. In the wake of the 1995 New York torching of a subway token booth, then Senator Dole used the occasion to lash out at Hollywood during his campaign for the Republican presidential nomination. In his speech, Dole mirrored the sentiments of law enforcement officials who were calling the violent incident a copycat crime based on the film, *Moneytrain.* Dole's insight and political rhetoric decrying violence in film renewed a public debate about the ability of film to influence public behavior.[11] Later, President Clinton picked up on the call for Hollywood to reform itself, reinforcing the notion that film has the ability to affect lives, to influence behaviors, and to propagate beliefs. If this is true, then it is important for both the makers of film and the consumers of culture to recognize that film is a powerful medium that has the ability to influence attitudes and actions. As Joel Martin points out, Michael Ryan and Douglas Kellner argue in *Camera Politica* that films "often foreshadow political developments" and can shape collective ideology, that stories given life in film provide a significant way to formulate and shape collective values.[12]

If society mirrors film in this way, if action and behavior are affected by Hollywood, then we need to consider carefully the context and the impact of films like *Natural Born Killers* and *Pulp Fiction.* Such films are considered dangerous by some because they create an atmosphere of conflict and lead to a desensitization to violence in society.[13] The slippery-slope theory holds that we see violence on the screen, we become immune to its horror, we accept it in the social context, and violence then perpetuates itself simply because the public no longer is outraged by it. A graphic example that supports this theory dates to 1998, when two teenagers killed their victim by enacting scenes from the movies *Scream* and *Scream 2.* One of the teenagers confessed, suggesting that repeated exposure to movie and TV violence not only desensitized him to violence but enticed him to be violent as well.[14] If this type of desensitization occurs as routinely as suggested, we might also be concerned about seemingly innocuous films or non-violent films. Films might perpetuate all types of ideologies, not simply an ideology of violence.

Films also have the power to influence individuals and communities positively, not just negatively. So, if we are to blame Hollywood for glorifying violent tendencies, we should also praise the movie industry for communicating hope in films like *The Shawshank Redemption*; forgiveness in *Places in the Heart*; grace in *The Fisher King*; redemption in *The Spitfire Grill*. There are scores of films that showcase human nature in its most flawed, most vulnerable, and consequently most noble state. These films appeal to our higher nature. Positive or negative, the scope and intensity of the debate shows that our culture recognizes the power of film to affect or at least reflect values and beliefs; therefore, film has the potential to act religiously.[15]

Many religion scholars who are interested in the role films play in values, ethics, religious beliefs, and attitudes tend to focus on the power of film to shape and change ideologies. Margaret Miles's *Seeing and Believing* focuses on the reformative role of films in society.[16] In addition, Robert Johnston eloquently shares a personal story about the power of film that helped transform his life by viewing film "as the occasion not only to know about God but to know God."[17] Sandra Gravett explores the rich possibilities of the *Twilight* series in this regard. In a recent article in "Christianity Today," Gravett explores how the *Twilight* narratives bring to the forefront "issues related to faith, redemption, and hope as well as demonstrate positive values ..."[18] Gravett goes on in that article to explore the difficult concepts of free will and moral responsibility in Christian thought and how the *Twilight* stories negotiate this aspect of Christian theology. The implication here is that these narratives can at least help provoke dialogue on ideology and perhaps affect change in perspective.[19]

On the other hand, some commentators suggest that films do not influence attitudes so much as they reflect reality. Thus, films do not encourage violence; they simply reflect a violent society by choosing subject matter from the culture.[20] This argument fundamentally removes the movie industry from responsibility and fights off the censor's scalpel. It seems fair and reasonable to acknowledge that films both reflect and affect society's attitudes, beliefs, values, and hopes. Included in these beliefs are worldviews and religious attitudes. Religion and films are both cultural products. As such, they define and represent who we are and what we believe. Films and religion can show us where we fail yet applaud our more noble state. Rarely does either do only one. As a result, films constitute an important cultural medium for the study of the intersection of religion and cultural forms.

The interdisciplinary study of religion and film is a fairly new area and has yet to emerge as a truly interdisciplinary field. Like religion and literature, this study is best done between disciplines, and one of the goals of the exploration of religion and film is to encourage film studies, religious studies, and popular culture studies scholars to communicate better with one another. In the past, as Joel Martin reminds us, religious studies scholars and film studies scholars have largely ignored one another as well as the content of the others' discipline.[21] When attempts have been made to study religion and film, the result more often than not has been disciplinary, coming from one discipline or another rather than from between the disciplines. Since I am trained in religious studies, my approach to religion and film tends to rely upon methods from religious studies and religion and literature as they are applied to film. This approach is insufficient, because there is a long established tradition of film studies that needs to be incorporated into such analyses as these. Cooperative interdisciplinary work that draws upon the expertise of film studies scholars, religious studies scholars, and scholars from various religious traditions will yield insightful views of culture and religion.[22] Religion and film as a cultural studies project will mature into a discipline when this layering of expertise from across and between the disciplines and traditions coalesce. For example, from the film *The Matrix*, my students and other Christian interpreters are tempted to view the character Neo as a messiah figure and to invoke the all-too-familiar Christ figure image. But many scholars warn us against this easy assumption. Alice Bach, for example, reminds us that not all victims need be Christ figures in her analysis of *One Flew Over the Cuckoo's Nest*.[23] So if not every victim in film need be a crucified Christ, neither does every messianic figure need be a savior Christ. Neo, in *The Matrix*, might as easily or more so be construed a bodhisattva from the Buddhist tradition.[24] That so many of my students peg Neo as a Christ figure demonstrates how uninformed Americans can be about various religious traditions beyond Christianity. But even if religious studies scholars begin dialoguing more across traditions, religion and film work is still too oriented to religious studies. In addition to realizing that religious imagery beyond Christian imagery might exist in popular movies, we need also to learn more from film studies about special effects or from psychologists about mind control: how would this change our view of Neo as religious messiah in *The Matrix*? We need also to consider that Neo may not be representing any religious imagery at all—perhaps he is just Neo.

Such interdisciplinary, intercultural, and collaborative work continues to expand, but several questions must be addressed if the disciplines of religious studies and film studies are to work constructively together. As obvious as it might seem, a definition of religion must be agreed on. Outside religious studies, religion is often defined as a set of truth claims, as an institution that considers itself the guardian of orthodoxy. A religious studies definition of religion will be more constructive for an interdisciplinary approach to the study of film. In short, rather than defining religion as a set of truth claims, we should define religion as a process of making and searching for meaning. Thus, instead of religion being the antithesis of heresy, it is the combatant of nihilism. This broad definition of religion will prevent a study of religion and film from being defined by one orthodoxy or another, thus allowing each discipline to work unhindered by ideological allegiance.

This functional definition will work for an interdisciplinary study of religion and film but can be misleading as well. Consider the distinction M. S. Mason makes between "what makes a film 'religious' as opposed to one that uses religious imagery …"[25] In a commentary for *The Christian Science Monitor*, Mason writes about contemporary film's use of the image of Jesus in movies like *The Last Temptation of Christ* or *Jesus of Montreal*. These films tend to "exploit the metaphors and symbols of Jesus' life …" The movies so "trivialize Jesus' whole life" that they cannot function religiously, that is, they cannot treat concepts like forgiveness and evil seriously for a contemporary audience.[26] So, Mason's criticism suggests these films use religious imagery but might not be "religious" in the sense that they function religiously for contemporary audiences. In this case, these seemingly religious films (because of subject matter) might fail to function religiously and should not be considered religious in the sense of the above definition.

Contrast this to films like *Places in the Heart* or *The Fisher King*. *Places in the Heart* is full of religious images and portrays religion as a cultural product, but it also functions religiously in that it translates religious concepts such as forgiveness and evil for contemporary audiences. In addition, *The Fisher King* is based upon the legend of the Holy Grail, so it occupies a prominent place in our religious cultural heritage. But it also functions religiously because it raises religious questions for the audience. Mason writes, "it is really about the hunger for redemption …"[27] Mason quotes Richard LaGravenese, who wrote the screenplay; for LaGravenese, redemption is "the only subject" for a contemporary American movie.[28] So, *The Fisher King* functions religiously because it challenges contemporary audiences to grapple with theological questions, not because its subject matter draws upon religious cultural symbols.

One can further see the complexity of looking at films like this by considering Joel Martin's discussion in *Screening the Sacred* of *Rocky*, a film that is not obviously religious in any way.[29] On one level, the film treats religion as a cultural phenomenon as Rocky Balboa's Catholicism becomes a backdrop for the story to contextualize Rocky's ethnicity. On another level, one could interpret rich religious imagery in the film such as the opening scene of a close-up of the face of a Byzantine Christ in light of the Christ figure that Rocky embodies. On a third level, we might consider what makes the film religious, that is, how does the film function religiously for the audience? Does it represent some sort of faith in justice for the oppressed? Does this represent a religious ideology? It is this third level, the functional level, that is the trickiest but also the most rewarding. And although I will be concerned with these three ways of considering religion and film, the third consideration will attract most of the attention in this chapter.

With the assumptions that film provides a medium for studying the religious dimensions of culture, that film can function religiously for individuals and for society, that film can reflect as well as affect beliefs and behaviors, and that film is a powerful communicator of values, I turn to this exploration to better understand how such beliefs and values interact in the public sphere. First, we will consider briefly the state of the religion and film field (if it can be considered a field); second, we will look at the future of the field; third, we will focus on how contemporary culture and traditional religion interact by viewing religion in film in light of the secularization thesis of this book. I will illustrate the secularization thesis by looking at what the contemporary world has done with a traditional religious category—the idea of the apocalypse.

The state of religion and film as a discipline

To refer to religion and film as a discipline is probably premature. As noted above, the study is very new and is still being shaped and explored by scholars in religious studies and film studies. For the most part, there has been little dialogue between the two disciplines. As Joel Martin points out in *Screening the Sacred*, much of the early work done by religion scholars focused on classic or art films (this is particularly true in Europe), and much of the work by religious studies scholars has been theological in nature.[30] However, these generalities are beginning to change, and we have seen increased interest in popular films in books like *Screening the Sacred* and *Reel Spirituality*. And interest in the interdisciplinary nature of the topic, which is obvious from the exploration of religion and film at religious studies conferences, American studies conferences, and cultural studies conferences, is balancing the theological viewpoint and adding diverse perspectives. More and more emphasis is being placed on popular films because of their potential for reaching mass audiences and, thus, affecting popular ideology. These changes map out the predominant direction of this proto-discipline and suggest agenda items for the future of religion and film, if it is to continue as a viable interdisciplinary project. If work in religion and film continues, and if this proto-field continues to develop, methodology must come to the forefront of discussion and the work must move beyond traditional theological approaches.

Developments along both fronts have characterized the work in the field. Works have appeared that have begun to explore methodology. The 1995 book edited by Joel Martin and myself, *Screening the Sacred*, consists of collected essays dealing only with popular films. And to avoid parochialism either of theological or disciplinary bent, the book is organized around three approaches to the study of film: theological, mythological, and ideological. In this typology is an incipient method for studying films that attempts to address shortcomings of any one method. The book argues that theological criticism treats religion traditionally and tends to find religion in films through theological categories such as grace, redemption, evil, sin, and forgiveness. The problem with theological criticism is its narrow focus, usually arising from Western symbols and religions. Mythological criticism universalizes the study of religion and film by treating religion as it is recognized through universal archetypes, symbols, and rituals. And finally, ideological criticism understands religion as it exists in relation to that which is not religion and includes categories ranging from the social order to gender relationships and race and class distinctions. By mapping out a three-fold typology for the study of religion and film, the authors and editors of *Screening the Sacred* attempt to broaden the discussion to include a wide variety of understandings about what is religious in society.

Additional work on religion and film is emerging as noted scholars in religious studies are directing their attentions to the topic at national conferences and in manuscripts in process. Thus, there seems to be a future for this pursuit in academia. In addition, if the anecdotal reports concerning pedagogy are any indication, using films in the classroom as an effective teaching tool seems to have a promising potential. If research and teaching in this proto-field are to be successful, we can map out a few items scholars will have to accept as the field develops. Most of these challenges are already indicated in the scholarly works that exist at present. I will explore some of these issues here in hopes of stimulating dialogue about new approaches to the study of religion and film. In doing so, I will reflect on the future direction of religion and film studies but also suggest ways the film experience might mimic aspects of religious experience.

First, most of the current work on religion and film done by religious studies scholars and theologians grew out of and employs methodological procedures from literary and narrative studies. After all, as scholars, we have been trained to examine and produce texts, not films, and it is natural for us to proceed in this way. Although the approach has served the field well, it is necessary to explore methods unique to the film genre, and religious studies scholars need to learn more from the methods and insights of film studies. While we know how to "read" a film like literature, we might not know how to "see" a film critically.

Jann Cather Weaver has been sensitive to these questions on methodology and helps us to learn how to "see" films critically by differentiating between "seeing" and "watching" films. "Seeing" a film, for Weaver, goes beyond passive "watching" for entertainment. "Seeing is a disciplined task, … the critical discipline of delving beneath surface, affective, and customary (culturally-coded) appearances…"[31] Weaver gives religion and film scholars a vocabulary and working model for a methodology of seeing. In particular, Weaver, like Mason, challenges us to see the difference between films that are religious (function religiously) and films that merely employ religious symbols or draw upon the cultural context for religious images (i.e. the Christ figure or the Bible). Her method seems very effective in moving us "beyond watching, beyond the perpetual quest for the filmic Christ figure, and beyond using film as ILLUSTRATION of doctrine, moral lessons, or of a current religio-social issue."[32] The other real strength of Weaver's perspective is that it empowers the viewer and it transfers power from the film producers/industry to the film viewers/consumers, both as individually engaged viewers and as a community of viewers.

Weaver's perspective implies that simply transferring the methods from literary studies is not sufficient because films represent a layering of narrative and images that is in many ways more complex than literature. This layering and intensification become clear when we look at the creative forces behind literature and film. When we deal with literature, we can usually focus on the author as the creative force behind the narrative; however, with film we must deal with layers of creative forces including the screenplay writer, the director, and perhaps the author of a book if the screenplay was adapted from a novel. This complicates the critical task, as Alice Bach has reminded us in her work. As she implies in her comments on Bible films, the layering of film introduces contemporary culture into the process of interpretation of the subject matter. As a result, Bible films might reflect the contemporary situation more than the biblical one.[33] This is true of non-biblical films as well, such as movies like *The Scarlet Letter*. *The Scarlet Letter* is based on a screenplay that takes liberties with the novel's story line. Such changes are not unusual when a novel is adapted for a screenplay, and revisions often reveal much about what contemporary audiences will tolerate in their entertainment. In this case it tells us as much about twentieth-century preoccupations as about Nathaniel Hawthorne's nineteenth-century ones. Yet, much of the critical analysis of the movie focuses simply on pointing out the changes made in transferring the classic novel to the screen rather than in trying to unravel the layering of intent and meaning behind the changes. This type of simple comparative analysis to the novel is not a sufficient standard of criticism because it does little to explore what the contemporary version tells us about our society or our sensibilities as a movie-going public. We must explore new ways to deal with the dynamics of revision rather than simply judge the movie in relation to the book that bears the same title. We must fully consider this layering of creative intent.

But the creative force behind film is not the only element that is layered and intensified when moving from literature to film. All the traditional elements of narrative undergo intensification. If in literary analysis we focus on character development, we must extend that examination with films to include not only the character in the screenplay but the actor's or actress's portrayal of that character. If with literature we look at setting, with a film the setting is intensified because of the images, special effects, and computer-generated visuals available to film makers. And if plot analysis is our prime area of examination in literature, we must note that plots in films unfold much more quickly (the action takes place in film time rather than in reading time), and filmic plots often unfold nonsequentially. With the elements of film, there is an intensification of effect, and perhaps of influence, and we need to search for more productive ways to measure both effect and influence.

I have argued that images are extremely important in imparting meaning in our contemporary culture, perhaps even superseding texts for the task. If visual images are indeed replacing written texts as the conveyors of information and meaning, it might have important implications for religious ideas.[34] And in film, visual images are further intensified by soundtracks and other auditory effects. The result is an integrative experience unfolding before the moviegoer that is more intense, more riveting, more involving, and perhaps more participatory than the texts of previous generations. Add to this our own "realist" assumptions about what we see (i.e. seeing is believing),[35] and we can begin to sense the power attached to film images and their presentation. At least film seems to function powerfully in this way for my students, who are much more willing to watch a movie than to read a novel, and we need to be more sensitive to the effects of this integration of sensations.

This integrative experience of visual images and auditory presentations is unfolding in more and more compact and graphic forms. For example, music videos represent a development of the film form that deserves serious attention. As conveyors of violence, sexual images, and plot lines, music videos are particularly effective in reaching a society that often does not demonstrate the patience for a two-hour plot to develop, let alone the several-hour experience of the novel. Perhaps the next technological development to deliver images will be virtual reality, which might be accompanied by tactile sensation as well. In any event, technology has made the proliferation of video images and auditory sensations possible and profitable, and can provide the viewer a type of transcending possibility. One of the possibilities for the future of the study of religion and film must be to explore film's ability to provide this experience of transcendence, and it is through transcendence that we sense and explore the ways film might mimic religious experience.

Film gives us creative ways to approximate transcendence. Technology allows film makers to transport viewers to another world graphically, not simply through description.[36] Films can visually take us to outer space, to the jungles of the Congo, to a prehistoric rain forest inhabited by dinosaurs, or to a post-apocalyptic setting. This transference takes us beyond ourselves and generally deals with topics that are beyond the ordinary, mundane experiences of our lives. As I wrote previously in *Screening the Sacred*, many popular films are characterized by "excess"; for example, violence and explicit sexuality. When films focus on excess, on that which is beyond the ordinary, they act religiously by allowing transcendence, freedom, and escape.[37] This transcendence through escape of the ordinariness of everyday life allows us to tap into what Janice Rushing and Richard Maltby identify as corporate beliefs through shared myths and ideals.[38] If films function in this way, then they function religiously or even mythically by shaping and reflecting shared values.[39]

This suggests that film provides an important way to study religion in contemporary America. In an age and society marked by individualism, films highlight societal and cultural truths. Richard Gollin comments on this by focusing on film's power to create in viewers the need to "sacrifice whatever their personal indulgences and rededicate themselves to higher public purposes."[40] So films like *Natural Born Killers* and *Pulp Fiction* tell us about ourselves, but so do films like *Apollo 13* and *Forrest Gump*. How are these films instructive about our society and, in Gollin's words, our "ideological covenants and obligations?"[41] Can they provide corporate truths and images? I am arguing that they can, and that other forms of our popular culture work on the societal level religiously by reflecting and affecting fundamental values and even behaviors.[42]

This corporate function of film as a clue to what society values suggests we must be cognizant of the audience and of how meaning is relayed to that audience. We cannot simply assume the same type of audience we assume for a novel. Reading a novel is a solitary activity—watching a film, at least in the theater, has the potential for being a communal and thus ritualistic one.[43] We can ask questions concerning the communal consumption of film and what this means for the audience and the critic. We can also make assumptions and judgments about the effects of the DVD player, rental movies, and other forms of cable and satellite TV that bring films into our living rooms. These technologies change a communal experience into a solitary one, in some ways paralleling the shift from storytelling to novel reading—a shift that requires a change in audience from communal to individual.

Therefore, our future study of popular film and religion should include sensitivity to what happens or might happen in the movie theater or at home and what consequences this might hold for individuals and society. In other words, we must be concerned with the psychology of film and with what media experts call reception theory. Many scholars have suggested that popular culture can be a clue to understanding society's values and to recognizing what motivates individual and collective behavior.[44] The task for students of religion and film is to develop better ways to measure how films function religiously and how they might affect values and behaviors.

Religion, film, and secularization

The secularization thesis that forms the basis of this book is important to consider in light of film because film is the only cultural product studied here that is essentially a product of the postmodern world. As secularization is generally associated with Western culture since the Enlightenment, film is the only cultural form considered here with its entire history during the era when the secularization of Western culture has been at its height. This positions film uniquely to take over the functions religion is transferring to secular culture.

One of the major arguments underlying my work hinges on the idea that the secular and the religious worlds can coexist without religion becoming less significant. I am assuming that secularization does not destroy religion, and, for the purposes of this study, I am defining secularization as a sociological process that blurs the boundaries between the sacred and the secular. Western religion is based upon the idea of a transcendent God (a wholly and Holy Other) and on a sacred realm that is completely separate from our mundane, secular, profane world. This division of reality into sacred and profane has also characterized much religious studies work. But in the postmodern era, the strict boundaries separating sacred and profane have become flexible, and from these flexible boundaries we see secularization taking place in two directions.[45] First, there is a tendency for tradition to secularize—for religious institutions to employ secular and popular cultural forms like television and the movies to make religious teachings relevant for a contemporary audience.[46] In this instance, we see contemporary religion making concessions to secular cultural forms. The second way secularization is proceeding is by the dispersion of the religious sensibility through a variety of contemporary, secular cultural forms. As I argued in *Screening the Sacred*, when religious institutions no longer dominate culture they forfeit some of their proprietorship over sacred sensibilities. With this loss of cultural hegemony, religious concerns surface elsewhere, so that secular culture can function religiously. In postmodern society, the religious impulse is disseminated through a variety of cultural forms like film, which are external to traditional religious institutions and expressions.[47]

As I have written previously in *Screening the Sacred*, the result of this secularization is a postmodern society defined by a secular paradox—a society that is uncomfortable with institutionalized and public religion but is often defined by religious categories through popular culture. As secularization of society continues, so does the dissipation of functions formerly reserved for religious institutions. We find popular culture functioning in some of the same ways as institutionalized religious ritual so that popular culture provides a context for understanding values, belief systems, and myths.[48] To illustrate this, I will discuss how popular films have provided a secular context for understanding a traditional Western religious concept, the apocalypse, mirroring the two directions of secularization.

Study guide

Important words and concepts

Film and politics
Image-rich culture
Orthodoxy
Power and influence of film
Religion and film movement
Sensory intensification

Discussion questions

(1) Why are films an ideal medium for studying the relationship of religion and culture?

(2) How might movies function religiously?

Guided "Seeing/Hearing"

(1) Read chapter 2, "Teaching Religion and Film: A Fourth Approach," from the book, *Teaching Religion and Film*.[49] Experiment with the exercises in that chapter for isolating image and sound in a film. What does this tell us about the intensified sensory experience of films?

9

A cinematic secular apocalyptic imagination

In the pages that follow, I discuss how popular films have provided a secular context for understanding a traditional Western religious concept, the apocalypse, mirroring the two directions of secularization. Among theological images arising from Western—in particular, Jewish and Christian—religions, none has received more popular attention recently than images associated with the end of the world. This preoccupation with the end of things is connected in a real way with the postmodern context that tends to deny anything absolute. With the destruction of absolutism, with the loss of certainty, it makes sense that theories and conspiracies about the end of the world would arise—if the absolute falls, so falls all else. But the end of the world does not simply result in the end of things, at least not theologically or in the movie versions. Almost invariably, the end brings about the ascendency of something to authority—some greatness to believe in. In a sense, the end-of-the-twentieth-century preoccupation with the end of things was a response to postmodernism's relativism. This is seen very clearly in the recent theatrical preoccupation (particularly if you look at the pre-Y2K setting) with the end of the world or at least with the end of life as we know it. By examining what movies have done with the Western concept of apocalypse, the cataclysmic end of the world, we can see how film secularizes a theological concept in the court of popular culture. And in doing so, the movies have recaptured and reinterpreted the Jewish and Christian concepts of the apocalypse where the context of a cosmic battle between good and evil destroys the Earth, results in a sovereign God (good) defeating the forces of evil, and pictures a new kingdom, a transcendent, heavenly empire (a sacred realm) that replaces the destroyed world (the contemporary secular realm).

If we take the Jewish and Christian apocalyptic traditions and compare them to film's communication of those traditions, we can see some interesting dynamics taking place between postmodernity and tradition. For example, when the Christian apocalypse, John's Revelation, was written, it was produced by and for a group of Christians who were marginal and on the fringes of society. This marginalized group, persecuted by the Roman Empire at the end of the first century, produced and embraced a vision of the apocalypse that overturned the ruling powers. World destruction was pictured as God's sovereign vengeance on an evil empire that had oppressed the righteous. In other words, John's Revelation was an anti-secular manifesto, warning against the ways of the world, condemning the world and those whose allegiance was the world because the world would be destroyed and only the righteous would inherit the kingdom of God.

Fast-forward 20 centuries: Where are the Christian apocalypticists now? By and large they are not in the mainstream of Christianity because the church has become so secularized, so worldly. In fact, mostly since Constantine's legitimization of Christianity in the fourth century, visions of the apocalypse have come from the fringe of the Christian tradition. The mainstream of the tradition, the secularized and worldly majority in the tradition, cannot sustain a critique of worldliness because a secularized church is so heavily invested in the world. In the modern church community, only those who reject secular culture can truly embrace an apocalyptic vision. The result is that the Christian version of the apocalypse in contemporary society has become muted. A secularized church might have some vague understanding of the end of time, but it does not act like it believes in an imminent apocalypse because it continues to raise money and build buildings.

So, the situation is this: outside of those fringe groups in the Christian tradition, a real apocalyptic consciousness as an anti-secular theological position is largely missing from contemporary, Christian theology. The exception is found in some segments of the evangelical community that invest heavily in a pre-millennial, dispensationalist view of world conquest, but at the same time this community is often more secularized than ever, so the anti-secular edge of the apocalyptic consciousness is muted. Does this mean that, religiously, apocalyptic concerns have ceased to exist? Undoubtedly not, for fascination with the end of the world is strong—as witnessed by the proliferation of end-of-the-world movies and books, some from religious organizations and some from secular, popular culture. My guess is that anxiety over human contingency invests in apocalyptic scenarios. Secular apocalypses have supplemented religion in establishing an apocalyptic imagination in popular culture because a secularized church (because of its investment in the world) often avoids the topic.

Why does the apocalyptic imagination have the power to transcend theology and persist in the secular imagination? It persists because it is a fundamentally religious category, a way of making sense out of our world. The apocalyptic imagination is essentially a way of overcoming our angst over the realization of our finitude. Apocalypticism is a Western concept that is basically egocentric in origin. We see life around us and we observe it beginning and ending; we know birth and death, and, as we imagine our own birth and death, we extrapolate and hypothesize world creation and world destruction as a way to make sense of time and a creation that outlives us. Hypothesizing egocentrically, we believe that if we are born and die then surely the world had a beginning and will have an end. However, this reasoning works only if we reduce the totality of existence to the restrictive life of individuals; when we look at humanity or the world as wholes, origins and ends are not so obvious—humanity recycles itself, as does nature across the evolutionary cycle. Therefore the apocalyptic imagination results when we construct a worldview based on our egocentric beliefs concerning life and time. As Frank Kermode has written, "[T]he paradigms of apocalypse continue to lie under our ways of making sense of the world" by helping us to order our lives and time with a beginning and an end point that has some meaning.[1]

This egocentric angst about the end is accentuated in contemporary culture because mainstream, secular religion has essentially dropped the apocalypse as a meaningful notion, so we seek other outlets for overcoming our anxiety about the end of things. We find these secular apocalypses in the burgeoning fascination with the end of the world in the film industry and in the Hollywood version of Armageddon—a secularized reappropriation of the traditional Christian apocalypse. Scores of secular movies as diverse as *Pale Rider, Apocalypse Now, Natural Born Killers, Independence Day, 2012*, and Jim Henson's children's epic, *The Dark Crystal* explore various notions about the end of things. In addition, there are also movies about the end produced by evangelicals who try to counter secular philosophy with an evangelical version of the end of time. *The Omega Code* and the film version of *Left Behind* provide two examples of evangelical visions attempting to reclaim defining the apocalypse in popular culture. Virtually all of these films, secular or Christian, participate in the secularization of religion by secularizing the apocalypse in one of two ways. The evangelical films try to render traditional theology through the secular medium of film and thus demonstrate secularization in the first direction, the secularization of the sacred. The secular films arise from a completely secular vantage point but tap into a theological context that has been borrowed from traditional religion. As such, these secular apocalypses sacralize the secular by raising secular philosophies through the context of religious ideas. These approaches both participate in secularization but issue in radically different visions of the end of the world based on fundamentally different worldviews. Because we find both secularists and conservative theologies competing in the secular arena of the theater to portray a vision of the end of the world, we see how thoroughly secularization has produced a blurring and bending of boundaries between the sacred and the secular.

The secularization of the sacred

The Bible and the evangelical apocalypse on the screen

Despite evangelical suspicion about secular culture, the evangelical tradition, at least in the twentieth century, has not been at all shy about employing secular culture to spread the Christian message. Christian radio, television, and music all employ secular tactics and media very effectively. Film, as well, constitutes fertile ground for the portrayal of religious topics, sometimes by religious people and sometimes by secular. When religious groups adopt secular forms, media, or tactics for presenting a message they perceive to be sacred, then we see the secularization of the sacred in our secularization process. The blurring of distinctions continues, here promoted by the religious community.

An example of this willingness to adopt a secular medium to spread the sacred message comes through the very successful evangelical book on Jesus by Philip Yancey, *The Jesus I Never Knew*. Yancey, editor-at-large at *Christianity Today* magazine, wrote the book as an outgrowth of a Sunday School class he was teaching in Chicago in which he used portrayals of Jesus in film to study Jesus's life. The book chronicles the effect films about Jesus had on Yancey personally (in Yancey's words, "the films helped restore Jesus' humanity for me"[2]) and suggests that films can be powerful tools for communicating the evangelical message. The book, published by Zondervan, is accompanied by teaching materials and a video that uses clips from movies about Jesus. *The Jesus I Never Knew* was phenomenally successful in evangelical circles, winning the 1996 Gold Medallion Christian Book of the Year Award by the Evangelical Christian Publishers Association. The success of Yancey's pedagogy and book demonstrates again the blurring of sacred and secular realms in our culture, particularly evident in films.

Almost from the beginning of film, religious topics have found their way into this medium, and religious controversy has arisen in the context of film and the popular audience. In *Reel Spirituality*, Robert Johnston includes a chapter on the relationship between the church and the movies and provides an excellent brief history of religious themes and controversies through the history of the cinema. As he points out, many early films featured religious subjects and were made by religious people. As the cinema evolved, so did the presentation of religion and the Bible, but much of the subject matter was still biblical, such as Cecil B. DeMille's *The Ten Commandments*.[3] Alice Bach has written an insightful article on film and the Bible in which she differentiates between films about biblical subjects and films where analysts claim to find biblical influence. She rightly advises caution when dealing with film and reminds us not to go looking for biblical themes that may or may not be present.[4] Similarly, Jeffrey Mahan balances some of the theological and cultural concerns of presenting Jesus on film in his recent article, "Celluloid Savior: Jesus in the Movies,"[5] while Anton Karl Kozlovic has written an article entitled "Superman as Christ-Figure: The American Pop Culture Movie Messiah."[6] And a more recent volume edited by George Aichele and Richard Walsh, *Screening Scripture*, explores the enduring influence of biblical themes on secular movies.[7] I mention these examples from many to point out that, from the beginning of film, the Bible has and continues to influence the medium in terms of subject matter, theme, symbolism, and interpretive criticism. Sometimes this connection is made by religious moviemakers, sometimes by secular moviemakers, and sometimes by critics and analysts. So it should be no surprise that with the recent fascination with the end of the world there would be movies depicting the apocalypse from a conservative Christian perspective as well as from a secular perspective. After all, what better topic than cosmic cataclysm could one hope for, given special effects in contemporary movies? The challenge to depict Satan, Armageddon, the rapture, and other eschatological images presents the right sort of task for special-effects crews and make-up artists.

During a paper presentation at a conference a few years back, I wondered aloud about the absence of major motion pictures depicting the apocalypse from a distinctly biblical perspective. In quick succession came films like *The Omega Code*, *Left Behind*, and *Megiddo: The Omega Code II*, all three films based on biblical rather than secular visions of the end times and all three coming from the perspective of evangelical Christianity. That these films appeared among other, secular end-of-the-world movies makes for a fascinating comparison of world-views. For while the medium, film, might be the same, the premise and message differ greatly.

One of the most intriguing issues arising from these evangelical films about the apocalypse is how much the forces behind the films want them to be a success— not only in the evangelical world but also in popular culture. These films are not an attempt to reach believers so much as they are an attempt to tap into the secular culture on a popular mass-audience level. In a *Gentlemen's Quarterly* (*GQ*) interview with Jim Nelson, Matt Crouch, the producer of *Megiddo*, describes his goal of reaching an evangelical movie audience, but he also admits his method was to use the "quality of Hollywood" to communicate the Christian message.[8] In addition, Tim LaHaye sued Namesake Entertainment and Cloud Ten Pictures in July 1999 because, at least in part, the film *Left Behind* did not realize the antici-pated mass and blockbuster appeal.[9] And Peter Lalonde, one half of the Lalonde brothers who made the movie *Left Behind*, exclaimed in the same interview mentioned above, "Jack Nicholson! ... How good an Antichrist would that guy be?"[10] Clearly, Crouch, LaHaye, and the Lalondes all want to render a film faithful to the biblical story of the apocalypse, but they want these films to be successful in the same sense that Hollywood blockbusters with Hollywood stars are successful with a popular audience. At the conclusion of the *Left Behind* video, Kirk Cameron, star of the film, urges viewers to spread the word so the film will have a greater popular effect.

However, these film makers are sensitive to the subtle blurring of lines involved when using secular media and forms for sacred purposes. In his article for *GQ*, "God is on Line One," Jim Nelson recognizes the discontinuity. These evangelical films about the apocalypse require "fictive jumps ... to fictionalize what you believe to be true."[11] The film makers and screenplay writers recognize this and accept responsibility for fictionalizing parts of the story that are not spelled out in the Bible in order to make the story credible. They are careful not to contradict the Bible in their writing, however.[12] So the result is a movie that stays mostly true to the biblical accounts of the apocalypse, however they may be interpreted, and that uses modern special effects and filming techniques to bring the more fantastic and visual parts of the story to life on the screen. The result is sometimes dazzling, sometimes horrific, and often effective, especially with the proper audience.

After a brief review of *The Omega Code*, *Left Behind*, and *Megiddo: The Omega Code II*, I will suggest some common characteristics of these few attempts at popular Christian apocalyptic movies before examining the more common and numerous examples of popular secular apocalyptic movies.

The Omega Code and *Megiddo: The Omega Code II*: the secularization of the sacred apocalypse

The Omega Code, a surprisingly successful evangelical vision of the apocalypse from 1999, is based upon the notion that the Bible contains a secret code that will reveal the events of the end time. The idea that whoever controls the code can control the eternal souls of humans motivates the antichrist, embodied by the character Stone Alexander (played by Michael York), to steal the code and initiate the events that will lead to the end of time. An elaborate computer program allows Bible scholars and Stone to unravel the Bible code by reading the text in three dimensions. The plot of this action thriller proceeds as Stone tries to wrest control of the final code from the film's protagonist, Gillen Lane (played by Casper Van Diem), a self-absorbed, human-potential guru who in the end undergoes a religious conversion through his struggle to thwart the antichrist. The film ends ambiguously with the revelation of the final code that points to the new millennium as the beginning of the end. Whether the antichrist controls events and initiates his hellish kingdom or the kingdom of God is inaugurated awaits resolution in *Megiddo: The Omega Code II*.

The film's main characters, Stone and Gillen Lane, are introduced early in the film, and it is not clear at first who is supposed to represent the antichrist. Lane is a young, brilliant, handsome, and precocious Ph.D. in world religions and mythology from Cambridge. He has achieved success and fame as a human empowerment speaker and writer who appears as an evangelist for a secular humanist gospel. As the film progresses, it becomes clear that Lane is not the embodiment of evil, but is simply the paradigm of human fallibility and sinfulness. While his motivational speeches and work appear to save others, he cannot save himself—he suffers from demonic visions and nightmares, his marriage is falling apart, and he is powerless to stop the film's more demonic character, the antichrist Stone Alexander. So the evangelical perspective of the film becomes clear—the battle in the movie is for the human soul, represented in concentrated form by the brash, confident Lane. And human pride in one's ability to save oneself becomes the chief avenue for falling into evil. Nevertheless, by the end of the film, Lane, tormented still by his demonic visions, prays a simple prayer for salvation. At once his visions are lifted and his demons vanquished, and, while it is unclear if this prayer will deliver Lane and humanity from the evil of the antichrist, it is clear that Lane (and thus human beings) cannot save themselves but must depend on the saving grace of Jesus Christ. The movie obviously operates from an evangelical perspective, and the message is clearly enunciated through the transformation of Lane. That the action takes place in the context of the apocalyptic drama gives us a clue to the motivating force behind the film.

The film's other main character, Stone Alexander, the embodiment of evil, the antichrist, appears as a benevolent world leader who uses technology to solve problems of drought and food production while using his charisma to unite people under his goal of a one-world government. While his actions appear to benefit humankind, they produce a smokescreen that hides his evil intent to capture the souls of human beings and enslave them in his ungodly kingdom. This vision of the antichrist is in accord with the teachings of some who study biblical prophecy with a view toward the apocalyptic drama—a false peace breeds deception and blindness. Stone's demonic and supernatural nature unfolds as the plot does, particularly when he is resurrected after dying from a gunshot wound to the head, thereby fulfilling the prophecy associated with the beast, who "seemed to have a mortal wound ... [to the head that] was healed."[13] From that point on, it is clear that the antichrist is embodied in Stone and that the cosmic battle is underway. Stone represents pure evil arrayed against God, while Lane represents human frailty. The battleground is Earth—the spoils of victory, the souls of human beings.

The plot is difficult to follow without some grounding in the apocalyptic tradition that lies behind the film. Hal Lindsey, who wrote *The Late Great Planet Earth* in 1970, served as consultant to the film, and the apocalyptic drama unfolding bears the mark of the tradition he represented during the latter part of the twentieth century. In the video version of *Megiddo*, the sequel to *The Omega Code*, Lindsey appears before the movie starts to reassert his position that the film chronicles the "precise pattern" of events that are foretold in biblical prophecy. He asserts his belief that the antichrist is now alive and that the second coming of Jesus is not long in the future. Paul Crouch (executive producer of the film and father of Matt Crouch, the producer of both *The Omega Code* movies), also appears in a short cameo to vouch for the veracity of the belief that we are situated at the end of time on Earth when Bible prophecy points to the coming of the antichrist and the battle of Armageddon. *Megiddo* takes the viewer to that battle made famous in John's Revelation in the climax of the movie.

The 2002 *Megiddo: The Omega Code II* is a more sophisticated movie than *The Omega Code*. The plot is more suspenseful, less punctuated by the esoteric code that drives the action. And the movie makers use special effects more liberally and with more dramatic results than in the earlier film: Stone Alexander spews from his mouth a plague of what appears to be locusts; a hellish scene of the battle of Armageddon (the hill of Megiddo) plays out under the red light of a sun turned to blood; a shaft of heavenly light descends from heaven; Stone is transformed into a beastly and horrific Satan who is cast into and chained in the lake of fire. With *Megiddo*, Crouch employs cinematic special effects to portray the events in Revelation. The effect is dramatic, and this is the most interesting point about the movie. With *Megiddo* we see clearly the blurring of secular and sacred lines through the use of media, which the film decries, to help visualize a sacred story. The power of image, made possible by a secular, popular film medium, becomes part of creatively telling and recasting a sacred story. By presenting it in visual form, part horror film, part science fiction, part religious drama, the film makers take a bold step in exploring popular avenues for a sacred message.

After an initial narration by the antichrist, *Megiddo* begins in 1960 when Stone is a young boy and chronicles the development and maturation of the evil of antichrist. At a party, the young boy overhears a conversation between his father and a friend about the 1960 presidential election. Stone's father predicts Nixon cannot win the presidency because of his unsightly appearance on television and offers his assessment that television will play a major role in shaping public opinion. He boldly asserts this in a not-so-subtle foreshadowing of the role the media will play in the rise of the antichrist to world dominion. Later in the movie, Stone murders his father in order to control his father's media empire, because it is the key to distributing his message. In a bit of thematic irony, the film portrays mass media as the tool the antichrist will use to ascend to popularity while at the same time this story is told through the same mass media. In fact, as mentioned earlier, contemporary evangelicals have been adept at using various media formats for spreading the message, so it is not media *per se* that is evil. The point here is that secular media can be used for good or evil, and that it is suspect at best.

After Stone attempts to kill his baby brother, he is sent to military school in Rome where he receives the military training and leadership skills he later employs in his attempted rise to world dominion. The film chronicles Stone's rise to head of the European Union and ultimately to Chancellor of the United World Union, seemingly bringing peace and ending world hunger through his attempts to create a unified world government, a united world with one currency and one language. Such a vision of world dominion has long been associated with the antichrist by some apocalypticists, so the plot is a predictable one based on this particular prophetic tradition. As in *The Omega Code*, Stone has a human obstacle to battle and overcome, his brother David (played by Michael Biehn), whom he had tried to murder as a baby. David (messianic overtones?) ascends from the vice-presidency of the United States when Stone kills the president, and Stone then tries to force David to join the United World Union. The United States had been the chief hold-out, joined tentatively by China and the "Latins," in their suspicion of Stone and his one-world government. Of course, David refuses, and the forces are quickly aligned—Stone and his United World Union against the United States with its allies, the "Latins" and China.

This good-versus-evil scenario quickly develops as David is discredited by Stone and by treasonous forces within the U.S. government, goes into hiding, and, seeking strength through prayer, ultimately tries to assassinate Stone. He fails, and, as in *The Omega Code*, the potential human savior falls short. Even David, with his goodness and honesty, with the force of the United States and its allies, cannot defeat the beast—this task must be left to the supernatural. The movie comes to its climax with the aforementioned battle of Armageddon, the appearance of the kingdom of God, the casting out of evil, and the establishment of God's kingdom. The last image of the movie is of a renewed Earth: the scene abruptly changes from hellish battlefield to Eden-like paradise punctuated by a cascading waterfall.

Left Behind

Left Behind, the 2000 movie based on the novel by the same name, was produced by the Canadian filmmaking duo Peter and Paul Lalonde. The film comes in a line of apocalypse theme movies written and produced by the brothers including *Apocalypse*, Revelation, and *Tribulation*. The Lalondes' and Cloud Ten Pictures' earlier movies were not largely known, although *Tribulation* boasted a sizeable budget and a cast with known names like Gary Busey, Margot Kidder, Howie Mandel, and Nick Mancuso. But *Left Behind* received the benefit of the block-buster novel series by Tim LaHaye and Jerry Jenkins. Kirk Cameron, Brad Johnson, Chelsea Noble, and Clarence Gilyard give the movie recognizable stars, and the action-packed plot containing political intrigue gives the evangelical message a viable vehicle to attract a popular audience.

Many of the elements found in *The Omega Code* movies are present here: the plot revolves around eschatological interpretations of biblical prophecy; underlying tensions in Jerusalem between Jews and Muslims are key to the end of time; a charismatic and powerful antichrist rises to world popularity through the United Nations by combating world hunger and offering world peace; a global currency and global community are instituted; rebuilding the Temple in Jerusalem is planned. Yet, this film focuses on another element in the escha-tological drama based on biblical prophecy. The premise of *Left Behind* turns on the rapture, the belief that true Christians will be caught up in heaven and mysteriously disappear in order to escape the prophesied tribulation period. This intriguing element adds drama to the film as people disappear from planes and cars, and chaos and panic result. As dazzling as the special effects of Armageddon are in *Megiddo: The Omega Code II*, capturing the chaotic results of the rapture are much more believable, having a visceral and palpable impact. The movie ends with the revelation of the antichrist, the world poised on the brink of the seven-year period known as the tribulation, but with the assertion that "faith is enough."

The other major element that sets this film apart from *The Omega Code* movies is a more pronounced evangelical appeal. *Left Behind* portrays successful, attractive people making rational decisions to follow Jesus Christ, praying for forgiveness and guidance in light of the events of and following the rapture. By shifting focus from antichrist and Armageddon to rapture, this film is less like a horror film and more like an intriguing action flick, albeit with an evangelical message. The video, which was released before the movie came to theaters, ends with an appeal by star Kirk Cameron to spread the word about the film project so that others will see it but also so that Hollywood will take notice—notice that an audience exists who will pay to see movies with a spiritual message. The film becomes a purposeful evangelical tool to spread the message to as many people as possible through the use of secular media. The hope that other such films will be produced by Hollywood lies at the core of the project. These evangelical Christian film makers understand the power of images and film to shape beliefs and attitudes and are beginning to capitalize on this aspect of the postmodern psyche.

This brief review of some evangelical films that have chosen the apocalyptic drama as their subject allows us to isolate a few characteristics of the seculari-zation of the sacred drama. While each film has its own individual characteristics, they share the following emphases to one degree or another:

(1) These films reflect a particular evangelical interpretation of the end of time that is tied to linking biblical prophecy to contemporary events. Not all evangelicals share this interpretation of the biblical apocalyptic literature,

but there does exist a community that seeks within contemporary events signs that the end is approaching, based on clues in the Bible. This stance involves an interpretive leap—beginning with the notion that the Bible is the key to understanding all of life, this evangelical apocalyptic stance believes that there are also hidden clues that will reveal the key to understanding the conclusion of history.

(2) In these dramas, there is a focus on the apocalyptic antichrist rather than on a savior figure. This makes sense because in the evangelical apocalyptic drama, the savior is the risen and returning Christ, and none of the films depict the return of Christ.

(3) The films accept the idea that the world is beyond saving and that events of the end are to be interpreted as those that will usher in God's kingdom.

(4) The apocalyptic conflict is a cosmic one between good and evil for eternity and for human souls.

(5) Human effort cannot save the planet or humankind—no human savior will be adequate. The final battle is a cosmic one waged on a supernatural level.

(6) Certain signs are key and repeat themselves as enduring symbols in this prophetic tradition: the establishment of Israel as a nation; Middle East conflict, particularly between Jews and Muslims; creation of a global community by erasing national boundaries and creating a world currency; weather patterns and natural disasters; the deceptive and charismatic rise of antichrist.

(7) Technology is key—a computer program unravels the secret code in *The Omega Code*, the media become the tools of the beast in *Megiddo*, and scientific technology to end world hunger is significant in all three movies.

(8) Violence characterizes all three films but is much less a part of *Left Behind* than *The Omega Code* and *Megiddo*. Of course, violence in these films should not surprise us, even though they are meant to be spiritual films, because the subject matter is violent—world conquest, the antichrist, evil incarnate, and so on, must come wrapped in a certain amount of violence.

(9) There can be no lasting world peace and no final solution to problems such as poverty and hunger. Peace and alleviation from suffering can only be achieved in God's kingdom

(10) The films use secular media and popular entertainment as vehicles for a particular sacred view of the apocalypse and constitute the secularization of the sacred. Filmmakers do this willingly in order to capture the imagination of a secular audience.

I enumerate these characteristics now in order to compare them to those found in apocalyptic films that begin from a secular viewpoint rather than from an evangelical one. The differences in worldview are interesting and enlightening.

The sacralization of the secular

Secular apocalypses[14]

Although it is not surprising to see evangelicals making films about the apocalypse (except for the fact that evangelicals have historically been suspicious of the medium), one finds it at least intriguing to see the various movies made (particularly in the 1990s) about end-of-the-world themes. As Y2K anxieties mounted, movie makers cashed in, and a surprisingly wide range of movies emerged about the end of the world. By the end of the first decade of the twenty-first century, the approach of 2012 had a similar affect. These secular apocalypses were made not from the religious point of view at all, yet they participated in a sacralization of the secular because in many ways they functioned religiously by imparting an ideology (if not theology) of the end times that captured the imagination of the public. In doing so, they took on sacred function. Commentators such as Daniel Wojcik view apocalypticism as rampant in American society. In his insightful work on popular culture and the apocalypse, *The End of the World as We Know It: Faith, Fatalism, and Apocalypse in America*,[15] Wojcik sees apocalypticism everywhere in culture and examines apocalyptic philosophies that give serious response to our hopes and visions. He points to popular culture as an effective medium for communicating contemporary apocalyptic visions and concerns accompanying them. When popular culture does this, it addresses a fundamental religious concern, so when secular cultural forms like movies tackle a worldview that has traditionally been ascribed to the religious imagination, we have secular culture taking up sacred functions, thus sacralizing the secular imagination. This sacralized, secular ideology communicated through diverse films, sets forth a few recurring themes. After reviewing these themes through reference to a variety of secular apocalyptic films, we will look at a few films in particular that embody the secular approach to the end of time. *Waterworld*, *12 Monkeys*, *Independence Day*, and *2012*, for example, provide us with illustrations of the extraordinary diversity of popular films based on eschatological themes. What will emerge is an apocalyptic consciousness in the popular, secular sphere that contrasts drastically with the one established in evangelical apocalyptic movies.

The first point to keep in mind with these secular, cinematic apocalypses is that, although many borrow image and symbolism from the Jewish and Christian apocalyptic dramas, most are not apocalyptic *per se* in the sense that Jewish and Christian apocalypses "unveil" or "reveal" God's sovereignty. While they focus on the eschatological characteristics of the tradition and view the end of the world through the lens of religious apocalyptic renderings, these cinematic dramas ignore some salient features of apocalyptic texts.

Second, the cinematic apocalyptic dramas draw as much from contemporary science fiction as they do from apocalyptic texts, so the stories appear in radically altered forms. For example, whereas demonic beasts might predominate in the evangelical films, these apocalyptic culprits wear contemporary clothing in secular films. The cinematic apocalypses contemporize evil, the Prince of Darkness, and the antichrist. No longer the beast of Revelation, modern evil comes packaged in nuclear weapons, global warming, killer viruses, and aliens—ideas that can excite the imagination of contemporary, secular audiences.

Third, in secular apocalyptic dramas, it is no longer the supernatural that initiates the apocalypse. Whereas, in traditional Jewish and Christian eschatology, the apocalypse comes from the transcendent realm,[16] in secular apocalypses the end comes about more often than not from human stupidity and greed (for example, in *Waterworld*). This is the ultimate secularization of the apocalypse, because world destruction has been removed from the realm of the sacred to the secular realm, from the hand of the supernatural to the will of humanity. The secular film version of the apocalypse removes the divine element from the apocalyptic drama yet retains religious symbolism, imagery, and language. Nor does it remove the notion of otherness as a necessary component of humanity's struggle with the end of the world. However, in these films, the divine Other is replaced by aliens, disease, meteors, and machines—an otherness that exists in "binary opposition" to humankind. So the secular apocalypse of film is postmodern in that it has undermined the binary opposition of God–human[17] by effectively removing God from the equation. Yet it retains a sense of opposition ("something–human") that is crucial for understanding threats to existence.

Fourth, in the traditional Christian apocalypse, the end of the world raises the righteous to the kingdom of heaven and judges the wicked, so Armageddon is something not only preordained to happen but welcomed by the righteous community. In the secular apocalypse, as I have noted in *Screening the Sacred*, there is no such fatalism and differentiation, and the emphasis is not on the end itself, but on avoiding or surviving the end. In fact, surviving the end is one of the characteristics of the secular apocalypse, and we find that human ingenuity, scientific adaptation, and heroism allow humanity to survive and outlive the apocalypse or to avoid it entirely. This makes sense—since the secular apocalypse has humanity initiating the end, it casts human beings in the role of messiahs, saviors from destruction.[18] This characteristic stands in stark contrast to the evangelical films, which picture potential human heroes as powerless against supernatural forces, both good and evil. Thus we see a secular apocalyptic imagination that removes Armageddon from God's hands and places it squarely in the hands of humanity—the fate of the world depends on no one but ourselves. This exclusion of God from the apocalypse defines the secularization of traditional apocalyptic imagination. This secularization of the end trivializes it, humanizes it, and makes it less threatening, if not inconsequential.

A fifth characteristic of the more recent apocalyptic films suggests a further refinement as well. Just a few years back, many apocalyptic films were based on the premise of nuclear holocaust, because at one time the idea of nuclear winter was foremost in our minds as the villain most likely to succeed in bringing about the end of the world as we know it.[19] Films such as the 1964 British black comedy, *Dr. Strangelove: Or How I Learned to Stop Worrying and Love the Bomb*, *Def-Con 4*, and *The Day After* illustrate an earlier preoccupation with world destruction by nuclear means. And the idea still arises. For example, nuclear war is implied in films like *The Book of Eli* and *The Road* but is not an integral part of either film. Also, in *Independence Day*, nuclear destruction of the world becomes a fear but is minimal in light of the other threat of world destruction, alien invasion. In fact, nuclear destruction is considered in *Independence Day* as a possible means of *saving* the world from apocalypse. Let us entertain the assumption that, with the end of the Cold War, the nuclear threat no longer dominates our fears as it once did, so imaginative film makers and artists have gone in search of other world-ending scenarios, such as global warming in *Waterworld*. We will see this transition clearly when we examine *12 Monkeys*, an apocalyptic scenario based on a killer virus. This film was inspired by a 1962 French film that envisioned the end of the world through nuclear destruction. While nuclear annihilation was a real fear in 1962, it was less so at the end of the twentieth century, so *12 Monkeys* had to go in search of a more convincing culprit. What we learn from our secular apocalypses is that we tend to continually reinterpret the apocalypse in light of contemporary consciousness and fears.

Finally, when apocalypticism focuses on the end of things, it becomes a way of overcoming our angst over the realization of our finitude. But when apocalypticism focuses on violence, it becomes a way to control chaos and evil by identifying it, as in *12 Monkeys*, or by defeating it, as in *Independence Day*. The paradigms of violence, like the paradigms of world destruction, help us to make sense of our world by transferring judgment to human control. It is an egocentric attempt to achieve the sovereignty that God claimed in the Jewish and Christian apocalypses. The violence we see portrayed so frequently on our movie screens, the violence we are so fond of calling gratuitous, functions apocalyptically, and thus religiously as well. Or at least it can. What did violence bring us in John's Revelation and in the evangelical apocalyptic movies?—the battle between good and evil and the ultimate destruction of evil. What does violence bring to the movie screen in secular apocalypses?—if not the destruction of evil, then at least the identification of it. This is an important role for movies to play in a secular world where belief in the devil as the embodiment of evil carries little if any importance.

Consider a few brief examples that flesh out the above characteristics of the secular, cinematic apocalypse. The notion that while the threat of the end is inevitable, hope that the destruction of humanity is avoidable runs through virtually all of the recent secular films with eschatological emphases or allusions.[20] These films reject the idea of human extinction in favor of imagining humanity's salvation or at least its survival. We see this in films like *12 Monkeys*, in which there is hope that humanity will be rescued from a killer virus, or in *Waterworld* that ends with an "ark" locating dry land, the promised land. In *Armageddon*, the sacrifice and heroism of one individual spares the world and humanity entirely. As a huge meteor bears down on the Earth, Harry Stamper (an oil rig driller played by Bruce Willis) and a rag-tag group of misfits (similar to those in *Independence Day*) are recruited to fly a space ship to land on the meteor, drill a hole, and drop a nuclear bomb into it to destroy it before it destroys the Earth. Besides a subplot involving a romance between Stamper's daughter (played by Liv Tyler) and his protégé (played by Ben Affleck), that is as deep as the plot gets. A multinational mission is successful, but only after Stamper, in a final act of selflessness, sacrifices his life to save Earth. The movie's plot is weak, but it works well to demonstrate Hollywood's secular apocalyptic premise—the end is avoidable.

Deep Impact employs a plot that is a bit more complex. In this movie, Earth is threatened by a comet. Government officials, led by the U.S. president (played compassionately by Morgan Freeman), scramble to devise a plan to save the Earth. The basic plan is the same—fly a spaceship into the comet and blow it up. This time the mission is led by an ex-astronaut (played by Robert Duvall), but the complexity of dealing with a comet makes it clear to our heroes and the government that some fragments will hit the Earth with catastrophic effects even if the mission is successful. Thus, the plot is more complicated, if only slightly so, and raises ethical questions about who will be saved and how. The heroic efforts of government ensure the survival of humanity even if it means great loss of life.

In *Contact*, we are treated to the movie adaptation of Carl Sagan's vision of humanity's first contact with alien intelligence in another world. We are also introduced to the idea that this event could bring mass extinction at the hands of an advanced and hostile civilization (similar again to *Independence Day*). Jodie Foster plays Dr. Eleanor Arroway, a brilliant young scientist who is obsessed with finding evidence of extraterrestrial life. The movie features a strong cast and does allow some debate of theology, even though most of the questions involve the existence of God rather than any serious consideration of eschatology. Nevertheless, the movie offers hope and comfort that humans are not alone to face the horror of extinction. Although not a guarantee, the notion that another intelligence exists out there comforts us. In this movie, government officials make it clear that they consider alien life a threat whether the aliens act aggressively or not, thus mirroring popular images of alien forces invading Earth. Yet, the alien "other" in *Contact* seems benign, fatherly, and almost divine to the secular, scientific mind in which God is functionally absent.

Contact, as secular apocalypse, communicates serene comfort from the calming presence of extraterrestrial life and presents a stark contrast to religious apocalypse that is portrayed through disturbing scenes in the movie in which religious fanatics are depicted as apocalyptic terrorists. Whereas religious apocalypticists in *Contact* use violence (they destroy the costly machine built to allow contact with an extraterrestrial civilization), in Hollywood's apocalyptic drama the threat of human extinction breeds harmony, not violence. The threat of the end tends to bring people together in a unified stand against annihilation, evolving from a deep faith in the powers of scientific ingenuity and human ability. This is also seen clearly in *Deep Impact* and *Armageddon* in which individuals and government combine forces to save the day. The message is clear: together we can beat this thing. (Note how different this is to the helplessness of humanity in the face of a divinely ordained apocalypse one finds in evangelical apocalyptic dramas.) So the secular apocalypse moves beyond some of the fatalism we often find in religious apocalypticism.

If the world is to be saved in these cinematic dramas, it must have a savior. While we see this messiah fixation in *12 Monkeys, Independence Day, Waterworld, Deep Impact, Armageddon,* and even *Contact,* we see it nowhere more powerfully than in *The Matrix.* In this film, a computer hacker (Keanu Reeves) who takes the name "Neo" stumbles onto secret and life-threatening information. Neo learns that his world is all an illusion, an elaborate hoax played on his mind to obscure the real world where machines, computers, and artificial intelligence have enslaved humanity. This "unveiling" reflects the revelatory intent of much religious apocalypse. The plot taps into the underlying fear that society is too dependent on the computer (particularly at that time in light of Y2K anxieties) and that dependence will lead to humanity's downfall (i.e. enslavement).

In *The Matrix,* fear is developed through a scenario in which machines breed and sustain humans as power sources. At the same time, the machines construct an elaborate shadow world (a cyberworld of illusion), and feed it to the imaginations of the catatonic human bodies. Neo is initiated into this awareness by an underground movement of humans who are seeking to overthrow the machines and establish a new city, the city of Zion, where hopes of restoration of the human race stay alive. A strong-willed Trinity (Carrie-Anne Moss) leads Neo to the leader of these revolutionaries, Morpheus (Laurence Fishburne), who is looking for a "chosen one" to lead them to freedom. Morpheus is convinced that Neo is the one. Neo gradually emerges as the one who will lead the underground resistance, and the movie ends not with restoration but with hope of such.

Note the strong religious imagery present in names: Neo (new); Trinity (Christian overtones); Morpheus (dream god from Greek mythology); city of Zion. This obvious use of religious language establishes Neo as one of the strongest messiah figures in contemporary apocalyptic movies. Religious language and devotion predominate in Morpheus's selection of Neo as "the One." And Neo's initiation into messianic ways becomes highly ritualized. Neo's training involves martial arts expertise and mind control, bringing an Eastern religious element into the picture as well. So Keanu Reeves becomes one in a line of macho messiahs (e.g. Bruce Willis and Kevin Costner) who use muscle and force to save humanity, but, unlike other messiahs, this one must use mind control as well. And his literal "waking up" from his catatonic state makes Neo as much a bodhisattva[21] as a Western-style messiah.

Neo's messianic cause brings to light yet another characteristic of the secular, cinematic apocalypse. With the exclusion of the divine from the apocalyptic formula, the secular apocalypse seeks new relevance in redefining the end through science and human effort. Angelic armies and beasts no longer suffice to usher in the end. Even though the secular apocalypse uses science and human ingenuity to overcome the fatalism of religious apocalyptic myth, often these secular versions employ religious language and images. In *Armageddon*, the United States, Russia, France, and Japan join in a cooperative effort to save humanity using technology, but the president of the United States refers to the Bible in his effort to create a unified mission to save the world from collision with a massive meteor. When at the end of the film catastrophe has been averted, the movie portrays mass celebration at religious shrines. So, while the thanks for salvation should go to science and human sacrifice, the movie cannot quite divorce itself from the divine implications of global disaster. In a similar vein, the plot of *Deep Impact* also relies on science and secular government to save a remnant of the Earth, but these actions are couched in religiously symbolic language. For example, the spaceship carrying the nuclear weapon that eventually destroys the comet threatening Earth is christened "the Messiah," while the operation that selects and transports selected Americans to safe bunkers so they can repopulate the Earth is dubbed Project "Noah's Ark." The impact of these symbols suggests that the cinematic apocalypse is thoroughly secular in terms of substance—the actors, saviors, and heroes are governments and individuals while the threat comes not from some divine power but from natural forces. Nevertheless, the apocalyptic moment still carries religious imagery and symbolism. This might be the most telling comment on our secular society's appropriation of religion—while our culture is substantively secular, we legitimize it with reference to religion, and if our culture functions religiously as well, it is sacralized.

After undermining the God–human dichotomy and rejecting the supernatural as the agency for the apocalypse, the contemporary apocalyptic imagination has been in search of a new apocalyptic cause. As suggested earlier, the contemporary eschatological movie has redefined the agency of the end several times in the last 30 or so years. At one time, eschatological fears were attached to our fears of nuclear annihilation, yet, by the late 1990s, nuclear weapons become the agency of salvation, as in *Deep Impact*, *Independence Day*, and *Armageddon*. Viruses (*12 Monkeys* and *Outbreak*), aliens (*Independence Day*), and global warming (*Waterworld*) have taken front stage as threats that concern contemporary Americans. And, more recently, *The Matrix* has explored the possibility of artificial intelligence giving rise to the end of the civilization that produced it. The theme of humanity against machine is not a new one and recalls the Frankenstein theme of a human creation turning against the human creator.[22] *The Matrix* uses fears surrounding technology (e.g. Y2K fears were based on nervousness that our culture had created a monster—a computer-driven world that would wreck civilization) to continue the "Garden motif" in which creation turns against the Creator.

This element of *The Matrix* allows a further refinement of the secular, cinematic apocalyptic myth made possible by the concept of virtual reality. To a greater extent than ever before in human culture, we can use technology to create a virtual reality. *The Matrix* raises an interesting question concerning the capabilities of this technology a couple of hundred years from now. The plot of the movie is based on the premise that computers have constructed an elaborate alternative reality that masks the post-apocalyptic world. To the extent that human beings exist in this world, they exist in ignorance of the real, actual state of their world or their lives. They have been duped by a virtual world that to them appears real. This contemporary revisiting of Plato's famous allegory of the cave and of the neo-Platonic dualism of real and ideal adds an interesting twist to the idea of the apocalypse and raises the possibility that the apocalyptic moment has already passed—both in reality and out of human memory. The role of Morpheus (the Greek god of dreams) as the character who introduces the real versus the shadow world in this movie only complicates the matter. How can we be sure Morpheus's version of the Matrix is not the "dream" masquerading as his "reality" that is based on "illusion?"

Most twentieth-century millennial groups are pre-millennial in their orientation and thus require a destruction scenario to fulfill their apocalyptic expectations. The secular cinematic apocalyptic drama capitalizes on this perception and stereotypes apocalyptic groups—this describes an additional characteristic of these cinematic apocalyptic dramas. Contemporary culture already tends to view apocalyptic groups as marginal, sometimes scary, sometimes dangerous, sometimes as the agents of mass destruction. This image certainly does not describe all religious groups that are millennial in orientation, but it does describe the way secular movies have portrayed religious groups focusing on apocalypse. As a result of this and other cultural characterizations, religion has largely forfeited its proprietorship of the apocalypse in our culture. In its place science has stepped in with its fantastic theories about origins and endings in our universe.

The conflict between faith and science in dealing with cosmology is a main theme in *Contact*. In this movie, the protagonist Dr. Arroway exhibits unyielding faith in science while religious representatives appear as kooks (the apocalyptic terrorist), as right wing zealots (Rob Lowe's character, Richard Rank), or as compromised and unconvincing (Matthew McConaughey's character, Palmer Joss). In the end, this works against the scientist Arroway when she asks the world to believe her story that cannot be proven or substantiated. In our secular eschatological dramas, science has wrested control of cosmic cataclysm away from religion, suggesting that the charges of secularists that religion is anachronistic (if not irrelevant) arise most convincingly over questions of eschatology. We have already witnessed more than a century of debate over creation and now see the movie medium sponsoring debate on the eschaton.

My main argument here is that a secularized apocalyptic imagination is fostered by or reflected in the contemporary film industry, and that this imagination of the end contributes in some way to a postmodern, secular vision of apocalypse that draws upon but revises the Jewish and Christian apocalyptic imagination. As such, films like the ones highlighted in the remainder of this chapter are re-visioning the apocalypse in ways that make sense to contemporary audiences and in ways that eclipse traditional religion's ability to do so. By eclipsing traditional religion's role in presenting apocalyptic themes, these secular apocalypses take on sacred roles and are witness to a sacralization of secular culture. Sometimes this process draws on the traditional apocalypse's heavy eschatological emphasis—sometimes more generally on the apocalyptic cataclysm that envisions justice and judgment through violence and death. All of these themes can be found in many popular films but especially in *Waterworld*, *12 Monkeys*, and *Independence Day*. These movies all function religiously in that they present a secular apocalyptic story that helps the viewer come to grips with human finitude and world fragility.

Waterworld

The highly publicized and critically abused film, *Waterworld*, provides a good example of an apocalyptic film based on a contemporary dilemma. *Waterworld* takes the warnings of global warming and, like any good science fiction work, asks the question, "What if …?" Then the film extrapolates a possible future scenario based on the idea of melted polar caps from a runaway greenhouse effect. The film is thus based on an Earth largely covered by water, a new flood requiring, as in Noah's day, adaptation to life entirely on water. A world covered in water not only poses challenges to the remnant of humanity that survives the eco-catastrophe, but it also created major headaches for the production crew. Determined to avoid shooting with a blue screen, Dean Semler's crew encountered incredible difficulty shooting the film on water, particularly on the unstable trimaran that is the Mariner's (played by Kevin Costner) ark. The technical demands and artistic difficulties of shooting on water led to what was then the most expensive film in history, at about $175 million, and to a Universal Pictures production record of 166 days.[23] For all this cost and trouble, director Kevin Reynolds and producer-star Kevin Costner did make a technically advanced film, and a good one at that,[24] and the film anticipated residual income on ventures such as "Waterworld Live," a live sea war spectacular and outdoor stunt show at Universal Studios Hollywood.[25]

The film itself follows a straightforward plot with predictable developments. The setting is a future, inundated Earth where survivors of the great eco-disaster exist on floating cities, atolls, or floating barges (mini-societies). Mariner is a loner, existing on his trimaran and adapting to life on the sea. The action of the movie begins when Mariner arrives at an atoll to trade for supplies. He possesses a few ounces of the most precious commodity in such a world, dirt, and seeks to trade his treasure for water and a scrubby tomato plant. The citizens of the atoll discover Mariner is a mutant with webbed feet and gills behind his ears. This mutation calls to mind the mutation themes of earlier post-nuclear films. Mariner is caged and sentenced to death when the atoll is attacked by a band of smokers (pirates) who are led by Deacon (Dennis Hopper). In the confusion, Mariner is rescued by a beautiful woman, Helen, and a little girl, Enola, and the three escape together on Mariner's trimaran.

The point of the story is revealed when we learn that Deacon is pursuing Enola because of a tattoo on her back that is a map leading to the mythical dry land. Obviously, in *Waterworld*, if someone could find and master dry land, that person could enjoy unimaginable riches and pleasure. The plot develops as Deacon captures Enola; Mariner discovers a drawing Enola leaves behind that matches an old copy of *National Geographic* picturing trees with the caption, "Paradise Lost"; Mariner surmises that perhaps the mythical dry land could actually exist and that Enola might hold the key to paradise after all. This makes her rescue crucial.

Mariner locates and infiltrates Deacon's floating colony, a huge oil tanker. In great feats of daring, he saves Enola, destroys the tanker, and defeats Deacon and his evil minions. Once evil has been destroyed, Helen and Mariner employ the help of Gregor, an old inventor from Helen's atoll, and decipher the tattoo on Enola's back. In the end, they find dry land, complete with fresh water and vegetation, and populate it with the survivors of the atoll where Helen and Enola began. The righteous community, as opposed to Deacon's evil society, occupies dry land, paradise. However, Mariner realizes he is not meant for dry land (remember his mutations) and, having played his part as epic hero and savior, he leaves the community behind and sails off alone.

The point of the story, the apocalyptic premise, is to find paradise, dry land, a flooded world's version of the kingdom of God. *Waterworld* thus defines a period of temporary trial and tribulation, a concept familiar to the Christian apocalypse, which will be followed by paradise. And the vicinity of dry land is signaled in the same way as it was following the biblical deluge, by the perching of a bird on the edge of the ark, in this case a balloon. Dry land is the metaphorical home for the inhabitants of Waterworld and literally home for Enola. When Enola arrives at their paradise, she exclaims, "I'm home." Enola had once lived on the island and was sent away when her parents were dying. Enola is a curious girl who has visions of and draws strange figures: what we know as trees and horses but what were to the Waterworld inhabitants strange unknown plants and animals. Her drawings came from her suppressed memories from early childhood. So, arrival at dry land is "going home" for humans who were not meant to live on water, just as the post-apocalyptic "new heaven and new Earth" meant going home for first-century Christians who were dispossessed in Roman society and for true Christians in the evangelical apocalyptic movies.

Dry land was all but destroyed in the apocalyptic scenario of *Waterworld*. Yet the promised land was never forgotten and attained mythic proportions, and the righteous eventually inherit paradise in the last scene of the movie. Mariner, who rescues Enola and leads the remnant to paradise, becomes the apocalyptic hero who appears on the scene in order to deliver (save) the righteous, guide them to paradise, and defeat the wicked, which Mariner does in his daring rescue of Enola. I have written in *Screening the Sacred* about another apocalyptic hero from an earlier film using apocalyptic imagery and categories, Clint Eastwood's *Pale Rider*.[26] In that story, Eastwood (Preacher) rides onto the scene as a young girl reads from the book of John's Revelation. During the course of the story, Preacher befriends the residents of a small community, defends their rights against the power of a large strip-mining company, and defeats the wicked en route to securing the happiness of the righteous community. At the closing of the movie, Preacher rides out of sight, just as Costner sails into the horizon in *Waterworld*. The apocalyptic hero protects, delivers, and defeats wickedness, but in the end the hero is of a different order and cannot remain with the righteous remnant.

As a secular apocalypse, *Waterworld* reflects contemporary, secular concerns rather than sacred ones in its depiction of the apocalyptic disaster. In this case, it is very clear the apocalypse occurred as an eco-disaster, which came about as a direct consequence of human action. Director Kevin Reynolds commented, "I'm very concerned with ecological issues, because I think they are the overwhelming problems the world faces right now and will result in our own self-destruction ... a whole world covered in water because of human stupidity and greed."[27] Note the emphasis on the apocalypse being self-induced—our secular apocalypse in this case will be self-destruction, not supernatural destruction, as in the evangelical apocalyptic movies.

The environmental theme is carried out with little subtlety in two major symbols of the movie. First, Deacon's tanker, the evil and ancient freighter in the story, turns out to be the Exxon Valdez, the infamous tanker that polluted the waters and was at the time of the movie a symbol of ecological disaster. And near the point when Mariner triumphs over Deacon, we learn that the patron saint of Deacon and his evil empire is none other than Captain Joe Hazelwood, the doomed captain of the Valdez.[28] So in this movie of eco-apocalypse, the predominant symbol of evil turns out to be a symbol of ecological and environmental disaster. The second apocalyptic and environmental symbol here is Enola, whose name brings to mind the *Enola Gay*, the airplane that dropped an atomic bomb on Hiroshima. In this movie, Enola delivers not the apocalypse but escape from it, not nuclear annihilation but the key to paradise. These two symbols draw upon contemporary ecological, environmental, and apocalyptic imagery to construct a secular apocalypse set on the watery world of our future.

12 Monkeys

From *Waterworld*, which is straightforward in terms of plot, we move to an examination of *12 Monkeys*, Terry Gilliam's convoluted story that jumps from future to past to past-future and back again. Gilliam, who also directed *The Fisher King* and the cult favorite, *Brazil*, is known for his "inventively convoluted design."[29] The inspiration for this movie came from Chris Marker's *La Jetée* (1962), a short work of stills that chronicles time travel after the apocalyptic nuclear destruction of Paris and, one would assume, the world. Gilliam Americanizes Marker's classic,[30] and in the process produces a challenging secular apocalyptic image for the twenty-first century.

The film is set in Philadelphia in 2035. Ninety-nine percent of the world's population has been destroyed by a killer virus that was released in 1996. The survivors of the virus have now retreated underground to a subterranean hell beneath the city. Scientists in this underground world send criminals to the surface periodically to monitor conditions. They decide to send one such subject, James Cole (played by Bruce Willis), on a time-traveling mission to 1996 to locate the source of the virus, thus allowing them to plot a strategy to defeat the bug and once again populate the Earth's surface—in other words, to go home. The scientists believe a group called the Army of the 12 Monkeys was responsible for the outbreak. Cole is selected partly because of his keen powers of observation and memory (he is haunted by a childhood memory of a man shot down in an airport). Cole's first foray into the past lands him by mistake in Baltimore in 1990, where his mad apocalyptic ranting leads to his confinement in a mental hospital as a schizophrenic. There he meets Dr. Kathryn Railly (Madeleine Stowe), a psychiatrist, and Jeffrey Goines (Brad Pitt), a mental patient he befriends. Cole's attempts to contact the future fail, but he is finally returned to 2035, where his scientist interrogators make a second attempt and land him in 1917 in the middle of World War I. There, Cole is shot in the leg before landing in Baltimore in 1996. The time travel sequences confuse past, present, and future so much that not only the viewer but Cole himself begins to doubt the reality of the quest. When Cole locates Dr. Railly in 1996, she is giving a lecture about a doomsday scenario based upon a great plague. Her lecture is complete with references from John's Revelation, apocalyptic prophecies, and artwork symbolizing the end. Cole and Railly begin an adventure that leads them to the Army of the 12 Monkeys, which is headed by none other than Goines. Dr. Railly begins to believe Cole's story when she discovers the bullet in his leg is from World War I. In the meantime, it turns out that the Army of the 12 Monkeys had nothing to do with the virus but was an animal activist group aimed at freeing the research animals in the lab of Dr. Leland Goines (Jeffrey's father). An assistant to Dr. Goines, Dr. Peters, an "apocalypse nut" in the words of Dr. Railly, plans to scatter the virus.

Believing they had communicated sufficient information to the future and averted the release of the virus, Cole and Dr. Railly travel to the airport to pursue an amorous life together. Once at the airport, they encounter Dr. Peters, realize he is the one releasing the virus, and Cole tries to stop him. In the process, Cole himself is shot down by a security guard as a younger James Cole watches (hence the vivid memory of the adult Cole who saw or imagined his own death as a child). The movie ends aboard a plane with a scientist from the future seated next to the plotting Dr. Peters.[31] One assumes the scientist acquires the needed information, returns to the future, defeats the virus, and allows humankind to go home, to once again populate the Earth, or to establish a new world.

One of the most remarkable characteristics of this secular apocalypse is the time travel element. With this tool, the viewer is allowed to see that human initiative both created the apocalypse and perhaps averted it; therefore, the confusion of time (which could also be considered a characteristic of postmodernity based on relativity theory) is the central element driving this plot. Jeffrey Beecroft, production designer for the movie, comments: "[Y]ou have pieces of the past and the future and the present in all scenes …" so that the plot ends with Cole's past memory of his future death.[32]

Beecroft's comment brings to mind an interesting possibility in terms of interpreting this film. In Marker's classic, *La Jetée*, time travel seems to be imaginative mind extension,[33] so the possibility exists that the same is true in *12 Monkeys*. Since the story is told from Cole's point of view, it is not at all clear whether it depicts reality or the distorted view of a real schizophrenic. In other words, the viewer has no way of knowing whether the story is based in 1990 in the mind of mental patient or in 2035 with time travel and futuristic scientists. This apocalyptic scenario could present the eschaton, or simply the delusions of a psychologically disturbed man rather than the real eschaton.[34]

The movie could be about an apocalypse that is human-caused with the help of a virus and human-averted with the help of futuristic ingenuity. This option fits our paradigm of secular apocalyptic movies, because it places world destruction at the feet of humanity and reinterprets the apocalypse in light of contemporary fears, mutated viruses and biological terrorism. However, the other option, the imagined eschaton, raises some interesting possibilities for our secular apocalypse as well. If James Cole's illness leads to a vision of the end,[35] then the movie is less about a scenario of the end than it is about the visionary experience. Now, let us imagine another famous visionary, John of Patmos, and the psychological dynamics that went into play in producing his revelation, his vision. If we look at *12 Monkeys* in the same way, we can understand apocalyptic scenarios as visionary attempts to imagine our own finitude (i.e. Cole's vision of his death) in a world that continues without us. In John's case, this scenario drew upon a storehouse of Jewish and Christian images to produce a vision of world destruction and God's kingdom. In Cole's case, he could have drawn upon a store of images from his twentieth-century paranoia and anxieties concerning deadly germs to produce a hellish end to civilization and the possibility of establishing a new Earth. The end being unimaginable, Cole then fabricates an alternative ending that saves humankind.

This alternative interpretation of *12 Monkeys* supports the idea that apocalyptic concepts are born out of Western and human egocentrism as a way of dealing with human finitude. Since time inscribes humanity to a limited existence, in a secular apocalyptic imagination it makes sense that transcending time (time travel) could free humanity. John's apocalypse freed humanity by transcending space, by ascending to and viewing the kingdom of Heaven. But the secular apocalypse, which has no transcendent realm in its arsenal of images, transcends time, the great limiter of human experience. And it is this transcendence of time that defines the end and the thwarting of the end for this secular apocalypse. With no transcendent kingdom of heaven, the secular apocalypse is limited to envisioning a new, regenerated Earth, a secular kingdom. In doing so, it sacralizes the secular.

Independence Day

With *Independence Day*, we have a movie that includes a different perspective of the apocalypse than our other two films. Whereas *Waterworld* and *12 Monkeys* were both "post-apocalyptic" in respect to the events that bring about the end (they take place between the destruction and re-inhabitation of the Earth—they are about going home), *Independence Day* portrays events that threaten to bring about the end. By the time humans figure out what is going on, the world's major cities have been destroyed and a 36-hour countdown to complete world destruction is underway. So, *Independence Day* is less about going home than it is about saving home; less about finding a new Earth than it is about saving the old.

The premise is an old one lifted directly from H. G. Wells's *War of the Worlds*, in which the fate of humanity and civilization is directly threatened by hostile aliens with superior technology bent on destroying human life and conquering Earth. The film opens on July 2nd with views of an American flag planted on the moon and appropriate American symbols like Washington monuments and the Statue of Liberty. Then we see a huge alien ship approach the planet. The mother ship then dispatches smaller ships (still 15 miles in diameter) that travel to and hover over major cities like Washington, Los Angeles, and New York. The gargantuan ships dwarf the cities and provide eerie apocalyptic scenes as they arrive at their appointed destinations around the globe. As they approach, they come from the sky in mountains of fire and smoke, like some fiery chariots from another world. And when they arrive they darken the skies and threaten total annihilation from another world. With governmental officials scrambling to respond appropriately and with the cities in panic, the aliens attack on July 2nd and destroy the targeted cities—millions die around the world. The images are dramatic, sensational, and highly symbolic—major buildings and monuments are obliterated, the Statue of Liberty lies face down with a destroyed Manhattan in the background, and, in a scene that is the ultimate apocalyptic image for American civil religion, the White House is destroyed.

July 3rd begins with the cities in ruin and government officials at a loss for what to do. We learn that the U.S. government knew about these aliens from a crashed ship from years ago and that there is a top-secret area (Area 51—a creative reference to the theorized Roswell secret military installation) where scientists have been studying the aliens with little success for years. The secretary of state and former CIA director knew about the facility but failed to tell the president; the implication is that, because of governmental secrecy, more people will die. So, even though the apocalypse in this movie comes from above, human action and inaction and governmental deception are at least partly responsible for the disaster. With this twist in the film, it is probably appropriate that the movie was shot largely at Hughes Aircraft in Culver City, California, where top-secret weapons were designed and built during the Cold War.[36]

Meanwhile, an unlikely coalition of heroes begins to emerge who ultimately team up to save the world. The U.S. Air Force is gearing up to respond with one of the movies heroes, Captain Steven Hiller (Will Smith), emerging as a top-gun fighter pilot who wants to join the NASA shuttle team. Russell Casse (Randy Quaid), one of the great comic characters of the movie, is a drunken crop duster who suffers from post-combat trauma from his service in Vietnam. Casse was also abducted by aliens in the past and wants payback. David Levinson, an electronics specialist played by Jeff Goldblum, emerges as an eccentric genius inspired by his equally offbeat father (Judd Hirsch). And, of course, President Whitmore (Bill Pullman) provides inspirational leadership, pulling together a force of fighter pilots and even strapping himself into a jet fighter to do battle with the aliens (the president had been a fighter pilot during the Gulf War). As the movie develops, our team of saviors is a politically correct coalition of African-American, Jewish, and WASP heroes who are undergirded by the strength and inspiration of women and the elderly and who join talents to defeat evil. Levinson conceptualized the plan to defeat the aliens and flies with Captain Hiller to plant a computer virus on board the mother ship. Captain Hiller flies an alien craft to the mother ship and returns home safely and heroically with Levinson. Casse sacrifices his life to destroy the aliens. And Whitmore provides the energy and leadership to inspire his warriors in a wonderful speech just before climbing into a fighter jet: in his speech he declares the Fourth of July no longer an American holiday but worldwide Independence Day when humankind will join forces to gain "freedom from annihilation," i.e. freedom from apocalyptic destruction.

Our heroes are successful, the alien threat is defeated, and somehow humankind is able to put aside its political differences, to join together in a united effort against a common foe, and to save the world. This rather trite point of the movie demonstrates the seriousness of the secular apocalyptic idea—apocalypse is a real threat that will require extraordinary means to defeat, but the apocalypse can be avoided, even if it is initiated by some greater force. It can be averted through human ingenuity, technology, and unity. Again, this avoidance of the end is one of the characteristics of the secularization of the apocalypse—no longer do we picture the apocalypse as beyond our control, initiated by supernatural forces as in evangelical apocalyptic movies. Also, in this and in other secular apocalyptic movies, we see world unity as a key to avoiding the end, while in evangelical movies world unity is a sign of the antichrist.

Nevertheless, *Independence Day* introduces a new element into our secular apocalypse. In this movie, and others, the impending doom is not the direct result of human failure, as it was in *Waterworld* and *12 Monkeys*, but comes from a force greater than and beyond our control. As Caron Schwartz Ellis has argued, aliens constitute another type of otherness,[37] so that aliens can become our secular "other," descending from the heavens, the transcendent realm. And this is problematic for a postmodern, secular worldview that basically no longer accepts the idea of a transcendent realm. So how does *Independence Day* deal with this dilemma? It familiarizes the alien and makes it vulnerable. In one of the great comic lines of this movie (and by the way, this is a very humorous film—no dark disaster film here), U.S. pilots are plotting strategy for counterattack when Captain Hiller is reprimanded by his superior officer for talking during the meeting. When called down by his officer, Hiller quips: "I'm just a little anxious to get up there and whup ET's ass." This comic line makes the aliens, the other, vulnerable and familiar, because we immediately recall the loveable and vulnerable Spielberg creation, ET. This is how the secular apocalypse deals with otherness: it makes the alien familiar and less threatening as a way of controlling what is beyond our control. This is one of the characteristics of our secular apocalypses. They bring the potential of world destruction and those forces that threaten to destroy the world under human control. There is no helplessness in the face of the Almighty here, and in our secular, cinematic apocalyptic dramas, humankind, not God, emerges as sovereign.

2012, the movie

2012, the date, has been on my mind lately. For a year now, my daughter and her teenage friends have been talking about it. They're mildly concerned, and it has occurred to me that their media, songs, films, popular culture and the like, are filled with references to the end of time. And for the millennial generation, 2012 is the first popular, mass marketed end-of-time scenario with a tie to religion, popular culture, and mass appeal. The teenagers I talk with are at least peripherally knowledgeable concerning the Mayan long count calendar and the film, *2012*. Further, as I sit at my computer and compose the first words on the film, *2012*, I notice the date: 11/11/11. As strange as it looks, stranger still is the article that pops up on my screen that associates 11/11/11 with the Mayan apocalypse. We are more than a year out from the supposed end of the Mayan calendar, and yet we cannot escape its presence in the popular culture. As I read the article with mild interest,[38] I did not learn much new. Some see significance in the number 11 and particularly in the sequence of 11s. The symmetry of the repeated 11s for some carries metaphysical significance, and apparently the New Age blogosphere has been bombarded with entries concerning the date, including those who see 11/11/11 as the beginning of the metaphysical year leading up to the fateful winter solstice of 2012. Our collective imagination seems destined to be drawn to such phantasmal imagery about the end of time, not because we are inherently a superstitious lot but because such symbols bring order to something that would otherwise be chaotic and horrific. The beauty inherent in the symmetry of 11/11/11 suggests that, whatever 2012 might bring, it must be part of some grand cosmic plan, ordered and predictable, frightening yet part of the underlying ordering of the cosmos. This desire for order and symmetry, I argue, lies within our fascination with the apocalypse and drives our culture's hunger for all things ultimate.

Roland Emmerich, the director of *2012*, is a veteran of end-of-time movies, having also directed *The Day After Tomorrow* and *Independence Day*. He skillfully weaves stories of heroism and hope through the grim and graphic images of this masterfully crafted special effects production. While images of destruction are horrific, they also unfold with a kind of surreal beauty as characters in the film await violent destruction with a peace borne of awe before the awesome power of nature's destructive will. Images of destruction are powerful and symbolic: Christ the Redeemer in Rio de Janeiro collapses; the ceiling of the Sistine Chapel cracks right between the outstretched hands of Michelangelo's God and Adam, undoing the work of creation with the act of apocalypse; the White House is crushed by a giant tsunami and the aircraft carrier *John F. Kennedy*. But the most arresting image, one of horrific destruction, is also one of sublime beauty and peace. In an image reproduced as poster art, a Buddhist monk calmly stands at the top of the world while the tsunami crashes among the mountain tops of Tibet. The monk's serenity reproduces the attitude of many in the final moments before the end. Is this the underlying apocalyptic message of the film? The end, while violent, will be preceded by that moment of clarity and serenity—the transcendent moment when the end is inevitable and the conscious mind is enveloped with the awe of time and space collapsing.

Like many other end-of-world films, *2012* operates on the premise that the end of the world is survivable, at least by a few. Also, like *Deep Impact*, this film raises ethical issues concerning who is saved and who is left behind. We learn that governments around the world work in secret for three years to produce ships that turn out to be "arks" built to survive the cataclysmic events that scientists learn about and to repopulate the Earth from a pool of a fraction of Earth's total population. Money, power, and genetics turn out to be just a few of the factors for selection, and this, of course, raises ethical issues concerning the decisions about who and what is allowed on the arks. It turns out that selected works of art and books and species of animals (just like on Noah's Ark) are also included on the checklist of world civilization and life worth carrying over to the new world. Since the primary destructive force turns out to be huge tsunamis produced by massive earthquakes, the ark imagery is a not-so-subtle but apt one. This time there are six arks, not one, and governments, not God, coordinate their construction and planning. In this way, *2012* is a secularized story of the biblical flood and ark. However, this film based upon the Mayan calendar that some believe forecasts the end on the winter solstice in 2012 is also rich with religious imagery from the world's major religions. It is a film that explores the permeable boundaries between sacred and secular visions of the end of time.

The story opens in India in 2009, when scientists discover unprecedented solar flare activity that is causing neutrinos to heat the Earth's core. Computer projections predict that the crust of the Earth will shift on the heated interior causing massive quakes and tsunamis, predictions that come true in 2012. The governments of the world coordinate efforts to deal with the impending disaster under the leadership of the U.S. President Thomas Wilson, played skillfully by Danny Glover. The president recruits Adrian Helmsley, a talented young geologist, to help coordinate the project. The efforts are kept highly secret, partly in order not to panic the public, but mostly because the plan to deal with the disaster is a plan to save only a small portion of humanity. The large portion of the human population will perish in the cataclysm that cannot be averted. In this sense, the story follows closely the biblical flood story. However, the element of divine judgment is completely missing, as the cataclysm this time is caused by sunspots, not a regretful creator. A subplot develops when Jackson Curtis (played by John Cusack), a struggling writer who is estranged from his family, accidentally learns of the plot from his employer's actions (Russian billionaire Yuri Karpov) but mostly from his encounter in Yellowstone National Park with the eccentric conspiracy theorist, Charlie Frost (played masterfully by Woody Harrelson). Charlie is an eccentric prophet, bordering on insanity, operating on the periphery of society, preaching to an audience which goes largely unhearing—but he is the prophet of truth, heralding as prophets of old the message of a coming world-ending cataclysm. Charlie has a map of the ark locations, a map that later allows Curtis to save his family. Most of the action of the film involves Curtis racing against time to get his family to China aboard the arks.

As the destruction begins, the film astonishes and mesmerizes the viewer with images and action. The special effects are remarkable for their realism and scale. The destruction allows the film to focus on stories of heroism. President Wilson decides to stay behind rather than board an ark, in order to stand with the doomed populace. In his final address to the nation, he reads from Psalm 23 before the broadcast comes to an end; Helmsley gives a rousing speech that convinces the various governments to allow extra people on board the arks, endangering their own lives to save others; even the self-serving Yuri sacrifices his life to save his sons. This is the stuff we come to expect from disaster adventure films, and *2012* does not disappoint. The adventure genre often highlights the worst and the best of human nature, and here the best shines forth with a force that saves not only individuals, but world civilization.

As the film reaches its climax, the arks are boarded, and the countdown to the tsunami crashing into the arks proceeds, we learn that many of the original passengers will be left behind because one of the arks is damaged. The arks have been sealed and prepare to navigate to safety when the realization that many will perish sinks in for those safely on board. In an effort to save those still to board, Helmsley tries to convince the world leaders to reopen their arks and let the "extras" in. It is a risky request since it would endanger those on board and the entire project in order to save a relative few. Carl Anheuser (played by Oliver Platt), who is the political head of the United States' ark, opposes the plan on practical terms: Helmsley's plan would threaten the whole project, the chance of saving civilization, and the ultimate goal of repopulating the Earth. Helmsley presses on through impassioned speech and makes his case based on the higher nature of human empathy and a particularly important passage from a book that is meaningful to him. The book is Jackson Curtis's book, *Farewell Atlantis*, a book that flopped, has obvious apocalyptic overtones, but that nonetheless will become a cornerstone for a new civilization since Helmsley saved it and is a fan of the book. Helmsley reads from the book about what it means to be human, "the moment we stop fighting for each other, that's the moment we lose our humanity." He argues that to start a new future based on an act of cruelty and abandonment would be to reject the one thing that makes us human—our ability to exercise empathy to overcome our selfish tendencies. His speech has the desired effect, the arks open their gates to the remaining passengers, and most make it on without incident. But in a dramatic turn of events the gates on the U.S. ark jam, threatening to sink the U.S. effort to save its citizens. The pending disaster requires more acts of heroism and sacrifice, but in the end the ark is sealed and the passengers saved. Helmsley's vision of human nobility wins the day, and the future of humanity is built upon this hope: the hope that in the face of self-extinction, being human means acting selflessly.

In the final scenes, three of the arks set sail for a new land mass on Day 27 of the Month 01, in the year 0001. Satellite images show that the continents seem to have merged in the shape of Africa. The new era of human civilization will begin with all humanity as one, arising out of its original home, Africa. The apocalypse has ushered in a new creation, and a new human era will begin, based as it is on an act of humanity. There is hope for this new world, a new Earth. This secular apocalypse, based on a sacred story from the Bible and a sacred Mayan calendar, provides a new vision of a new Earth and new civilization to be built upon an act of kindness rather than an act of cruelty. While it is not at all clear whether religion will be part of civilization that was chosen to be saved, the movie at least implies that in this new world the biblical myth of creation and cursing will be reversed. In the biblical myths, Adam's disobedience led to the murder of Abel by Cain, an act of cruelty and selfishness that stands at the beginning of human civilization. This time, in the new world, humanity's obedience to their higher natures will give humankind another chance. This time, an act of kindness and selflessness defines the beginnings of civilization, and one only hopes that the new world will follow suit.

Post-apocalyptic survival guides: *The Book of Eli* and *The Road*

The traditional Christian apocalypse ushers in the Kingdom of God. The secular apocalypse avoids the end. But what do you do if you cannot avoid the apocalypse yet the Kingdom of God does not replace the destruction the apocalypse brings? Sometimes human effort fails and the world is destroyed, or nearly so, despite how splendid humanity sees itself. What do you do if the world ends but you do not? This is the question of many post-apocalyptic films, with their grim representations of life after civilization destroys itself. A destroyed Earth, without the redemptive hope of religious apocalypse, presents a very grim picture indeed—a postmodern aesthetic unbridled. Two recent films fall into this category, yet amidst the distressing picture of post-apocalyptic America there flickers a small flame of hope, something dim yet present to carry hope of a reborn, yet distantly future, civilization. There are no aliens in the picture, no killer viruses, no unforeseen global or cosmic catastrophe; there is just the very worst of human nature and its destructive impulses and the very best of human moral consciousness. And if one can bear the bleak, hellish filmic presentation of a burned Earth without civilization's restraints, then one can find there the spark, be it divine or human, that promises our angels will guide us through the desert.

The Book of Eli and *The Road* are similar in many ways. Both films are set in a post-apocalyptic America where the earth has been burned, where life barely continues, and where brutish impulse to survive seemingly has taken over the vestiges of humans who are left after the conflagration. *The Road* is set a few years after the apocalyptic event; *The Book of Eli* is set 30 years after the "flash." The difference in time is believable in that, in the latter film, survivors have begun to organize into settled communities, while in the former there are only loners and loose bands of nomads. Both films chronicle a journey: in *The Road*, a man and his son travel to find warmer weather near the ocean, and in *The Book of Eli*, Eli journeys west. In both films, the road is a dangerous place, filled with outlaws, desperados, and even cannibals, but in both films the road is the way, both literally and metaphorically, out of darkness and toward light. In both films, the protagonists carry something with them (actually in them) that separates them from evil, and it is this something that provides the note of hope in the films.

The Road is a particularly difficult film to watch. It is based on the book by the same title by Cormac McCarthy, a book which is equally difficult to read. The pages of the book and the scenes of the film are filled with despair and hopelessness, as a father and his son struggle to survive in the most horrific situations of hunger, fear, cold, pain, and danger. The greatest fear is to become victim to cannibals, and the father keeps a gun designated as an instrument for suicide to avoid the horrors of falling into the hands of cannibals. The father constantly reassures the son that they are the good guys and would never give in to the evils they witness around them. The son pressures the father to help others, even though to do so would hinder their chances of survival. What holds the two to a thin thread of sanity is their love of one another, their assurance that they are among the "good guys," and that they carry and preserve "the fire." The fire of civilization, the fire of love, the fire of humanness, this is what father and son carry within and mean to preserve. In the end, the son, bereaved after his father's death to sickness, carries on with another family, a good family, and the reader/viewer is left with that glimmer of hope that the fire will continue, that civilization will again rise from the ashes, and that humanity will not succumb to brutishness but will be elevated by goodness and by the spirit born by love for others.

These themes are present in *The Book of Eli* as well, but in more explicitly religious/Christian terms. Eli (played by Denzel Washington) is on a 30-year quest to deliver a copy of the King James Bible to a place where it will be safe and become part of a collection of civilization's great productions. Following "the war" that Eli references, virtually all Bibles were burned, and apparently Eli has the last one. If he is successful, the Bible will become a cornerstone of the rebirth of human civilization. He encounters many challenges, but his greatest comes when Carnegie (played by Gary Oldman) discovers that Eli has the Bible. Carnegie is the leader of a small community and rules the "town" by fear and through his control of a clean water source. He has been looking for a copy of the Bible because he believes that having the words of the Bible will provide him with a source of ultimate power. For Eli, religion will save civilization; for Carnegie, religion will deliver "divine" power into his hands. Throughout, Eli quotes scripture, acknowledges the golden rule as the supreme message of the Bible, offers grace and prayer, and "walks by faith, not sight" to complete his mission. In the end, he surrenders his Bible to Carnegie to save the life of Solara (Mila Kunis). But in the ultimate plot twist, the Bible which Carnegie has in his possession does him no good since it turns out to be written in braille. Eli did walk by faith, not sight, and his faith delivered him to Alcatraz Island, where he dictated the entire memorized Bible to the curator there before dying from a mortal wound that Carnegie had inflicted upon him. It is clear that Eli is given the strength to complete his mission from a divine source, and, as Solara prepares to return to her home, it is clear that a new civilization will dawn eventually, raised from the desolate landscape by light (Solara) and God (Eli).

Both of these films bring our study of apocalyptic themes in films full circle: from the traditionally religious story based on religious texts, to the secular story where human effort replaces God; to the post secular hope that humankind's folly will find forgiveness in God's redemption. In this way, some secular apocalypses recapture the original meaning of the Jewish-Christian apocalyptic drama to cross the permeable sacred–secular divide and to provide an apocalyptic hope based on redemption, rebirth, and renewal.

Summary

My contention here is that the process of secularization has affected some of our traditional religious categories, one of them being the idea of the apocalypse. With a sacred worldview, one that dichotomizes the transcendent realm and the world, cosmic cataclysm initiated from another realm to destroy the world makes sense and is almost inevitable. However, in a secular world, where our worldview no longer dichotomizes the transcendent and this world, where we view reality through a secular lens rather than a sacred one, we have difficulty conceptualizing world destruction from the hands of a sovereign ruler. Part of the process of secularization involves raising humanity to the sovereign level so that humans control their own destiny, and this has even spilled over into our ideas of the apocalypse. Because mainstream religion by definition has become so secularized it rarely deals with the scenario of the apocalypse, one might think it would simply go away. But the apocalyptic imagination is alive and well, because the human imagination (at least the Western imagination) must incorporate the endpoint in order to make sense of time and death. So, with religion's minimization of the eschaton because of the secularization of mainstream traditional religion, popular culture has co-opted what was the religious business of apocalyptic thinking. In that it provides an apocalyptic consciousness, it functions religiously and is witness to the sacralization of a secular viewpoint. Popular movies have taken up the charge and created an alternative secular apocalyptic imagination in which the end is less threatening and can even be avoided.

The secularization of the apocalyptic consciousness in movies, like elsewhere in our popular culture, takes place in two directions: 1) evangelical apocalyptic films start with a sacred worldview and portray the apocalypse using secular media and contexts, thus secularizing the sacred; 2) secular apocalyptic films proceed from a secular worldview and substitute a secular vision of the end for the traditional religious apocalypse. That this new vision functions religiously to deal meaningfully with the problem of the end of existence results in a sacralization of the secular. In either case, we see the secularizing blurring of boundaries between the sacred and secular unfold in our end-of-time imaginations.

Study guide

Important words and concepts

Apocalypse
Apocalyptic
Armageddon
Eschatological
Eschaton
Evangelical apocalyptic films—characteristics
Fatalism
Secular apocalyptic films—characteristics

Discussion questions

(1) What are the key differences between religious apocalyptic movies and secular apocalyptic movies, as outlined in this chapter?
(2) How does the role of the supernatural differ in the various movies under consideration?
(3) Will the apocalyptic imagination pass if the year 2012 passes without incident? Why, or why not?

Guided reading

(1) Read John's Revelation in the New Testament. Write a short essay in which you answer the following question: What role has the book of Revelation played in shaping a contemporary, popular apocalyptic consciousness? Focus on movies with apocalyptic themes to write your paper.

Part Four
Con-text

10

Communitas/Con-text

On a typical Sunday morning across America, one might observe or participate in any number of activities in the name of Christian worship. A priest dispenses the Holy Sacrament in solemnity and dignity; a former drug addict "testifies," dressed in biker leathers and do-rag; a teenager in shorts and sandals fetches donuts and coffee while the band plays loud "praise" music; a man clutches a hymnal and sings heartily "The Old Rugged Cross;" a young woman lifts her hands high to God, and her hands are full of writhing rattlesnakes; a preacher gives a carefully constructed and highly technical talk; another preacher pounds the pulpit and delivers a fiery, improvised sermon; a cowboy, head bowed in prayer, stares at his dusty boots; a young boy is raised from a chilly stream, beaming and saved. All of this and more—all of this in the name of Jesus—all of this within a few miles radius—all of this to define and bind a community of believers and to give that community a context for working out the highly variable belief system that is American Christianity.

The variety of religious practice in America is astounding, developing out of the free tradition of practice as established in the United States since the revolutionary period. R. Laurence Moore effectively argues that religion in America is diverse because religious practice has had to compete in the marketplace of ideas and activities in order to survive and thrive.[1] Moore's thesis provides an effective and insightful way of looking at the fundamental dynamics of the evolving American religious landscape by placing this evolution in the context of free market forces. And if one extrapolates from this basic idea, it is easy to see that the free market will eventually give the public what it wants. All it takes is a stroll down any aisle of any department store to see where this leads. There are not just a few varieties of shampoo or breakfast cereal on the shelves. Rather, there is a confusing array of products designed to serve niches and address certain needs. Do you need a great-tasting cereal that gives you an ample supply of fiber? There's a box for you. Do you need a shampoo that gives extra body while making your hair smell great and repairing your split ends? There's a bottle for you. Do you need a soap that exudes a rugged manly smell while moisturizing your skin? There's a bar for you. And do you need a religion that meets your standards of orthodoxy and quotient for entertainment without making unreasonable demands upon your life? Well, there's a religious community for you, too.

One might call the proliferation of niche religious communities "lifestyle Christianity." And lifestyle churches provide communities that are comfortable for seekers. These communities have long served to provide comfortable worship contexts for varying social and class levels. For example, in colonial America, the Anglican Church provided a high-profile position for the privileged elite in society. The lay vestries of Virginia had status and power, and the position of vestryman provided for religious operation but also for social propping. Perhaps an even better example of religion and social propping can be found in Lee Smith's short story, "Tongues of Fire," where Smith suggests one's social status is reflected in one's choice of worship community.[2] In the town where I grew up, and in many communities across America, we often find stereotypical associations with religious communities that include not only Christian denominations but other religions as well.

From this, one can begin to understand the importance of community in religious affiliation—or even lack of it. One's identity is in part wrapped up in one's religious affiliation or lack thereof, whether in reality or only in perception. In this sense, one's religious context (con-text) or communitas is important for understanding the curious interaction between sacred and secular that is explored in this book. In this fourth section, we move beyond pre-text, text, and post-text to discuss con-text, the various realities that shape our religious sensibilities and projections. If "we are what we eat," and if "clothing makes the man," then contextually our religious sensibilities and projections must come from what we "ingest" spiritually and the spiritual "clothes" we don every day. The company we keep helps to define us, for better or worse, and at some level personal worth is judged by religious context. The focus in the following sections is on the religious and quasi-religious communities that blur distinctions between secular and sacred. This blurring, the secularization of the sacred, usually takes place in a particular "context" of religious community. While we might not give great credence to the role of religion in everyday life, religious affiliation often becomes a litmus test for legitimacy to perform certain social roles or adequacy to represent a particular social status.

We can see this clearly in the way religion and politics interact in contemporary American society; for example, in the very public conflict that arose between President Barack Obama's critics and Obama's religious mentor, the Reverend Jeremiah Wright. Barack Obama had attended Trinity United Church of Christ in Chicago where the Reverend Wright was senior pastor. The Reverend Wright was well known for prophetic sermons in the tradition of black liberation theology.

His prophetic utterances led to controversy, especially when harsh-sounding segments were aired as sound bites on the evening news and radio talk shows. Particularly controversial were quotes by the Reverend Wright that seemed to condemn America and even blame America for the 9/11 terrorist attacks in New York City and Washington, DC. There was little attempt in the media to put these comments in the context of black liberation theology or in the community setting from which it came. Rather, the sound bite ruled, separated from its context and taking on a whole new dimension. Not wanting to disown the Reverend Wright, Obama issued statements on race in America and distanced himself from those controversial remarks. Eventually, Barack Obama dissociated himself from the Reverend Wright to avoid association with the controversy surrounding the Reverend Wright's statements.

In this example, President Obama's context, his communitas, was a predominantly and prominent African-American urban church, and Obama's spiritual "clothing" was very publically "hung out to dry" when the more controversial elements of Wright's preaching became public. While this is certainly a legitimate communitas in the socially progressive segment of Protestant Christianity, association with it began to damage Obama politically because it was presented with racially charged implications, socially liberal or even radical associations, and anti-American or unpatriotic-sounding rhetoric. Barack Obama's belief system was being defined by his spiritual context. Whether or not Wright was using metaphor; whether or not Obama agreed with his controversial statements; whether or not the media presentation of Wright was fair does not matter. What matters is the dynamic that allows communitas to define the individual and the assumption that contextual values are equivalent to personal values and beliefs. To avoid being labelled unpatriotic, radical, or racial, Obama was forced to disavow his communitas and re-contextual his religious status.

More recently, at the beginning of the 2012 presidential campaign, one of the Republican frontrunners, Mitt Romney, has garnered close scrutiny due to his religious communitas. Romney is a Mormon, a member of The Church of Jesus Christ of Latter-day Saints. A prominent Baptist minister, the Reverend Robert Jeffress, made headlines during the fall 2011 campaign by publically claiming that Mormonism was a "cult" and not Christian. It is difficult to say at this time what effect these aspersions against Mormonism will have on Romney's candidacy, but no doubt he will have to defend his communitas. What has yet to be seen is how this will define Romney. Will his Mormonism establish him as a values candidate with unquestioned moral sensibilities? Or will the specter of cultism taint him with false associations with polygamy and other controversial aspects of Mormon history? Whatever the reaction, Mormonism will help contextualize Romney's individual status and will most likely play some role in the candidate's future.

Thinking about context and communitas helps us to understand some of the trends in the contemporary Christian community in America. For years we have been hearing that traditional affiliation in America is becoming less important. People are instead opting for "lifestyle" churches or churches of convenience. Feeling comfortable with a social setting is probably more important to Christian Americans than theological affiliation. People might choose a church based on programs, location, facilities, class, or even popularity of a minister, rather than on denomination or theological affiliation. What Americans are putting into practice is contextualization—churches play an important role in establishing one's communitas, and Americans are practicing greater freedom in choosing that communitas than in the past. It is not surprising, then, that contemporary America displays great religious mobility, at least within dominant traditions. American Christians move in and out of religion, between denominations, and even between Christian and non-Christian traditions. More and more, American Christians are more likely to attend multiple types of services or to blend Christian beliefs with non-Christian beliefs. For example, 22 percent of Christians surveyed by the Pew Forum profess a belief in reincarnation, and Americans are more likely than ever to mix spiritual and non-Christian super-natural beliefs with their Christianity.[3] What we are witnessing is not a loss of fidelity but rather an expression of religious freedom to define ourselves in the context of communitas.

The process of religious mobility in America can be seen clearly in a contemporary movement often referred to as the Emerging Church movement. Chapter 12 of this book examines this movement in more detail as an example of a secularizing trend within a sacred community. For now, suffice it to say that the Emerging phenomenon is one of the most important trends to affect the Christian Church in the latter twentieth and early twenty-first centuries. Emerging Christianity has grown out of dissatisfaction with Christian institutions and focuses on alternative worship patterns, alternative mission strategies, and new ways of conceiving Christianity. Some refer to the Emerging Church as post-Christian, and it is certainly postmodern in its deconstruction of familiar patterns within the Christian community. The Emerging movement provides alternative communities for worship within the Christian world, but, perhaps even more importantly, Emerging Christianity has forced a rethinking within traditional denominations about what church is and how church works. Emerging Church paradigms have challenged church culture and theological education. Churches have added new worship paradigms to satisfy the desires of those who do not respond to traditional services. Divinity schools have added new degree programs to meet the demand of praxis-heavy models of church organization. In some Divinity programs, theological sophistication has taken a back seat to engagement with praxis and programmatic sophistication. What the Emerging

Church demands, and what contemporary Christianity has begun to respond to, is engagement with culture.

Theologies, such as post-liberal theology or narrative theology, have developed to support this new paradigm. These theological commitments do for theology what in literary studies reader response theory does for literature. These theological positions could be analogously understood as believer response or faith response theory, and they open theology up to society as a real force by shifting the locus of power toward the laity. These perspectives allow praxis to come to the fore and they de-center authority, empowering those who have the greatest transformative potential in society—local leaders and parishioners. These theological perspectives, whether known by the post-liberal or narrative label, or by a host of other potential labels—dialogical, relational, engaged, or the like—represent the most important theological movements in the postmodern era because they have shifted authority and allowed for more engagement at local levels and because they force an engagement with popular, secular culture. So as post-liberal theologies and Emerging paradigms continue to develop, we see within these movements a secularization of the sacred.

The Emerging phenomenon provides yet another opportunity for religious mobility in America—mobility away from tradition and toward individual definition within a communitas. This process of "defining" is analogous to the process of "othering," discussed in chapter 1. "Defining" in this sense establishes a "persona," a religious persona, which reflects who we wish to be based on free choices of association. In the remaining chapters, I will examine examples of communitas where the context exists solely to establish a persona (e.g. religious motorcycle groups and cowboy churches). But the phenomenon also helps explain evolving trends in the Christian community such as the so-called "Emerging Church" movement and exotic traditional practices such as snake handling. Emerging Christians are in part exercising a post-tradition focus on praxis as a way of defining who they are rather than what they believe. And movements that are most identified with an activity or sacramental ritual such as snake handling are defined by what they do more than by a belief structure. This focus on identification marks a shift in American cultural religion where religious affiliation is based perhaps more on the Jungian concept of "persona" than on theological commitment to a belief statement or creedal affirmation. In Jungian psychology, the persona is the social face one presents to the world. This face both presents an image to the external social world and also, perhaps, hides a true identity as a metaphorical mask. In psychology, this concept is generally related to developmental stages and contributes to the development of a healthy ego. As used here, I will adopt the fundamental role of persona in defining the social and public person while hiding the private identity. As with Jungian thought, the danger lurks that one will become wholly identified with the persona and thus lose one's true identity.

When someone "defines" themselves spiritually or religiously through the adoption of a persona, they are propping up a social identity by which they are known and by which they wish to be known. One can shed a particular social designation and exchange it for another by shedding a former religion and adopting a second. Likewise, one can stake out alternative ground within a traditional community by defining a persona. For example, the member of a local Methodist Church who also rides a Harley and is a member of the Christian Motorcyclists Association does this when she wears her CMA vest to a traditional worship service. She identifies with the Methodist tradition, but she defines her status with the CMA by creating an alternative persona from her fellow conservative Methodists. She becomes a barrier buster, and, like other cultural movements examined in this book, her persona allows her to negotiate the permeable boundaries between the sacred and secular in society.

But why would we see so much definition in contemporary society, so much concern with contextualizing or building communitas. The answer, I think, lies within contemporary culture, where complexity and diversity have threatened to destroy sense of community. In some ways, the postmodern concern with political correctness is an attempt to do away with the special status attached to community and exclusivity. If it is true that authentic community is vanishing, then it would not be surprising to see individuals in collectives try to re-establish community, even of the artificial or fleeting kind. Victor Turner wrote about communitas and ritual.[4] To borrow that concept, I am using communitas here to refer to intense community feelings of solidarity, equality, and purpose, often organized around a cause that produces a sense of unity. If our postmodern society has produced a culture where community is rare, it would follow that such a culture would be bereft of the transcendental potential to be achieved through communitas. In such a culture, we would expect to see movements arising, claiming such communitas, searching for purpose, and generally defined in some way as an alternative to the predominant culture that prevents such community from occurring. For some individuals, absent a community that locates them meaningfully in society, the adoption of a persona allows them entrance into an alternative group that provides that sense of meaningful communitas. Such groups provide much of what might be rare in the postmodern, deconstructed social order where group identification carries certain impolitic implications: rituals of passage, sense of belonging, group identification and commitment, and individual validation within a group on the margins of society.

Con-text/Communitas: Beyond Text/Beyond Community. These are concepts that allow us to glimpse the ever-changing landscape of America's religious communities from the perspective of an individual's status in society. One might be contextualized by religious affiliation, as were President Obama or Mitt Romney. One might actively "define" oneself through adopting a persona, as a member of a religious motorcycle group defines their alternate ego by adopting a lawless persona and wrapping it with religious intent. In any event, the boundaries between the secular and sacred in our society are often blurred in this on-going dance between persona and communitas, individual and community.

Study guide

Important words and concepts

Communitas
Context
Emerging church
Lifestyle religion
Persona
Postliberal theology
Praxis
Religion and politics
Religion and social status

Study questions

(1) Define communitas.
(2) Why does this chapter use "communitas" instead of community?
(3) Think about ways in which you have experienced the connection between religion and social status. How are the connections communicated in popular culture?
(4) Define the difference between focusing on praxis as opposed to focusing on orthodoxy.

Guided reading

(1) Read President Lincoln's Second Inaugural Address (1865). After a long civil war that divided the country and exposed the scourge of racial divide, Lincoln sought to begin national healing with this address. Write an essay in which you demonstrate the themes that Lincoln develops in this speech that point toward the elements that build "communitas."

11

The motorcycle as American icon and symbol of sacred journey

A quick computer search indicates that American culture is filled with motorcycle groups and clubs. Of course, motorcycle groups like the Hells Angels and Outlaws have been part of the popular culture scene for some time. Other groups, like the Harley Owners Group (HOG), have international chapters. But there are also groups that claim a religious allegiance of a type: Bikers for Christ, for example, and a whole host of Biker Churches dot the landscape. Some of these groups have members who sport long hair, tattoos, leathers, chains, and other biker parapher-nalia, and the only thing separating them from so-called gangs is a mission statement centered on religious fellowship and support, missions outreach, and sometimes substance abuse support. These are traditional-looking bikers with a religious purpose and focus. So the term lifestyle takes on a more intricate meaning for these religious bikers—is it the biker lifestyle or the religious lifestyle, or both? The term lifestyle is actually key here, for it seems that association with a particular lifestyle or image is what motivates many of the biker groups or clubs. The adoption of a persona[1] allows religious bikers to inhabit two worlds, one respectable and the other sketchy.

Just as religious groups adopt the motorcycle lifestyle as a way of gaining entrance into another, alien, world, so have motorcycle advertisers adopted religion as a way of marketing a product, particularly by adopting anti-religion or the dark side of religion. For example, in a recent motorcycle magazine publi-cation, *Motorcyclist*, November 2011, we can see the language of religion used in several ways to tap the dark side of the motorcyclist persona. One of the featured motorcycles in that publication was the Ducati Diavel, which means "devil."[2] Since marketers are hired to sell bikes, the name must be meant to tap into the "dark hero" persona rather than suggest something about the bike's handling or reliability. The same issue of the magazine sported a Harley-Davidson ad for its "Night Rod Special" with a caption that read "The Meek Inherit Nothing." Of course, this ad plays off the beatitude in Matthew's gospel, "the meek shall inherit the earth." Once again, the language of religion is co-opted to express a counter-Christian value represented by the leather-clad biker on a black bike. Again, in the same issue, a motorcycle gear company uses religious language to describe a new jacket: "Seven Sins" describes seven antisocial attributes of motorcycling. But the language of sin, which would normally be used in a religious sense to repel, is used here to attract.

Much has been made in popular culture about lawyers and doctors who ride Harleys on weekends to escape respectability for a short time and adopt an alter ego. Perhaps this is part of what motivates religious bikers. The motorcycle in popular American culture has supported a "bad-boy" or counter-cultural image. For evangelical Christians to adopt that particular image provides street cred, so to speak, among an alternative culture. Many Christian riders claim that it provides acceptance among a fertile group needing to be evangelized or helped. Others say that hanging out with counter-cultural toughs allows them to model a positive image, a sober image, of a drug-free existence for a crowd that might not be so inclined. In this sense, the adopted persona actually makes possible a type of mission that would otherwise not be open. Whatever is going on with the motorcycle persona, the existence of religious biker groups provides a prime example of what otherwise would be a secularized group taking on sacred significance. But even beyond the persona-building aspect of religious bikers, there are other components of the biker lifestyle that promote the sacralizing of the secular activity of motorcycling. The motorcycle itself appears as a secular icon with sacred significance in American popular culture.

The Harley-Davidson Corporation, and most if not all motorcycle manufacturers, present their products around an image of the motorcycle as an icon of freedom, individuality, and independence. This image is more than a marketing ploy, however, and has roots in American popular culture through film and literature. In particular, a classic American film, *Easy Rider*, and a classic American book, *Zen and the Art of Motorcycle Maintenance*, have helped establish the motorcycle mystique in our art and culture. Both film and book revolve around the element of travel as spiritual journey and sacred activity but develop this notion in radically different ways. But the mystique involves deeper spiritual connections as well. In essence, the motorcycle has become a type of spiritual talisman in our culture, imbuing its rider with magical powers and transcendence. The motorcycle has come to function in our culture as an icon, fetish, and talisman, while motorcycle communities act as support groups that sponsor pilgrimages and gatherings with fanatical devotion. As with many forms of popular culture in America, the motorcycle and its attending activities function religiously from many perspectives, including ceremonial, ritual, communal, and experiential.

As for the communal aspect of motorcycling, many motorcyclists talk about the transcendent feeling gained from riding and the feeling of connection with other motorcyclists. When one biker meets another, their connection is immediate and unquestioned—they have shared the experience of freedom and transcendence so many motorcyclists describe. They have been renewed of mind and spirit and recognize that in one another. Their connection transcends place, circumstance, motorcycle brand loyalty, class, gender, and race. The motorcycle becomes the common denominator of experience that binds strangers together through a shared communion of the road. Tim Kessel expresses this "common bond" in an essay by that title in a recent edition of *Motorcyclist* magazine. Kessel described a recent trip he took across the Mexican border on a very expensive and technologically advanced motorcycle. Stopping in a poverty stricken, and perhaps risky, area a middle-aged man pulled up next to Kessel on his small, 250cc, Mexican-made motorcycle. The two motorcycles, and motorcyclists for that matter, could not have been more different, yet the two felt an immediate bond. Neither could speak the other's language, yet for a sustained time they communicated through the language of their bikes. Their differences did not matter; "All that mattered was ... a common bond that transcends ..."[3] This is communitas: that experience of community which is able to transcend difference and create an equality of being; that context or status which connects people meaningfully at a level beyond themselves and their individuality; that experience of shared humanity which operates on the mythic level.

The connection of motorcycles to popular mythological experience and religious practice comes in many different guises: para-religious groups such as the Christian Motorcyclists Association, King David Bikers, and Soldiers for Jesus attend rallies and sponsor pilgrimage journeys; the unofficial biker credo bolsters a particular version of American civil religion that places value on freedom and individuality, symbolized by the motorcycle, the ultimate "freedom machine"; the biker image sets up a peculiar American dualism where the outlaw persona plays the part of the dark hero; the motorcycle redefines space and time in a culture that is conflicted about both; motorcycle brand loyalty and customization approach a type of fetishistic obsession to machine and desire; a motorcycle communitas exists that develops the idea of brotherhood, sisterhood, and solidarity in the presence of danger. I will examine all these ideas in this chapter but will focus on two themes that relate to the presentation of the motorcycle and motorcyclist in popular culture. The first is related to fetishism, masculinity, and sexuality and grows from the popular bad-boy image of motorcyclists promoted in films like

Easy Rider and *The Wild One.* The second is related to the idea of pilgrimage and, while present in many films, is best represented by *Easy Rider* and the classic book, *Zen and the Art of Motorcycle Maintenance.*

A quick look at several motorcycle films will give you an idea about the image of motorcyclists in popular films: *Easy Rider* stars Peter Fonda, Dennis Hopper, and Jack Nicholson; *The Wild One* portrays Marlon Brando as a gang leader; *Born to Ride* features John Stamos as a military hero; Robert Blake is a cop in *Electra Glide in Blue*; *Knightriders* features Ed Harris as the leader of Knights on motorcycles; *Rebel Rousers* has Jack Nicholson and Bruce Dern as motorcycle gang members; Sylvester Stallone and Henry Winkler play motorcycle rebels in *The Lords of Flatbush.* Another film, *Girl on a Motorcycle*, features a young woman (Marianne Faithfull) clad in a leather jump suit who runs away from her newlywed husband on a Harley-Davidson bike to reunite with her former lover. While this film picks up on the anti-establishment theme of the others, its female lead character adds another dimension to the filmic image. Nevertheless, the portrayal of a leather-clad, sexually liberated female motorcyclist probably does more to fuel the fetishistic fantasies of men than to broaden the cultural image of the biker. These films, and others, are testosterone-charged portrayals of bad-boy, leather-clad, anti-culture rebels who often play a type of anti-hero in the film. So much motorcycle marketing, imaging, and association plays on this cultural image—the motorcycle denotes masculinity, sexuality, and anti-establishment values. And while there continues to be a growing number of female motorcyclists, the popular images of motorcycling remain focused on masculinity and fetishism as it pertains to motorcycles and bikers in our popular culture. In particular, three types of fetishistic desire surface in relation to motor-cycle culture: religious fetishism; commodity fetishism; and sexual fetishism—all three relate to transcending power—the motorcycle as fetish transfers some type of superhuman power to the motorcyclist.

In religious studies, "fetishes are material objects believed to embody supernatural powers that aid or protect the owner."[4] Fetishes are connected to uncertainty and danger and provide power to the one facing danger. The element of danger in riding motorcycles is obvious—small mistakes are occasionally made when riding and the consequences of such mistakes can easily be serious. In this context, the customization of bikes acts as a kind of fetish building that empowers the owner. Motorcycle owners often spend thousands of dollars customizing their bikes with parts that increase performance or beautify the motorcycle—chrome, leather, stuffed animals, flags, and other additions give bikes a unique quality, a one-of-a-kindness that owners take pride and comfort in. The customizing comes with the addition of talisman-like objects and decorations. And except for perfor-mance modifications, these customizations have only symbolic value that usually conveys power, magical power.

So the motorcycle has a kind of magical power of the fetish, and we see this very clearly in the marketing of the motorcycles with symbolic and mythological names and other more visual symbols. Here are a few model names for motorcycles: Shadow, Vulcan, Ninja, Rune, Bandit, Intruder, Valkyrie, Marauder, Warrior, Ulysses, and Diavel. Savvy motorcycle companies tap into mythology to give bikes an aura of power and magic that is, of course, transferred to its owner. Sometimes this mythology taps into the "dark side," thus highlighting the kind of counter-cultural image that is often associated with motorcyclists. One advertisement for Honda's Rune pictured the motorcycle in a darkened, mist-shrouded forest with a black knight on a black horse behind it. Caption reads: "MSRP: Your Soul."[5] A Harley-Davidson ad posed its "Night Rod" model by a tree filled with bats. Part of the ad reads, "It's time the world had a hero from the dark side."[6] Religious and mythological fetishism transfers to the possessor of the fetish magical power. Even the nearly ubiquitous helmet recalls a knightly or warrior presence and power—thus clad in appropriate armor (leather and padding), the helmeted knight mounts his/her steed and becomes Vulcan, Marauder, Warrior, Ulysses, or Bandit.

Besides the religious connection to power and myth, the motorcycle might also function as fetish in a more general sense. As Slavoj Zizek writes, fetishes work through disavowal, where a fetish substitutes for an object of one's real desire.[7] Zizek and Jean Baudrillard both explore Marxist thinking about "commodity fetishism," where a material object or commodity replaces or substitutes for social relationships. Marx writes about the ability of capital to be fetishized, to attain a socially accepted symbolic power that appears to be real.[8] When Baudrillard expands this concept, he writes about a commodity's or an object's ability to stand in for, to signify, to become part of, or to define personal identity. Object fetishism occurs when one consumes an object that is perceived to have power, and that object in turn bestows some status upon the consumer. Therefore, objects of consumption have exchange value in a particular culture and can grant the consumer various attributes such as attractiveness or social prestige.[9] In this way, objects help establish personal identity or one's persona. Furthermore, commodities or objects have values that help to define how they describe personal identity: objects may have a "functional logic of use value," which describes the purpose of a commodity; "an economic logic of exchange value," "a logic of symbolic exchange," which is an arbitrary value of the object in relation to the owner of the object; and "a logic of sign value," which relates what social status a particular object bestows upon a subject. In his "logic of signification," objects achieve "the status of an *instrument*, a *commodity*, a *symbol*, or a *sign*."[10] The last of these, "sign," particularly comes into play with objects purchased with "discretionary income," money not needed for utility or symbol.[11] One can do a quick commodity value inventory of the motorcycle to see how motorcycles might function as social fetishes.

First, in terms of functional value, the motorcycle is limited. A motorcycle's function is to transport, and, in the days of high gas prices, the high fuel mileage of some motorcycles might give this function higher value. Nevertheless, the motorcycle as a means of transport is very limited unless you live in Southern California or somewhere with a similar climate. Bad weather makes a motorcycle unreliable and unsafe; limited storage capacity makes it difficult to transport anything other than lunch and a change of clothes; transporting more than two people at one time is not impossible but is not recommended. All in all, as a means of transportation, the motorcycle has less functional value than a car or truck. Second, the exchange value of a motorcycle is highly variable depending on size, make, and other factors. A very reliable, functional, and pretty bike can sell for as little as $6000; the average Harley retails for more than double that in the $12,000—$19,000 range, and can go much higher; a Honda Rune used to retail for about $27,000; and the one-off custom chopper can easily reach $70,000 or more. But in terms of exchange value, a motorcycle does not approach the value of other means of motorized transport like cars, and often quick depreciation can lead to very inexpensive motorcycles in the pre-owned market.

But while motorcycles do not compare well to cars in terms of functional or exchange value, the story changes when one considers symbolic exchange value and especially sign exchange value. While these are hard to measure, we might say something like the symbolic exchange value of a motorcycle is freedom or individuality within the social context. Isn't this what motorcycles symbolize in popular culture—freedom, individuality, and power? Yet these are arbitrary and agreed-upon symbols that may not have anything to do with the reality of the motorcycle. One is much less free on a motorcycle than in a car—on a motorcycle there are all sorts of limitations: weather, limited fuel capacity, few service outlets, and a motorcycle trip requires much more planning than one in a car. And individuality? While one major motorcycle manufacturer (Star motorcycles, a subsidiary of Yamaha) recently launched an ad campaign stressing its motorcycles' ability to reflect the rider's individuality, there is a circulating joke about bikers, those rugged individualists—thousands of individualists who wear the same leather boots, the same logo on t-shirts, and the same leather jackets while riding clones of the same motorcycles. Finally, there is sign exchange value, the value of an object in a system of objects. While a motorcycle may cost less than a car, they are not seen as a necessity, so their value in a system of transportation objects is higher. Motorcycles are often purchased with discretionary income. A particular motorcycle confers social status: new, expensive Harleys are owned by middle-aged, white-collar workers, doctors and lawyers; sport bikes are cheap and fast and are popular among the young, carefree set; Goldwings are for old folks; real patriots should only ride American-made motorcycles. Image and social status are symbolized by the bikes people ride in a way that Mercedes and BMWs also confer a particular social status upon the owners of those cars. So, from an analysis using the concept of commodity fetishism, one might argue that the motorcycle as fetish replaces, defines, and establishes certain social relationships in our culture. The motorcycle carries a mystique that helps to establish one's persona.

Finally, one type of defined social relationship established by and reinforced by motorcycle culture relates overtly to sexuality and gender. Biker rallies such as those held at Sturgis, Daytona Beach, and Myrtle Beach feature scantily clad women on the back of bikes. Part of the culture involves "breast flashing" for attendees at the rally or for the camera. Motorcycle websites are filled with bikini clad or nude "biker babes" posing seductively with motorcycles, with rally pictures featuring wet t-shirt contestants, breast flashers, or other nudity, and with more suggestive photos of nude female models in sexually provocative poses using a motorcycle as a sexual prop. Sometimes these models sit astride the bike and pose with the bike as a sexual substitute. Such an obvious manipulation of the bike with sexual overtones begs the question about sexual fetishism and the connection with masculinity.

Sigmund Freud's work on sexual fetishism highlights an obsessive equation of objects with body parts. For Freud, sexual fetishism occurs when the "normal sexual object is replaced by another which bears some relation to it, but is entirely unsuited to serve the normal sexual aim."[12] Normally, we think of underwear fetishes or leather fetishes (which may not be entirely irrelevant when talking about biker apparel) or foot fetishes. But what about the motorcycle as sexual fetish where the motorcycle itself is sexualized? Time and again we see advertisers making the connection. For example, a company called Hotbodies sells undertail exhausts and markets them alongside female models who display their tightly skirted derrieres. Another company markets bike exhaust pipes called "Jug huggers" and has used a buxom model wearing a tight shirt that partially exposes a breast to draw attention to the product. Motorcycle cylinders are often referred to as jugs, and the exhausts are attached to them, hug them so to speak. But this advertiser makes explicit what is only marginally implicit. Okay, so sex sells, and these could be just examples of how savvy companies try to get the attention of the predominantly male motorcycle riding community. But even motorcycle journalists use an abundance of sexual innuendo to sexualize motorcycles, as evidenced by a description of three adventure touring bikes in a review article. *Cycle World* described the BMW R1200GS, the Buell XB12X Ulysses, and the Ducati Multistrada 1000DS in the following way: "It's all long legs and short skirts when gazing at this semi-naked trio. If that doesn't arouse your adventuresome spirit, a ride aboard any of the three surely will."[13]

But motorcyclists not only sexualize motorcycles by substituting bikes for female bodies. Motorcycles can also perform the fetish function by serving as a phallic substitute. I already mentioned that female models are often depicted in sexually provocative poses with motorcycles—not only in advertisements but also in visual presentations completely separate from the need to sell something. In this sense, motorcycles can become phallic substitutes in subtle ways, and, again, I refer to Freud, where the fetish can substitute for the missing phallus in overview of the female anatomy. Thus, the fetish comes into play in male castration anxiety.[14] By substituting for the phallus, the fetish object can magically protect against castration. So, phallus substitutes, as fetishes, protect and promote virility and masculinity, and the motorcycle might function in this way through transference of power from the machine to its rider. In this case, it is most often the size of cylinder displacement that suggests the power of the motorcycle and reflects the power and masculinity of its rider. (Other measures of power are horsepower and torque, but displacement is the quintessential measure of strength.) Motorcycle companies compete for displacement supremacy, with recent years witnessing a marked increase in displacement size among all major motorcycle manufacturers. Touring bikes were once built in the 750–900cc ranges. Now mid-size cruisers sport 1100–1500cc engines and some top 2000cc. By comparison, the car I drive has a 1600cc engine, and the previous car I owned sported an 1100cc engine. If you don't think that size makes a statement in the motorcycle community about masculinity, ask someone who rides Harley-Davidson's smallest bike, the Sportster 883. While not small by historic standards at 883cc and over 500 pounds, this bike is known in the Harley world as a "chick bike" because of its "small" size. Men tend to opt for the 1200cc Sportster or one of Harley's larger models.

In any event, the motorcycle as sexual fetish seems to operate religiously by facilitating sexual prowess and power. The implication is that the motorcyclist will harness increased sexual attractiveness, the fetishized object acting as a type of aphrodisiac, stirring the sensual appetite of the rider and the desired companion. This implied connection to prowess becomes explicit in one of Harley-Davidson's television advertisements from a few years back. In this ad, a series of masculine men are left speechless and kissless on the doorstep by their dates, who end the dates abruptly. The frustration is etched upon each man's face. However, in the last scene of the commercial, the viewer does not see the expected jilted dater but rather a motorcycle (a Harley-Davidson motorcycle) parked by the curb with a red, lacy bra hanging from the handlebars. In the background, giggles emanate from the house. The implication, to put it politely, is that the Harley-Davidson man gets the girl.

Postmodern theorists essentially view fetishes as objects that stand in for, replace, or protect a missing or absent desire or a desire that is threatened in some way—power, beauty, wealth, virility; these desires are embodied in fetishes that in turn help to create the identity of those for whom the object serves as fetish. But postmodern theorists and Freudian thinkers tend to be myopic. It is one thing to use theory as a mode of analysis in order to provide an interesting perspective from which to observe and appreciate behavior and activities; it is quite another thing to say these theories actually tell us what is going on with the behaviors under observation.

Whether or not motorcycles function as fetishes to define identity and social relations in American culture, motorcycles have functioned as an icon in popular American culture for more than a century—more so since the 1960s and 1970s. I think part of this reflects the influence of two cultural products of the time period: the 1969 movie, *Easy Rider*, and the 1974 novel, *Zen and the Art of Motorcycle Maintenance*. Both reflect the mood of the times, and the motorcycle in each serves as the vehicle for counter-cultural values and spiritual journey. The bikers in these works, while very different from one another, share the road that offers a spiritual journey unmediated by the trappings of contemporary life. The motor-cycle, both in these stories and in the dreams of countless bikers and would-be bikers, symbolizes freedom, journey, escape, and immediacy of experience, while contemporary society seems to promote conformity and predictability.

Easy Rider chronicles the cross-country journey of Wyatt (Captain America) and Billy on choppers while rock-and-roll tunes like Steppenwolf's "Born to Be Wild" and The Byrds' "I Wasn't Born to Follow" provide the appropriate soundtrack. The journey takes Wyatt (Peter Fonda) and Billy (Dennis Hopper) in and out of the lives of farmers, hippies, and the like, highlighting the cultural fissures that characterized the 1960s. Rock-and-roll music, drugs, counter-culture values, hippie idealism, and freedom from responsibility characterize the duo, yet, far from being idealized in the movie, such values lead to confusion, depression, and ultimately murder. Nevertheless the motorcycle, with all its attendant associations and images, characterizes the journey and highlights the social disil-lusionment of the 1960s counterculture. Near the beginning of the movie, Wyatt, Captain America, tosses his watch and begins his journey, thus freeing himself and Billy from the constraints of time, past and future, and embarking on the timeless spiritual odyssey that marks their adventure.

From that point, the journey of Captain America and Billy is an epic one of spiritual import. Based on the ideals championed by Jack Kerouac in the novel *On the Road* (1957) and a generation of Beat poets and philosophers, Wyatt and Billy are wanderers on a barren landscape, restless in their world, seeking enlightenment through a series of encounters, characters, and a pilgrimage to New Orleans. However, these wanderers, pilgrims, who are beyond time and place (no watch, no roots), beyond traditional ethics and morality (no responsi-bilities, few limits on indulgences such as sex and drugs) end up dead by the road side after being gunned down by stereotypical rednecks in a pickup truck. The rednecks represent a society that is threatened by the independence and limitless freedom of these easy riders, a society that will stop at nothing to prevent that type of unfettered idealism. As pilgrims who are liberated from space and time, Wyatt and Billy transcend the limits of society and become true spiritual pilgrims, limitless in possibility and magnitude. And, like any true spiritual visionary, their transcendent state cannot be understood or tolerated by those bound by time and space, and they are martyred by the unenlightened.

And this is the spiritual power Captain America has bequeathed American motorcycle culture. The promise of pilgrimage; the promise of sacred power through a journey that is timeless and transcendent of space resonates and persists through the motorcycle persona, the image, the myth, and the machine. *Easy Rider* cemented into American popular consciousness the image of motorcycles as chariots of the spiritual journey—a powerful chariot that continues to be threatening to some and liberating to others.

In 1974, Robert Pirsig published *Zen and the Art of Motorcycle Maintenance*, a classic American book that builds on the image of the motorcycle as freedom and pilgrimage chariot. In Pirsig's autobiographical novel, the narrator takes the reader on a cross-country motorcycle trip with his son and friends. Along the way, the narrator treats the reader to a "chautauqua," a series of lectures on metaphysics and philosophy that are interspersed into the travel journal. The book is complex and operates on several levels. Motorcycle maintenance is metaphorical not only of work done to keep a machine in working order but of work done to allow the individual to experience virtue, to experience "living right." The narrator reasons: "The real cycle you're working on is a cycle called yourself."[15] The narrator works on this "cycle" with religious devotion throughout. When the narrator occupies himself with the unpleasant task of cleaning the cycle, he does so with ritualistic care in "the way people go to church—not so much to discover anything new … but mainly to reacquaint myself with the familiar."[16] The care the narrator gives his motorcycle is ritual, reacquaintance, renewal. And when the narrator performs the more interesting and novel maintenance tasks, he does so with religious devotion. As he adjusts the tappets on his motorcycle, the narrator muses, "I always feel like I'm in church when I do this … The gage is some kind of religious icon and I'm performing a holy rite with it."[17]

Perhaps the primary metaphor at work in the book revolves around the motorcycle trip that provides the plot parameters for Pirsig. The journey carries the pilgrimage motif with it, and Pirsig's narrator becomes a "pioneer … looking onto a promised land."[18] The motorcycle journey becomes metaphorical on at least three levels: the narrator is on a journey to reestablish a relationship with his son; the narrator is on a journey to reestablish a relationship with himself, a self that was lost to electroshock therapy and mental illness; the narrator is on a journey to the heart of the Western philosophical system in order to dismantle and rebuild Western philosophy by replacing Truth and rationality with Quality and virtue. But the spiritual journey motif is at the heart of the book at every level, symbolized by the motorcycle that makes these journeys possible, and the narrator tells the reader why it must be a motorcycle and not a car. There is an immediacy to experience on board a motorcycle that is not available in a car—the "concrete whizzing by five inches below your foot" demands immediacy of attention, "immediate consciousness," and reminds one constantly of the rider's vulnerability or contingency.[19] Such contingency is preliminary and preparatory to real enlightenment. Furthermore, the motorcycle enlarges the rider's sight to allow for alternative visions. Car riders are restricted to a vision that is framed and scripted by the boundaries set by windows and windshields. Like watching television, they can see no more than the frame allows. By contrast, the rider has no restriction—the field of vision is unlimited[20]—Vision in the sense of Emerson can take place—alternative worlds can be imagined—reality beyond what society has prescribed and narrowly allowed can be discovered.

Thus liberated, the narrator in *Zen and the Art of Motorcycle Maintenance* embarks upon a spiritual journey that presents the reader a new way of envisioning reality; a new worldview built partly from Buddhist humanism and partly from the teachings of the Sophists. The motorcycle allows the narrator to envision reality without the frame and to see anew the roots of Western philosophy. Once Western philosophy is liberated, a whole new metaphysics emerges into relief. But this new metaphysics is simply the rediscovery of an ancient metaphysics, based upon the Good represented by the Sophists, which lost out to the philosophy of the True, represented by Plato. The mind and soul of Western thought turned on that distinction, according to Pirsig,[21] and that has made all the difference. Pirsig challenges the reader to imagine Western civilization had the Sophists won the argument, and in his metaphysical musings one can see the nascent murmurings of postmodern challenges to Truth. The result of embracing the new metaphysics is visionary, enlightening, revelatory, and liberating. And the motorcycle journey/pilgrimage makes this spiritual enlightenment and power possible and available by breaking the frame and expanding vision. Like *Easy Rider*, this book depends on the motorcycle as a vehicle of freedom that leads to enlightenment and release from the constricted seeing of traditional society and values. Unlike *Easy Rider*, *Zen and the Art of Motorcycle Maintenance* ends with a note of hope: father and son connect; insanity and sanity merge; Western philosophy is redefined in ways allowing for spiritual expansion. In any event, these two pop culture products have given us an image of the motorcycle that has persisted. The motorcycle is a "freedom machine," and in that independence lies power: raw, sexual, and symbolic, this power comes as spiritual energy begetting vision, transcendence, and the means to journey to the horizon of reality and to leave time and space behind.

Profiles of religious motorcycle organizations

Biker churches have begun to proliferate across my part of North Carolina and are common in other places across the country. These churches are quite disparate in terms of their association with the symbols and caricatures one normally associates with the biker community; however, most of them are built on the foundation of a mutual love of motorcycling and Christ. In addition to these biker churches, national and international organizations exist that combine the love of riding and commitment to a religious persuasion. Most of these groups depend on the cultural associations with motorcycling in either a positive or a negative way: positive association involves using the metaphorical freedom valued by bikers to illustrate the spiritual freedom promised through religion; negative association often taps the cultural bad-boy image of bikers to model the power of religion to turn lives around—to save one from the road to perdition, so to speak. Nevertheless, whatever the focus, biker churches and religious motorcycle organizations have become part of the American cultural landscape that represents the permeable boundaries between secular and sacred.

Most religious motorcycle organizations highlight their group in terms of creating a brotherhood or sisterhood and, thus, focus on the communitas aspect of motorcycling. Motorcyclists tend to be tribal anyway, identifying with a particular biker culture based on the brand or type of bike they ride. Of course, there are Harley riders and Harley "culture," but there are also café racers, BMW elitists, Goldwing tourers, dual sport adventurers, sport bike hooligans, vintage connoisseurs, dirt bike athletes, and the like. Many riders identify along the lines of kinship based on brand or type, and this reinforcement of communitas can be felt through both belonging and exclusion throughout the motorcycling community—e.g. only Harleys are welcome at some rallies. Likewise, the religious motorcycling groups emphasize communitas based on faith. The King David Riders feel that riding reinforces their connection to Judaism and other Jews. The Christian Motorcyclists feel a special connection to brothers and sisters in Christ. Motorcycling, an activity that seemingly has nothing to do with religion, has co-opted a sacred context to create a communitas depending on both a religious context and larger context of bikers in the culture. As such, these religious biker communities mimic the tribalism intrinsic in much of motorcycling and represent the sacralization of the secular in American popular culture.

Biker churches—Freedom Biker Church

Biker churches are everywhere. I chose to highlight the Freedom Biker Church because of its proximity to my home. The Freedom Biker Church is a network of biker churches headquartered in Angier, North Carolina. According to their website, the churches in the network are committed to freedom and brotherhood: the freedom of the road and the freedom of Christ; the brotherhood of bikers and the brotherhood of believers. The website declares: "We are a brotherhood of bikers bound by a faith relationship in Jesus Christ, a passion for bikers and the freedom of the open road; bikers reaching bikers with the message of true freedom in Jesus Christ."[22] One of the header bars of the website reads "Black Leather. Tattoos. And Jeans {Proper Sunday Attire}."[23] This, plus the photos of bikers on the webpage, advertise the potential clientele for the church, but the site also suggests all bikers are welcome and has photos of at least one sportbike rider in racing leathers. The Core Value statement includes a "*real*, personal Relationship with Jesus Christ," but also affirmation of "the Biker way of life."[24] While it is not clear what is meant by the Biker way of life, brotherhood and freedom seem to be the main elements of this lifestyle. I would also add acceptance of Biker appearance to be a main attribute to this value. The website also includes a Statement of Faith that includes traditional views of the Trinity, substitutionary atonement, and Baptist views on Ordinances. The Statement of Faith is partly modeled on and even references the Southern Baptist Faith and Message.[25]

The Freedom Biker Church website at first glance could be any biker website full of leather, tattoos, and bearded bikers. It even has a space for Biker B.A.B.E.S. (Bold and Beautiful Eternal Sisters). But this is no ordinary biker website. It is clear that this community, while tapping into the cultural biker context, establishes a different communitas, one built on the dual affiliation to biker culture and Christian ecclesia. While the brotherhood and sisterhood of this ecclesia may look different from that at the First Baptist Church, it is no less real, and it is reinforced by the real communitas established by sharing biker values as well.

Religious biker groups

Apart from the growing number of biker churches springing up around the country, there also exist a number of organizations with clubs and chapters that are sponsored by religious groups or that constitute a religious organization. Christian Motorcyclists Association, for example, and King David Bikers exist to organize like-minded religious riders for rides, pilgrimages, missions, or other religiously oriented activities. Unlike the biker churches, these groups usually do not have set meetings in set places with set congregations. Rather they are more loose-knit groups each bound by common values and a common religious commitment. The fact that they like to ride gives them an additional reason to congregate and meet for group rides. Sometimes the focus is on establishing and reinforcing communitas, as it is with the King David Bikers, which mentions on its website the need to nurture community within the Jewish population.[26] And sometimes the focus seems more externally focused, as might be the case with the Christian Motorcyclists Association, which was founded in part to provide a positive Christian witness at motorcycle rallies.[27] So there seems to be a dual purpose for such organizations: to nurture communitas and to provide a means of outreach to the larger motorcycling community.

King David Bikers

King David Bikers was established as a Jewish motorcycle riders' organization founded to promote fellowship and education for Jewish motorcyclists in south Florida. The group sponsors rides, maintains a newsletter and website, and supports Jewish charities and causes. The two prerequisites for membership are a "passion to ride" and "faith as a Jew."[28] The group was started in 2004 and is affiliated to the Jewish Motorcyclists Alliance (JMA).[29] This Alliance is an umbrella organization for a variety of Jewish motorcycle groups, such as Hillel's Angels of New Jersey.[30] Having never attended a JMA event, it is difficult to characterize the group with accuracy, but given the information about them on the websites and in the media, it appears this group of bikers gather for the same reason any others do—for the ride. Nevertheless, Jewish faith and observance are never far from the center of their meetings. King David Bikers even hosts an unofficial rabbi, Rabbi Zig Zag. While King David Bikers seems to use motorcycles to reinforce the religious identity of its members, it could be just the other way around. Perhaps it is the identity as Jewish American that reinforces the camaraderie experienced through their passion for riding.

It is in this dialectic that the role of communitas in establishing social and religious context comes into play. While the members of King David Bikers are bound by a common faith, it is a faith that in many ways has been "othered" in American culture (see chapter 1). To the extent that Jewish Americans feel "other than" other Americans due to their religion or their culture, their common interest in motorcycling, a distinctive part of American culture, aids in forging a communitas outside of the minority religious community. So, while the context of the King David Bikers is Judaism, the communitas of bikers allows them to embrace and be embraced by the broader American culture. In this way, King David Bikers allows its members to actively contextualize their community in a way that affirms the group (positive othering, see chapter 1). In a wonderful YouTube video, Rabbi Zig Zag talks about the King David Bikers' dual context as Jews and as bikers. He explains the group's purpose as reinforcing Jewish observance and identity in a positive way. For Rabbi Zig Zag the teffilin act as metaphors just as the motorcycle leathers—in both instances, the leather is protection. The teffilin is God's protection, and, like the freedom one experiences on the bike, it breaks "through limitations" and brings "the spiritual into the physical world" by "taking something physical and ... transcending it into something Holy."[31] But Rabbi Zig Zag also affirms that putting on the teffilin connects him to every other Jew in the world much like riding the motorcycle connects him to others in the group—the motorcycle, like Judaism, creates communitas, and it is in this context that the group maintains identity and power.

Christian Motorcyclists Association

On October 22, 2011, Herb Shreve, the founder of the Christian Motorcyclists Association (CMA), died. Herb founded the CMA in 1975 as an evangelistic outreach to the motorcycling community. Today, there are over 1000 chapters of the CMA, and the Association boasts international chapters as well. In 2011, the CMA was able to donate in excess of 3.7 million dollars to its partner ministries and has donated more the 40.7 million dollars in the past 24 years.[32] These totals represent significant accomplishments for the group, and the CMA should be considered a major para-religious group in the United States and even internationally. The main focus of the CMA is evangelical outreach, and the group achieves this vision through both a positive presence at motorcycle rallies and the significant gifts it makes through its Run for the Son program. The doctrinal statement on the CMA website is Trinitarian with fundamentalist influence, proclaiming beliefs in an infallible scripture, virgin birth, substitutionary atonement, sanctifying power of the Holy Spirit, and second coming.

But why motorcycles—there are plenty of evangelical outreach missions that do not involve biker rallies and events. In the case of the CMA, it seems that motorcycles are the primary purpose of such an evangelical community. It is important for this group to be part of that communitas that identifies with bikers, largely, it seems, because the biker community has such a reputation for "bad-boy" behavior. Nevertheless, the ministry is focused on the biker community, and the CMA sponsors several ministries that address the needs of bikers at rallies, including ministries that sponsor biker games and mechanical services. This is a true niche organization that has a powerful presence in the motorcycling community, and for its members tribal association is proclaimed through vest patches, clothing, tattoos, and other identifying markers that help to create and reinforce communitas. Once again, a secular cultural activity, motorcycling and attendance at motorcycle rallies, has been sacralized by the CMA in a way that bends and blends the boundaries defining secular and sacred activities.

"Before there were motorcycles …"

… there were horses … and cowboys. If motorcycles are an American icon that allows one to blend the sacred and secular around the concept of communitas, then certainly a meta-narrative centered on the mythos of the American West would prompt such a socio-cultural sacralizing tendency. The myth of the American West, built on virtues such as individualism, honor, freedom, and masculinity, almost exactly parallels the mythos of the motorcycle context. Whether in the saddle of a horse or a motorcycle, the rider forges an identity and context with fellow riders. Motorcyclists and cowboys alike engage in dangerous activity, and this risk-taking behavior helps to forge their community bond. Faith surviving danger is a faith magnified ... just ask any snake handler. So it should be of no surprise that faith communities center on high-risk activities and the attendant feeling of transcendence that survival of such activities bring. Horse-back riding, bull riding, rodeo, guns—all this makes up the mythos at the heart of "cowboy churches" that can be found across the American landscape.

The American Fellowship of Cowboy Churches[33] and small cowboy congregations across the country blend the Western mythos and the Christian faith in a way that attempts to create a more authentic faith—one that is untainted by the by-products of our industrial and technological ages. Cowboy Churches locate true connection to God spatially in the outdoors, chronologically in the pre-industrial American West, and theologically in a simple, straightforward gospel that seeks authenticity through a way of life, the cowboy way, and the virtues that accompany it (honesty, goodness, thrift, and honor). It is a gospel of salvation based on grace, but is also a gospel of proverbs based on behavior. And those who follow this gospel reinforce it through group activities and even group dress. Cowboy clothing includes proper boots, Western jeans, belt buckles, authentic hats, and shirts with snaps rather than buttons. Communitas is behavior-, belief-, and lifestyle-based, and the context, the cowboy context, reinforces the Christian commitment. Once again, the secular is sacralized in boundary-bending communitas building.

Love Valley, which was highlighted in chapter 5, did not host a cowboy church for most of its history. Now, however, along with the Love Valley Presbyterian Church, there is also the Cowboy Christian Fellowship, a non-denominational, Love Valley-based, cowboy church. The existence of a cowboy church in Love Valley, the quintessential cowboy town in western North Carolina, makes perfect sense. However, long before the appearance of this congregation, the utopian experiment that defines Love Valley had established a meta-narrative based on the cowboy mystique and mythos. Since the 1950s, Love Valley has based life on a sacred appropriation of the cowboy myth, and communitas has depended on reality maintenance of that myth. What one sees in the "sacred cowboy persona" in Love Valley or in the cowboy church, one also sees in the biker persona of King David Bikers—an identity forged through connection not only with a group but with a context—an identity built through communitas, sacred and secular, and honed at the edge of danger through awe and transcendence.

Study guide

Important words and concepts

C. G. Jung

Commodity fetishism

Communitas

Cowboy church

Disavowal

Fetishism/fetish

Metaphysics

Para-religious group

Persona

Sigmund Freud

Sophism

Talisman

Study questions

(1) How do religious motorcycle groups or Cowboy Churches build communitas through establishing a particular persona for their members?

(2) Describe fetishism.

(3) What role do motorcycles play in popular culture?

(4) Think of a para-religious group that you have encountered from your own experience. How do concepts like communitas, persona, and fetishism play out in these groups?

Guided watching and reading

(1) Watch the film *Easy Rider*. Read the section entitled "Pilgrimage" from the Qur'an. What elements do the sacred prescriptions for pilgrimage in the Qur'an share with the secular pilgrimage of the protagonists from *Easy Rider*.

12

Emerging Religion: Machine guns, post-Christian churches, the Internet, snakes, and science

Sam Childers, a.k.a. the "Machine Gun Preacher," shares a compelling story. What brought him to the Southern Sudan and locked him in battle with groups like the Lord's Resistance Army to rescue and liberate children who had been kidnapped and enslaved? What led him to choose building an orphanage in the Sudan rather than pay his mortgage back home in Pennsylvania? What possessed him to risk life and limb, to sleep with an AK-47 and a Bible, and to continue to lead raids to find and liberate children? What turn of events created the Shekinah Fellowship Church in Central City, Pennsylvania, the spiritual home of the "Machine Gun Preacher," and the core of Sam's vision of missions in a world with "No borders. No restraints." The answer, according to Sam, is clear. While doing mission work in the Southern Sudan, Sam heard God speak.[1]

If the above profile is not remarkable enough, it should also be noted that Childers accomplished these things after turning from a life of violence, crime, and drugs. A hard-living biker, Sam was constantly in trouble until he turned to God through the influence of his wife, Lynn. The story is not so different from thousands of testimonials given by Christians who found in religion meaning and purpose; salvation and life, except by degrees of intensity. Sam's story pushes the boundaries, and while some have challenged parts of his story and even the legitimacy of his orphanage, the results of Sam's efforts as told in his autobiography are nothing short of remarkable. Sam is a gun toting preacher who liberates enslaved children in Africa, who rides his bike and looks every bit the part of a hardened biker gang member, and who travels the country speaking about the dangers of drug addiction and alcohol abuse—this should be the stuff of movies, not real life. But now we have an example of art imitating life, because the film industry has noticed the story, and the 2011 movie, "Machine Gun Preacher," stars Gerard Butler as the unconventional Childers.

As engaging and exhilarating as Childers' story is, his is but a paradigm of a late-twentieth- and twenty-first-century pattern of what some see as a kind of postmodern and even post-Christian church. Childers embodies the type of Christianity that has abandoned the traditional institutional structures, the age-old theologies, and the stolid and stilted worship patterns of the past. The pattern sees non-denominational movements that focus more on praxis than theological sophistication—doing rather than believing. And while not all of these late twentieth-century praxis oriented religious groups carry machine guns into the Sudan, the sentiment is the same—if Christianity is to be relevant in a postmodern or even post-Christian world, it must be a Christianity that has gravitas around the globe, a Christianity that is responsive to pain and suffering, a Christianity that makes a difference with "boots on the ground," so to speak. This is religion that illustrates emerging into being, emerging into significance, and emerging into culture. This is religion that is embracing being, embracing significance, and embracing culture. This is religion that is experimental, bold, and barrier busting. And this is religion that more than anything else challenges the church of the twenty-first century to break out of worn molds and to emerge on the scene with something tangible to offer, something redeeming to grasp, and something real to claim.

This new paradigm, more than anything else, depends on redefining communitas, or context, and that is why it is so challenging to the traditional church. Childers, ecumenists, and many others experimenting with the new patterns of the "Emerging Church," all have something in common. They have found the traditional institutional structures and the context they foster to be lacking. They have found the traditional communitas to be shackled, quaint, and sequestered in safe, orthodox, and creed-bound communities. The new post-Christian vision of communitas involves redefining that part of the religious order so as to expand more inclusively what it means to be a community in relation to God. To see this more clearly, imagine that a reality, metaphysically defined, is made up of a triadic relationship of being.[2] The triad relates God, the individual, and the communitas as in the Figure 12.1.

The triad is not unlike the social order as envisioned by Confucius for ancient Chinese society. For Confucius, the self, or the individual, has no existence except in relation to a communitas, the various orders of society defined by filial piety: the family, the society, the government, the world. In the words of Hustin Smith,

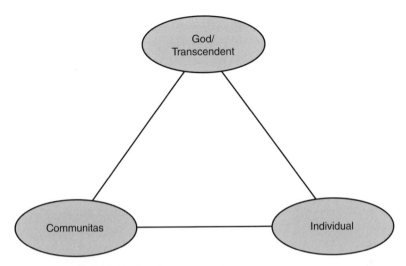

Figure 12.1 God, the individual, and the communitas.

"The self *is* a center of relationships. It is constructed through its interactions with others and is defined by the sum of its social roles."[3] And in Confucian society, all social roles were legitimized by the decree from Heaven through the emperor, so the divine intrudes into this relationship between individual and communitas as a third partner. Thus, self-centered and selfish concern is countered by family, community, national, and human responsibilities, all arranged by a transcendent and metaphysical order.[4] Shifting demands of the communitas necessarily create appropriate response or consent from the other two partners in the trinity, and vice versa. The goal of the individual is to so order life that proper actions strengthen the communitas and respond to the needs of the context. In doing so, the context, the communitas, is changed in subtle and sometimes not-so-subtle ways. This is what Sam Childers and others are doing—they are defining and responding to the needs of a particular communitas in light of what they believe to be transcendent (divine) order. As a result, they bring into relief the failure of existing forms of communitas by revising and restructuring a new context that moves the triadic relationships toward harmony.

Such a paradigm is also implied by the Puritan experiment in the New World. Sensing an imbalance in the nature of relationship between self, community, and God, the Puritan "city on a hill" was an attempt to rebalance the triad. Often, the Puritan community in the New World is portrayed as a hierarchical society that subjugated individuals through authoritarian dictates from religious leaders who acted for God. Nathaniel Hawthorne helped to perpetuate this view of Puritan society through his novel, *The Scarlet Letter*. And while there might be some truth to this portrayal of the Puritan worldview, especially seen through the

Enlightenment lens that ultimately shaped the founding of the United States, the Puritan experiment is better understood by using the triadic relationship as a template. The Puritans understood individual concern and action in the context of religious community, and the religious community was organized by divine mandate. So, however, oppressive twenty-first-century Americans might believe Puritan society to have been, it was meant to be an experiment in redefining communitas in such a way that established mutual responsibility between the three parties of the triad. When all parties lived up to their responsibility, then harmony in society was maintained. If one individual or the community or even, in theory, if God were to shirk duty, then harmony would be disrupted. A sermonic form, the "jeremiad," was formulated to bring prophetic insight to the source of breakdown when judgment seemingly visited Puritan society.[5] The Puritans understood this harmonic balance in terms of "covenant" based on their understanding of the covenantal relationship God established with Abraham and the people of Israel. Intrinsic to this covenant from Jewish history is the triad: God, Abraham, Israel.

In these two examples, ancient Confucian society and Puritan Covenantal society, reality was understood as a harmonic triad relating the individual to communitas in light of transcendent dictate. What Confucius and the Puritans achieved was a reorganization of the social structure in light of this triadic relationship. In both cases, the prevailing context for community was redefined and a new communitas emerged. This is what is happening with Sam Childers, religious bikers, and various contemporary church paradigms. Whether known as ecumenism or, more specifically, as the Emerging Church, the Christian community can no longer ignore the Sam Childerses of the world, or the meeker and milder Brian McLarens.

The Emerging Church paradigm

While the ministers, leaders, and theologians of the phenomenon known as the Emerging Church normally do not carry guns, they do carry a big stick, and at least some of them hope to bring a radical change to the Christian landscape on the order of Luther's society-transforming reformation of the sixteenth century.[6] The leaders of the Emerging Church sense a redefinition of the prevailing church context and are seeking to create a new and revolutionary communitas that brings fundamental change to traditional worship and religious communities. Assuming the above triadic relationship accurately describes the social construct of religious reality, this means that fundamental changes to how individuals operate in the religious context are in order and that fundamental changes to how they perceive the transcendent are demanded. Perhaps this means also that the transcendent realm itself must evolve and change in light of the reordered communitas.[7] This, I believe, is exactly what is implied by the changing paradigms instituted by the Emerging Church movement. The metaphor can be extended in light of triadic relational theology: An emerging church demands emerging Christians AND an emerging God.

What is the Emerging Church? Depending on one's relationship to the movement, it might be seen as the next grand departure of the Church that will continue to grow around the world or the beginnings of the Church's descent into irretrievable darkness. Whatever its character, the Emerging Church should rightly be understood as a movement or direction in the Christian community that is largely responding to postmodern developments and post-foundationalist thought within theological circles. Some believe the foundations of the movement can be traced to the post-liberal theological constructions of the latter twentieth century. John Franke traces the origins of the emerging movement to the post-liberal agenda of Hans Frei, a Yale theologian. Franke identifies emerging thought as reacting against the foundationalism of the modern, Enlightenment variety and, thus, establishes emerging thought as thoroughly postmodern. Franke discards modernist labels like conservative and liberal as descriptors of truth for less restrictive non-foundationalist ways of talking about "commitments" rather than truths.[8] If we combine all these potential points of origin and influence, postmodern, post-foundational, and post-liberal, we can isolate a pattern that is repeated in the emerging phenomenon.

Postmodernism has, more than anything, called into question the assumption that there are certain undeniable and universal truths, which exist independent of cultures and cultural products like language and religion. The postmodern critique of culture eventually became engaged in the politics of power as previous foundational, cultural truths were questioned, struck down, and replaced. Postmodern assumptions as applied to philosophy and theology go hand in hand with a position sometimes called post-foundationalism, the philosophical perspective that there can be no normative or objective truth in reality.[9] Such thought has sometimes been located in postliberal theological thinking, which includes the position that Christian belief and faith are part of culture and language. Such a position gives great power to the contemporary communitas, because it is the community of faith that becomes the arbiter of truth. Biblical interpretation becomes an outgrowth of the communitas, and truth is truth only to the extent that truth is sanctioned by the communitas. For those drawn to this postliberal perspective, postmodernism frees the community from anachronisms and irrelevant creedal positions while liberating the community to discover relevance in texts, language, and religious positions. One might say that culture trumps tradition in defining what is true or what is important, and that religion, if it is to remain relevant, must yield to contemporary culture. This becomes another example of the blurred and permeable boundaries that exist between secular culture and religious culture, and in this instance represents the secularization of the sacred—the movement of sacred reality constructions toward contemporary cultural constructions of truth. In literary theory, this outgrowth is sometimes called "reader response criticism," where the meaning of a literary work is unpacked based on what type of reality perspective the work creates with the reader. This reality perspective produces the only truth of the book, apart from meaning that might have been intended by the author and despite whatever canonical or orthodox truth tradition might have held for the text. As applied to religion, we might call this perspective "cultural response faith" where truth is defined more by contemporary culture than by unchallenged original sources or traditional interpretations.

Whether the emerging phenomenon is based on this or not, it certainly has been influenced by this line of thinking, and the result is an ecumenical approach to creating Christianity that is ultimately and mostly responsive to contemporary culture. Such a perspective tends to favor praxis/practice over creed and consensus over orthodoxy. Critiques of this perspective suggest that emerging thinkers allow truth to be sacrificed, or at least hedged, for expediency. Proponents tend to see truth as a moving target, relative to the situation and communitas, so, once again, the communitas emerges as a powerful agent in the process of defining religious significance and truth. The emerging community tends to be dissatisfied with traditional forms of worship, missions, and ways of defining communitas and has set out to redefine "church" in light of contemporary demands. This willingness to suspend attachment to tradition and to forge new patterns of allegiance is aptly illustrated with the rather long and satirical byline of Brian McLaren's book, *A Generous Orthodoxy*. McLaren, a leading proponent of the emerging movement, adds an explanation to the cover of his book that is not exactly a subtitle but that lays out the direction of his "generous orthodoxy" project. McLaren adds, "WHY I AM A missional + evangelical + post/protestant + liberal/conservative +mystical/poetic + biblical + charismatic/contemplative +fundamentalist/ calvinist + anabaptist/anglican + methodist + catholic + green + incarnational + depressed-yet-hopeful + emergent + unfinished CHRISTIAN".[10] By including his litany of labels, McLaren suggests that no label is sufficient and that all labels are deficient. Or he attempts half-heartedly to be all-inclusive with his generous orthodoxy, allowing that all labeled Christians are welcome. The litany capitalizes the first four words and the last, so that one way of reading this "subtitle" is that the titles that separate Christians represent unimportant, traditional, creedal institutions that claim a certain truth when the only thing of importance is "WHY I AM A ... CHRISTIAN." Thus we have McLaren's, and the emergent community's, basic starting point—any institution that claims exclusive, objective truth must be discarded in exchange for a more universalistic and inclusive set of cultural needs/truths represented by the universal title, CHRISTIAN.

The Emerging Church is less a church, if church is defined as institution, and more an ecclesia, or community that outstrips institutional affiliation. So, the emerging community does not want to be thought of as a denomination in the same way as Methodists, Baptists, or Presbyterians think of themselves. Neither do the emergents want to be considered a tradition in the way we think of the Roman Catholic or Orthodox traditions. In this way, proponents of emerging Christianity consider themselves a model of the New Testament community, with the emphasis on communitas more than anything. But it is certainly not New Testament culturally because emergent theology demands that communitas be defined in light of contemporary culture rather than ancient. The emerging movement strives to be responsive to the changing cultural landscape rather than base a community on principles/truths held by the early church of the first century. For example, Paul's admonition (in 1 Corinthians, ch. 11) for women to veil themselves should appear to be a ludicrous suggestion for the emerging Christians by their own emphasis on contemporary culture. But what the emerging Christian should be concerned with is the multiple ways women are symbolically or in reality held in submissive and oppressive roles in contemporary society, especially where Christianity tends to be silent or passive.

If the Emerging Church is not a church in the institutional sense, how do we know it when we see it? If a duck is known by its appearance and sound, as in "if it walks like a duck and quacks like a duck," then how do we recognize an emerging community when we see one? The first thing to note is that the emerging movement is certainly not homogenous. In fact, many go to great lengths to distinguish between the words "emerging" and "emergent." Emergent is associated with the Emergent Village, a more official, if not institutional, organization founded on the principles of emerging thought. It is thought by many to be too much aligned with institutional trappings and, thus, representative of what emerging thought should be emerging from. Surely the Emergent Village itself recognizes this contradiction as it uses strained and stretched language on its website to avoid presenting itself as an organization: the Emergent Village is a "friendship," not a church; a "group," not an institution, a "network," not an organization. And when finally the word "organization" is used to characterize the Village, it is used to describe "an organization around our friendship."[11] So, if an organization like the Emergent Village disdains being an organization, and if many within the emerging movement distance themselves from organized religion, it is difficult to point to something in emerging Christianity and say, "if it looks like this, it must be emerging." If one can do this, then the emerging group probably comes too close to something that could be identified as an institution.

The fear of institutionalization is central to this movement in that it began, at least in part, in disillusionment over the institutional character of traditional

Christianity. Many fear something akin to the development within Barton Stone's movement whose followers wished to be known only as "Christians" but which later joined the Campbellites and developed into the "Christian Church" or "Disciples of Christ." This tendency to denominationalize is exactly what emerging leaders do not want, but the temptation to organize is almost too much to overcome. At least for the present, if one cannot point to the "Emerging Denomination" in the traditional sense and isolate a creed or structure by which to identify the movement, one can isolate common characteristics in the emerging movement. Once these common traits are identified, it becomes easier to recognize these characteristics among existing churches and institutions rather than to create something we can identify as an Emerging Institution. In fact, emerging trends have played a large role in creating change among traditional institutions in terms of worship patterns and even theological positions.

What, then, are some emerging tendencies? As mentioned earlier, this is not a homogenous movement, but it is one that promotes certain ideals. In an article for *Christianity Today*, Scot McKnight isolates "five streams" or tendencies within emerging thought. The first stream is "prophetic rhetoric" that is "deliberately provocative."[12] It should be noted what is the target for emerging provocative rhetoric. The target is not secular culture or the traditional Church's alliance with culture. Rather, emerging tendencies align themselves with popular culture and speak out against the traditional Church's resistance to change. The second stream is postmodernism in a variety of flavors. The essential element is that emerging thought challenges long-held absolutist truth narratives in favor of culturally imbedded truth narratives. Third, emerging thought is praxis- or practice-oriented. Emerging Christians tend to be creative in worship, focused on a living faith based on ethical standards, and missional, the word used to describe outreach that is centered on redemptive, humanistic work in society and among individuals. Fourth, emerging Christians tend to be post-evangelical, by which McKnight means "post-systematic" theology and inclusive rather than exclusive. Finally, McKnight suggests that emerging movements tend to be political in a social gospel, social work sort of way—they are involved in and through the political process in much the same way emerging folk tend to embrace the larger culture.[13] McLaren spends a book trying to get at what emerging Christianity is, and perhaps his most concise statement is the nonsensical and comically creedal proclamation "that relativists are right in their denunciation of absolutism ... absolutists are right in their denunciation of relativism ... they are both wrong because the answer lies beyond both absolutism and relativism."[14] Yet, it is never quite clear what or where that beyond might be found.

It seems that the emerging movement is attempting to emerge *from* something but its own limitations will not allow it to emerge *to* something else. It wants to emerge from the hierarchies and anachronism of traditional faith communities; however, its egalitarian and unfettered ideals will not allow it to become something other than tendencies or guidelines or directions. The movement resists institutionalization as the end of "emergence," yet it cannot quite grasp what the movement is evolving *toward*. For something to fully emerge, it must come into being at some point, and it seems that this is the evolutionary step that frightens or baffles emergent leaders. In the end, emergent movements will probably either become what they fear most or cease to be a relevant and substantial force in the Church.

Up to now, the Emerging Church has been characterized as postmodern, as if this is an evolutionary movement out of modernism toward some new horizon. But if there is no horizon that can be sighted, the movement will lose its way and become not a forward-looking revolutionary movement but rather a backward-looking retreat behind what it is rebelling against. The emerging movement is defined against modernism, and it runs the risk of being more reactionary than revolutionary if it fails to articulate a consistent and realizable vision. If this danger is realized, the Emerging Church will die the relativist's death—once the current milieu ceases to resonate, so will the emerging milieu's defined cultural products cease to attract. Peter L. Berger points to the Catholic Church's attempt to embrace contemporary culture through its program of updating known as "aggiornamento" following the Vatican II Council. For example, says Berger, the accommodations made to contemporary society, such as saying Mass in the vernacular, led to the most unsettling period of the Church's history since the Protestant reformations.[15] While the Catholic Church has not ceased to exist, the irony of this example should be obvious—in the attempt to make worship more palatable, the Church created a crisis. This is the danger of rebelling against tradition by aligning with contemporaneity. The contemporaneous passes quickly, and without underlying substance, so will that which is aligned with the moment. The Catholic Church had tradition to rescue it from the difficulties following Vatican II. It is not clear that the Emerging Church has that anchor or the ability to note the passing moment. If all the emerging phenomenon has to commend it is rebellion against modernism, it will witness itself pass into post-emerging status.

In the same article mentioned above, Peter L. Berger describes a process called "demodernization." By demodernization, he does not mean postmodern. Rather, Berger describes demodernization as a tendency to react against the alienation brought about in society by modern developments and progress. This reaction is akin to or grows out of "nostalgia," a longing for a lost "wholeness," which is perceived to be obscured by modernist commitments.[16] Demodernization can be seen at work in twentieth-century utopian communities that wish to reach back to a simpler life as a way of overcoming fragmentation and reclaiming "wholeness." Is this the dynamic of the emerging movement? The movement does not claim to be reaching back, but one wonders. Certainly, the emerging community is reacting against modernism and the fragmentation modernism seems to have accelerated in the Christian community. Certainly, the emerging community sees overcoming fragmentation in the church and in society as its greatest challenge. Certainly, there are some primitivist and reconstructionist tendencies in the anti-institutional bias of the emerging ethos. Yet, the emerging movement sees the solution to this dilemma in contemporary society, in the secular culture, in the de-centered authority structures of the postmodern agenda. By reaching out to culture, adopting culture, accommodating to culture, the emerging movement, consciously or not, secularizes the sacred.

The emerging movement seeks to redefine communitas by making it more egalitarian and contemporary, more engaging and redemptive, more accessible and open. The purpose is to reestablish harmony based on the triadic relationship between God, communitas, and the individual. The emerging movement searches for this harmony in a reconceived communitas that allows the individual to overcome modern isolation. Will such a communitas survive? Or will it fall victim to the alienation tendencies fostered by decentering? Whether the emerging movement can create a Village of "friendship" across geographical space as the Emergent Village hopes, or whether the emerging ethos will end in an isolated suburbia of dead ends is yet to be seen. But, for certain, the Emerging Church movement has provided the traditional church with its greatest challenge of the late twentieth and twenty-first centuries, for the emerging movement has demanded that the Christian Church redefine its own context and the way communitas is envisioned and embodied.

Virtual communitas?

With the proliferation of the virtual world and online communities created by Facebook, Twitter, and other social networking sites, it makes sense to ask the questions: Are there virtual religious communities, and do these constitute what is described here as communitas? The answer to the first question is, yes, indeed. The answer to the second is, maybe. If industrialization and urbanization helped produce the modern affliction of social and individual isolation, what can be said of the technological revolution? Have technology and the changes brought by rapid technological advances in the twentieth and twenty-first centuries exacerbated social alienation? Certainly this argument can be made and seen everywhere in society. Children used to spend hours together before they spent hours in front of the TV before they spent hours on the computer. Were they less isolated then? Of course, in one sense, because every hour someone spends on the computer, they are not spending time in socialization. But this does not necessarily mean that they are isolated. In fact, with wide circles of acquaintances readily available through a few keystrokes on a wallet-size cellphone, perhaps young people are more connected to others than ever before. Without a doubt, the concepts of community and even friendship (who have you defriended today?) have been changed by contemporary technology.

Enter religion. The sacred has been perhaps more secularized through digitization than through any other means—it is everywhere present on my computer screen, and, with a little creative searching, I can connect with just about any type of religious community I wish. Religious marketing has taken on new dimensions in the digital world, even to the extent that the computer has become a conduit of the sacred (more on this later). The point is that new technologies have generally been adopted by the various aspects of culture and have changed culture for the better or the worse, and digital technology is no different. What is potentially different about digital technology is its ability to bust the boundaries that space and time have traditionally imposed upon society and individuals. Now communities transcend those elements that have in times past separated individuals and cultures. Digital friendships, ever expanding digital communities, digital relationships—this is the world we inhabit. It should then be no surprise to find God on the Web.

Need absolution? There's an app for that. Well, not exactly. Even though the Catholic Church still requires going to a priest for absolution, the Church has approved the use of a "confession app" to aid in the process of contrition. Just go to iTunes, and there it is: "Confession: A Roman Catholic App."[17] Hyped as "the perfect aid for every penitent," this app costs just $1.99 and includes a personal and confidential conscience examination, an ongoing history of confession, an ability to add sins that might not be included, and a choice of different acts of contrition. The app was designed in cooperation with Roman Catholic priests and received an imprimatur from Bishop Kevin C. Rhodes.[18] It's the real thing and an ingenuous appropriation of cultural tools by the Church to reach out to parishioners through digital technology. While grace does not transport through the digital conduit, it is certainly close to that step. And although the Confession App is not the first tool to advocate digital confession, it is the first to receive legitimacy through its sponsorship by an organization with the worldwide clout of the Roman Catholic Church. The Church is apparently banking on the notion that the app will encourage more participation in the confession sacrament, something that has been in decline among contemporary Catholics.

The app is not a replacement for traditional confession but rather an aid in examining one's conscience that the tech-savvy Catholic can use prior to or during the confession. The app is password protected and confidential, so, unless one wants to pour out one's heart on some type of social medium, the user need not worry about their latest indiscretions being posted publically. One of the neat features of the app is its age-appropriateness. The question prompts are appropriately gauged to highlight what would be the likeliest temptation traps for users according to gender and age. As an examination of conscience, then, the app is designed to help the user measure their acts and omissions of acts that would constitute sin as defined by the moral standards of the Church. In this sense, the app is not so different from written examinations through history. But the iPhone app has the added advantages of being portable and more user specific.

And specific it can be—and quite personal if you will. Father Edward L. Beck, C. P., religion contributor for ABC News, offered a quick review of the Confession App on a "Moment of Faith." Father Beck views the app as a friendly way to encourage Catholics back into the confessional booth because the confessional experience has the potential of being so powerful. He also gives an example that demonstrates the highly personal nature of the app. Under the sixth commandment is a question about treating one's body with purity. If the user signs in as a 40-year-old male and works with this question, one of the prompts asks the user if he is guilty of masturbation. Under various profiles, the app will also quiz the user about contraception practices. This is how the app leads one to consider actions that may or may not have occurred to them without the examination of conscience. So, when the user goes to confession, they have done the homework, completed a thorough examination, and could have even used the app to organize their confession to the priest. The implication is that it is easier to be examined by an impersonal iPhone and then to answer the iPhone's questions, than it is to be examined by a priest. But the confession still needs to be made to the priest. If this app works, and there is no reason to think that it does not, one wonders if it does not speak to the contemporary culture's obsession with the digitization of our lives. We are apt to post personal items in the new social media, so the Confession App takes this a step further. Now there is an outlet that allows us to post confidentially matters that are presumably more sensitive in nature. What is it about digitizing our thoughts and acts that is so appealing?

As virtual community, the Confession App allows the user to change the context of one of the most intimate sacramental moments. The app's mystery acts almost as transcendent inquisitor, reading one's thoughts and deeds, yet not exposing one's failures. The app is non-judgmental in that way and becomes an arbiter of grace and forgiveness for the psyche if not the soul. And the app connects the user to Catholics and non-Catholics who examine their conscience using the Catholic Church's moral standards as a guideline. Working with the app makes one feel either guilty or more virtuous, depending on the perspective, but it also connects the user with a community of believers who strive to better their lives and moral actions, and in that sense redefines their moral communitas by using technology.

The Catholic Church is not the first to use digital technology as a confessional outlet, however. The Internet is filled with confession online sites where one can anonymously but also publically confess one's actions and where the curious can read them. Does it somehow make us feel better about ourselves by reading what others are presumably suffering in their lives? Is this the point in these types of online communities of pain and suffering? If one way to deal with guilt is to be reminded that others have committed similar acts that are causing them guilt, then the appeal of these sites can be understood. And, of course, they also appeal to the more prurient and curious aspects of human nature. Online confessional communities allow users to spy on the private lives of others, or what is paraded as the private lives of others. In this, observers of the sites can become a community of priests, hearing confession and passing judgment from a position of moral superiority or taking solace in the company of sinners. Whatever the case, the online confessional creates and promotes a whole new context for establishing a community for confession and grace.

Do these online confessional tools bring great promise or danger? Perhaps both. The promise is expressed by those who promote the Confession App. Used properly, the app can encourage people to be better or it can encourage them to return to a sacramental ritual they perhaps have abandoned. However, it seems that a danger does exist and that would be the danger of completely redefining communitas and context. In the Catholic Church, while it is not meant to replace confession, it seems the Confession App in some fundamental way replaces the context of complete trust built between the priest and parishioner. With the Confession App, the parishioner becomes one step removed with a bit of technology shielding the user from the priest. If the relationship is subtly changed, then the communitas changes as well. In non-Catholic online confession sites, the balance is disrupted even further. Without official confession oversight, the implication is that one can confess and even receive absolution minus any communitas except that provided by the site itself. In this case, communitas is defined digitally and absolution occurs between person and machine. Have we, thus, digitized God?

Confession is not the only aspect of online religion. Religion is all online now, and for many it seems that online spirituality and church have met a need that actual church attendance has not. Sites like lifechurch.tv offer a glimpse at what might become the future. While lifechurch does not advocate replacing virtual church with physical church, and promotes church attendance, it does offer alternatives to traditional church attendance. One can form or join a LifeGroup either physically or virtually, and young children can get the virtual church experience through lifekids.tv. Church online should be no surprise, and its popularity should not shock a society that shops online, meets romantic partners online, buys cars online, and posts intimate details of everyday life online. Why should such a culture not embrace God online as well? This digitization of religion holds consequences concerning communitas, however, and the more of life we outsource to a digital community, the more our lives become disconnected, isolated, and depersonalized. At some point, we have to ask how much of community we have redefined and how much we have lost completely. Can we really be connected with others through a digital interface in the same way or as meaningfully as we can face to face?

Sander Vanocur raised the alarm years ago concerning the increasing depersonalization of society in relation to television and TV's failed promises. In an essay entitled, "TV's Failed Promise," he warned that media can be used with tremendous propaganda potential, and TV, with its image rich format, can create greater confusion between reality and illusion.[19] The Internet, with its greater availability and reach, only takes this confusion to greater heights than we could have imagined. Digital manipulation of images displayed professionally on the computer screen makes deception easier than ever, and uncritical viewers of images are duped more readily than ever before. Virtual worlds take us where we could not have gone before, but they also take us away from the real. Some, I am afraid, are all the more ready to trade a real communitas for the virtual without a sense of loss or fear. If this applies to virtual religion, then the institutional church has reason to worry. Once a virtual context can replace or redefine the physical worship experience and fellowship, then even the emerging church might become passé.

Communitas defined as anti- or a-secular

Through the examination of motorcycle and cowboy communities, we looked at how secular groups can be sacralized to serve a transcendent purpose. By considering emerging churches and online churches, we have witnessed how the sacred can accommodate the secular and we can see how secularizing the sacred can result in redefining one's religious context. By using these groups as examples, I do not mean to suggest that all groups experience such permeable boundaries between the sacred and secular, although these permeable boundaries do seem to characterize our postmodern age in relation to religion and spirituality. Some religious groups do not wish to secularize and cannot accommodate to popular culture or secular societal standards without fundamentally changing their character and being. In fact, some groups purposefully define themselves against secular society and contemporary culture and by doing so define their own character, charter, or mission. Two examples will suffice to illustrate this anti-secular or a-secular stance. The snake handling Christians of the southern Appalachian Mountains must maintain an anti-secular position because of secular legal standards, and the various Creationist and Intelligent Design groups must maintain an anti-cultural stance by aligning their philosophy against science.

Handling serpents as "secular disobedience"

The ritual practice of handling dangerous serpents in church is seen by practitioners as obedience to divine law that requires disobedience of civil or secular statutes, unless the activity is done in West Virginia where it is legal. In every other state in the United States, handlers break the law when they take up snakes in a worship setting. When handlers engage in an illegal activity that also has the potential for leading to death, they create a context with an extremely powerful communitas. This communitas stands alone against non-practitioners and against the secular authorities, insisting that what binds them together comes from a higher authority. Empowered by, as they believe, the Holy Ghost, or Holy Spirit, these snake handling believers follow a mandate and in doing so bring themselves into communion with a small number of like-minded believers in the United States. Their self-imposed status as outsiders on the periphery of the Christian world reinforces their sense of separateness. However, this sense of separateness creates a strong sense of legitimacy for their practice. For the snake handlers, there is a palpable sense that they alone practice and maintain truth against all odds, and it is their status as law-breakers, in part, that grants their practice authority. Much like the early church that was periodically persecuted by the Roman Empire, snake handlers are set against secular powers whenever they practice what they believe to be authentic Christianity. They are in good company with Christians who have been persecuted by secular authorities throughout history. For this reason, the snake handlers cannot accommodate to secular society, for to do so would be to forfeit that which most defines their belief.

Religious snake handling has been transcultural through the ages, but the particular form of serpent handling identified here dates to the early twentieth century. George Went Hensley was certainly not the first person in history or even in Appalachia to pick up poisonous serpents as a ritual act, but his name more than any other is associated with the revival of this act in the southern Appalachian Mountains. In 1909, Hensley was in his early thirties and pastor of a Church of God in Tennessee. He had been troubled for some time about a particular verse in chapter 16 of the gospel of Mark. The verses read, "And these signs shall follow them that believe; In my name shall they cast out devils; they shall speak with new tongues; They shall take up serpents; and if they drink any deadly thing, it shall not hurt them; they shall lay hands on the sick, and they shall recover."[20] Being of holiness and Pentecostal persuasion, Hensley was already practicing some of the signs and had seen others, perhaps even snake handling,[21] so it is not difficult to understand his curiosity about all the signs mentioned in Mark's gospel. The story has it that Hensley was walking on top of White Oak Mountain near Chattanooga while meditating on Mark's verse when he happened upon a rattlesnake. He prayed, was empowered, picked up the snake, and was not bitten. Shortly after that Hensley returned to his church, handled the snake, and others took up the practice in like manner.

For most snake handlers, picking up serpents as a ritual act is an act of faith in response to God's injunction to "them that believe … [to] take up serpents." Handlers are careful to insist that, before taking up a serpent, they should receive an anointing from the Holy Spirit, and the Spirit empowers the handler to take up the snake without harm. The snakes handled in services are generally rattlesnakes and copperheads or moccasins, but they are all potentially deadly. The snakes are grasped, sometimes in handfuls, tossed, draped around necks and heads, sometimes whipped or trodden on, and otherwise handled as the Spirit directs, BUT they rarely bite. When they do bite, the faithful refuse to seek medical attention, citing faith in God's will to oversee the outcome. Bitten participants rarely but sometimes die from their bites. Some snake handlers also drink poison in what would appear to be lethal doses in response to the injunction in Mark's passage—few die. All this takes place in the context of exuberant and ecstatic dancing, shouting, convulsing, praying, and other behavior on the part of the handlers and those present but not handling. From the outsider's perspective, the ritual is fascinating, mesmerizing, frightening, and exotic. For the insider, the ritual is the result of Spirit anointing and faithful response to God. The outsider witnesses altered states of consciousness and what might be described as spirit possession. The insider feels the power of the Holy Spirit to face death with the faith that the Spirit of God will protect them. Regardless, serpent handling is a fascinating ritual, and it is illegal in most places.

It is the illegality of the ritual that is relevant to this section on religious context and communitas. As mentioned above, snake handling is illegal in every state except for West Virginia. So when worshipers pick up snakes, they are not only obeying God's command, defying secular command, and risking their lives, but they are also defining clearly their communitas. It would be hard to imagine a more strict line drawn between insider and outsider than the one drawn by defying secular authority and life-threatening behavior. For the serpent handling believers, their communitas exists in direct opposition to secularism, and any accommodation would be to change the context beyond recognition. Unlike many cultural activities that cross the sacred–secular permeable boundaries, the wall between handlers, non-handling Christians (the great majority), and secular culture/law is tightly prescribed and clearly demarcated. The snake handlers situate themselves in a small but clearly identifiable communitas with strict sociological boundaries. With these boundaries come strong legitimating forces, using Berger's terms,[22] and the fact that a few hundred or more serpent handling believers prove to themselves and promote to the world that they are the only true believers reinforces the social cohesion of their communitas, which in turn reinforces the individual's status in the divine context. In other words, snake handlers establish their sacred communitas by maintaining a strict exclusionary community against the outside world. Such a strict sacred community has little tolerance for secular intrusion.

Religion and science: the same side of different coins

A similar act of exclusion can be seen in contemporary standoffs between certain religious perspectives and the scientific community. While it is tempting to say that current science and religion debates represent much ado about nothing, it is hard to dismiss an argument that has been ongoing since the Enlightenment and particularly hateful since Darwin. The science and religion debates are not limited to Darwinian evolutionary theory, as they encompass a wide range of ethical debates ranging from right to life to genetic engineering to epistemological debates concerning theory and method. But it is in the "Creation" debates that the divide between science and religion, secularism and sacredness, are most clearly drawn and fiercely fought. The debate rages most enthusiastically between biologists and creationists, and the contested ground of origins unfortunately overshadows potential areas of cooperation and dialogue among physicists and theologians.

The creation debates center on theories of origins, and in the balance is whether or not a transcendent reality is even in the mix. While there are many scientists who are believers, and many believers who accept Darwinian evolutionary thought as a valid scientific theory, the attention goes to those staking out positions on the extremes: on one side are those who view origins arising from chance without design or supernatural agency; on the other are those who argue that evolutionary theory does not adequately account for a supernatural element of design in creation. The side of the coin in question is how one understands the world and its origins. The two different sides are religious and scientific worldviews. The two extreme views cannot be reconciled, not because adherents are not trying but because the answers are found on two radically different coins: one coin is constructed from the scientific worldview; the other uses religious cosmology—the answers cannot be the same, and one wonders if the questions are even the same. So why does religion expect science to give a religious answer, and why does science demand religion surrender its worldview?

The scientific evolutionary versus creationist views of origins and the debates surrounding the dichotomous views are convoluted and difficult. The presentation of these debates here is not meant to be a comprehensive view of the various positions and sources of inspiration or theory: creationism, scientific creationism, intelligent design, young earth versus old earth creationism, atheism, evolutionary biology, geological record, scientific method—all these and more must be fully explored in a study of the issues at stake. What I wish to point out in this short description is that those Christians who hold to a fully literal rendition of the Genesis story of creation have staked out a position that is fully aligned against science and, thus, against a secular worldview since science is roundly accepted as a valid approach to understanding our world. This type of hard-core creationism creates an impermeable boundary much in the same way the snake handlers close themselves off from secularism. It is not illegal to believe in creationism as it is to handle serpents, but it is certainly impractical, and it carries a similar kind of cultural derision that goes along with activities like handling rattlesnakes. Creationists are viewed by the scientifically minded to have their heads in the sand, and creationists believe they are a minority being persecuted by a secular culture that has bought a bill of goods from the scientific community. The characterization of fundamentalists during the infamous Scopes trial gave popular culture an image of religious fanatics who were uninformed and ignorant. This characterization in many ways carries over to creationists today. Creationists are seen by scientists as superstitious heaven gazers while creationists view evolutionists as elitist secularists, or worse, atheists. The boundary that separates them is so firmly established as to discourage further dialogue—in this case, sacred views and secular, scientific theories are irreconcilable.

Nevertheless, one development out of this debate seeks to make those boundaries less stringent and more permeable, at least from the religious side. Creation science, or scientific creationism, was a movement that was most evident in the United States from the 1960s through the 1980s. Creation science challenges the underlying science of evolutionary theory and attempts to replace this with a scientific basis for the stories of creation in the book of Genesis. The idea is that, if biblical creation stories can be shown to be supported by science, then creation science could be taught in the public school science classes alongside of Darwinian evolutionary theory as an alternative theory of origins. Court cases in the 1980s discredited creation science as science, and that project was largely abandoned or replaced by the Intelligent Design proponents of the 1990s. The point here for our discussion is that creationism attempted to co-opt a foreign method to make its case in the secular setting. Creationism, a religious commitment, tried to make a scientific case, called creation science, built on religious presuppositions. It did not work. Not only was the move roundly criticized by scientists as phony science, but it was recognized by the courts for what it was, a religious commitment. The important thing to recognize in the light of this book is that creation science represents a failed attempt to secularize the sacred. The proponents of this position used the methods and language of a secular commitment to try to gain acceptance by a secular audience, public schools. But this type of permeable boundary cannot be manufactured or forced—where such boundaries occur, they grow organically. In this instance, the secularization of the sacred could not be sustained.

It is worth noting that the sacred–secular/scientific divide here goes deeper than the intellectual disputes concerning theories of origin. In fact, the disagreement expands to a cultural debate that reaches to public education. Creationists do not like the Darwinian scientific curriculum and see it as a secular doctrine that is hostile to religion. Of course, scientists, and for the most part, the courts, see creationism, Intelligent Design, creation science, and the like as religious cosmologies masquerading as science in the attempt to infiltrate a secular curriculum. As such, these approaches have been deemed mainly unconstitutional in that they violate the First Amendment prohibition against an establishment of religion. So the science versus religion debate is a small part of a larger cultural debate that pits secularism against certain sacred beliefs and practices. The separation here is firm and very public, and when it comes to certain parts of the disagreement, the boundaries between sacred and secular are impermeable and solid. The religious and scientific answers and questions surrounding origins represent different coins in a sphere where the prevailing authority demands a unified currency, and in such an economy, balance comes when one currency is perhaps inflated as the other is devalued. In the contemporary world, when it comes to understanding origins it certainly seems that the stock of science is trading at astronomical levels in relation to religion.

The sacred and secular context of religious communities

Throughout this book, I have attempted to explore the various ways the sacred and secular interact in our culture. The lines are generally not definitively drawn, and what we witness are postmodern permeable boundaries between the sacred and the secular. This cultural predilection extends to what are normally considered sacred communities, and we see church communities take on secular characteristics in the attempt to redefine the context of church. The result is a new way of defining communitas where sacred communities cozy up to secular patterns and commitments. We see this clearly in "emerging communities" and online religious communities. But this pattern is not universal among twenty-first-century religious communities, as our quick survey of snake handlers and creationists suggests. Some communities depend upon strict boundaries between them and predominant secular values in order to maintain their context and define their communitas. We are well advised to understand these dynamics sociologically, for, whether one identifies with a sacred or secular communitas, the context is one of social relationship which has at a minimum the relationship of the individual to the communitas as its base. For those who understand the world as sacred, the added element of the transcendent defines reality as a triad.

Nevertheless, even the most ardent secularist entertains that third leg of the triad. They might call it truth or socially constructed values or some other name, but the third leg is there, providing the standards by which one is related to society. In either case, communitas (social context) becomes the defining organizing principle by which we relate meaningfully to others and to that which is beyond ourselves.

Study guide

Important words and concepts

Communitas
Demodernization
Emerging Church
Filial piety
Foundationalism
Missional
Postliberalism
Primitivism
Reconstructionism
Religion and science
Triadic relationship
Virtual community/church/religion

Study questions

(1) Describe how the Emerging Church phenomenon challenges traditional paradigms for the Christian church.
(2) How does post-liberal theology establish an ideological foundation for the emerging phenomenon?
(3) How does the Emerging Church support the thesis of this book?
(4) How do contemporary snake handlers illustrate the uneasy alliance between sacred and secular visions of reality?
(5) Can science and religion be reconciled? Should they?

Guided watching

(1) Watch the film *Machine Gun Preacher*, based on the life of Sam Childers. How does this story illustrate the shift in many contemporary and emerging

communities from orthodoxy and tradition to praxis? How does this help to understand a challenge to the traditional understanding of communitas? Now read Paul's Letter to the Galatians in the New Testament. Paul also tries to redefine communitas. Do you see any parallel emphases between Paul's and Childers's understanding of communitas?

Conclusion: Theological appropriation of secularization: A cooperative model

When she was small, I enjoyed driving my daughter to and from preschool to begin and end the workday. Sometimes those short 20-minute commutes passed with hardly a word spoken, sometimes in chatty silliness. I fielded the types of penetrating questions that make the most hardened parent cringe, and I helped make up nonsense rhymes and songs. Those rides were sacred time, because they were ritualized; because they would take me beyond myself, my daily concerns, and my work worries; because they introduced me to another's world; and because the interactions sharpened my awareness and consciousness more than hours of prayer or meditation. Never was I more focused than during those too-few moments of the day—focused on driving safely for one, but also focused on the surrounding environment that was for my daughter a source of endless curiosity and questioning.

During those rides, I noticed things I failed to notice before. For example, I read bumper stickers at stop lights because I never knew when I might have to answer a question about one. I learned there are developed theologies on the bumpers of automobiles ranging from apocalyptic predictions to glorification of the goddess. And I noticed a curious "evolution" of symbols on the backs of cars that highlights the ever-shifting boundaries that merge sacred and secular. Consider the following:

Most of us have seen the familiar Christian symbol of the fish. In its most rudimentary form, it appears as two curves, meeting at one end to form a head and crossing near the opposite end to create a tail. The use of the symbol dates to early Christianity and is deeply ingrained into Christian iconography. It appears in churches, on Christmas trees, on billboards, in advertisements, and on cars. The Greek word for fish, ichthus, is an acronym for a Christian confession: Jesus Christ,

Son of God, Savior. Early Christians could identify themselves secretly during times of persecution by initiating or completing the fish symbol in the presence of someone they suspected of sharing their faith. So the contemporary, public display of the fish symbol represents a quiet and respectful proclamation of faith, not an aggressive evangelistic tool or social commentary—simply an unobtrusive way of claiming faith. It is not surprising that a fair number of these fish symbols (at least where I live) are displayed on automobiles—some of them are plain and some have Jesus or the Greek letters for ichthus printed inside of them.

A while back, another symbol began to appear on the backs of cars that at first glance resembled the simple ichthus. However, upon closer examination, one could see that the ichthus had sprouted legs and that in the new symbol, now an amphibian, the word Jesus had been replaced by the name Darwin. The editorial comment is clear: this Darwinian amphibian is a direct response to the Christian declaration of faith through display of the fish. The secular response proposes to replace the fish with a more highly evolved creature, science, through its evolutionary representative, Darwin. The display of the Darwinian amphibian suggests that Christianity is antiquated and inferior to science and to rationalism and that a sacred worldview is to be discarded for a secular one. What at first appeared to be an attempt at clever commentary presented some interesting and disturbing questions as I began to think about the evolution of ichthus. Why would a secular-minded person want to co-opt a religious movement's symbol and openly mock the underlying commitment attached to the symbol? There was no provocation in displaying the fish—why the deliberate insult in response?

The exchange does not end with the appearance of the evolved amphibian. The next evolution in popular cultural exchange appeared a bit later when I spotted on the back of the car in front of me a new version of the symbol. This time, the Darwinian amphibian was being swallowed by a bigger fish that had "TRUTH" inscribed inside it. With this Christian response, this time provocative, the symbol co-opts not only the secular symbol (Darwinian amphibian) but also the secular philosophy behind it (survival of the fittest) to debunk the secular "truth." The irony is obvious. The secular amphibian used the Christian fish to attack Christian thought while the Christian response used secular philosophy to attack the secular amphibian.

The exchange is instructive and brings to light an attempt from both perspectives to mount a worldview/culture war that pits Christian fundamentalism against science, the sacred against the secular. The stakes are high—Truth. This public exchange also demonstrates the level of public, secular saturation of religion and religious dialogue. The evolution of the ichthus represents an ideological debate on the nature of creation and on the validity of the sacred worldview. The crux of the debate is not so much creationism versus evolutionary theory as it is about the basic worldview behind these theories: sacred versus secular.

Nevertheless, I was careful above with my choice of words. I suggested this exchange represents an attempt to mount a culture war, not the actual pitting of worldviews against one another. I believe the deeper truth found within this apparent conflict is not irreconcilable positions but rather an assimilation of one worldview into another—a melding of one into the other—a blurring of boundaries between secular and sacred, not retrenchment into clearly defined worlds. Each evolutionary step of the ichthus incorporates elements of the opposing worldview to develop its own stance: the secular amphibian incorporates the Christian fish just as the Christian carnivore assimilates the secular. The secular amphibian's existence is based upon something more fundamental, the presence of ichthus. Thus, the secular amphibian embodies the ichthus. Conversely, and even more telling perhaps, if the popular adage, "We are what we eat" holds, then the Christian carnivore takes into itself (sacramentally?) the secular amphibian and becomes the secular worldview. The secular is sacralized by incorporating the ichthus; the sacred is secularized by eating the amphibian. We see this exchange everywhere—the process of these dissolving boundaries between sacred and secular is secularization.

Looking elsewhere for secularization

Popular culture is a rich repository for evidence of this secularization process. As I have noted throughout this book, the process takes place in two directions. What we normally consider sacred culture or institutions constantly adopt secular means to an end. They take on secular ways when convenient or advantageous. This secularization of the sacred is inherent in Western religion and marks the history of Christianity from virtually the beginning. But secular culture also participates in secularization by taking on religious functioning on many levels. When culture functions to create ideologies that grant meaning to individuals or cultures, we have secular ideologies functioning religiously, and we witness the sacralization of the secular. The two directions mark a dialogue in society, a two-way reaching out that blurs the distinctions and boundaries we sometimes like to imagine existing between the secular and the sacred. Such a dialogue of blurring is the secularization process.

I have organized this book around four aspects of culture: space, text, image, and community. I chose these four because it seems to me that we see most clearly—in the spaces we construct for specific purposes, the texts we revere, the images we view, and the communities we join—the attempts to define certain objects as sacred, certain functions as secular, and so forth. In other words, in our culture, we tend to divide space, text, image, and community into sacred and secular camps. I chose these four as well because they define interrelated ways of conveying meaning. Before texts, we had spaces, and more recently we tend toward images, which in some ways brings us full circle to a pre-textual situation where spaces and their arrangements become supreme in conveying meaning. In all of this, we have community, a context for arranging space, sharing texts, and creating images. I hope that, by looking at these four areas, my thesis that sacred and secular are in constant dialogue in society has been strengthened.

However, it should be noted that space, text, image, and community as I have treated them here do not exhaust the areas of culture where one finds the secularization process. Many other areas of popular culture might be examined—popular magazines help define issues of gender in our culture;[1] television might help shape adolescent appropriations of violent attitudes;[2] art has long been allied to religious expression as well as to secular; music, and more recently music videos, seem to act in particularly powerful ways to capture the attention of adolescents and potentially shape their ideologies.[3] These and other products of culture neatly fit into or are related to one of my four organizing categories, space, text, image, or community. However, music in some sense does not fit these categories and in some sense fits them all. While music is neither space, text, image, nor community, in some ways it embodies spatial, textual, visual and contextual characteristics— the spatial arrangement of sound through rhythm and speed is reflected in music texts with notation and often punctuated by images accompanying community performance. In any event, music in our culture operates in many of the ways our other categories do and can be used to illustrate the secularization thesis. And when music becomes music video, then it definitely contains aspects of at least text and image. Music alone and music with video demonstrate not only the secularization process but also how we can construct a postmodern theology of popular culture that is large enough and open enough to allow both sacred and secular religious functioning.

We need look no further than the genre of music known as "Christian pop" or "Christian rock" to see the secularization of the sacred in full swing. Some of what passes as contemporary Christian music is hardly recognizable from the Top 40 music that plays constantly on commercial stations. The only difference arises with the lyrics, which are distinctly Christian. Some of this music has a hard edge to it and resembles rock and roll in every respect except for lyrics. From light rock to rap to punk to hard rock—these forms have been adopted by the contemporary Christian music scene. The popularization of Christian rock/pop music witnesses to a purposeful adaptation of a secular medium for the propagation of the Christian message. The strategy is to tap into youth culture and Christianize it.

The genesis of this movement in the evangelical community seems to have been motivated by the desire to give evangelical youth what they wanted (pop music) but at the same time to make sure it was ideologically in line with evangelical truths. So early contemporary Christian music appealed to a subculture of evangelical youth and could be purchased in Christian bookstores. However, by the mid-1990s, the music began to reach beyond Christian bookstores and musicians began to play in secular venues. The direction of the music changed—no longer an internal cultural form, the music was directed to secular audiences, using secular forms with Christian lyrics to become an evangelical tool. By 1995, the growing Christian music empire was moving beyond evangelical audiences and was gaining ground in the secular mainstream. The growing popularity of the movement was due, probably in large part, to popular cross-over artists like Amy Grant who performed secular songs as well as songs with Christian lyrics. With this growing popularity in the secular realm, Christian music moved from the shelves of Christian bookstores to the aisles of Wal-Mart.[4] Whether or not this music is reaching an expanded secular audience or simply reaching the evangelical market in secular venues is difficult to determine. But, with the recent popular success of MercyMe, it appears that this music is reaching into the mainstream, partly perhaps because of marketing and the adoption of a secular music format. MercyMe's 2001 hit, "I Can Only Imagine,"[5] imagines what it must be like to be in heaven before God. The song is a popular worship song, but by 2004 the song had crossed over to adult contemporary stations. By 2010, it had gone platinum. It was marketed in secular markets, and it is not clear how far into the mainstream this music has reached. However, it is clear that such marketing of the message marks a definite adoption of the secular medium for theological purposes.

This secularization of Christian music creates some confusion with many fans and critics of Christian music. For example, Amy Grant, who is one of the most popular and successful stars of the contemporary Christian music scene, has often confused and even dismayed followers of the genre. Winner of several Grammy and Dove awards, her huge popularity among evangelicals was translated to the popular music scene by the mid-1980s as Grant was able to move almost seamlessly between the worlds of secular pop and Christian music. That the Christian music diva could record such songs as "Baby Baby" created suspicion among some evangelical fans.

The release of her album *Behind the Eyes* created another round of confusion and doubt over the intent of her music from some evangelical circles. Even though the songs on that album deal with themes such as temptation, struggle, love, and fidelity (Christian themes if ever there were some), the lyrics are hard to identify as Christian. As a result, some religious radio stations chose not to play the album because it contained "no evangelical bent, no mention of God."[6] So, while the most recognizable artist in the Christian music scene continues her crossover success, some are uncomfortable with what they consider the secularization of sacred music, or at least the secularization of a sacred music artist.

This discomfort is directed at other Christian artists as well and demonstrates that the secularization of this cultural form is perhaps proceeding more completely than with others, those marked by space, text, image, or community. Perhaps it is more difficult to draw the lines with music. Some religious fans of contemporary Christian music seem to believe that some artists adopt the forms of secular culture too well in their attempts to be relevant. For example, the Christian ska group (ska has been characterized as upbeat punk rock with horns[7]) "Five Iron Frenzy" has seemingly crossed the line with some fans. The group is fond of playing secular venues and tends to shy away from "preaching" at their concerts. And they seem to have offended some Christian fans when they donned Star Trek outfits for one of their concerts. Some critics seem to question the band's commitment to its Christian cause because there exists little to distinguish the group from secular ska bands. Nevertheless, the group's lead singer defends their style by suggesting that some audience members are "saved" by attending their concerts rather than through preaching.[8] While disagreement remains among evangelicals concerning the appropriate limits of adopting secular culture as a vehicle for the sacred message, there seems to be unanimity that the purpose for using secular media in the first place is for propagation of the gospel. So, the purposeful secularization of the sacred is meant to reach the secular audience with the sacred message.

We even see this same secularization tendency in more traditional "gospel" music formats. Record production companies are purposely pushing gospel music and artists into the secular arena to garner more mainstream audiences and venues. According to Jazzy Jordan of Verity Records, "[G]ospel artists are starting to resemble a lot of secular artists ... bringing the hip-hop beats and feel of the street to gospel ..."[9] Pulling off such a secularizing market strategy is no easy task, as recognized by Demetrus Alexander-Stewart of Atlantic Christian in the following comment for *Billboard* magazine concerning imaging of the secularized gospel music: "The mainstream side didn't want it to look too churchy and, for gospel, it couldn't look too worldly, so we were trying to strike a balance."[10] This perceived balance gives us a clue to the extent that blurring of boundaries has taken place. No longer do sacred musicians reject secular culture, nor do the fans and promoters of sacred music. Rather, extensive blurring of malleable boundaries between the sacred and secular components of our culture is not only accepted but manipulated from the sacred side and, as we shall see, also from the secular side.

Just as contemporary Christian musicians use a secular medium to communicate a sacred message, we also see secular artists whose seemingly secular music communicates religiously meaningful lyrics. That represents the sacralization of the secular in which originally secular cultural forms take on sacred or religious functions through the subject matter or presentation of the art. Examples abound: Tori Amos singing "God" or "Muhammad My Friend"; Joan Osborne's lyrics asking "What if God Was One of Us?"; Garth Brooks singing about "unanswered prayers"; Carrie Underwood asking for Jesus to "take the wheel." These secular folk, pop, and country songs represent a small fraction of many contemporary secular songs that employ religious language, themes, or images to create a kind of secular theology through music. Religion is everywhere in popular music and videos, and it is not coming from religious bodies or from any recognizable religious community. Perhaps the most interesting pop star whose work touches upon and implicates religious themes is Madonna, whose work includes songs and videos such as "Like A Prayer" and music where she chants "Om Shanti."[11] And perhaps the most interesting recent star whose work sacralizes the secular is Carrie Underwood.

Carrie Underwood broke in to the Country and Western music scene after winning the 2005 season of American Idol. An immensely talented singer and popular musician and pop icon, Underwood has won several awards and has risen to the top of the country music world. While Underwood is squarely in the country genre, she often sings songs with religious messages, and, in her performances, the country song morphs into a sacred offering, sacralizing the secular musical genre. Underwood talks openly about her faith, and grew up singing in her church, so it is no surprise that her faith would spill over into her craft; but rarely has an artist been able to pull this off with such emotion and success. Two songs in particular illustrate how this crossover artist takes the country format and uses it to communicate emotionally charged, religion-saturated messages.

As in so much country music, these two songs employ lyrics that construct a narrative. In "Jesus, Take the Wheel,"[12] a mother is driving home with her baby to see her parents on a snowy Christmas Eve. She loses control on the slick roads and prays for Jesus to take the wheel. She gives up control of the car and ends up safely on the shoulder. The incident leads her to evaluate her life and is a metaphor for her decision to give up control of her life to Jesus. The young mother prays for Jesus to take the wheel of her life. This metaphor is one of the central messages of the evangelical message—Christians should turn their wills and lives over to Jesus. In the second song, "Temporary Home,"[13] the lyrics describe three scenarios of broken lives: a six-year-old boy who bounces from foster home to foster home and sees each stop as a "temporary home"; a young mother looking for a job, living in a halfway house, who tells her baby that the halfway house is only a "temporary home"; and finally, an old man on his death bed, who comforts his visitor by insisting that this is just his "temporary home." The song uses the transiency of life's situations as a metaphor for expressing hope in an eternal home beyond this one. The message reiterates the Christian hope of a heavenly home while implying that earthly life is temporary and sometimes unjust. These two songs are beautiful, emotional, and religion-saturated, and their crossover appeal and broad popularity demonstrate how effectively a secular musical genre can sacralize a story.

Carrie Underwood's use of religious themes in her work rings with authenticity and honesty, her art acting as a vehicle for her faith. But the same cannot be said of all popular music that employs religious imagery or themes. Sometimes the religious theme becomes a prop for something else, as it is in a pair of pop tunes that play off the "end of the world" scenario. I realized something was up with pop culture when my daughter and her friends would occasionally ask me about the end of the world, 2012, and whether or not I believed the world would end in 2012. I knew that pop culture was full of 2012 predictions, but I did not realize that such end-of-the-world images were also popping up in popular song lyrics. Of course, I watched *Apocalypse Now* along with everyone else of my generation, and I am well aware that music may be appropriated to lend a heavy apocalyptic sense to films and videos or simply to popular music.[14] As The Doors' "The End" belted out at the beginning and end of the movie, I could not help but remember that the song originally recalled the end of a love relationship, yet it was the perfect song to attach to tap the feeling of *Apocalypse Now*. But I had not listened to the songs my daughter and her friends were listening to, in particular Britney Spears's song "Till the World Ends"[15] and Jay Sean's song "2012."[16] At first, I thought these pop songs must be sacralizing the secular, using secular music to tap into anxiety about the eschaton. But, when I listened, I realized that these were dance songs, using the popular fascination with the end of the world to promote a "live for the moment" mentality. The end of time is no more than a point of departure for advocating a party spirit. Spears's song advocates dancing to the eschaton, and the later video is set at a dance party on December 21, 2012.[17] The party is more bacchanalian excess than anything: with scantily clad dancers performing sexually suggestive moves, interspersed with apocalyptic scenes of urban destruction, the anticipated apocalypse is met, if not welcomed, with abandon. Jay Sean celebrates the party spirit as well and advocates partying until the eschaton, even though the lyrics make it clear that the world is not really ending. To the extent that these songs have incorporated sacred categories, they have done so in only a peripherally religious manner.

What can we make of this contemporary sacralization of secular music? It witnesses the extent to which our society has become religion-saturated throughout its popular culture in and through venues that are distinct from and separate from religious institutions and official religious bodies. Does this mean that religion, far from losing power through secularization, might actually be more potent in our culture than ever, albeit without the official backing of institutions? The possibility exists that religion, dissipated throughout the culture, arising authentically in the hands and creations of representatives who are removed from the restrictions of orthodoxy, can become a religion that empowers and functions to grant meaning to a more diverse population than can official religious bodies alone.[18]

If this in fact is happening, is there something about music that inspires a more powerful religious response than other cultural forms? We can at least recognize, as does the work of Andy Bennett, that popular music operates collectively in political and social ways.[19] Music can be a powerful means to express theology, or ideologies of any sort, and is thus an important vehicle for the secularization of popular culture and religion. Consider the important work of James C. Scott in *Domination and the Arts of Resistance: Hidden Transcripts*,[20] and of theo-musicologist Jon Michael Spencer in *Blues and Evil*.[21]

Scott argues that the relationship between dominant and subordinate groups in society is often marked by public and hidden transcripts. Because of their subordinate status, marginalized groups are not free to publicly communicate some messages. Therefore, these groups create hidden transcripts, messages that can be understood within the group but that are hidden from the dominant group. In this way, the subordinate group can communicate rebellious or factious messages.[22] Such hidden transcripts can function to bolster morale or create group cohesion, and they constitute important ideologies of groups. It is often within the hidden transcripts of a group that one finds truth. In this way, African-American religious traditions could operate in the South to make religion meaningful even in the context of slavery and Jim Crow. Therefore, gospel music and other forms of African-American hidden transcripts gave voice within the African-American community to a meaningful version of Christianity that promised social reversal while critiquing white Christianity and society.

Spencer's work on blues music recalls this social dynamic as he examines some of the stereotypes surrounding blues music. He contends that blues music contains an essentially religious character even though it is often characterized as the devil's music. This misinterpretation of the genre results when critics from outside the tradition misread the hidden transcripts contained within the music. Spencer goes on to construct mythologies of the blues based on African traditions and Christianity; theologies of the blues, which allow blues music to function religiously in the African-American community while critiquing the traditional church; and theodicies of the blues, that function religiously in addressing oppression of African-Americans. In these theodicies, Spencer suggests that code in blues lyrics equates white oppressors with evil, and that such music establishes a rebellious theodicy. Thus, embedded within blues music as an African-American cultural product lie a mythology, theology, and theodicy (theological categories) that authenticate African traditions while critiquing white religion and society.[23] In this case, it is blues music, generally considered secular, that represents an authentic theological stance within the black community, not the black church and certainly not the white. Where the religious institutions fail, the secular culture functions religiously, and the secular is sacralized to become more powerful than sacred institutions in functioning religiously.

Jon Michael Spencer spoke at a conference in 1996 where he eloquently elaborated on this point.[24] In making the case for theo-musicology, Spencer suggested that secular music contains layers of theological meaning. He noted that popular music has contributed to American spirituality and has affected behavior, and it is perhaps better suited for these purposes than sacred music. Whereas sacred music is defined by, bounded by, and limited by doctrine and dogma, secular music has no such limitations. Thus, according to Spencer, it is in secular music that we learn what we really believe, and it is through our response to secular music that we can fashion an ethics that is meaningful and relevant. Secular music, therefore, provides a more reliable measure of authentic belief, relevant ethics, and real commitment than sacred music, which can be defined by standards of belief that are no longer owned by those in the tradition.

Scott's thesis and Spencer's enlightened work on blues demonstrate the power music can claim in the religious sphere and in constructing values and ethics that we live by and respond to. That music claims this power to create all kinds of ideologies and value systems has been well documented in the literature, and we find sociologists, theologians, and even pediatricians writing about the powerful effect music can have on society and individuals. The effectiveness of music to create and strengthen ideologies and behaviors seems to be multiplied when music is coupled with image to produce the very popular cultural form, the music video.[25] Music videos are short, visually rich, intense, loaded with images of violence and sexuality, and are devoured by young people in such a way that they affect values and attitudes toward gender, sexuality, and violence.[26] With this in mind, we need to be cognizant of the power music and music videos exert in shaping the attitudes of young people, for example, because these forms function in a most meaningful way—by acting religiously, they shape ideological covenants.

Much of the work on music and music videos centers on the extent to which they help shape youth attitudes, particularly toward sexuality and violence. The concern comes from the shared assessment that the values being transmitted through popular music and videos are harmful. As early as the 1930s we see popular music playing a significant role in portraying women using a complex combination of images ranging from innocent sweetheart to sexual vixen.[27] Many scholars now agree that contemporary popular music plays a significant role, perhaps even a leadership role, in constructing and deconstructing gender images in the culture.[28] The problem arises because it seems the predominant images conveyed in popular music lean toward objectifying women as sexual objects and often portray women as victims of sexual violence. Much of the literature suggests that music videos promote stereotypes about sexuality and dramatize sexual relationships through a model of antagonistic relationships between men and women that cast women in submissive roles.[29] The disturbing implication is that popular music and music videos perpetuate certain myths of sexuality and gender relationships that youth incorporate uncritically from the culture.

Sut Jhally has created an important and provocative video that supports the above research suggestions, that music videos create and support cultural stories of sexuality. Jhally challenges us to think critically about the impact of those stories on the consumers of music videos (mainly young people). Jhally's videos, *Dreamworlds* and the updated *Dreamworlds II*, argue with narration that accompanies video and music clips that music videos create cultural stories about sexuality based on male "adolescent fantasy." These stories are potentially harmful to women because of objectification within a dreamworld of sexual fantasy.[30] Jhally's videos argue persuasively that the dreamworld of music video portrays women from a male perspective that is absorbed into youth culture. The women in these videos play a "decorative role," exposing their bodies through undressing, bathing, and stripping. These women are schoolgirls, teachers, and prostitutes, and the dominant behavior they exhibit is nymphomania. The implication is that all women, schoolgirls as well as prostitutes, exhibit strong, aggressive sexual desire. In the music video dreamworld, these women make themselves available to men through easy, casual sexual encounters, devoid of any meaningful relationship.

The most disturbing aspect of this male dreamworld, according to Jhally, takes this "decorative role" to its logical conclusion. If videos support a cultural story that puts women's bodies on display for males, then women's bodies become nothing more than objects, women in the videos "lose subjectivity" and, thus, their humanity. In the dreamworld, men do not have to respect women or sexual boundaries, because women have no subjective status. This, according to Jhally, leads to attitudes that legitimize and normalize the sexual violation of women. Jhally underscores this warning by ending the video with a clip of a gang rape from the movie, *The Accused*, while interspersing clips from music videos and by posting statistics that suggest that adolescent attitudes demonstrate a disturbing acceptance of sexual violence. If Jhally is right and music videos create a powerful cultural story that promotes an ethos of easy sex with women as objects, then we see this cultural form playing a significant religious role by functioning to create and grant validity to moral and ethical standards that stand in contradiction to many other religious teachings on sexual morality and the value of persons and bodies. These secular stories function as mythic truth and thus sacralize the secular.

Music and the music video provide powerful avenues for teaching youth through their culture. Thus, Jhally's film is disturbing and illustrates the negative power of religious functioning. However, music and music videos do not have to solely promote negative values, no more than full-length films only promote violence and sexuality. Music can also function religiously in positive ways, making meaningful transcendence of the mundane possible and enlightening. Music can function as an avenue to enlightened and heightened living, not simply degraded living. There are no doubt many positive examples of popular music and popular music videos, but a uniquely American form of popular music, jazz, captures the essence of the sacralizing possibility of secular music.

If Ferdinand "Jelly Roll" Morton did not give birth to jazz music according to his own claims, then he at least was midwife to the movement. It is probably more accurate to consider him one of the earliest important composers of jazz music in the early twentieth century.[31] It was in jazz that Jelly Roll located the power of truth and a type of transcendent immortality. As a jazz composer, Jelly Roll sometimes found himself defining jazz differently than those jazz musicians who found the power of jazz in improvisation, the original creation of music in unscripted fashion. But Jelly Roll did not reject improvisation, he simply jealously guarded his composition and limited improvisational freedom to a select few musicians.[32] Thus we find in Jelly Roll a type of elitism of talent, but for those talented individuals, himself and a handful of musicians, finding power in the creative process was a reality. For a few enlightened and blessed individuals, jazz could become a means to achieve a heightened relation to creativity and could lead to a type of transcendent approach to truth.

This brings to mind the philosophy of transcendentalism, of Emerson and Thoreau. For the transcendentalists, Emerson especially, only those who achieve a heightened awareness, communicated through metaphors of "seeing," could claim "Imagination, ... a very high sort of seeing" and could become poets of "true naming."[33] Emerson's poetic awareness, Thoreau's walking meditation, Jelly Roll's meditative improvisation all suggest that transcendence is available to those who can imagine the poetry or the melody, and that truth is available through the creative relationship of artist and the divine. Through music, secular as well as sacred, we hear the possibility of transcendence through creativity—music is poetry, music is myth, music is vibration that resonates not only physically but at the deepest level of our consciousness—as such, music functions religiously as an avenue to truth. Music allows us to participate in the creative moment, the transcendent moment, and can become an important transmitter of cultural truths and power, of Scott's "hidden transcripts," of Spencer's "mythologies," of Jhally's "cultural stories," of gospel music's secular gospel, of Jelly Roll's creative transcendence. As such, we see music and its accompanying images and trappings functioning in the ongoing secularizing process, both secularizing sacred music and sacralizing secular tunes, blurring and bending the boundaries between sacred and secular.

The postmodern secularization of religion

Meditative improvisation

We know that religious diversity in America is increasing;[34] people are redefining God, as Wade Clark Roof reminds us, in more personal and individualistic ways;[35] Robert Wuthnow points out that contemporary Americans feel comfortable searching for religious meaning in extra-ecclesiastical activities and institutions;[36] we see our popular culture influencing religion in very public ways. Does all this suggest, as some have argued, that religion in our culture, or at least traditional religious institutions, are falling by the wayside, that they will lose power over culture or over individual lives, that secularization will result in the obliteration of religion as a major part of American culture? Far from it. Leigh Eric Schmidt has eloquently described the process of secularization in *Consumer Rites: The Buying and Selling of American Holidays*. Schmidt recalls Reinhold Niebuhr's sacred–secular "paradox" to suggest that we witness in our culture "a dance of the sacred and the secular, sometimes graceful, sometimes awkward."[37] Secularization is not warfare where one side will acquiesce; rather, it is Schmidt's dance, with partners in relation, touching and separate, flowing and faltering, self-conscious and confident, seducing and holding at arm's length. Secularization, as dance, flows into dissolving and bending boundaries as sacred and secular exist in relation to one another.

So, we want to see secularization not through a paradigm of antagonism but through a model of relational tension, in which one cannot exist without the other and where each mutually props up the other. Secularization describes a situation of co-dependence. The antagonistic model of secularization is a postmodern attempt to explain a modern challenge to a Christian worldview. In its postmodernity, secularization theory has tended to deconstruct truth claims and ideologies and is dependent on such deconstruction to explain reality. Deconstruction itself suggests antagonism between authority structures in society, so religion as authority structure has come under attack as part of the larger postmodern challenge to authority. Thus, postmodernism has attempted to describe the modern, scientific deconstruction of Christianity as secularization, but has failed to demonstrate that such deconstruction is actually happening.

Nevertheless, the antagonistic, deconstructing model, which reached its peak in postmodern critique but maintains its roots in modernism's rationalism, is beginning to soften. We can reconstruct the evolution of sacred–secular co-dependence by looking at the concept of "binary opposition"[38] as fundamental in reality construction. If we can say that pre-modern binary opposition is defined by a God–human dichotomy, the modern opposition became sacred–secular, and the postmodern negates the sacred from the dichotomy entirely with the ascendancy of the secular. So with postmodernism's deconstruction of the sacred, binary opposition is defined solely in secular terms, as in human–human, human–nature, human–machine, or the like. However, as John McClure has argued, we may now find ourselves in a "post-secular culture," a post-postmodernism if you will, where philosophical, theological, and popular voices alike "refuse to silence" either sacred or secular voices but draw from each in non-dualistic ways.[39] McClure points out that representatives of the oppositional model such as Edward Said recognize a return to religion in postmodern culture but decry it as regressive. McClure then reviews other secular philosophers such as Michel Foucault, Jürgen Habermas, and Jacques Derrida, who maintain more openness to religious worldviews. What we see in McClure's work is the possibility of religious meaning in a secular world that can be free from dogmatism and be embedded in popular cultural forms.[40] Thus, our postmodern binary oppositions become more cooperative binary relations.

What we have then is a more cooperative view of the sacred–secular continuum that replaces the oppositional model, that moves beyond acceptance of a sacred–secular dichotomy revealed by modern rationalism, and that unveils the long partnership that has characterized the relation between sacred and secular since before the rise of modern worldviews. This model of partnership holds that sacred and secular are not dichotomous in Western culture but dialogic in constant relation. The secularization/sacralization process as described in this book predates modernity, the Enlightenment, and the rise of modern science. The partnership is as old as notions of transcendence, because it is the birth of the ideal of the transcendent, something beyond self, that gives rise to the search for meaning beyond self, an objective rather than subjective truth. This objectification battles the existential horror of imagining nothing beyond the self, existential aloneness. Once truth is objectified, the sacred and the secular become the partnered repositories of truth tucked away in transcendental as well as this-worldly reality. Both realms became external and objective places for truth, which is external to the self and to subjective reality, to reside.

What postmodernism tries to do is to re-subjectivize truth by under-mining truth claim systems—Christianity, capitalism, Marxism, Americanism, as examples. In this sense, postmodern deconstruction can be seen as a corrective to objectification. This is where classical secularization theory has risen to supremacy in the effort to undermine the idea of the sacred as a way of decon-structing the idea of ultimate truth. However, secularization theory does not undermine the idea of ultimate truth but merely replaces the sacred with the secular as the repository of such truth. Classical secularization theory, based on oppositional models, simply replaces one kind of objective truth with another, and this postmodern approach to re-subjectivize truth fails. What we have instead are sacred–secular, other–this, beyond–here, transcendent–immanent tandem polarities of externalized truth claims that represent in different ways the human need to objectify truth. We see this even in the postmodern task of undermining truth claims, because if postmodernism refuses to adopt an ethic or morality and depends on subjective appropriation of principles, we face the prospects of unchallenged evil, injustice, slavery, and other atrocities that arise throughout human history.[41] And postmodernism ultimately fails in that it either replaces one set of truth claims for another or, as Robert Royal in his quotation of G. K. Chesterton points out, through the process of undermining a truth claim only solidifies that claim, pushing it to unprecedented dogmatism.[42] Thus, postmodernism either objectifies itself or that which it hopes to undermine, undercutting the notion of subjectivity, undermining the attempt to undermine, imploding, or shall we say, deconstructing itself.

So, rather than seeing sacred and secular as oppositional where one must capitulate to the other, it is more helpful to see sacred and secular world-views on a continuum along which we attempt to define "the good, the true, and the beautiful"[43] in commonly held value structures including religion, popular culture, literature, music, and community. Be it categorized as secular or conceived as sacred, the compartmentalization of culture matters less than legitimation of value for a group, either formally or informally, conceived within a common cultural context. So postmodernism brings not the end of religion, not even the end of religious institutions. But it can lead to a secularization of religion wherein the sacred and the secular exist in dialogical, reciprocal, and cooperative relationships.

We can see this in the United States where there exists less separation of sacred and secular values than there is separation of the sources of authority for those values. While sacred worldviews may differ from secularly conceived reality structures in terms of their authoritative ground, two supposedly opposed worldviews may in fact espouse similar value systems because they exist in cooperative, not oppositional, relationship, especially in popular culture. Likewise, values from sacred and secular realms are shared in America in social context because the sources of authority for values nurture one another and support one another, defined as they are in relation to one another. So we can have civil religious dialogue that falls in line with religious institutions because of common cultural grounding, even though American civil and governmental institutions and religious institutions maintain a formal separateness. This does not separate sacred and secular values, only institutional sponsorship.

The non-establishment clause of the First Amendment to the U.S. Constitution maintains secular, political neutrality (and thus secular independence) toward sacred matters while the freedom of worship clause seeks religious independence from secular powers. And in this separation that we hold sacrosanct, the real cooperative relationship emerges—both religion and government are independently defined but inextricably bound: one's freedom is defined through relation to the other. If no one religion is established, then all or none are valid harbingers of truth while secular philosophy guides the process. If U.S. citizens are free to choose or not choose, then secular powers validate all or none. The relationship between religion and the secular in the United States is not separate if, by separate, one means oppositional. Quite the contrary; they are separate in their reciprocity, which defines a broadly diverse religious landscape that is closely connected to and dependent on secular life.

The pluralist experiment in the United States guarantees that no one truth position can claim authoritative ascendancy, thus the legitimacy of all is established and upheld by secular authority, and the pluralistic religious situation legitimizes the philosophical ideological base that allows it. In other words, the American religious-political experiment demands, and at the same time depends on, a vital religious pluralism. A vital religious pluralism in turn depends on recognition of varieties of religious truth claims and at least implicitly encourages and supports infidelity toward denominationalism and dogmatism. This infidelity is what we see in contemporary America—appropriate and expected infidelity toward dogmatic formulation, not toward religion itself. This infidelity toward institutionalized doctrine and ritual has been misconstrued as secularization that leads to the demise of religion. While secularization in America rightly might lead to the demise of institutional dogmatism, it does not spell the end of religion; in fact, it gives us a more vital and multifarious religious landscape than would exist without the secular mandate. Infidelity to institutionalized religion does not equate with illegitimacy—one can be devoted to truth while not devoted to any particular truth claim. So the reciprocal, cooperative relationship that exists between secular worldviews and sacred realities can breed a cooperative quest for "the good, the true, and the beautiful"[44] when this transcendental journey beyond self can be directed toward the world as easily as toward the heavens.

If such a quest toward meaning is to lead to healing rather than to disruption, to reconciliation rather than to demonizing, it must be predicated upon the recognition that religious truth is larger than any dogmatism, larger than any institution, and can be glimpsed by embracing the sacred–secular dance, by remaining open to truth where and when it arises, by "departing the text"[45] with mindful awareness of truths rather than Truth. Such a quest must be meditative in intent and open to surprise at any moment. Such an approach requires improvisation rather than enslavement to notation and mindful awareness rather than mindless faith. Meditative improvisation allows us to glimpse truth in the midst of this sacred–secular partnership.

Final words

Secularization paradigms are usually based on the sacred–secular dichotomization, which in turn arose out of Western dualism and was heightened by modernism as historicism and empiricism rose to primacy through science. In many manifestations of this dualism, religion takes a reactionary stance toward the secular while the secular remains suspicious of religion. Perhaps postmodernism, which in its most trenchant forms reinforces the sacred–secular antagonism, will lead us beyond the postmodern disenchantment with the sacred to a place where sacred and secular are not oppositional but rather integrated and infused with one another. This perspective must recognize and maintain healthy and legitimate theological tension between the two, for any merger carries risk. The danger of sacralizing the secular is that it can occur without moral or ethical grounding and can become relativistic to the extent of meaninglessness.[46] The risk of the secularization of the sacred is functional. If the sacred adopts secular functions while refusing to revise its theological orientation, then it runs the risk of de-legitimizing that particular theological perspective (the example is the church that becomes so identified with secular culture that it loses its prophetic voice in society).[47]

Risks aside, if the contemporary church can accept a cooperative model for secularization and embrace the world, its travails and its beauties, perhaps then the world can embrace religion, its truths and its ecstasies. Herein lies grace: when reconciliation between the world and religion, between the secular and the sacred, occurs, then so, in the words of Andrew Johnson, "the lion and the lamb shall lie down together."[48]

Study guide

Important words and concepts

Contemporary Christian music
Crossover music
Hidden ideologies in culture
Ichthus

Study questions

(1) Drawing upon your own favorite music, describe how music can communicate certain values or ideologies in culture.

(2) What characteristics of music make it effective in communicating religious messages?

(3) How does understanding the role music plays in contemporary culture contribute to the overall theme of this book?

Guided listening

(1) Find a quiet time when you are likely to not be interrupted. Listen to various types of music: Beethoven's Ninth symphony; something from Woodstock; Asian melodies; African folk music; Top-40 tunes; blues; jazz; Country and Western. Make notes as you listen—how does each genre make you feel? Are any of these feelings the same feelings you might associate with religious emotions? What make music a universal experience?

Notes

Chapter 1

1. See Alfred North Whitehead, *Process and Reality (Corrected Edition)*, (eds), David Ray Griffin and Donald W. Sherburne (New York: The Free Press, 1978). (Originally published by Macmillan, 1929.)
2. Joseph Campbell, *Reflections on the Art of Living: A Joseph Campbell Companion*, sel. and ed. Diane K. Osbon (New York: HarperPerennial, 1991), 179.
3. Richard M. Gollin, *A Viewer's Guide to Film: Arts, Artifices, and Issues* (New York: McGraw Hill, 1992), 214.
4. See Elie Wiesel, "Night," Bantam 1982, orginally published 1960 (Hill and Wang), p. 2 for questioning God as dialogue.
5. I began to think about relativity in relation to God through a discussion with Dr. Michael Vines. Dr. Vines uses the vast distance between God and humanity to illustrate God as Other. I use it here to challenge that notion. Relativity does not establish God as Other but establishes a relative scale of difference of great proportions.
6. See *The Examined Life: Introduction to Philosophy*, dir. Sally V. Beaty, Intelecom, 1998, #116, "Does Science Give Us Truth" for the Bohr–Einstein comparison.
7. See Georg Wilhelm Friedrich Hegel, *Phenomenology of Spirit*, trans. A. V. Miller (Oxford: 1977).
8. See Rudolf Otto, *The Idea of the Holy* (Oxford: Oxford University Press, 1923).
9. Peter L. Berger, *The Sacred Canopy: Elements of a Sociological Theory of Religion* (New York: Anchor Books, 1969), 7–15.
10. Berger, *The Sacred Canopy*, 29–33.
11. See Whitehead, *Process and Reality*.

Chapter 2

1. The evolution of the theory of secularization presented in this chapter and book runs throughout my work in two previous books. My thanks to the publishers of those books for their cooperation in my use of previously published material. See Conrad E. Ostwalt, Jr., *After Eden: The Secularization of American Space in the Fiction of Willa Cather and Theodore Dresier* (Lewisburg: Bucknell University Press, 1990) and Conrad E. Ostwalt, Jr., "Conclusion: Religion, Film, and Cultural Analysis," in Joel W. Martin and Conrad E. Ostwalt, Jr., *Screening the Sacred: Religion, Myth, and Ideology in Popular American Film* (Boulder: Westview Press, 1995).
2. Claudia Glenn Dowling, "A Light in the Desert," *Life*, June 1996, 72.
3. Howard Dorgan, *Giving Glory to God in Appalachia* (Knoxville: University of Tennessee Press, 1987), ch. 2.
4. Joan Osborne's "One of Us," and Madonna's "Like a Prayer" music videos.

5. This understanding of the relationship between religion and secularization exists throughout the scholarly literature. For a good articulation of the predominant attitude, see Bernard Eugene Meland, *The Secularization of Modern Cultures* (New York: Oxford University Press, 1966).

6. Peter L. Berger, "Secularism in Retreat," *The National Interest* (winter 1996/97): 4.

7. Ibid., 5, 6.

8. Mark Chaves, "Secularization as Declining Religious Authority," *Social Forces* 72:3 (March 1994): 749, 750. Other writers such as David Yamane support this line of thinking and uphold the old secularization thesis while incorporating newer revisions and insights. See David Yamane, "Secularization on Trial: In Defense of a Neosecularization Paradigm," *Journal for the Scientific Study of Religion* 36, no. 1 (1997): 109–22. The roots of this revision can be seen as early as the mid-1970s in work such as Bryan Wilson's "Aspects of Secularization in the West," *Japanese Journal of Religious Studies* 3, no.4 (December 1976): 259–76 where Wilson points to religion's powerlessness in Western, contemporary society (276).

9. Andrew Greeley, "The Persistence of Religion," *Cross Currents: The Journal of the Association for Religion and Intellectual Life* 45, no. 1 (spring 1995): 24–41.

10. See Rodney Stark and William Sims Bainbridge, *The Future of Religion: Secularization, Revival and Cult Formation* (Berkeley: University of California Press, 1985); Daniel Bell, "The Return of the Sacred? The Argument on the Future of Religion," *British Journal of Sociology* 28 (December 1977): 419–49; and Robert Booth Fowler, *Unconventional Partners: Religion and Liberal Culture in the United States* (Grand Rapids, Mich.: Eerdman's, 1989).

11. Stephen L. Carter, *The Culture of Disbelief: How American Law and Politics Trivialize Religious Devotion* (New York: Basic Books, 1993), 15–16.

12. See Carter, "The Culture of Disbelief." This is how he understands religion. See also Wade Clark Roof and William McKinney, *American Mainline Religion: Its Changing Shape and Future* (New Brunswick, NJ: Rutgers University Press, 1987).

13. See N. J. Demerath, III, "Varieties of Sacred Experience," presidential address at the Society for the Scientific Study of Religion, Boston, Mass., November 6, 1999, *Journal for the Scientific Study of Religion*, 39, no. 1 (March 2000), 1–9.

14. Peter L. Berger, *The Sacred Canopy: Elements of a Sociological Theory of Religion* (Garden City, NY: Doubleday and Company, 1967).

15. Ibid., 27–8.

16. See also Bryan Wilson, "Secularization: The Inherited Model," *The Sacred in a Secular Age: Toward Revision in the Scientific Study of Religion*, ed. Phillip E. Hammond (Berkeley: University of California Press, 1985), 9–20; and David Martin, *The Religious and the Secular* (New York: Schocken Books, 1969).

17. See Demerath, "Varieties of Sacred Experience."

18. See Greeley, "Persistence of Religion." See also Demerath. "Varieties of Sacred Experience," and James Mathisen, "From Civil Religion to Folk Religion: the Case for American Sport," in *Human Kinetics*, ed. S. J. Hoffman (Champaigne, Ill.: University of Illinois Press, 1992.)

19. Chaves, "Secularization as Declining Religious Authority."

20. See E. M. Adams, *Religion and Cultural Freedom* (Philadelphia: Temple University Press, 1993), 1–4; Owen Chadwick, *The Secularization of the European Mind in the*

Nineteenth Century (Cambridge: Cambridge University Press, 1975), 432. Even if religion is connected to neurosis as Freud thought, it is still a fundamental human characteristic. See Sigmund Freud, *The Future of an Illusion*, trans. and ed. by James Strachey (New York: W. W. Norton), 1961.

21. Chaves, "Secularization as Declining Religious Authority."

22. See Stark and Bainbridge for the idea that revival and new religion formation could result from the secularization process.

23. R. Laurence Moore, *Selling God: American Religion in the Marketplace of Culture* (New York: Oxford University Press, 1994).

24. See R. Stephen Warner, "Work in Progress toward a New Paradigm for the Sociological Study of Religion in the United States," *American Journal of Sociology* 98, no. 5 (March 1993): 1044–93 and Nathan O. Hatch, *The Democratization of American Christianity*. (New Haven, Conn: Yale University Press, 1989).

25. Paul Nathanson, *Over the Rainbow: The Wizard of Oz as a Secular Myth of America* (Albany: State University of New York Press, 1991), 17–18.

26. Ibid., 17.

27. See Meland, "Secularization of Modern Cultures," 145–6.

28. Jon Michael Spencer, *Blues and Evil* (Knoxville: The University of Tennessee Press, 1993).

29. See Demerath, "Varieties of Sacred Experience," 3.

30. See W. Warren Wagar, "Introduction," *The Secular Mind: Transformations of Faith in Modern Europe*, ed. W. Warren Wagar (New York: Holmes and Meier Publishers, 1982), 2.

31. Berger, *The Sacred Canopy*, 106.

32. See Bryan Wilson, "Secularization: The Inherited Model," in *The Sacred in a Secular Age*, ed. Phillip E. Hammond, 11; Andrew Greeley, "The Persistence of Religion," *Cross Currents: The Journal of the Association for Religion and Intellectual Life* 45, no. 1 (spring 1995), 41; and James Drane, *The Possibility of God: A Reconsideration of Religion in a Technological Society* (Totowa, NJ: Littlefield, Adams, and Company, 1976), 98–9.

33. See Ninian Smart, *Beyond Ideology: Religion and the Future of Western Civilization* (San Francisco: Harper and Row, 1981), 208ff.

34. See Drane, *The Possibility of God*, 99–100.

35. See William Lloyd Newell, *The Secular Magi: Marx, Freud, and Nietzsche on Religion* (New York: The Pilgrim Press, 1986).

36. See Owen Chadwick, *The Secularization of the European Mind in the Nineteenth Century* (Cambridge: Cambridge University Press, 1975), 14–15, and 156; and Wagar, "Introduction," 2.

37. See Nathanson, *Over the Rainbow*, 14.

38. Greeley, "Persistence of Religion," 38.

39. Berger, *The Sacred Canopy*, 108.

40. Steve Bruce, ed., *Religion and Modernization: Sociologists and Historians Debate the Secularization Thesis* (Oxford: Clarendon Press, 1992), 6.

41. Stephen L. Carter, *The Culture of Disbelief: How American Law and Politics Trivialize Religious Devotion* (New York: Basic Books, 1993), 23–4, 6, and 277.

42. See Chaves, "Secularization as Declining Religious Authority," 752; and David Martin,

A General Theory of Secularization (New York: Harper and Row Publishers, 1978), 12. See also Wilson, "Secularization: The Inherited Model."

43. See Nathanson, *Over the Rainbow*, 14; and Meland, "Secularization of Modern Cultures," 116.

44. Wilson, "Secularization: The Inherited Model," 11–12. See also Olivier Tschannen, "The Secularization Paradigm: A Sytematization," *Journal for the Scientific Study of Religion* 30, no. 4 (1991): 395–415. See Nathanson, *Over the Rainbow*, for his use of this quotation.

45. Roy Wallis and Steve Bruce, "Secularization: The Orthodox Model," *Religion and Modernization: Sociologists and Historians Debate the Secularization Thesis*, ed. Steve Bruce (Oxford: Clarendon Press, 1992), 11, 22.

46. Berger, *The Sacred Canopy*, 107–8.

47. Meland, *Secularization of Modern Cultures*, 36–42. The quotation is found on 42.

48. R. Laurence Moore, *Selling God: American Religion in the Marketplace of Culture* (New York: Oxford University Press, 1994), 4. Moore cites a report on a survey conducted by the Graduate School of the City University of New York, *New York Times*, April 10, 1991.

49. Roger Finke, "An Unsecular America," *Religion and Modernization: Sociologists and Historians Debate the Secularization Thesis*, ed. Steve Bruce (Oxford: Clarendon Press, 1992), 163.

50. See Mark Hulsether, "Interpreting the 'Popular' in Popular Religion," *American Studies* 36, no. 2 (Fall 1995), 129–31. See also Jon Butler, *Awash in a Sea of Faith* (Cambridge: Harvard University Press, 1990).

51. David Martin, *The Religious and the Secular* (New York: Schocken Books, 1969), 10ff.

52. Chadwick, *Secularization of the European Mind in the Nineteenth Century*, 4. See also Hammond, *The Sacred in a Secular Age*.

53. Jeffrey K. Hadden, "Desacralizing Secularization Theory," *Secularization and Fundamentalism Reconsidered: Religion and the Political Order, Volume III*, ed. Jeffrey K. Hadden and Anson Shupe (New York: Paragon House, 1989), 3–4.

54. Greeley, "Persistence of Religion," 39.

55. Ibid., 25–6, 29–31, 39.

56. See Laurence Iannaccone and Rodney Stark, "A Supply Side Reinterpretation of the 'Secularization' of Europe," *Journal for the Scientific Study of Religion* 33, no. 3 (1994), 230–52; Rodney Stark and William Sims Bainbridge, *The Future of Religion: Secularization, Revival and Cult Formation* (Berkeley: University of California Press, 1985); Mark Chaves, "Secularization as Declining Religious Authority," *Social Forces* 72, no. 3, 749–74; and Peter L. Berger, "Secularism in Retreat," *The National Interest* (winter 1996/97), 3–12.

57. Meland, *Secularization of Modern Cultures*, 117.

58. Wagar, "Introduction," 4. See also Harvey Cox, *The Secular City: Secularization and Urbanization in Theological Perspective* (New York: Macmillan,1966); and Martin E. Marty, *The Modern Schism: Three Paths to the Secular* (New York: Harper and Row, 1969), 11.

59. See Frank J. Lechner, "The Case Against Secularization: A Rebuttal," *Social Forces* 69 (1991), 1103–19; Chaves, "Secularization as Declining Religious Authority," 749; Chadwick, *The Secularization of the European Mind*; and Hammond, *The Sacred in a Secular Age*.

60. Stark and Bainbridge, *The Future of Religion*, 429–30.

61. Ibid., 1–2.

62. See Demerath, "Varieties of Sacred Experience."

63. Peter Iver Kaufman, "Religion on the Run," *Journal of Interdisciplinary History*, xxv, no. 1 (summer 1994), 85–6. See also C. John Sommerville, *The Secularization of Early Modern England: From Religious Culture to Religious Faith* (New York: Oxford University Press, 1992).

64. Nathanson, *Over the Rainbow*, 318.

65. See Chaves, "Secularization as Declining Religious Authority."

66. George M. Marsden and Bradley J. Longfield, (eds), *The Secularization of the Academy* (New York: Oxford University Press, 1992), 5, 13–41.

67. Chaves, "Secularization as Declining Religious Authority," 755–6.

68. Ibid., 749.

69. Berger, *The Sacred Canopy*, 110–18. The quotation is found on 118.

70. Ibid., 123.

71. David Martin, *A General Theory of Secularization* (New York: Harper and Row Publishers, 1978), pp. 100–1.

72. Sommerville, *The Secularization of Early Modern England*, 3–5. See also Vernon Pratt, *Religion and Secularization* (London: Macmillan, 1970), 1–5. See also Tschannen, "The Secularization Paradigm: A Systematization." See Timothy Husband and Jane Hayward, The Metropolitan Museum of Art, *The Secular Spirit: Life and Art at the End of the Middle Ages* (New York: E. P. Dutton, 1975), 11.

73. See Wagar, "Introduction," 6. See also Timothy Husband and Jane Hayward, *The Secular Spirit: Life and Art at the End of the Middle Ages* (New York: E. P. Dutton, 1975), 11.

74. See Wagar, 5 and 12.

75. David Nash, *Secularism, Art and Freedom* (Leicester: Leicester University Press, 1992), 8–27.

76. Carter, *The Culture of Disbelief*, 7.

77. Ibid.

78. Meland, *The Secularization of Modern Cultures*, 15 and 58ff. See also Arnold Toynbee, *An Historian's Approach to Religion* (New York: Oxford University Press, 1956).

79. Wagar, "Introduction," 9. See also Vernon Pratt, *Religion and Secularization* (London: Macmillan, 1970), 11–20.

80. Pratt, *Religion and Secularization*, 13.

81. See Bernard Eugene Meland, *The Realities of Faith: The Revolution in Cultural Forms* (New York: Oxford University Press, 1962), Preface.

82. James Drane, *The Possibility of God: A Reconsideration of Religion in a Technological Society* (Totowa, NJ: Littlefield, Adams, and Company, 1976), 87–9.

83. Stark and Bainbridge, *The Future of Religion*, 430–4.

84. Ibid., 432–3.

85. Wagar, "Introduction," 8.

86. See Meland, *The Secularization of Modern Cultures*, 35; and Ninian Smart, *Beyond Ideology: Religion and the Future of Western Civilization* (San Francisco: Harper and Row, 1981), 209–11.

87. Phyllis H. Stock, "Proudhon and *Morale Independante*: A Variation of French Secular

Morality," in *The Secular Mind: Transformations of Faith in Modern Europe*, ed. W. Warren Wagar (New York: Holmes and Meier Publishers, 1982), 102ff.

88. Newell, *The Secular Magi*, xiv.
89. Nathanson, *Over the Rainbow*, 311.
90. Husband and Hayward, *The Secular Spirit*, 12.
91. See David Martin, *A General Theory of Secularization*, 1–8 in particular.
92. Wagar, "Introduction," 5–6.
93. See David Spadafora, "Secularization in British Thought, 1730–1789: Some Landmarks," in Wagar, *The Secular Mind*, 36.
94. Greeley, "Persistence of Religion," 34–5, 27.
95. Carter, *The Culture of Disbelief*, 44–5, 51.
96. See Fowler, *Unconventional Partners*, 2. See also Kenneth D. Wald, *Religion and Politics in the United States* (New York: St. Martin's Press, 1986), 9.
97. Alexis de Tocqueville, *Democracy in America*, Harvey C. Mansfield and Delba Winthrop, (eds), (Chicago: University of Chicago Press, 2000).
98. See Mark Hulsether, "Interpreting the 'Popular' in Popular Religion," *American Studies* 36, no. 2 (fall 1995), 127. See also Paul Boyer, *When Time Shall Be No More: Prophecy Belief in Modern American Culture* (Cambridge University Press, 1992), 2–3 and 13–15; and George Gallup, Jr. and Jim Castelli, *The People's Religion: American Faith in the 90s* (New York: Macmillan Publishing Company, 1989).
99. Carter, *The Culture of Disbelief*, 51ff and 67.
100. Peter L. Berger, "Religion in Post-Protestant America," *Commentary* (May 1986), 4; and Berger, "Secularism in Retreat." See also Robert Booth Fowler, *Unconventional Partners: Religion and Liberal Culture in the United States* (Grand Rapids: Wm. B. Eerdman's Publishing Co., 1989), 3; and Jon Butler, *Awash in a Sea of Faith*.
101. Moore, *Selling God*, 67ff.
102. Ibid., 11. See also Hulsether, 128.
103. See Moore, *Selling God*; Roger Finke and Rodney Stark, *The Churching of America, 1776–1990: Winners and Losers in Our Religious Economy* (New Brunswick: Rutgers University Press, 1992); Laurence Iannaccone, "The Consequences of Religious Market Structure: Adam Smith and the Economics of Religion," *Rationality and Society* 3 (April 1991), 156–77; Steven H. Warner, "Work in Progress toward a New Paradigm for the Sociological Study of Religion in the United States," *American Journal of Sociology* 98, no. 5 (1993), 1044–93.
104. Greeley, "Persistence of Religion," 27.
105. Moore, *Selling God*, 10.
106. Clifford Geertz, "Thick Description: Toward an Interpretative Theory of Culture," in *Interpretation of Cultures* (New York: Basic Books, 1973), 3.
107. Fowler, *Unconventional Partners*, 3.
108. Moore, *Selling God*, 8.
109. James G. Moseley, *A Cultural History of Religion in America* (Westport, CT: Greenwood Press, 1981), 161–2. See also Clifford Geertz, "The Interpretation of Cultures," 87–125.
110. Greeley, "Persistence of Religion," 36.
111. Moore, *Selling God*, 9 and 275.

112. See George M. Marsden, *Fundamentalism and American Culture: The Shaping of Twentieth-Century Evangelicalism 1870–1925* (Oxford: Oxford University Press, 1980), vi and 3ff.

113. Butler, Awash in a Sea of Faith, 4.

114. Adams, *Religion and Cultural Freedom*, 25 and 56.

115. See Moore, *Selling God*; and Allen C. Guelzo, "Selling God in America: How Christians Have Befriended Mammon," *Christianity Today* 39, no. 5 (April 24, 1995), 27–30.

116. Moore, *Selling God*, 5–6, 13ff., 91, 120, 221–2. See also Michael T. Gilmore, *American Romanticism and the Marketplace* (Chicago: University of Chicago Press, 1985); and Nathan Hatch, *The Democratization American Christianity* (New Haven: Yale University Press, 1989).

117. See Moore, *Selling God*, ch. 8; and Hulsether, "Interpreting the 'Popular' in Popular Religion," 128–9.

118. See Paul Galloway, "Media are Poor Substitute for the Family," *Chicago Tribune*, *The Charlotte Observer*, June 3, 1996, 9A. See also Quentin Schultze, *Winning Your Kids Back From the Media* (Westmount, Ill.: InterVarsity Press, 1994).

119. Langdon Gilkey, *Society and the Sacred: Toward a Theology of Culture in Decline* (New York: Crossroad, 1981), 3–4.

120. Conrad Ostwalt, "Conclusion: Religion, Film, and Cultural Analysis," in Joel Martin and Conrad E. Ostwalt, Jr., *Screening the Sacred: Religion, Myth, and Ideology in Popular American Film* (Boulder: Westview Press, 1995), 157–8.

121. See John Storey, *An Introductory Guide to Cultural Theory and Popular Culture* (Athens: The University of Georgia Press, 1993), 154–9.

122. See Storey, *Cultural Theory and Popular Culture*, 159–61; and Jean-François Lyotard, *The Postmodern Condition: A Report on Knowledge* (Manchester: Manchester University Press, 1984).

123. Storey, *Cultural Theory and Popular Culture*, 162–5; and Jean Baudrillard, *Simulations* (New York: Semiotext(e): 1983). For the *JFK* reference, see Ostwalt, "Conclusion," *Screening the Sacred*, 156.

124. See Storey, *Cultural Theory and Popular Culture*, 166–72; and Frederic Jameson, "Postmodernism, or the Cultural Logic of Late Capitalism," *New Left Review* 146 (1984); "The Politics of Theory: Ideological positions in the Postmodernism Debate," *The Ideologies of Theory Essays* 2 (London: Routledge, 1988); "Postmodernism and Consumer Society," in *The Anti-Aesthetic: Essays on Postmodern Culture*, ed. Hal Foster (Port Townsend, Washington: Bay Press, 1983), 111–25.

125. See Ostwalt, "Conclusion," *Screening the Sacred*, 156–7. See also Conrad Ostwalt, "Dances with Wolves: An American *Heart of Darkness*," *Literature/Film Quarterly* 24, no. 2 (1996): 209–16.

126. David Jasper, paper presented at the Southeastern Conference for the Study of Religion, March 1996, Columbia, South Carolina.

127. See Ostwalt, "Conclusion," *Screening the Sacred*, ch. 4.

128. Moore, *Selling God*, 5.

129. Gabriel Vahanian, *The Death of God: The Culture of Our Post-Christian Era* (New York: George Braziller, 1961), 60–6.

130. See Newell, *The Secular Magi*, xiv.

131. See Stark and Bainbridge, *The Future of Religion*, 435–86.

132. Moore, *Selling God*, 3, 41–2, 44, 49, 50–2, 251–2, and ch. 9.

133. Ibid., 209–18.

134. Nathanson, *Over the Rainbow*, 17.

135. Jacqulyn Weekley, quoted in Julie Slaven, "Lights! Camera! Religion!," *The Charlotte Observer*, June 1, 1996, Section G1 and 4.

136. Timothy C. Morgan, "Cyber Shock: New Ways of Thinking Must be Developed for the Church to Keep Pace in the Coming Information Age," *Christianity Today* 39, no. 4 (April 3, 1995), 78–86.

137. Gustav Niebuhr, "Where Religion Gets a Big Dose of Shopping-Mall Culture," *The New York Times* (April, 16 1995), 1, col. 1.

138. Bill Leonard, quoted in Niebuhr, "Shopping Mall Culture," 14.

139. Gustav Niebuhr, "The High Energy Never Stops," *The New York Times* (16 April 1995), 14; and Niebuhr, "Shopping-Mall Culture," 14; and Trip Gabriel, "MTV-Inspired Images, but the Message for Children Is a Moral One," *New York Times* (April, 16 1995), 14.

140. Niebuhr, "Shopping-Mall Culture," 1.

141. Julie Slaven, "Lights! Camera! Religion!," 1, 4.

142. Dowling, "A Light in the Desert," 66–73.

143. See Conrad Ostwalt, "Conclusion."

144. See Moseley, *A Cultural History*, xv–xvi, 161. See also Edwin S. Gaustad, Darline Miller, and G. Allison Stokes, "Religion in America," *American Quarterly* 31, no. 3 (1979), 250.

145. See Gilkey, *Society and the Sacred*, x; Fowler, *Unconventional Partners*, 3; and Peter W. Williams, *Popular Religion in America: Symbolic Change and the Modernization Process in Historical Perspective* (Englewood Cliffs, NJ: Prentice-Hall, 1980, 1989).

146. See Moore, *Selling God*, 17, 221–2.

147. Nathanson, *Over the Rainbow*, xviii. See also Husband and Hayword, *The Secular Spirit*, 11.

148. Mark Twain, quoted in Moore, *Selling God*, 147.

149. See Smart, *Beyond Ideology*, 221–32; and W. Warren Wagar, "World's End: Secular Eschatologies in Modern Fiction," in Wagar, *The Secular Mind*, 239.

150. See John Lukacs, "It's the End of the Modern Age," *The Chronicle of Higher Education* (26 April 2002), Section 2, B9. Lukacs discusses the return to a "pictorial" orientation in contemporary society that mimics the Middle Ages.

Chapter 3

1. Abraham Lincoln, "Gettysburg Address," November 19, 1863.

2. ABC's Wide World of Sports Introduction included these words, written by Stanley Ralph Ross.

3. Michael Novak, *The Joy of Sports: End Zones, Bases, Baskets, Balls, and the Consecration of the American Spirit* (New York: Basic Books, 1976), 33.

4. Novak, *The Joy of Sports*, 123.

5. Ibid., 126.

6. Ibid., 125 and 124.

7. http://www.Packers.com/lambeau-field/stadium-info/history

8. See G. R. Potter, *Zwingli* (Cambridge: Cambridge University Press, 1976).

9. The descriptions of the ICF worship service and of contemporary Zurich are based on my visit to Zurich during September, 1996. Additional information on ICF came from the organization's promotional literature and Website www.icf.ch/

10. Leo Biggers, pastor of the ICF. Interview by author, August 15, 1996.

11. See "Pope Accepts Theory of Evolution," *The News and Observer*, Raleigh, North Carolina, October 25, 1996, 1A and 16A.

12. See R. Laurence Moore, *Selling God: American Religion in the Marketplace of Culture* (New York: Oxford University Press, 1994).

13. Cathy Lynn Grossman, "Charting the Unchurched in America," *USA Today* (7 March 2002), 4 (www.usatoday.com). Grossman quotes Ronald Inglehart for these statistics.

14. Peter L. Berger, *The Sacred Canopy: Elements of a Sociological Theory of Religion* (Garden City, NY: Doubleday and Co., 1967).

15. Mark Noll, *A History of Christianity in the United States and Canada* (Grand Rapids: Wm. B. Eerdmans, 1992), 92–3.

16. See Noll, *History of Christianity*, 227.

17. For an examination of the history of evangelical use of media, see Bill Jarrett, "The Lively Experiment: American Evangelicalism and Twentieth-Century Technology," paper presented at the North Carolina Religious Studies Association, Boone, NC, October, 1993.

18. Stephen Board, "Moving the World with Magazines: A Survey of Evangelical Periodicals," in *American Evangelicals and the Mass Media: Perspectives on the Relationship Between American Evangelicals and the Mass Media*, ed. Quentin J. Schultze (Grand Rapids: Zondervon, 1990), 137.

19. See Harold E. Metcalf, *The Magic of Telephone Evangelism* (Atlanta: Southern Union Conference of Seventh-Day Adventists, 1967); and Richard N. Ostling, "Many Are Called: Dialing for Jesus," *Time*, February 27, 1989, 79.

20. See Everett C. Parker, Elinor Inman, and Ross Snyder, *Religious Radio: What to Do and How* (New York: Harper and Brothers Publishers, 1948); and Dennis Benson, *Electric Evangelism* (Nashville: Abingdon Press, 1973).

21. Quentin J. Schultze, "The Invisible Medium: Evangelical Radio," in Schultze (ed.), *American Evangelicals and the Mass Media*, 171–2.

22. Merrill McCloughlin, "From Revival Tent to Mainstream," *U.S. News and World Report*, December 19, 1988, 52–7.

23. See Stewart Hoover, "The Meaning of Religious Television: The '700 Club' in the Lives of Its Viewers," in Schultze (ed.), *American Evangelics and the Mass Media*, 234.

24. Peter G. Horsfield, *Religious Television: The American Experience* (New York: Longman, Inc., 1987).

25. See Stewart M. Hoover, *Mass Media Religion: The Social Sources of the Electronic Church* (Newbury Park, California: SAGE Publications, 1988).

26. Joel Gregory, *Too Great a Temptation: The Seductive Power of America's Super Church* (Fort Worth: The Summit Group, 1994), xiii.

27. See Lyle E. Schaller, *The Seven-Day-A-Week Church* (Nashville: Abingdon, 1992); and John N. Vaughan, *The Large Church: A Twentieth-Century Expression of the First-Century*

Church (Grand Rapids: Baker Book House, 1985).

28. Gregory, *Too Great a Temptation*, xiv.

29. Ibid., xiii.

30. Scott Thumma, "Exploring the Megachurch Phenomena: Their Characteristics and Cultural Context," Hartford Institute for Religion Research, hirr.hartsem.edu, 12.

31. Robert Schuller, interview by G. A. Pritchard in *Willow Creek Seeker Services* (Grand Rapids: Baker Books, 1996), 50.

Chapter 4

1. Charles Trueheart, "The Megachurch," *The Sunday Oregonian: Forum*, September 22, 1996, E 1. See also Scott Thumma, "Exploring the Megachurch Phenomena," Hartford Institute for Religion Research (hirr.hartsem.edu); and Scott Thumma, *The Kingdom, the Power, and the Glory: Megachurches In Modern American Society*, dissertation, Emory University, 1996.

2. Trueheart, "The Megachurch."

3. Bryan Wilson, "New Images of Christian Community," in *The Oxford History of Christianity*, ed. John McManners (Oxford: Oxford University Press, 1993), 617, 587–9.

4. R. Laurence Moore, *Selling God: American Religion in the Marketplace of Culture* (New York: Oxford University Press, 1994), 5.

5. Bernard Eugene Meland, *The Secularization of Modern Cultures* (New York: Oxford University Press, 1966), 145–6. See also William Lloyd Newell, *The Secular Magi: Marx, Freud, and Nietzsche on Religion* (New York: The Pilgrim Press, 1986), xiv.

6. See Mark Hulsether, "Interpreting the 'Popular' in Popular Religion," *American Studies* 36, no. 2 (fall 1995): 133.

7. Paul Nathanson, *Over the Rainbow: The Wizard of Oz as a Secular Myth of America* (Albany: State University of New York Press, 1991), 17. See also Julie Slaven, "Lights! Cameras! Religion!" *The Charlotte Observer* (June 1, 1996) G1 and G4. See also Thumma, "Exploring the Megachurch Phenomena."

8. Gustav Niebuhr, "Where Religion Gets a Big Dose of Shopping-Mall Culture," *The New York Times* (16 April 1995): 1, 14.

9. James Wall quoting Steve Johnson, Chicago Tribune critic, in James Wall, "Viewing the Megachurch: Between a Gush and a Smirk," *Christian Century* 112:10 (March 22, 1995): 315–16.

10. See Thumma, "Exploring the Megachurch Phenomena," and *The Kingdom, the Power, and the Glory*; and G. A. Pritchard, *Willow Creek Seeker Services: Evaluating a New Way of Doing Church* (Grand Rapids: Baker Books, 1996).

11. Niebuhr, "Where Religion Gets a Big Dose of Shopping-Mall Culture," 1.

12. Eric Reed, "Willow Creek Church Readies for Megagrowth," *Christianity Today* 44, no. 5 (April 24, 2000): 21–4. See also http://www.believe.com/church/willowcreek/

13. Pritchard, *Willow Creek Seeker Services*, 11–12. See also Pritchard's dissertation, a comprehensive study of Willow Creek Community Church that numbers over 800 pages. The dissertation is rich with citations and is available through Communication Institute, Washington, Illinois.

14. For the history of Willow Creek from its roots in Son City, see Pritchard, *Willow Creek Seeker Services*, 31–49.

15. George G. Hunter, III, *Church for the Unchurched* (Nashville: Abingdon, 1996), 26–34. See also James L. Kidd, "Megachurch Methods," *Christian Century* 114, no. 16 (May 14, 1997): 482–5. Kidd quotes Hunter in his review of the book.

16. Pritchard, *Willow Creek Seeker Services,* 49–50, 52.

17. Trueheart, "The Megachurch," E7, quoting Kenton Beshore, senior pastor at Mariners Church, Newport Beach, California.

18. Mark O'Keefe, "The Megachurch: Oregon," *The Sunday Oregonian: Forum* (September 22, 1996), E7, quoting the Reverend Marilyn Sewell of First Unitarian Church in Portland, Oregon.

19. Niebuhr, "Where Religion Gets a Big Dose of Shopping-Mall Culture," 14.

20. Bishop Charles Blake interview by Duncan Moon, "Morning Edition," National Public Radio (April 20, 2001), transcript, hour 2, National Public Radio, 15.

21. Ibid.

22. Slaven, "Lights! Camera! Religion," G1, quoting Jacqulyn Weekly.

23. Blake interview by Moon, 16.

24. See Rodney Stark and William Sims Bainbridge, *The Future of Religion: Secularization, Revival and Cult Formation* (Berkeley: University of California Press, 1985, 436; and R. Laurence Moore, *Selling God: American Religion in the Marketplace of Culture* (New York: Oxford University Press), 65 and 209–18.

25. Pritchard, *Willow Creek Seeker Services*, 123.

26. Trueheart, "The Megachurch," E1.

27. Pritchard, *Willow Creek Seeker Services*, 223.

28. See Pritchard, *Willow Creek Seeker Services*, 138; and Lee Strobel, *Inside the Mind of Unchurched Harry and Mary: How to Reach Friends and Family Who Avoid God and the Church* (Grand Rapids: Zondervon, 1993), 66. See also Blake interview by Moon, 16–17.

29. See Moore, *Selling God*.

30. Staffers at the Willow Creek Association, interview by the author, August 13, 1996.

31. Leo Bigger, leader of the ICF, interview by author, October 2, 1996.

32. Leo Bigger, interview by author, August 15, 1996.

33. Bryan Wilson, "New Images of Christian Community," in *The Oxford History of Christianity*, ed. John McManners (Oxford: Oxford University Press, 1993), 593.

34. Pritchard, *Willow Creek Seeker Services*, 206, 128–9.

35. Hybels, quoted in Pritchard, *Willow Creek Seeker Services*, 73.

36. See Trueheart, "The Megachurch."

37. The marketing theory followed at Willow Creek is based on Philip Kotler, *Marketing Management: Analysis, Planning, Implementation, and Control,* 6th edn (Englewood Cliffs, N.J.: Prentice Hall, 1988). See also Pritchard, *Willow Creek Seeker Services*, 68–70.

38. See James Emery White, "Churches, Listen to the Unchurched," *The Charlotte Observer* (March 27, 1995), 7A.

39. David S. Luecke, "Is Willow Creek the Way of the Future?" *Christian Century*, 114, Issue 16 (May, 14 1997): 479–83.

40. Pritchard, *Willow Creek Seeker Services*, 25–9. See also Thumma, "Exploring the Megachurch Phenomena."

41. Pritchard, *Willow Creek Seeker Services*, 64–5.

42. Ibid., 23–4.
43. See Luecke, "Is Willow Creek the Way of the Future?"
44. Trueheart, "The Megachurch," E7.
45. Pritchard, *Willow Creek Seeker Services*, 59.
46. Trueheart, "The Megachurch," E7.
47. Leo Bigger interviews, October 2, 1996 and August 15, 1996. This impression is also based on the September 1, 1996 Seeker Service at the ICF.
48. Trueheart, "The Megachurch," E7.
49. Wilson, "New Images of Christian Community," 596–7.
50. Peggy Hill and Bishop Kenneth Ulmer, interview by Duncan Moon. Morning Edition, National Public Radio, April 20, 2001, transcript, hour 2, p. 16.
51. See Pritchard, *Willow Creek Seeker Services*, 51ff. for an assessment of the Schullerian approach.
52. Ibid., 42.
53. *ICF Church News*, no. 4, 1996.
54. www.icf.ch
55. Wilson, "New Images of Christian Community," 606.
56. See Moore, *Selling God*.
57. See Pritchard, *Willow Creek Seeker Services*, 81–2.
58. Ibid., 89–91.
59. See Neil Postman, *Amusing Ourselves to Death* (New York: Viking Penguin, 1985); David Wells, *Turning to God* (Grand Rapids: Baker, 1989); and Lee Strobel, *Inside the Mind of Unchurched Harry and Mary: How to Reach Friends and Family Who Avoid God and the Church* (Grand Rapids: Zondervon, 1993).
60. See O'Keefe, "The Megachurch: Oregon," E1. See also Trueheart, "The Megachurch," E7; and Pritchard, *Willow Creek Seeker Services*, 89.
61. Leo Bigger interview August 15, 1996; and *ICF Church News*, no. 4, 1996, 4.
62. Mailer, Mecklenburg Community Church.
63. *In Touch*, Mecklenburg Community Church's newsletter, November, 1993.
64. There are dozens of testimonials from seekers about the services they attend, descriptions like "fun," "entertaining," "relevant," and "engaging" abound. See Ken Garfield, "Nontraditional church appealing to many," *Charlotte Observer*, May 24, 1993.
65. Pritchard, *Willow Creek Seeker Services*, 33–6. See also Thumma, "Exploring the Megachurch Phenomena."
66. Wilson, "New Images of Christian Community," 596.
67. See Thumma, "Exploring the Megachurch Phenomena," 5ff.
68. See James Wall, "Viewing the Megachurch," 315–16.
69. Pritchard, *Willow Creek Seeker Services*, 153.
70. Ibid., 53.
71. Ibid., 57–8 and 154–6.
72. See Ibid., 154–6 and 227. Examples of psychology self-help books widely read at Willow Creek are Melody Beattie, *Codependent No More*, David Keirsey and Marilyn Bates, *Please Understand Me*, and Henry Cloud, *When Your World Makes No Sense*.
73. See James Kidd, "Megachurch Methods," *Christian Century* 114, Issue 16 (May 14,

1997): 482–4. See also George G. Hunter, III, *Church for the Unchurched* (Nashville: Abingdon, 1996).

74. Wilson, "New Images of Christian Community," 593.

75. Ibid., 608.

76. Trueheart, "The Megachurch," E7.

77. Ibid.

78. Haya El Nasser, "Giant Churches Irk Some Neighbors," *USA Today* online, September 23, 2002.

79. Wilson, "New Images of Christian Community," 595.

80. Trueheart, "The Megachurch," E7.

81. Pritchard, *Willow Creek Seeker Services*, 81–2.

82. Moon interview, transcript, 16.

83. Trueheart, "The Megachurch," E7.

84. Ibid., E7.

85. See Rodney Stark and William Sims Bainbridge, *The Future of Religion: Secularization, Revival, and Cult Formation* (Berkeley: University of California Press, 1985).

86. See Slaven, "Lights! Camera! Religion," G1; and Pritchard, *Willow Creek Seeker Services*, 192–4.

87. See Peter L. Berger, *The Sacred Canopy: Elements of a Sociological Theory of Religion* (Garden City: Doubleday, 1967), 156, for the "accommodation and resistance" roles of the church. Pritchard raises this concern focusing on the tendency to compromise eternal truth to relative cultural standards. See Pritchard, *Willow Creek Seeker Services*, 192–4.

88. Pritchard, *Willow Creek Seeker Services*, 244–9. See also James Wall, "Viewing the Megachurch."

89. James D. Hunter and Stephen C. Ainlay, (eds), *Making Sense of Modern Times: Peter L. Berger and the Vision of Interpretive Sociology* (New York: Routledge and Kegan Paul, 1986), 151–2. See also Pritchard, *Willow Creek Seeker Services*, 249.

90. Pritchard, *Willow Creek Seeker Services*, 239.

91. See David Luecke, "Is Willow Creek the Way of the Future," for his quote of Lyle Schaller.

Chapter 5

1. This biblical reference from Matthew 5.14 is used in a famous sermon by John Winthrop to characterize the New World religious and social experiment. Ronald Reagan also referenced the image in his farewell presidential address. The image of the city upon a hill has a firm foundation in America's civil religious understanding.

2. This section of the chapter on Love Valley as sacred space is based in part on a paper I delivered at the annual meeting of the American Academy of Religion, Nashville, Tennessee, November 2000, and on a response to four papers presented at the annual meeting of the American Academy of Religion, Boston, Massachusetts, November 1999. The papers and authors are as follows: Jay Blossom, "'An Ideal Summer Resort for Christian Families': Wholesome Entertainment in Early-20th-Century Winona Lake"; Thomas S. Bremer, "From Pilgrims' Sacred Topography to Tourists' Sacred Landscape: A Brief Tour of Western Religious Travel"; John Powers, "Shangri-la Comes to Hollywood, Or Hollywood Comes to Shangri-la: Tibet and Popular Culture in the 1990s"; Robin Sylvan, "Burning Man and Rave Culture: A

Pre-Millennial, Postmodern, Future Primitive Popular Religious Revival."

3. See Conrad Ostwalt, *Love Valley: An American Utopia* (Bowling Green, OH: Bowling Green State University Press, 1998), 2; David Kimbrough, *Taking Up Serpents: Snake Handlers of Eastern Kentucky* (Chapel Hill: University of Chapel Hill Press, 1995), 7–8; William Lynwood Montell, *The Saga of Coe Ridge: A Study in Oral History* (Knoxville: University of Tennessee Press, 1970), viii, xviii.

4. Sylvan writes about the landscape and human body as a "blank canvas" at the Burning Man Ceremony (Burning Man and Rave Culture) while Powers discusses the "myth-making process" in conjunction with popular images of Tibet (Shangri-la Comes to Hollywood).

5. Powers writes about "otherness tinged with menace" in his paper on Tibet, "Shangri-la Comes to Hollywood." See also Bremer, "From Pilgrims' Sacred Topography to Tourists' Sacred Landscape."

6. Sylvan notes the unofficial creed at the Burning Man Ceremony is "no observers, only participants" in his paper, "Burning Man and Rave Culture." Also see Bremer, "From Pilgrims' Sacred Topography to Tourists' Sacred Landscape."

7. See Bremer, "From Pilgrims' Sacred Topography to Tourists' Sacred Landscape."

8. For a complete treatment of Love Valley, see Ostwalt, *Love Valley: An American Utopia*; and Conrad Ostwalt, "Love Valley, A Utopian Experiment in North Carolina," *North Carolina Humanities* 1, no. 1 (Fall 1992): 101–8.

9. This paragraph vignette was previously published in Conrad Ostwalt, "Love Valley: A Utopian Experiment in North Carolina," 101, and is reprinted here by permission. The remainder of the section on Love Valley is based on that article, pp. 101–8, and upon Ostwalt, *Love Valley: An American Utopia* (reprinted by permission).

10. See Ostwalt, *Love Valley: An American Utopia*, 9. The letter was dated February 1, 1945 and was recorded by D. L. Morris in an unpublished manuscript housed in the Appalachian Collection at Appalachian State University, Boone, NC. See Morris, ch. 4, p. 4

11. Ostwalt, *Love Valley: An American Utopia*, 16. See also Jim Taylor, "Dude Ranch Shaping Up in North Iredell Valley, *Statesville Record and Landmark*, June 4, 1954: 1, 8.

12. See Ostwalt, *Love Valley: An American Utopia*, chs 6 and 7, for details.

13. See Ostwalt, *Love Valley: An American Utopia*, 11. Lyrics and music of "Love Valley" are by Loonis McGlohon.

14. See Ostwalt, *Love Valley: An American Utopia*, 113–14. Don Berg wrote the song, "Love Valley, U.S.A."

15. See Ostwalt, *Love Valley: An American Utopia*, 142–6.

16. Ostwalt, quoting Arizona, in *Love Valley: An American Utopia*, 136.

Chapter 6

1. See Stephen Prothero, *Religious Literacy: What Every American needs to Know—And Doesn't* (San Francisco: HarperSanFrancisco, 2007).

2. See William G. Doty, *Contemporary New Testament Interpretation* (Englewood Cliffs, New Jersey: Prentice-Hall Incorporated, 1972), 53.

3. Tim O'Brien, *The Things They Carried* (New York: Broadway Books, 1990), 179.

4. Writers as disparate as Joseph Campbell and Thomas Cahill recognize that centrality of metaphor to religious meaning. See Joseph Campbell, *Reflections on the Art of Living:*

A Joseph Campbell Companion, ed. Diane K. Olson (New York: HarperCollins, 1991), 168–71. In this short essay we find Campbell distinguishing between metaphorical and historical readings of the Bible. See also Thomas Cahill, *The Gifts of the Jews: How a Tribe of Desert Nomads Changed the Way Everyone Thinks and Feels* (New York: Nan A. Talese Doubleday, 1998), 49. In a few eloquent phrases, Cahill describes metaphor as the basis of "all language and all meaning" and, thus, "all religion."

5. Herman Melville, *Moby Dick* (New York: New American Library, 1961), 129. See also Conrad Ostwalt, *After Eden: The Secularization of American Space in the Fiction of Willa Cather and Theodore Dreiser* (Lewisburg: Bucknell University Press, 1990), 118–25.

6. See Ostwalt, *After Eden*.

7. See Phyllis Carey, ed., *Wagering on Transcendence: The Search for Meaning in Literature* (Kansas City: Sheed and Ward, 1997), xv and xviii, for the possibility of finding "transcendence in literature."

8. Mircea Eliade, *The Sacred and Profane: The Nature of Religion*, trans. Willard R. Trask (New York: Harcourt Brace Jovanovich, 1959), 4–14. See also Ostwalt, *After Eden*, 119.

9. See Lynn Ross-Bryant, *Imagination and the Life of the Spirit: An Introduction to the Study of Religion and Literature* (Chico, California: Scholars Press, 1981), 16. See also Langdon Gilkey, *Naming the Whirlwind: The Renewal of God Language* (Indianapolis: Bobbs-Merrill Company, 1969) and Ostwalt, *After Eden*, 119.

10. Giles Gunn, *The Interpretation of Otherness: Literature, Religion, and the American Imagination* (New York: Oxford University Press, 1979), 187, 171. See also Ostwalt, *After Eden*, 118.

11. In a sense, sacred and secular exist only in relation to one another, so to separate them invalidates any sense of meaning they maintain as concepts. See Cesareo Bandera, *The Sacred Game: The Role of the Sacred in the Genesis of Modern Literary Fiction* (University Park: The Pennsylvania State University Press, 1994), 16; and John Milbank, *Theology and Social History: Beyond Secular Reason* (Oxford: Basil Blackwell, 1990), 3.

12. David Jasper, "Art and the Biblical Canon," keynote address, RLA Conference 1994, as quoted in Michael Griffin, "Religion, Literature and the Arts (RLA) in Australia": An Introduction to this Special Issue of *Literature and Theology*, *Literature and Theology: An International Journal of Theory, Criticism and Culture* 10, no. 3 (September 1996), 202–3.

13. See Gunn, *The Interpretation of Otherness*; and Eric Ziolkowski, "History of Religions and the Study of Religion and Literature: Grounds for Alliance," in *Literature and Theology: An International Journal of Religion, Theory and Culture* 12, No. 3 (September 1998), 305–25.

14. David Jasper, *The Study of Literature and Religion: An Introduction* (Minneapolis: Fortress Press, 1989), 97.

15. Ibid., 4–5.

16. Ibid., 3.

17. See Gunn, *The Interpretation of Otherness*, 13–23 and 5–6.

18. Noel Rowe, "The Choice of Nothing," *Literature and Theology: An International Journal of Theory, Criticism and Culture* 10, no. 3 (September 1996), 228.

19. T. S. Eliot, "Religion and Literature," in *Selected Essays* (New York: Harcourt Brace Jovanovich, 1932). Reprinted in G. B. Tennyson and Edward E. Ericson, Jr., (eds), *Religion and Modern Literature: Essays in Theory and Criticism* (Grand Rapids: Wm. B. Eerdmans,

1975), 21–30.

20. Jasper, *The Study of Literature and Religion*, 7–8. See also Gregory Saylor, "Introduction," in Gregory Saylor and Robert Detweiler, (eds), *Literature and Theology at Century's End* (Atlanta: Scholars Press, 1995), 1; and David Hesla, "Religion and Literature: The Second Stage," *JAAR* 46, no. 2 (Summer 1978), 181–92.

21. See Gunn, *The Interpretation of Otherness*, 30ff.

22. G. B. Tennyson, "Introduction," in Tennyson and Ericson, *Religion and Modern Literature*, 11–12.

23. See Gunn, *The Interpretation of Otherness*, 56–7; and R. W. B. Lewis, "Hold on Hard to the Huckleberry Bushes," in Tennyson and Ericson, *Religion and Modern Literature*, 56–7.

24. For Scott's status as an apologist, see Gunn, *The Interpretation of Otherness*, 30–2.

25. Jasper, *The Study of Literature and Religion*, 6.

26. See Gunn, *The Interpretation of Otherness*, 34.

27. Peter L. Berger, *The Sacred Canopy: Elements of a Sociological Theory of Religion* (Garden City: Doubleday and Company, 1969), 4.

28. Jasper, *The Study of Literature and Theology*, 63. Wesley Kort writes about "the three moments in the aesthetic circle ..." referring to author, text, and reader. Wesley Kort, *Narrative Elements and Religious Meaning* (Philadelphia: Fortress Press, 1975), 3.

29. R. W. B. Lewis, "Hold on Hard to the Huckleberry Bushes," *The Sewanee Review* LXVII, no. 3 (summer, 1959).

30. Gunn, *The Interpretation of Otherness*, 5–6.

31. Wesley Kort, *Narrative Elements and Religious Meaning* (Philadelphia: Fortress Press, 1975).

32. See Irena Makarushka, "Framing the Text: A Reflection on Meanings and Methods," paper written at Bowdoin College, Brunswick, Maine, October 1993. See also, Cleanth Brooks, *Community, Religion and Literature* (Columbia: University of Missouri Press, 1995); and Alfred Kazin, *God and the American Writer* (New York: Alfred A. Knopf, 1997).

33. Gunn, *The Interpretation of Otherness*, 76.

34. Jasper, *The Study of Literature and Religion*, 8.

Chapter 7

1. Wesley Kort, "'Religion and Literature' in Postmodernist Contexts," *Journal of the American Academy of Religion* LVIII, no. 4 (winter 1990): 582–3.

2. Flannery O'Connor, *Mystery and Manners: Occasional Prose*, ed. Sally and Robert Fitzgerald (New York: Farrar, Straus, and Giroux, 1957), 58. See also Michael McFee, "'Reading a Small History in a Universal Light': Doris Betts, Clyde Edgerton, and the Triumph of True Regionalism," *Pembroke Magazine*, no. 23, 1991, 59.

3. Clyde Edgerton by W. Dale Brown, in *Of Fiction and Faith: Twelve American Writers Talk About Their Vision and Work* (Wm. B. Eerdmans Publishing Company, Grand Rapids, Michigan, 1997), 122 and 124.

4. Kenn Robbins, "Clyde Edgerton's *Killer Diller*," *Southern Quarterly* 30, no. 1 (fall 1991), 67.

5. Angeline Godwin Dvorak, "Cooking as Mission and Ministry in Southern Culture: The Nurturers of Clyde Edgerton's *Walking Across Egypt*, Fannie Flagg's *Fried Green Tomatoes at the Whistle Stop Café* and Anne Tyler's *Dinner at the Homesick Restaurant*, *Southern Quarterly* 30, nos. 2–3 (winter-spring, 1992), 90–2.

6. Robbins, *Killer Diller*, 67. See also Edgerton, Brown interview, in *Of Fiction and Faith*, 120–1 on the influence of Edgerton's Southern Baptist upbringing on his writing.

7. Kenn Robbins, "A Conversation with Clyde Edgerton," *Southern Quarterly* 30, no. 1 (fall 1991), 60–1.

8. See Kort, *Narrative Elements and Religious Meaning* (Philadelphia: Fortress Press, 1975), 20–39. Among the narrative elements, atmosphere not only limits and provides boundaries, but it also allows for possibilities. This characteristic of atmosphere lends narratives a religious quality.

9. Allen Kromer examines *Raney* in light of Northrop Frye's category of Romantic Comedy with a particular focus on 'resolution.' See Allen Kromer, 'Clyde Edgerton's Comic Vision,' M.A. Thesis, Baylor University, 1992.

10. Clyde Edgerton,quoted in Susan Ketchin, *The Christ-Haunted Landscape: Faith and Doubt in Southern Fiction* (Jackson: University Press of Mississippi, 1994), 368.

11. Ibid., 353–4.

12. The material on Lee Smith was published previously in Conrad Ostwalt, 'Witches and Jesus: Lee Smith's Appalachian Religion' in *The Southern Literary Journal* XXXI, no. 1 (fall 1998): 98–118. Copyright 1998 by *The Southern Literary Journal* and the University of North Carolina at Chapel Hill Department of English and Comparative Literature of the University of North Carolina at Chapel Hill. Published by the University of North Carolina Press. Used by permission of the publisher. www.uncpress.unc.edu. Reprinted with permission.

13. See Lisa Cade Wieland, 'Old Times Not Forgotten: Family and Storytelling in Twentieth-Century Southern Literature.' Ph.D. diss., Marquette University (Milwaukee, Wisconsin, 1998), 23 and chs. 3 and 4.

14. There are many recent good books for studying the history, variety, and beliefs of Appalachian religious traditions. The best comprehensive study is Deborah Vansau McCauley's *Appalachian Mountain Religion: A History*. Other recent studies that are helpful but more limited in scope include Thomas Burton's *Serpent-Handling Believers*; Howard Dorgan's *The Airwaves of Zion: Radio and Religion in Appalachia*, *Giving Glory to God in Appalachia: Worship Practices of Six Baptist Subdenominations*, and *The Old Regular Baptists of Central Appalachia: Brothers and Sisters in Hope*; David Kimbrough's *Taking Up Serpents*; James L. Peacock and Ruel W. Tyson, Jr., *Pilgrims of Paradox: Calvinism and Experience among the Primitive Baptists of the Blue Ridge*; and Jeff Todd Titon's *Powerhouse for God: Speech, Chant, and Song in an Appalachian Baptist Church*.

15. According to Lee Smith, her regional fiction particularizes and, thus, stands out in "a world that's changing so fast and becoming so same." Her characterization of Appalachian religion is a case in point. See "Lee Smith: Interviewed by Nancy Parrish," *Appalachian Journal* 19 (summer 1992): 398. In an interview with Susan Ketchin, Smith suggests that in Appalachia, church affiliation partially determines social identity. See "Lee Smith Interview," in Ketchin, *The Christ-Haunted Landscape*, 52. See also William M. Teem, IV, "Let Us Now Praise the Other: Women in Lee Smith's Short Fiction," *Studies in Literary Imagination* 27, no.2 (fall 1994): 63–73.

16. For an examination of this technique, see Howard Dorgan, *Giving Glory to God in Appalachia: Worship Practices of Six Baptist Subdenominations* (Knoxville: The University of Tennessee Press, 1987), 55–85.

17. Ibid., 18.

18. Smith's fiction demonstrates irreverence for traditional religion that can be traced to newspaper articles she wrote as a student at Hollins. Nancy Parrish points out that many of her articles challenged traditional religious and social codes. See Nancy C. Parrish, *Lee Smith, Annie Dillard, and the Hollins Group: A Genesis of Writers* (Baton Rouge: Louisiana State University Press, 1998), 177, 179–181.

19. Fred Chappell, "Family Time," *The Southern Review* 28 (October 1992): 941.

20. See Rebecca Goodwin Smith, "Gender Dynamics in the fiction of Lee Smith: *Examining Language and Narrative Strategies*" (diss., University of North Carolina at Chapel Hill, 1993), 88–93. Smith argues that the sexual and spiritual power embodied by Red Emmy is that of the archetypal sibyl figure and that this mythic goddess symbolism is suppressed by society. Tanya Long Bennett argues that Ivy's letters in *Fair and Tender Ladies* undermine traditional Christian theology but suggest the existence of a profound spiritual life associated with nature. See Tanya Long Bennett, "The Protean Ivy in Lee Smith's *Fair and Tender Ladies*," *Southern Literary Journal* 30. no. 2 (spring 1998): 76–8, 80–1. See also Dorothy Combs Hill, *Lee Smith* (New York: Twayne Publishers, 1992).

21. See "Lee Smith Interview" in Ketchin, *The Christ Haunted Landscape*, 46–8.

22. See Elisabeth Herion-Sarafidis, "Interview with Lee Smith," *The Southern Quarterly* 32 (winter 1994): 7–18.

23. Rosalind B. Reilly, "*Oral History*: The Enchanted Circle of Narrative and Dream," in *Southern Literary Journal* 23 (fall 1990): 79–92.

24. Ibid., 82.

25. For a discussion of the circle imagery, sacred place, and sacred time in *Oral History*, see ibid., 79–92.

26. This passage is from the Revised Standard Version of the Bible.

27. See Elke Worley Payne, "In Search of the Female Voice: Religious Experience in the Fiction of Lee Smith," (M.A. thesis, Western Carolina University, 1997): iv, 4,; see also Bennett, "the Protean Ivy," 76–8, 80, 86.

28. Reilly, "*Oral History: The Enchanted Circle*," 80.

29. Gloria Jan Underwood has pointed out that memory is a key to understanding wholeness in Lee Smith's novels. Crystal, in *Black Mountain Breakdown*, loses herself because she loses her history. Likewise, Ivy does not, because she accepts her memories. See Gloria Jan Underwood, "Blessings and Burdens: Memory in the Novels of Lee Smith (diss., University of South Carolina, 1991), 28ff., 110, 140.

30. Underwood, "Blessings and Burdens," 28ff., 110, 140.

31. See Edwin T. Arnold, "An Interview with Lee Smith," *Appalachian Journal* 11 (spring 1984): 244-46.

32. Ibid., 246.

33. "Lee Smith Interview," in Ketchin, *The Christ-Haunted Landscape*, 47, 53.

34. Virginia A. Smith, "Luminous Halos and Lawn Chairs: Lee Smith's *Me and My Baby View the Eclipse*," *The Southern Review* 27 (April 1991): 484. See also Virginia A. Smith, "Between the Lines: Contemporary Southern Women Writers Gail Godwin, Bobbie Ann Mason, Lisa Alther, and Lee Smith," (diss. Pennsylvania State University, 1989).

35. Rebecca Smith examines the role of the "strong, sacred, sexual female" and its accompanying spirituality as opposed to patriarchal religion as it appears in *The Devil's Dream*. See Rebecca Smith, "Writing, Singing, and Hearing a New Voice: Lee Smith's *The Devil's Dream*," *The Southern Quarterly* 32 (winter 1994): 48–62. Dorothy Combs Hill characterizes this as a "redemptive quest." See Hill, *Lee Smith*, 18–19.

36. See Lee Smith's Interview in Ketchin, *The Christ-Haunted Landscape*, 45–6, in which Smith speaks of the inseparability of "religion and sex." See also Lee Smith interview with Claudia Loewenstein, "Unshackling the Patriarchy: An Interview with Lee Smith," *Southwest Review* 78 (autumn 1993): 486–505, for the connection between spirituality and sexual awakening.

37. See Linda J.Byrd, 'The Reclamation of the Feminine Divine: 'Walking in My Body Like a Queen' in Lee Smith's *Fair and Tender Ladies*' in *He Said, She Says: A RSVP to the Male Text*, ed. Mica Howe and Sarah Appleton Aguiar (London: Fairleigh Dickinson University Press, 2001).

38. Anne Goodwyn Jones, "The World of Lee Smith," *The Southern Quarterly* 22 (fall 1983): 120.

39. Ibid.,129.

40. Debbie Wesley points to Smith's strong female characters who bring meaning through creative connection to their bodies. See Debbie Wesley, "A New Way of Looking at an Old Story: Lee Smith's Portrait of Female Creativity," *Southern Literary Journal*, 30, no. 1 (fall 1997): 88-90.

41. See Smith, "Gender Dynamics" and "Writing, Singing, and Hearing," and Teem, "Let Us now Praise the Other."

42. Virginia A. Smith, "Luminous Halos and Lawn Chairs," 484.

43. Lee Smith interview by William Walsh, in Linda Tate, ed., *Conversations with Lee Smith* (University of Mississippi Press, Jackson, MS, 2001).

44. Jones, "The World of Lee Smith," 121.

45. See Arnold, "An interview with Lee Smith," 244. Lee Smith discusses her fiction as a way of chronicling a time and place.

46. "This image of Ghostland is Lee Smith's contemporary portrait of Appalachia" —an Appalachia that has lost its pristine nature and has become commercialized. See Nancy D. Parrish, "'Ghostland': Tourism in Lee Smith's *Oral History*," *The Southern Quarterly* 32 (winter 1994): 37–47.

47. Victoria Chen, 'Chinese American Women, Language, and Moving Subjectivity,' in Harold Bloom, Editor, *Amy Tan* (Philadelphia, Chelsea House Publishers, 2000), 83–92. The quote is from page 83.

48. See Thomas Tweed and Stephen Prothero, *Asian Religion in America: A Documentary History* (New York: Oxford, 1999), 357 ff.

49. 'The Spirit Within,' *The Salon Interview: Amy Tan*. Available from Http://www.salon.com/12nov1995/feature/tan.html

50. See E. D. Huntley, *Amy Tan: A Critical Companion* (Westport, Connecticut: Greenwood Press, 1998), 114.

51. See Huntley, 142–49.

52. Randall Kenan interview by V. Hunt, "A Conversation with Randall Kenan," *African American Review* 29, no. 3 (Fall 1995), 413–16.

53. Randall Kenan quoted in Susan Ketchin, *The Christ-Haunted Landscape*, p. 296.

54. Matthew Guinn, *After Southern Modernism: Fiction of the Contemporary South*

(Jackson, MS, University Press of Mississippi: 2000), 138 and 139.

55. Ibid., 158.

56. Kenan quoted in Susan Ketchin, *The Christ-Haunted Landscape*, 296. For Kenan's recounting of his experience with the death of his uncle, see Ketchin, 281-84.

57. J.K. Rowling, *Harry Potter and the Sorcerer's Stone*, chapter One, New York: Scholastic, 1997.

58. Rowling, *Harry Potter and the Sorcerer's Stone*, p. 1.

59. Connie Neal, *The Gospel According to Harry Potter: Spirituality in the Stories of the World's Most Famous Seeker*, Louisville: Westminster John Knox Press, 2002.

60. For Jung on archetypes, see C.G. Jung, *The Collected Works of C.G. Jung*, G. Alder and R. F. C. Hull, (eds),. and trans., vol. 9, pt. 1, "Archetypes and the Collective Unconscious," Princeton: Princeton University Press.

61. See Joseph Campbell, *The Hero with a Thousand Faces*, 2nd ed., Princeton: Princeton University Press, 1972.

62. Rowling, *Harry Potter and the Sorcerer's Stone*, p. 85.

63. Rowling, *Harry Potter and the Sorcerer's Stone*, pp. 297–301.

64. Rowling, *Harry Potter and the Chamber of Secrets*, New York: Scholastic, 1999, p. 333.

65. Rowling, *Harry Potter and the Prisoner of Azkaban*, New York: Scholastic, 1999, pp. 425–28.

66. See Rowling, *Harry Potter and the Goblet of Fire*, New York: Scholastic, 2000, pp. 597–604; *Harry Potter and the Order of the Phoenix*, New York: Scholastic, 2003, pp. 820–44; *Harry Potter and the Half-Blood Prince*, New York: Scholastic, 2005, pp. 500–11.

67. Rowling, *Harry Potter and the Deathly Hallows*, New York: Scholastic, 2007, pp. 706–23.

68. Rowling, *Harry Potter and the Deathly Hallows*, p. 758.

69. Rowling, *Harry Potter and the Sorcerer's Stone*, p. 137.

Chapter 8

1. See Conrad Ostwalt, "Conclusion: Religion, Film, and Cultural Analysis," in Joel W. Martin and Conrad E. Ostwalt, Jr., (eds), *Screening the Sacred: Religion, Myth, and Ideology in Popular American Film* (Boulder: Westview Press, 1995), 153.

2. Parts of this chapter were previously published and are reprinted in edited version by permission of *Currents in Research: Biblical Studies*, Sheffield Academic Press, and Continuum. The full reference is Conrad Ostwalt, "Celluloid Religion: Reading Religion Scholars Watching Films: A Supplementary Response to Alice Bach's 'Cracking the Production Code: Watching Biblical Scholars Read Films'," *Currents in Research: Biblical Studies* 8 (2000): 146–61, copyright © Sheffield Academic Press Limited, 2000. Portions of this chapter were also previously published in Ostwalt, "Conclusion: Religion, Film, and Cultural Analysis," 152–9 and are reprinted or adapted here by permission of Perseus Books. Portions of this chapter originally appeared in the "Journal of Religion and Film," vols. 4, 1 (April 2000); 2, 1 (April 1998); and 2, 3 (December 1998) and are reprinted here with permission of the "Journal of Religion and Film."

3. George Aichele and Richard Walsh, (eds), *Screening Scripture: Intertextual Connections Between Scripture and Film* (Harrisburg, PA: Trinity Press International, 2002).

4. Robert K. Johnston, *Reel Spirituality: Theology and Film in Dialogue* (Grand Rapids: Baker Academic, 2000).

5. Margaret Miles, *Seeing and Believing: Religion and Values in the Movies* (Boston: Beacon Press, 1996).

6. Martin and Ostwalt, *Screening the Sacred.*

7. Clive Marsh and Gaye Ortiz, (eds), *Explorations in Theology and Film: Movies and Meaning* (Oxford: Blackwell, 1998).

8. John R. May, ed., *New Image of Religious Film* (Kansas City, MO: Sheed and Ward, 1997).

9. Michael Bliss, *The Word Made Flesh: Catholicism and Conflict in the Films of Martin Scorsese* (Lanham, Md: Scarecrow Press, 1995).

10. See Robert Johnston, *Reel Spirituality*, 31–9; also ibid. 19–30 for a discussion on the power of film to change life.

11. Tom Hays, "Hollywood Gets Blame over Booth Torching," Associated Press, *Charlotte Observer*, November 28, 1996: 2A.

12. Joel Martin, "Redeeming America: Rocky as Ritual Racial Drama," in Martin and Ostwalt, *Screening the Sacred*, 126. See also Michael Ryan and Douglas Kellner, *Camera Politica: the Politics and Ideology of Contemporary Hollywood Film* (Bloomington: Indiana University Press, 1988).

13. See D. Grossman, "Trained to Kill," in *Christianity Today*, 1998 (August 10, 1998: 30–9.

14. Associated Press report, "Get Used to It," in *Reader's Digest* (November, 1999): 155–6.

15. For a discussion of this, see Ostwalt, "Conclusion," in *Screening the Sacred.*

16. Miles, *Seeing and Believing.*

17. Johnston, *Reel Spirituality*, 29–30.

18. Sandra L. Gravett, "Destiny vs. Free Will in 'Twilight'," *Christianity Today*, www. christianitytoday.com, November 21, 2011, p. 1.

19. See also Sandra L. Gravett, *From Twilight to Breaking Dawn: Religious Themes in the Twilight Saga*, St. Louis: Chalice Press, 2010.

20. See Ostwalt, "Conclusion," in *Screening the Sacred*, 155–6.

21. Joel Martin, "Introduction: Seeing the Sacred on the Screen," in Martin and Ostwalt, *Screening the Sacred*, 4–5.

22. Martin, "Introduction: Seeing the Sacred on the Screen," 4–5, 12.

23. Alice Bach, "Cracking the Production Code: Watching Biblical Scholars Read Films," *Currents in Research: Biblical Studies* 7 (1999): 21–2.

24. Conrad Ostwalt, "Armageddon at the Millennial Dawn," *Journal of Religion and Film*, 4,1. Available online at http://www.unomaha.edu/jrf/armagedd.htm (accessed March 2, 2012). The bodhisattva reference first arose during a discussion following presentation of a paper on *The Matrix* at the American Academy of Religion Annual meeting in 1999.

25. Marilynne S. Mason, letter to the author, February 12, 1996.

26. M. S. Mason, "The Gospel According to Hollywood," *The Christian Science Monitor* (23 July 1990), 10–11.

27. M. S. Mason, "Terry Gilliam Grabs the Spotlight," *The Christian Science Monitor* (September 27, 1991), 13.

28. Richard LaGravenese, quoted by M. S. Mason in "Terry Gilliam Grabs the Spotlight."

29. Joel Martin, "Redeeming America: Rocky as Ritual Racial Drama," in Martin and Ostwalt, *Screening the Sacred*, 125–33.

30. See Martin and Ostwalt, *Screening the Sacred.*

31. Jann Cather Weaver, "Discerning the Religious Dimensions of Film: Toward a Visual Method Applied to *Dead Man Walking*," paper presented at the annual meeting of the American Academy of Religion, 1996, New Orleans, November, 1996.

32. Ibid.

33. Bach, "Cracking the Production Code," 13 and 16.

34. See Weaver, "Discerning the Religious Dimensions of Film", 2–3. See also Ostwalt, "Conclusion," *Screening the Sacred*, 153.

35. Richard M. Gollin, "Reading Films as They See Fit," *Christianity and Literature*, 42 (spring 1993), 392–3.

36. Ibid., 401.

37. Ostwalt, "Conclusion," *Screening the Sacred*, 155.

38. Janice Rushing, "Evolution of 'The New Frontier' in *Alien* and *Aliens*: Patriarchal Co-optation of the Feminine Archetype," in Martin and Ostwalt, *Screening the Sacred*, 94–6; Rushing, "Introduction to 'Evolution of "the New Frontier" in *Alien* and *Aliens*: Patriarchal Cooptation of the Feminine Archetype," unpublished, September 1993, 2 and Richard Maltby, "Introduction," in *Dreams for Sale: Popular Culture in the 20th Century*, edited by Richard Maltby (London: Harrap, 1989), 11. See also John Storey, *An Introductory Guide to Cultural Theory and Popular Culture* (Athens: The University of Georgia Press, 1993), 11ff.

39. See Matthew Fox, *Religion U.S.A.: Religion and Culture by Way of TIME Magazine* (Dubuque, Iowa: Listening Press, 1971), 7-10. Fox points out that secular culture has its own myths that reflect belief. See also Ostwalt, "Conclusion," *Screening the Sacred*, 155.

40. Richard M. Gollin, *A Viewer's Guide to Film* (New York: McGraw Hill, 1992), 180.

41. Ibid., 180.

42. See Ostwalt, "Conclusion," *Screening the Sacred*, 156.

43. Gollin, *A Viewer's Guide to Film*, 180.

44. This argument is common in studies dealing with popular literature. Kathryn Presley's work on popular literature in the Gilded Age draws upon a variety of works that establish a connection between popular literature and the social and moral values of an age. See William Darby, *Necessary American Fiction: Popular Literature of the 1850s* (Bowling Green: Bowling Green University Press, 1987) and Louis Schneider and Sanford M. Dornbush, *Popular Religion: Inspirational Books in America* (Chicago: University of Chicago Press, 1958). See also Catherine Albanese, *America: Religions and Religion*, 3rd (Belmont, California: Wadsworth Publishing Company, 1999), 468–72.

45. See Ostwalt, "Conclusion," *Screening the Sacred*,153–8.

46. Albanese, 17.

47. See Ostwalt, "Conclusion," *Screening the Sacred*, 158.

48. Ibid., 157–8.

49. Conrad Ostwalt, "Teaching Religion and Film: A Fourth Approach," in Gregory J. Watkins, *Teaching Religion and Film*, ed. New York: Oxford University Press, 2008, 35–54.

Chapter 9

1. Frank Kermode, *The Sense of an Ending: Studies in the Theory of Fiction* (London: Oxford University Press, 1967), 28, 3–5, and 17. See also Conrad Ostwalt, "Hollywood

and Armageddon: Apocalyptic Themes in Recent Cinematic Presentation," in Joel W. Martin and Conrad E. Ostwalt, Jr., (eds), *Screening the Sacred: Religion, Myth, and Ideology in Popular American Film* (Boulder: Westview Press, 1995), 61–2.

2. Philip Yancey, *The Jesus I Never Knew* (Grand Rapids, Michigan: Zondervan Publishing House, 1995), 22.

3. See Robert K. Johnston, *Reel Spirituality: Theology and Film in Dialogue* (Grand Rapids: Baker Academic, 2000), 31-37.

4. See Alice Bach, "Cracking the Production Code: Watching Biblical Scholars Read Films," *Currents in Research: Biblical Studies* 7 (1999).

5. Jeffrey H. Mahan, "Celluloid Savior: Jesus in the Movies," *Journal of Religion and Film*, 6, no. 1 (April 2002). See also Jeffrey H. Mahan, *Christianity and the Arts*, 8, no. 2 (spring 2001) for another version of the article.

6. Anton Karl Kozlovic, "Superman as Christ-Figure: The American Pop Culture Movie Messiah," *Journal of Religion and Film*, 6, no. 1 (April 2002).

7. George Aichele and Richard Walsh, (eds), *Screening Scripture: Intertextual Connections Between Scripture and Film* (Harrisburg, PA: Trinity Press International, 2002).

8. Matt Crouch, interview by Jim Nelson, "God is on Line One," *Gentlemen's Quarterly* (March 2001): 314.

9. Michael Smith, "Author LaHaye Sues 'Left Behind' Film Producers," *Christianity Today* 45 (April 23, 2001): 20.

10. Peter LaLonde, interview by Jim Nelson, "God is on Line One," *Gentlemen's Quarterly* (March 2001): 353.

11. Ibid.

12. Ibid.

13. The quotation is from John's Revelation, 13.3, Revised Standard Version. The bracket is mine to add the context of the head wound.

14. Portions of this chapter were previously published in *The Journal of Religion and Film* and are reprinted here in edited and expanded form by permission of the editor of the Journal. The full bibliographic records follow: Conrad Ostwalt, "Armageddon at the Millennial Dawn," (4,1); "Religion and Popular Movies," (2, 3); and "Visions of the End: Secular Apocalypse in Recent Hollywood Film," (2,1), all in *The Journal of Religion and Film* available online at http://www.unomaha.edu/jrf/ (accessed March 11, 2012).

15. See Daniel Wojcik, *The End of the World as We Know It: Faith, Fatalism, and Apocalypse in America* (New York: New York University Press, 1997).

16. See Norman Cohn, *The Pursuit of the Millennium* (Oxford: Oxford University Press, 1980), 15–22; and John J. Collins, *The Apocalyptic Imagination: An Introduction to the Jewish Matrix of Christianity* (New York: Crossroad, 1987), 9.

17. See John Storey, *An Introductory Guide to Cultural Theory and Popular Culture* (Athens, GA: The University of Georgia Press, 1993), 73–86, for a discussion of binary oppositions, particularly in the work on myth by Claude Levi-Strauss.

18. See Ostwalt, "Hollywood and Armageddon."

19. Ibid.

20. Ibid.

21. The ideas on *The Matrix* were initially presented at the 1999 American Academy of

Religion Annual Conference. The bodhisattva reference came from the discussion that followed the presentation of that paper.

22. The Frankenstein connection was suggested to me by Dr. Kelly L. Searsmith.
23. See Donald E. Williams, "An Oceanic Odyssey," *American Cinematographer* 76, no. 8 (August 1995), 40; Ron Magid, "The End of the World as We Know It," *American Cinematographer* 77, no. 7 (July 1996), 43–50; and Ron Magid, "Taking the Plunge on *Waterworld*," *American Cinematographer* 76, no. 12 (December 1995), 73–6.
24. See Stuart Kawans, "Films," *The Nation* 261, no. 6 (28 August 1995), 216.
25. See Robert Cashill, "Waterworld Live," *TCI* (April 1996), 38.
26. For a more comprehensive discussion of *Pale Rider*, see Ostwalt, "Hollywood and Armageddon."
27. Kevin Reynolds, quoted in Williams, "An Oceanic Odyssey," 40–1.
28. See Williams, "An Oceanic Odyssey," 41; and Jose Arroyo, "*Waterworld*," *Sight and Sound* 5, no. 9 (September 1995).
29. John Calhoun, "*12 Monkeys*," *TCI* (March 1996), 35.
30. See Thomas Delapa, "Deja vu ... again," *Boulder Weekly* (January 11, 1996), 24.
31. For a detailed plot analysis of the movie, see Philip Strick, "*12 Monkeys*," *Sight and Sound* 6, issue 4 (April 1996), 56ff.
32. Jeffrey Beecroft, quoted in Calhoun, "*12 Monkeys*," 36.
33. See Strick, "*12 Monkeys*," 56.
34. David Morgan, "Extremities," *Sight and Sound* 6, no. 1 (January 1996), 18–20.
35. Keith Simanton, "Terry Gilliam, La Jetee, and the Omega Man," 1996 review.
36. David Williams, "Worlds at War," *American Cinematographer* 77, no. 7 (July 1996), 32.
37. Caron Schwartz Ellis, "With Eyes Uplifted: Space Aliens as Sky Gods," in Martin and Ostwald (eds), *Screening the Sacred*, 83–93. For aliens as an example of cinematic otherness, see Ostwalt, "Conclusion," in *Screening the Sacred*, 155.
38. See Stephanie Pappas, "11/11/11: Is Date Tied to the Mayan Apocalypse?," available online at http://www.foxnews.com/scitech/2011/11/11/111111-is-date-tied-to-mayan-apocalypse/ (accessed March 11, 2012).

Chapter 10

1. R. Laurence Moore, *Selling God: American Religion in the Marketplace of Culture* (New York: Oxford University Press, 1994).
2. Lee Smith, "Tongues of Fire," *Me and My Baby View the Eclipse* (New York: Ballantine, 1990), 64.
3. Pew Forum Poll, "Many Americans Mix Multiple Faiths: Eastern, New Age Beliefs Widespread," December 9, 2009. Available online at http://www.pewforum.org/Other-Beliefs-and-Practices/Many-Americans-Mix-Multiple-Faiths.aspx (accessed March 13, 2012).
4. See Victor Turner, *The Ritual Process: Structure and Anti-structure* (Chicago: Aldine, 1969).

Chapter 11

1. See C. G. Jung, "Archetypes and the Collective Unconscious," in *The Collected Work of C. G. Jung*, vol. 9, pt. 1, G. Adler and R. F. C. Hull, (eds), and trans (Princeton, NJ: Princeton University Press, 1968).

2. See Tim Carrithers, "Smoking Guns: Shootout at the AAA Corral," *Motorcyclist*, November 2011: 48–52.

3. Tim Kessel, "Common Bond," *Motorcyclist*, December 2011, p. 34.

4. Arthur C. Lehmann and James E. Myers, *Magic, Witchcraft, and Religion: An Anthropological Study of the Supernatural*, 4th edn (Palo Alto, CA: Mayfield, 1997), 278–9.

5. See *Cycle World*, vol. 44, no. 7, July 2005: 4–5.

6. See *Cycle World*, vol. 44, no. 11, November 2005: 148.

7. Slavoj Zizek, *Interrogating the Real*, (eds), Rex Butler and Scott Stephens (London: Continuum, 2005), 50.

8. Karl Marx, *Das Kapital: A Critique of Political Economy*, vol. 1 (Chicago: H. Regenery, 1970).

9. See Jean Baudrillard, *For a Critique of the Political Economy of Sign*, trans. Charles Levin (St. Louis: Telos Press, 1981), 88–91.

10. Ibid., 66.

11. Ibid., 67.

12. Sigmund Freud, *Three Essays on the Theory of Sexuality* (New York: Basic Books, 1905, 1962), 19.

13. Don Canet, "Three Paths to Adventure," *Cycle World*, vol. 44, no. 9, September 2005: 48–51.

14. See Sigmund Freud, "Fetishism," *The Standard Edition of the Complete Psychological Works of Sigmund Freud*, vol. 21 (London: Hogarth Press, 1966), 147–57.

15. Robert Pirsig, *Zen and the Art of Motorcycle Maintenance* (New YorK:, William Morrow, 1974), 293.

16. Ibid., 286.

17. Ibid., 85.

18. Ibid., 79.

19. Ibid., 4.

20. Ibid.

21. Ibid., 335.

22. Freedom Biker Church website: http://freedombikerchurch.com (accessed March 12, 2012).

23. Ibid.

24. http://freedombikerchurch.com/about-us (accessed March 12, 2012).

25. http://freedombikerchurch.com/about-us/beliefs (accessed March 12, 2012).

26. http://kingdavidbikers.com (accessed March 12, 2012).

27. http://www.cmausa.org/ministry/history.asp (accessed March 12, 2012).

28. http://kingdavidbikers.com/aboutus.cfm (accessed March 12, 2012).

29. See http://kingdavidbikers.org and http://jewishbikersworldwide.com (accessed March 12, 2012).

30. http://hillelsangels.com/htdocs/home.html (accessed March 12, 2012).

31. http://www.youtube.com/watch?v=kVRWQyZS9GU (accessed March 12, 2012).

32. See http://www.cmausa.org (accessed March 12, 2012).

33. See http://www.americanfcc.org (accessed March 12, 2012).

Chapter 12

1. See http://www.machinegunpreacher.org (accessed March 13, 2012). See also Sam Childers, *Another Man's War* (Nashville: Thomas Nelson, Inc., 2009).

2 . See also chapter 1 of this volume, for another version of the triadic relationship.

3. Hustin Smith, The World's Religions (San Francisco: Harper, 1991), 180.

4. Ibid., 182.

5. See Sacvan Bercovitch, The American Jeremiad (Madison: University of Wisconsin Press, 1978).

6. See Phyllis Trickle, Foreword to Brian D. McLaren, A Generous Orthodoxy (Grand Rapids: Zondervan, 2004).

7. See chapter 1 of this volume.

8. John R. Franke, "Foreword," in McLaren, A Generous Orthodoxy, 14–16.

9. See David Kowalski, "Postmodernism and the Emerging Church movement," Apologetics Index, http://www.apologeticsindex.org/290-emerging-church (accessed March 13, 2012).

10. McLaren, A Generous Orthodoxy.

11. http://www.emergentvillage.com/about/

12. Scot McKnight, "Five Streams of the Emerging Church," Christianity Today, Available online at http://www.christianitytoday.com/ct/2007/february/11.35.html (accessed March 13, 2012).

13. See McKnight, "Five Streams," 2–6.

14. McLaren, Generous Orthodoxy, 42–3.

15. Peter L. Berger, "The Liberal as Fall Guy," Don't Just Do Something (Santa Barbara: The Center for the Study of Democratic Institutions, 1972), 63.

16. Ibid., 70–1.

17. http://itunes.apple.com

18. Ibid.

19. Sander Vanocur, "TV's Failed Promise," Don't Just Do Something (Santa Barbara: The Center for the Study of Democratic Institutions, 1972), 52, 56, and 60.

20. The Holy Bible, King James Version, 1769, Mk 16.17-18.

21. See Jimmy Morrow, with Ralph Wood, ed., Handling Serpents (Macon, GA: Mercer University Press, 2005), ch. 1.

22. See chapter 1 of this volume; and Peter L. Berger, The Sacred Canopy: Elements of a Sociological Theory of Religion (New York: Anchor Books, 1969).

Conclusion

1. See Linda Kalof, "Stereotyped Evaluative Judgments and Female Attractiveness," Gender Issues 17, no. 2 (spring 1999): 68–82.

2. See Michael Rich, Elizabeth R. Woods, Elizabeth Goodman, S. Jean Emans, and Robert H. DuRant, "Aggressors or Victims: Gender and Race in Music Video Violence," Pediatrics 101, no. 4 (April 1998): 669–74.

3. See Rich et al., "Aggressors or Victims," 670.

4. See Steve Rabey, "Pop Goes the Gospel: Contemporary Christian Music Secures an Unprecedented Secular Market Push," Christianity Today 39, no. 6 (May 15, 1995), 55.

5. MercyMe, "I Can Only Imagine," songwriter Bart Millard. "The Worship Project," 1999; "Almost There," by INO Records, August 14, 2001.

6. William D. Romanowski, "Where's the Gospel? Amy Grant's Latest Album has Thrown the Contemporary Christian Music Industry into a First-Rate Identity Crisis," Christianity Today 41, no. 14 (December 8, 1997), 44–5.

7. Ken Steinken, "Where No Ministry Has Gone Before: To Be More Effective Ministers, Five Iron Frenzy Resists the Packaging of Christian Rock Bands," *Christianity Today* 43, no. 6 (May 24, 1999), 74–5.

8. Steinken, "Where No Ministry Has Gone Before," 74–5.

9. Jazzy Jordan interview by L. C. in "Going Mainstream," *Billboard* 112, no. 32 (August 5, 2000): 46–8.

10. Demetrus Alexander-Stewart interview by L. C. in "Going Mainstream," *Billboard*, 46–8.

11. See Lama Surya Das, *Awakening to the Sacred: Creating a Spiritual Life From Scratch* (New York: Broadway Books, 1999), 308–9 for the spiritual significance of Madonna chanting.

12. Carrie Underwood, "Jesus, Take the Wheel," songwriters Brett James, Hillary Lindsey, and Gordie Sampson. Album "Some Hearts," by Arista Nashville. Released November 15, 2005.

13. Carrie Underwood, "Temporary Home," songwriters Zack Maloy, Luke Laird, and Carrie Underwood. Album "Play On," by Arista Nashville. Released November 2, 2009.

14. See Edward Whitelock and David Janssen, *Apocalypse Jukebox: The End of the World in American Popular Music* (Berkeley: Soft Skull Press, 2009).

15. Britney Spears, "'Till the World Ends," songwriters, Dr. Luke, Alexander Kronlund, Max Martin, and Kesha Sebert. Produced by Billboard. Released March 3, 2011.

16. Jay Sean, "2012 (It Ain't the End)," songwriters Jay Sean, Jared Cotter, and J-Remy. Produced by OFM. Released August 3, 2010.

17. Video directed by Ray Kay, released April 5 and 6, 2011.

18. In *The Transformation of American Religion*, Amanda Porterfield raises this question in the introduction to her book. See Amanda Porterfield, *The Transformation of American Religion: The Story of a Late Twentieth Century Awakening* (Oxford: Oxford University Press, 2001).

19. Andy Bennett, *Cultures of Popular Music* (Buckingham: Open University Press, 2001), 1.

20. James C. Scott, *Domination and the Arts of Resistance: Hidden Transcripts* (New Haven: Yale University Press, 1990).

21. Jon Michael Spencer, *Blues and Evil* (Knoxville: The University of Tennessee Press, 1993).

22. Scott, *Domination and the Arts of Resistance*.

23. This paragraph represents my understanding of Spencer's book, *Blues and Evil*.

24. Jon Michael Spencer, paper presented at the American Academy of Religion, New Orleans (November 25, 1996).

25. See Rich et al., "Aggressors or Victims."

26. See Rich et al, "Aggressors or Victims"; and Linda Kalof, "The Effects of Gender and Music Video Imagery on Sexual Attitudes," *The Journal of Social Psychology* 139, no. 3 (1999): 378–85.

27. See T. E. Scheurer, "Goddesses and Golddiggers: Images of Women in Popular Music of the 1930s," in *Journal of Popular Culture* 24, no. 1 (summer 1990): 23–38.

28. See Susan McClary, "Women and Music on the Verge of the New Millennium," *Signs: Journal of Women in Culture and Society* 25, no. 4 (summer 2000): 1283–6. McClary suggests that music might "foreshadow" developments and issues that occur in other cultural forms (p. 1285). See also Gayle Wald, "Just a Girl? Rock Music, Feminism, and the Cultural Construction of Female Youth," *Signs: Journal of Women in Culture and Society* 23, no. 3 (spring 1998): 585–610; Linda Kalof, "The Effects of Gender and Music

Video Imagery on Sexual Attitudes," *The Journal of Social Psychology* 139, no. 3 (1999): 378–85; Rich et al., "Aggressors or Victims."

29. See Rich et al, "Aggressors or Victims"; and Kalof, "The Effects of Gender and Music Video Imagery on Sexual Attitudes."

30. For this and other references to the Jhally video, see *"Dreamworlds II*: Desire, Sex, and Power in Music Video," written, edited, and narrated by Sut Jhally (produced by Media Education Foundation, 1995).

31. Alan Lomax, *Mr. Jelly Roll Morton: The Fortunes of Jelly Roll Morton, New Orleans Creole and "Inventor of Jazz"* (New York: Grosset and Dunlap, 1950), 68.

32. See Lomax, *Mr. Jelly Roll Morton.*

33. Ralph Waldo Emerson, "The Poet," *Essays* (Cambridge: Riverside Press, 1903 (1841, 44), III, 26.

34. See Susan Mitchell, *American Attitudes: Who Thinks What about the Issues that Shape our Lives*, 2nd and 3rd edns (Ithaca, New York, New Strategist Publications, 1998 and 2000).

35. Wade Clark Roof, quoted in Karin Evans, "Journeys of the Spirit," *Health* (April 2001): 123.

36. Robert Wuthnow, quoted in Evans, "Journeys of the Spirit," 123 and 178.

37. Leigh Eric Schmidt, *Consumer Rites: The Buying and Selling of American Holidays* (Princeton: Princeton University Press, 1995), 14. For the Niebuhr reference, see Reinhold Niebuhr, *Pious and Secular America* (New York: Scribner's Sons, 1958).

38. See John Storey, *An Introductory Guide to Cultural Theory and Popular Culture*, 2nd ed. (Athens: The University of Georgia Press, 1998), 78–81, for a discussion of binary oppositions, particularly in the work of Claude Lévi-Strauss.

39. John A. McClure, "Post-Secular Culture: The Return of Religion in Contemporary Theory and Literature," *Cross Currents* 47 (fall 1997): 340.

40. See McClure, "Post-Secular Culture," 334–41.

41. See Robert Royal, "Christian Humanism in a Postmodern Age," in Gregory Wolfe, ed., *The New Religious Humanists: A Reader* (New York: The Free Press, 1997), 94–5.

42. See Royal, "Christian Humanism in a Postmodern Age," 103. Royal quotes G. K. Chesterton from *Heretics* (New York: John Lane Company, 1909, 1905), 304–5.

43. Royal, "Christian Humanism in a Postmodern Age," 92.

44. Ibid.

45. Thank you to my daughter and her book, *Goodnight Opus*, by Berkeley Breathed (Boston: Little, Brown and Company, 1993). for giving me this wonderful phrase.

46. This is the danger suggested by Royal in "Christian Humanism in a Postmodern Age." See also Sam Keen, *To a Dancing God* (New York: Harper and Row, 1970) for the danger of losing a theistic perspective.

47. See Keen, *To a Dancing God.*

48. From *The Papers of Andrew Johnson*, ed. L. P. Graf and R. W. Haskins (Knoxville: University of Tennessee Press,1970), II, 176–7, as quoted in Winthrop S. Hudson, *Religion in America*, 4th ed. (New York: Macmillan, 1987), 149. See Dixon Wector, *The Saga of American Society* (New York: Scribner, 1937), 100; and Donald G. Mathews, *Religion in the Old South* (Chicago: The University of Chicago Press, 1977).

Works cited

Adams, E. M. *Religion and Cultural Freedom*. Philadelphia: Temple University Press, 1993.

Aichele, George and Richard Walsh, (eds). *Screening Scripture: Intertextual Connections Between Scripture and Film*. Harrisburg, PA: Trinity Press International, 2002.

Albanese, Catherine. *America: Religions and Religion*, 3rd edn. Belmont: Wadsworth Publishing Company, 1999.

Arnold, Edwin T. "An Interview with Lee Smith," *Appalachian Journal* 11 (Spring 1984): 240–54.

Arroyo, Jose. "*Waterworld*," *Sight and Sound* 5, 9 (September 1995).

Associated Press report, "Get Used to It," in *Reader's Digest* (November, 1999): 155–6.

Bach, Alice. "Cracking the Production Code: Watching Biblical Scholars Read Films," *Currents in Research: Biblical Studies* 7 (1999): 11–34.

Bandera, Cesareo. *The Sacred Game: The Role of the Sacred in the Genesis of Modern Literary Fiction*. University Park: The Pennsylvania State University Press, 1994.

Baudrillard, Jean. *For a Critique of the Political Economy of Sign*. Trans. Charles Levin. St. Louis: Telos Press, 1981.

—*Simulations*. New York: Semiotext(e): 1983.

Beattie, Melody. *Codependent No More*. San Francisco: Harper and Hazelton, 1987.

Beaty, Sally V., dir. The Examined Life: Introduction to Philosophy, #116, "Does Science Give Us Truth," Intelecom, 1998.

Bell, Daniel. "The Return of the Sacred? The Argument on the Future of Religion," *British Journal of Sociology* 28 (December 1977): 419–49.

Bennett, Andy. *Cultures of Popular Music*. Buckingham: Open University Press, 2001.

Bennett, Tanya Long. "The Protean Ivy in Lee Smith's *Fair and Tender Ladies*." *Southern Literary Journal* 30, 2 (Spring 1998): 76–95.

Benson, Dennis. *Electric Evangelism*. Nashville: Abingdon Press, 1973.

Bercovitch, Sacvan. *The American Jeremiad*. Madison: University of Wisconsin Press, 1978.

Berger, Peter L. "Religion in Post-Protestant America." *Commentary* 85, 5 (May 1986): 41–6.

—"Secularism in Retreat." *The National Interest*. (Winter 1996/97): 3–12.

—"The Liberal as Fall Guy." *Don't Just Do Something*. Santa Barbara: The Center for the Study of Democratic Institutions, 1972.

—*The Sacred Canopy: Elements of a Sociological Theory of Religion*. Garden City, NY: Doubleday and Company, 1967.

Blake, Bishop Charles, in an interview with Duncan Moon. Transcript of "Morning Edition" (April 20, 2001), Hour 2, National Public Radio, 14–17.

Blanchard, Kenneth H., Patricia Zigarmi, and Drea Zigarmi. *Leadership and the One-Minute Manager: Increasing Effectiveness Through Situational Leadership*. New York: William Morrow, 1985.

Bliss, Michael. *The Word Made Flesh: Catholicism and Conflict in the Films of Martin Scorsese*. Lanham, Md: Scarecrow Press, 1995.

Bloom, Harold, ed. *Amy Tan*. Philadelphia: Chelsea House, 2000.

Blossom, Jay. "'An Ideal Summer Resort for Christian Families': Wholesome Entertainment in Early-20th-Century Winona Lake," American Academy of Religion Annual Meeting, November 1999, Boston, MA.

Board, Stephen. "Moving the World with Magazines: A Survey of Evangelical Periodicals," in Quentin J. Schultze, ed., *American Evangelicals and the Mass Media: Perspectives on the Relationship Between American Evangelicals and the Mass Media*. Grand Rapids, MI: Zondervan, 1990.

Boyer, Paul. *When Time Shall Be No More: Prophecy Belief in Modern American Culture*. Cambridge: Cambridge University Press, 1992.

Breathed, Berkeley. *Goodnight Opus*. Boston: Little Brown and Company, 1993.

Bremer, Thomas S. "From Pilgrims' Sacred Topography to Tourists' Sacred landscape: A Brief Tour of Western Religious Travel," American Academy of Religion Annual Meeting, November 1999, Boston, MA.

Brooks, Cleanth. *Community, Religion and Literature*. Columbia: University of Missouri Press, 1995.

Brown, W. Dale. *Of Fiction and Faith: Twelve American Writers Talk About Their Vision and Work*. Grand Rapids, MI: Eerdmans, 1997.

Bruce, Steven, ed. *Religion and Modernization: Sociologists and Historians Debate the Secularization Thesis*. Oxford: Clarendon Press, 1992.

Burton, Thomas. *Serpent Handling Believers*. Knoxville: The University of Tennessee Press, 1993.

Butler, Jon. *Awash in a Sea of Faith*. Cambridge: Harvard University Press, 1990.

Byrd, Linda J. "The Reclamation of the Feminine Divine: 'Walking in My Body Like a Queen' in Lee Smith's *Fair and Tender Ladies*," in *He Said, She Says: A RSVP to the Male Text*, Mica Howe and Sarah Appleton Aguiar, (eds). London: Fairleigh Dickinson University Press, 2001.

Cahill, Thomas. *The Gifts of the Jews: How a Tribe of Desert Nomads Changed the Way Everyone Thinks and Feels*. New York: Nan A. Talese Doubleday, 1998.

Calhoun, John. "12 Monkeys," *TCI* (March 1996): 34–7.

Campbell, Joseph. *Reflections on the Art of Living: A Joseph Campbell Companion*, Diane K. Olson, ed. New York: HarperCollins, 1991.

Campbell, Joseph. *The Hero with a Thousand Faces*, 2nd edn. Princeton: Princeton University Press, 1972.

Canet, Don. "Three Paths to Adventure." *Cycle World*. 44, 9. September 2005: 48–51.

Carey, Phyllis, ed. *Wagering on Transcendence: The Search for Meaning in Literature*. Kansas City: Sheed and Ward, 1997.

Carrithers, Tim. "Smoking Guns: Shootout at the AAA Corral." *Motorcyclist*. November 2011: 48–52.

Carter, Stephen L. *The Culture of Disbelief: How American Law and Politics Trivialize Religious Devotion*. New York: Basic Books, 1993.

Cashill, Robert. "Waterworld Live," *TCI* (April 1996): 38–41.

Chadwick, Owen. *The Secularization of the European Mind in the Nineteenth Century*. Cambridge: Cambridge University Press, 1975.

Chappell, Fred. "Family Time," *The Southern Review* 28 (October 1992): 937–43.

Chaves, Mark. "Secularization as Declining Religious Authority," *Social Forces* 72, 3: 749–74.

Chen, Victoria. "Chinese American Women, Language, and Moving Subjectivity," in Harold Bloom, ed. *Amy Tan*. Philadelphia: Chelsea House Publishers, 2000.

Chesterton, G. K. *Heretics*. New York: John Lane Co., 1905–9.

Childers, Sam. *Another Man's War*. Nashville: Thomas Nelson, 2009.

Cohn, Norman. *The Pursuit of the Millennium*. Oxford: Oxford University Press, 1980.

Collins, John J. *The Apocalyptic Imagination: An Introduction to the Jewish Matrix of Christianity*. New York: Crossroad, 1987.

Cox, Harvey. *The Secular City: Secularization and Urbanization in Theological Perspective*. New York: Macmillan, 1966.

Crouch, Matt, in an interview with Jim Nelson, "God is on Line One," *Gentlemen's Quarterly* (March 2001): 310–15, 351–3.

Cycle World. Vol. 44, no. 7. July 2005: 4–5.

Cycle World. Vol. 44, no. 11. November 2005: 148.

Darby, William. *Necessary American Fiction: Popular Literature of the 1850s*. Bowling Green: Bowling Green University Press, 1987.

Delapa, Thomas. "Déjà vu … again," *Boulder Weekly* (11 January 1996): 24.

Demerath, N. J. III. "Varieties of Sacred Experience." *Journal for the Scientific Study of Religion* 39, 1 (March 2000): 1–11.

Dorgan, Howard. *The Airwaves of Zion: Radio and Religion in Appalachia*. Knoxville: The University of Tennessee Press, 1993.

—*Giving Glory to God in Appalachia: Worship Practices of Six Baptist Subdenominations*. Knoxville: The University of Tennessee Press, 1987.

—*The Old Regular Baptists of Central Appalachia*. Knoxville: The University of Tennessee Press, 1989.

Doty, William G. *Contemporary New Testament Interpretation*. Englewood Cliffs, NJ: Prentice-Hall Incorporated, 1972.

Dowling, Claudia Glenn. "A Light in the Desert," *LIFE* (June 1996): 66–72.

Dr. Luke, Alexander Kronlund, Max Martin, and Kesha Sebert. "Till the World Ends." Britney Spears. *Billboard*. March 3, 2011.

Drane, James. *The Possibility of God: A Reconsideration of Religion in a Technological Society*. Towota, NJ: Littlefield, Adams, and Company, 1976.

Dvorak, Angeline Godwin. "Cooking as Mission and Ministry in Southern Culture: The Nurturers of Clyde Edgerton's *Walking Across Egypt*, Fannie Flagg's *Fried Green Tomatoes at the Whistle Stop Café* and Anne Tyler's *Dinner at the Homesick Restaurant*." *Southern Quarterly* 30, 2–3 (Winter–Spring, 1992): 90–8.

Edgerton, Clyde. *Killer Diller*. Chapel Hill, NC: Algonquin Press, 1991.

—*Raney*. New York: Ballantine Books, 1985.

—*Walking Across Egypt*. Chapel Hill, NC: Algonquin Press, 1987.

—in W. Dale Brown, *Of Fiction and Faith: Twelve American Writers Talk About Their Vision and Work*. Grand Rapids, MI: Wm. B. Eerdmans Publishing Company, 1997.

—in Susan Ketchin, *The Christ-Haunted Landscape: Faith and Doubt in Southern Fiction*. Jackson: University Press of Mississippi, 1994.

Eliade, Mircea. *The Sacred and Profane: The Nature of Religion*, Trans. Willard R. Trask. New York: Harcourt Brace Jovanovich, 1959.

Eliot, T. S. "Religion and Literature," in *Selected Essays*. New York: Harcourt Brace Jovanovich, 1932. Reprinted in G. B. Tennyson and Edward E. Ericson, Jr., (eds), *Religion and Modern Literature: Essays in Theory and Criticism*. Grand Rapids, MI: Wm. B Eerdmans, 1975, 21–30.

Ellis, Caron Schwartz. "With Eyes Uplifted: Space Aliens as Sky Gods," in Joel W. Martin and Conrad E. Ostwalt, Jr., (eds). *Screening the Sacred: Religion, Myth, and Ideology in Popular American Film*. Boulder: Westview Press, 1995.

Emerson, Ralph Waldo. "The Poet," *Essays*. Cambridge: Riverside Press, 1903 (1841, 44), III.

Evans, Karin. "Journeys of the Spirit," *Health* (April 2001): 118–23, 178–9.

Finke, Roger. "An Unsecular America," in Steve Bruce, ed. *Religion and Modernization: Sociologists and Historians Debate the Secularization Thesis*. Oxford: Claredon Press, 1992.

Finke, Roger and Rodney Stark, *The Churching of America, 1776–1990: Winners and Losers in our Religious Economy*. New Brunswick, NJ: Rutgers University Press, 1992.

Fitzgerald, Sally and Robert Fitzgerald, (eds). *Mystery and Manners: Occasional Prose*. New York: Farrar, Straus, & Giroux, 1957.

Foster, Hal, ed. *The Anti-Aesthetic: Essays on Postmodern Culture*. Port Townsend, WA: Bay Press, 1983.

Fowler, Robert Booth. *Unconventional Partners: Religion and Liberal Culture in the United States*. Grand Rapids. MI: Wm. B. Eerdman's Publishing Co., 1989.

Fox, Matthew. *Religion U.S.A. : Religion and Culture By Way of TIME Magazine*. Dubuque: Listening Press, 1971.

Franke, John R. "Foreword," in Brian McLaren, *A Generous Orthodoxy*. Grand Rapids, MI: Zondervan, 2004.

Freud, Sigmund. "Fetishism." *The Standard Edition of the Complete Psychological Works of Sigmund Freud*. London: Hogworth Press, 1966.

—*The Future of an Illusion*. New York: W. W. Norton & Co., 1961.

—*Three Essays on the Theory of Sexuality*. New York: Basic Books, 1905, 1962.

Gabriel, Trip. "MTV-Inspired Images, But the Message for Children Is a Moral One," *New York Times* (Sunday, 16 April 1995): 14.

Galloway, Paul. "Media are Poor Substitute for the Family," *Chicago Tribune, The Charlotte Observer*, (Monday 3 June 1996): 9A.

Gallup, George and Jim Castelli, *The People's Religion: American Faith in the '90's*. New York: Macmillan, 1989.

Garfield, Ken. "Nontraditional Church Appealing to Many," *Charlotte Observer*, 24 May 1993.

Gaustad, Edwin S., Darline Miller and G. Allison Stokes, "Religion in America," *American Quarterly* 31, 3 (1979): 250

Geertz, Clifford. *The Interpretation of Cultures*. New York: Basic Books, 1973.

Gilkey, Langdon. *Naming the Whirlwind: The Renewal of God Language*. Indianapolis: Bobbs-Merrill Company, 1969.

—*Society and the Sacred: Toward a Theology of Culture in Decline*. New York: Crossroad, 1981.

Gilmore, Michael T. *American Romanticism and the Marketplace*. Chicago: 1985.

Gollin, Richard M. *A Viewer's Guide to Film: Arts, Artifices, and Issues*. New York: McGraw Hill, 1992.

—"Reading Films as They See Fit," *Christianity and Literature*. 42 (Spring 1993): 391–401.

Graf, Leroy P. and Ralph W. Haskins, (eds). *The Papers of Andrew Johnson*. Knoxville: University of Tennessee Press, 1970.

Gravett, Sandra L. "Destiny vs. Free Will in 'Twilight'," *Christianity Today*, November, 21, 2001: 1–4.

—*From Twilight to Breaking Dawn: Religious Themes in the Twilight Saga*. St. Louis: Chalice Press, 2010.

Greeley, Andrew. "The Persistence of Religion," *Cross Currents: The Journal of the Association for Religion and Intellectual Life* 45, 1 (Spring 1995): 24–41.

Gregory, Joel. *Too Great a Temptation: The Seductive Power of America's Super Church*. Fort Worth: The Summit Group, 1994.

Griffin, Michael, "Religion, Literature and the Arts (RLA) in Australia: An Introduction to This Special Issue of *Literature and Theology*." *Literature and Theology: An International Journal of Theory, Criticism and Culture* 10, 3 (September 1996), 202–3.

Grossman, Cathy Lynn. "Charting the Unchurched in America," *USA Today* (7 March 2002): 1–5.

Grossman, D. "Trained to Kill," in *Christianity Today*, (August 10, 1998): 30–9.

Guelzo, Allen C. "Selling God in America: How Christians Have Befriended Mammon," *Christianity Today* 39, 5 (April 24, 1995): 27–30.

Guinn, Matthew. *After Southern Modernism: Fiction of the Contemporary South*. Jackson: University Press of Mississippi, 2000.

Gunn, Giles. *The Interpretation of Otherness: Literature, Religion, and the American Imagination*. New York: Oxford University Press, 1979.

Hadden, Jeffrey K. "Desacralizing Secularization Theory," in Jeffrey K. Hadden and Anson Shupe, (eds), *Secularization and Fundamentalism Reconsidered: Religion and the Politicial Order*, vol. III. New York; Paragon House, 1989.

Hammond, Phillip E., ed. *The Sacred in the Secular Age: Toward Revision in the Scientific Study of Religion*. Berkeley: University of California Press, 1985.

Hatch, Nathan O. *The Democratization of American Christianity*. New Haven: Yale University Press, 1989.

Hays, Tom. "Hollywood Gets Blame over Booth Torching," Associated Press, *Charlotte Observer*, November 28, 1995: 2A.

Hegel, Georg Wilhelm Friedrich Hegel. *Phenomenology of Spirit*, trans. A. V. Miller. Oxford: Clarendon Press, 1977

Herion-Sarafidis, Elisabeth. "Interview with Lee Smith." *Southern Quarterly* 32 (Winter 1994): 7–18.

Hesla, David. "Religion and Literature: The Second Stage," *JAAR* 46, 2 (Summer 1978): 181–92.

Hill, Dorothy Combs. *Lee Smith*. New York: Twayne Publishers, 1992.

Hoover, Stewart M. *Mass Media Religion: The Social Sources of the Electronic Church*. Newbury Park, CA: SAGE Publications, 1988.

—"The Meaning of Religious Television: The '700 Club' in the Lives of Its Viewers," in Quentin J. Schultze, ed. *American Evangelicals and the Mass Media: Perspectives on the Relationship between American Evangelicals and the Mass Media*. Grand Rapids, MI: Zondervan, 1990.

Horsfield, Peter G. *Religious Television: The American Experience*. New York: Longman, Inc., 1987.

Howe, Mica and Sarah Appleton Aguiar, (eds). *He Said, She Says: A RSVP to the Male Text*. London: Fairleigh Dickinson University Press, 2001.

Hudson, Winthrop S. *Religion in America*, 4th edn. New York: Macmillan, 1987.

Hulsether, Mark. "Interpreting the 'Popular' in Popular Religion," *American Studies* 36, 2 (Fall 1995): 129–33.

Hunter, George G. III. *Church for the Unchurched*. Nashville: Abingdon, 1996.

Hunter, James D. and Stephen C. Ainlay, (eds). *Making Sense of Modern Times: Peter L. Berger and the Vision of Interpretive Sociology*. New York: Routledge and Kegan Paul, 1986.

Huntley, E. D. *Amy Tan: A Critical Companion*. Westport, CT: Greenwood Press, 1998.

Husband, Timothy and Jane Hayword. *The Secular Spirit: Life and Art at the End of the Middle Ages*. New York: E. P. Dutton, 1975.

ICF Church News, no. 4, 1996: 4.

Iannaccone, Laurence. "The Consequences of Religious Market Structure: Adam Smith and the Economics of Religion," *Rationality and Society* 3 (April 1991): 156–77.

Iannaccone, Laurence and Rodney Stark, "A Supply Side Reinterpretation of the 'Secularization' of Europe," *Journal for the Scientific Study of Religion* 33, 3 (1994): 230–52.

James, Brett, Hillary Lindsey and Gordie Sampson. "Jesus, Take the Wheel." Some Hearts. Carrie Underwood. Arista Nashville, November 2, 2009.

Jameson, Frederic. "Postmodernism and Consumer Society," in Hal Foster, ed. *The Anti-Aesthetic: Essays in Postmodern Culture*. Pottownsend, WA: Bay Press, 1983, pp. 111–25.

—"Postmodernism, or the Cultural Logic of Late Capitalism," *New Left Review* 146 (1984).

Jarrett, Bill. "*The Lively Experiment*: American Evangelicalism and Twentieth-Century Technology," paper presented at the North Carolina Religious Studies Association, October, 1993, Boone, NC.

Jasper, David. "Art and the Biblical Canon," 1994 RLA Conference Keynote Address, as quoted in Michael Griffin, "Religion, Literature and the Arts (RLA) in Australia: An Introduction to this Special Issue of *Literature and Theology*, *Literature and Theology: An International Journal of Theory, Criticism and Culture* 10, 3 (September 1996): 201–11.

—Paper delivered at the Southeastern Conference for the Study of Religion, March 17, 1996, Columbia, South Carolina.

—*The Study of Literature and Religion: An Introduction*. Minneapolis: Fortress Press, 1989.

Jhally, Sut. Dreamworlds II: Desire, Sex, and Power in Music Video. Media Education Foundation, 1995.

Johnston, Robert K. *Reel Spirituality: Theology and Film in Dialogue*. Grand Rapids, MI: Baker Academic, 2000.

Jones, Anne Goodwyn. "The World of Lee Smith," *The Southern Quarterly* 22 (Fall 1983): 115–39.

Jordan, Jazzy in L. C. "Going Mainstream." *Billboard* 112, 32 (August 5, 2000): 46–8.

Jung, C. G. *The Collected Works of C. G. Jung*. Ed. and trans. G. Alder and R. F. C. Hull. Princeton: Princeton University Press, 1978.

Kalof, Linda. "The Effects of Gender and Music Video Imagery on Sexual Attitudes," *The Journal of Social Psychology* 139, 3 (1999): 378–85.

—"Stereotyped Evaluative Judgments and Female Attractiveness," *Gender Issues* 17, 2 (Spring 1999): 68–82.

Kaufman, Peter Iver. "Religion on the Run," *Journal of Interdisciplinary History* xxv, 1 (Summer 1994); 85–94.

Kawans, Stuart. "Films," *The Nation* 261, 6 (August 28, 1995): 215–16.

Kazin, Alfred. *God and the American Writer*. New York: Alfred A. Knopf, 1997.

Keen, Sam. *To a Dancing God*. New York: Harper and Row, 1970.

Keirsey, David and Marilyn Bates. *Please Understand Me: Character and Temperament Types*. Del Mar, CA: Prometheus Nemesis, 1978.

Kenan, Randall. *A Visitation of Spirits*. New York: Anchor, 1990.

—in V. Hunt, "A Conversation with Randall Kenan," *African American Review* 29, 3 (Fall 1995): 413–16.

Kermode, Frank. *The Sense of an Ending: Studies in the Theory of Fiction*. London: Oxford University Press, 1967.

Kessel, Tim. "Common Bond." *Motorcyclist*. December 2011: 34.

Ketchin, Susan. *The Christ-Haunted Landscape: Faith and Doubt in Southern Fiction*. Jackson, MS: University Press of Mississippi, 1994.

Kidd, James L. "Megachurch Methods," *Christian Century* 114, 16 (May 14, 1997): 482–5.

Kimbrough, David. *Taking Up Serpents: Snake Handlers of Eastern Kentucky*. Chapel Hill: University of North Carolina Press, 1995.

Kort, Wesley. *Narrative Elements and Religious Meaning*. Philadelphia: Fortress Press, 1975.

—"'Religion and Literature' in Postmodernist Contexts," *Journal of the American Academy of Religion* LVIII, 4: 575–88.

Kotler, Philip. *Marketing Management: Analysis, Planning, Implementation, and Control*, 6th edn. Englewood Cliffs, NJ: Prentice Hall, 1988.

Kowalski, David. "Postmodernism and the Emerging Church movement," in *Apologetics Index*. Available online at http://www.apologeticsindex.org/ (accessed March 19, 2012).

Kozlovic, Anton Karl. "Superman as Christ-Figure: The American Pop Culture Movie Messiah," *Journal of Religion and Film* 6, 1 (April 2002).

Kromer, Allen. "Clyde Edgerton's Comic Vision," M.A. Thesis, Baylor University, 1992.

L. C. "Going Mainstream." *Billboard* 5 (August 2000): 46–8.

LaHaye, Tim, and Jerry Jenkins. *Left Behind: A Novel of the Earth's Last Days*. Wheaton, IL: Tyndale House Publishers, 1995.

Lalonde, Peter, in an interview with Jim Nelson, "God is on Line One," in *Gentlemen's Quarterly* (March 2001): 310–15, 352–3.

Lechner, Frank J. "The Case Against Secularization: A Rebuttal," *Social Forces* 69 (1991): 1103–19.

Lehmann, Arthur C. and James E. Myers. *Magic, Witchcraft, and Religion: An Anthropological Study of the Supernatural*, 4th edn. Palo Alto, CA: Mayfield, 1997.

Lewis, R. W. B. "Hold on Hard to the Huckleberry Bushes," *The Sewanee Review* LXVII, 3 (Summer, 1959).

Lincoln, Abraham. "Gettysburg Address," November 19, 1863.

Lindsey, Hal with C. C. Carlson. *The Late Great Planet Earth*. Grand Rapids, MI: Zondervan, 1970.

Loewenstein, Claudia. "Unshackling the Patriarchy: An Interview with Lee Smith." *Southwest Review* 78 (Autumn 1993): 486–505.

Lomax, Alan. *Mr. Jelly Roll Morton: The Fortunes of Jelly Roll Morton, New Orleans Creole and "Inventor of Jazz"*. New York: Grosset and Dunlap, 1950.

Luecke, David S. "Is Willow Creek the Way of the Future?" *Christian Century* 114, 16 (May 14, 1997): 479–83.

Lukacs, John. "It's the End of the Modern Age." *The Chronicle of Higher Education* . April 26, 2002: B9.

Lyotard, Jean-François. *The Postmodern Condition: A Report on Knowledge*. Manchester: Manchester University Press, 1984.

Magid, Ron. "The End of the World as We Know It," *American Cinematographer* 77, 7 (July 1996): 43–50.

—"Taking the Plunge on *Waterworld*," *American Cinematographer* 76, 12 (December 1995): 73–6.

Mahan, Jeffrey H. "Celluloid Savior: Jesus in the Movies." *Journal of Religion and Film*, 6, 1 (April 2002).

Makarushka, Irena. "Framing the Text: A Reflection on Meanings and Methods," Brunswick: Bowdoin College, October 11, 1993.

Maltby, Richard. "Introduction," in *Dreams for Sale: Popular Culture in the 20th Century*, ed. Richard Maltby. London: Harrap, 1989.

Marsden, George M. *Fundamenatalism and American Culture: The Shaping of Twentieth-Century Evangelicalism 1870–1925*. Oxford: Oxford University Press, 1980.

Marsden, George M. and Bradley J. Longfield, (eds). *The Secularization of the Academy*. New York: Oxford University Press, 1992.

Marsh, Clive and Gaye Ortiz, (eds),. *Explorations in Theology and Film: Movies and Meaning*. Oxford: Blackwell, 1998.

Martin, David. *A General Theory of Secularization*. New York: Harper and Row Publishers, 1978.

—*The Religious and the Secular*. New York: Schocken Books, 1969.

Martin, Joel. "Redeeming America: Rocky as Ritual Racial Drama," in Joel W. Martin and Conrad E. Ostwalt, (eds). *Screening the Sacred: Religion, Myth, and Ideology in Popular American Film*. Boulder: Westview Press, 1995.

Martin, Joel W. and Conrad E. Ostwalt, Jr., (eds). *Screening the Sacred: Religion, Myth, and Ideology in Popular American Film*. Boulder: Westview Press, 1995.

Marty, Martin E. *The Modern Schism: Three Paths to the Secular*. New York: Harper and Row, 1969.

Marx, Karl. *Das Kapital: A Critique of Political Economy*. Chicago: H. Regenery, 1970.

Mason, Marilynne S. "The Gospel According to Hollywood," *The Christian Science Monitor* (July 23, 1990): 10–11.

—"Terry Gilliam Grabs the Spotlight," *The Christian Science Monitor* (27 September 1991): 13.

Mathews, Donald G. *Religion in the Old South*. Chicago: University of Chicago Press, 1977.

Mathisen, James. "From Civil Religion to Folk Religion: The Case for American Sport," in *Human Kinetics*, ed. S. J. Hoffman. Champagne: University of Illinois Press, 1992.

May, John R., ed. *New Image of Religious Film*. Kansas City, MO: Sheed and Ward, 1997.

McCauley, Deborah Vansau. *Appalachian Mountain Religion: A History*. Urbana: University of Illinois Press, 1995.

McClary, Susan. "Women and Music on the Verge of the New Millennium," *Signs: Journal of Women in Culture and Society* 25, 4 (Summer 2000): 1283–6.

McCloughlin, Merrill. "From Revival Tent to Mainstream," *U.S. News and World Report*, 19 December 1988: 52–7.

McClure, John A. "Post-Secular Culture: The Return of Religion in Contemporary Theory and Literature," *Cross Currents* 47 (Fall 1997): 332–47.

McFee, Michael. "'Reading a Small History in a Universal Light': Doris Betts, Clyde Edgerton, and the Triumph of True Regionalism," *Pembroke Magazine* 23 (1991): 59–67.

McGlohon, Loonis. Lyrics to "Love Valley" song, 1960s.

McKnight, Scot. "Five Streams of the Emerging Church." *Christianity Today*. Available online at http://www.christianitytoday.com/ct/2007/february/11.35.html/ (accessed March 19, 2012).

McLaren, Brian D. *A Generous Orthodoxy*. Grand Rapids, MI: Zondervan, 2004.

McManners, John, ed. *The Oxford History of Christianity*. Oxford: Oxford University Press, 1993.

Mecklenburg Community Church's newsletter, *In Touch*, November, 1993.

Meland, Bernard Eugene. *The Realities of Faith: The Revolution in Cultural Forms*. New York: Oxford University Press, 1962.

—*The Secularization of Modern Cultures*. New York: Oxford University Press, 1966.

Melville, Herman. *Moby Dick*. New York: New American Library, 1961.

Metcalf, Harold E. *The Magic of Telephone Evangelism*. Atlanta: Southern Union Conference of Seventh-Day Adventists, 1967.

The Metropolitan Museum of Art, *The Secular Spirit: Life and Art at the End of the Middle Ages*. New York: E. P. Dutton and Company, 1975.

Milbank, John. *Theology and Social History: Beyond Secular Reason*. Oxford: Basil Blackwell, 1990.

Miles, Margaret. *Seeing and Believing: Religion and Values in the Movies*. Boston: Beacon Press, 1996.

Millard, Bart. "I Can Only Imagine." Almost There. Mercy Me. INO Records, August 14, 2001.

Mitchell, Susan. *American Attitudes: Who Thinks What About the Issues that Shape our Lives*, 2nd edn. Ithaca, NY: New Strategist Publications, 1998.

Montell, William Lynwood. *The Saga of Coe Ridge: A Study in Oral History*. Knoxville: University of Tennessee Press, 1970.

Moon, Duncan. Transcript of *Morning Edition*. National Public Radio April 20, 2001: 14–17.

Moore, R. Laurence. *Selling God: American Religion in the Marketplace of Culture*. New York: Oxford University Press, 1994.

Morgan, David. "Extremities," *Sight and Sound* 6, 1 (January 1996): 18–20.

Morgan, Timothy C. "Cyber Shock: New Ways of Thinking Must be Developed for the Church to Keep Pace in the Coming Information Age," *Christianity Today* 39, 4 (April 3, 1995): 78–86.

Morrow, Jimmy with Ralph Wood, ed. *Handling Serpents*. Macon, GA: Mercer University Press, 2005.

Moseley, James G. *A Cultural History of Religion in America*. Westport, CT: Greenwood Press, 1981.

Nash, David. *Secularism, Art and Freedom*. Leicester: Leicester University Press, 1992.

Nasser, Haya El. "Giant Churches Irk Some Neighbors," *USA Today*, September 23, 2002. http://www.usatoday.com/ (accessed September 2011)

Nathanson, Paul. *Over the Rainbow: The Wizard of Oz as a Secular Myth of America*. Albany: State University of New York Press, 1991.

Neal, Connie. *The Gospel According to Harry Potter: Spirituality in the Stories of the World's Most Famous Seeker*. Louisville: Westminster John Knox Press, 2002.

Nelson, Jim. "God is on Line One," *Gentlemen's Quarterly* (March 2001): 310–15, 352–3.

Newell, William Lloyd. *The Secular Magi: Marx, Freud, and Nietzsche on Religion*. New York: The Pilgrim Press, 1986.

Niebuhr, Gustav. "The High Energy Never Stops," *The New York Times* (April 16, 1995): 14.

—"Where Religion Gets a Big Dose of Shopping-Mall Culture," *The New York Times* (April 16, 1995): 1, 14.

Niebuhr, Reinhold. *Pious and Secular America*. New York: Scribner's Sons, 1958.

Noll, Mark. *A History of Christianity in the United States and Canada*. Grand Rapids, MI: Wm. B. Eerdmans, 1992.

Novak, Michael. *The Joy of Sports: End Zones, Bases, Baskets, Balls, and the Consecration of the American Spirit*. New York: Basic Books, 1976.

O'Brien, Tim. *The Things They Carried*. New York: Broadway Books, 1990.

O'Connor, Flannery. *Mystery and Manners: Occasional Prose*, Sally and Robert Fitzgerald, (eds). New York: Farrar, Straus, & Giroux, 1957.

O'Keefe, Mark. "The Megachurch: Oregon." *The Sunday Oregonian: Forum* September 22, 1996: E-1, 7.

Ostling, Richard N. "Many Are Called: Dialing for Jesus," *Time*, February 27, 1989: 79.

Ostwalt, Conrad. *After Eden: The Secularization of American Space in the Fiction of Willa Cather and Theodore Dreiser*. Lewisburg: Bucknell University Press, 1990.

—"Armageddon at the Millennial Dawn," (4,1); "Religion and Popular Movies," (2,3); and "Visions of the End: Secular Apocalypse in Recent Hollywood Film," (2,1). All in *The Journal of Religion and Film*, http://www.unomaha.edu/jrf/author.htm#O/ (accessed 19 March 2012).

—"Celluloid Religion: Reading Religion Scholars Watching Films: A Supplementary Response to Alice Bach's 'Cracking the Production Code: Watching Biblical Scholars Read Films.'" *Currents in Research: Biblical Studies* 8 (2000): 146–61.

—"Conclusion: Religion, Film, and Cultural Analysis," in Joel W. Martin and Conrad E. Ostwalt, Jr., (eds). *Screening the Sacred: Religion, Myth, and Ideology in Popular American Film*. Boulder: Westview Press, 1995.

—"Dances with Wolves: An American *Heart of Darkness*." *Literature/Film Quarterly* 24, 2 (1996): 209–16.

—"Hollywood and Armageddon: Apocalyptic Themes in Recent Cinematic Presentation," in Joel W. Martin and Conrad E. Ostwalt, Jr., (eds). *Screening the Sacred: Religion, Myth, and Ideology in Popular American Film*. Boulder: Westview Press, 1995, 55–63.

—"Love Valley, A Utopian Experiment in North Carolina," *North Carolina Humanities* 1, 1 (Fall 1992): 101–8.

—*Love Valley: An American Utopia*. Bowling Green, OH: Bowling Green State University Press, 1998.

—"Teaching Religion and Film: A Fourth Approach," in Gregory J. Watkins, ed. *Teaching Religion and Film*. New York: Oxford University Press, 2008: 35–54.

—"Witches and Jesus: Lee Smith's Appalachian Religion." *The Southern Literary Journal* XXXI, 1 (Fall 1998): 98–118. Copyright 1998 by *The Southern Literary Journal* and the University of North Carolina at Chapel Hill Department of English. Reprinted with permission.

Otto, Rudolf, *The Idea of the Holy*, Oxford: Oxford University Press, 1923.

Pappas, Stephanie. "11/11/11: Is Date Tied to the Mayan Apocalypse?" Fox News November 11, 2011. http://www.foxnews.com/scitech/2011/11/11/

Parker, Everett C., Elinor Inman and Ross Snyder, *Religious Radio: What to Do and How*. New York: Harper and Brothers Publishers, 1948.

Parrish, Nancy. "'Ghostland': Tourism in Lee Smith's *Oral History*." *Southern Quarterly* 32 (Winter 1994): 37–47.

—*Lee Smith, Annie Dillard, and the Hollins Group: A Genesis of Writers*. Baton Rouge: Louisiana State University Press, 1998.

—"Lee Smith: Interviewed by Nancy Parrish." *Appalachian Journal* 19 (Summer 1992): 394–401.

Payne, Elke Worley. "In Search of the Female Voice: Religious Experience in the Fiction of Lee Smith." M.A. Thesis. Cullowhee: Western Carolina University, 1997.

Peacock, James L. and Ruel W. Tyson, Jr. *Pilgrims of Paradox: Calvinism and Experience among the Primitive Baptists of the Blue Ridge*. Washington: Smithsonian Institution Press, 1989.

Pew Forum Poll. "Many Americans Mix Multiple Faiths: Eastern, Age Beliefs Widespread." December 9, 2011. http://www.pewforum.org (accessed summer, fall 2011 and March 2012).

Pirsig, Robert. *Zen and the Art of Motorcycle Maintenance*. New York: William Morrow, 1974.

"Pope accepts theory of evolution," *The News and Observer*, Raleigh, NC, October 25, 1996, 1A and 16A.

Porterfield, Amanda. *The Transformation of American Religion: The Story of a Late Twentieth Century Awakening*. Oxford: Oxford University Press, 2001.

Postman, Neil. *Amusing Ourselves to Death*. NewYork: Viking Penguin, 1985.

Potter, G. R. *Zwingli*. Cambridge: Cambridge University Press, 1976.

Powers, John. "Shangri-la Comes to Hollywood, Or Hollywood Comes to Shangri-la: Tibet and Popular Culture in the 1990s," American Academy of Religion Annual Meeting, November 1999, Boston, Massachusetts.

Pratt, Vernon. *Religion and Secularization*. London: Macmillian, 1970.

Pritchard, G. A. *Willow Creek Seeker Services: Evaluating a New Way of Doing Church*. Grand Rapids, MI: Baker Books, 1996.

Rabey, Steve. "Pop Goes the Gospel: Contemporary Christian Music Secures an Unprecedented Secular Market Push." *Christianity Today* 39, 6 (May 15, 1995): 55.

Reed, Eric. "Willow Creek Church Readies for Megagrowth," *Christianity Today* 44, 5 (April 24, 2000): 21.

Reilly, Rosalind B. "*Oral History*: The Enchanted Circle of Narrative and Dream." *Southern Literary Journal* 23 (Fall 1990): 79–92.

Rich, Michael, Elizabeth R. Woods, Elizabeth Goodman, S. Jean Emans and Robert H. DuRant. "Aggressors or Victims: Gender and Race in Music Video Violence." *Pediatrics* 101, 4 (April 1998): 669–74.

Robbins, Kenn. "Clyde Edgerton's *Killer Diller*," *Southern Quarterly* 30, 1 (Fall 1991): 66–69.

—"A Conversation with Clyde Edgerton," *Southern Quarterly* 30, 1 (Fall 1991): 58–65.

Roof, Wade Clark, and William McKinney, *American Mainline Religion: Its Changing Shape and Future*. New Brunswick, NJ: Rutgers University Press, 1987.

Romanowski, William D. "Where's the Gospel? Amy Grant's Latest Album has Thrown the Contemporary Christian Music Industry into a First-Rate Identity Crisis." *Christianity Today* 41, 14 (December 8, 1997): 44–5.

Ross, Stanley Ralph. Theme to ABC's Wide World of Sports.

Ross-Bryant, Lynn. *Imagination and the Life of the Spirit: An Introduction to the Study of Religion and Literature*. Chico, CA: Scholars Press, 1981.

Rowe, Noel. "The Choice of Nothing," *Literature and Theology: An International Journal of Theory, Criticism and Culture* 10, 3 (September 1996): 224–9.

Rowling, J. K. *Harry Potter and the Chamber of Secrets*. New York: Scholastic, 1999.

—*Harry Potter and the Deathly Hallows*. New York: Scholastic, 2007.

—*Harry Potter and the Goblet of Fire*. New York: Scholastic, 2000.

—*Harry Potter and the Half-Blood Prince*. New York: Scholastic, 2005.

—*Harry Potter and the Order of the Pheonix*. New York: Scholastic, 2003.

—*Harry Potter and the Prisoner of Azkaban*. New York: Scholastic, 1999.

—*Harry Potter and the Sorcerer's Stone*. New York: Scholastic, 1997.

Royal, Robert. "Christian Humanism in a Postmodern Age," in *The New Religious Humanists: A Reader*, ed. Gregory Wolfe. New York: The Free Press, 1997.

Rushing, Janice. "Introduction to 'Evolution of 'the New Frontier' in *Alien* and *Aliens*: Patriarchal Cooptation of the Feminine Archetype," unpublished essay, September 1, 1993.

Ryan, Michael and Douglas Kellner, *Camera Politica: the Politics and Ideology of Contemporary Hollywood Film*. Bloomington: Indiana University Press, 1988.

Saylor, Gregory and Robert Detweiler, *Literature and Theology at Century's End*. Atlanta: Scholars Press, 1995.

Schaller, Lyle E. *The Seven-Day-A-Week Church*. Nashville: Abingdon, 1992.

Scheurer, T. E. "Goddesses and Golddiggers: Images of Women in Popular Music of the 1930s." *Journal of Popular Culture* 24, 1 (Summer 1990): 23–38.

Schmidt, Leigh Eric. *Consumer Rites: The Buying and Selling of American Holidays*. Princeton: Princeton University Press, 1995.

Schneider, Louis, and Sanford M. Dornbush, *Popular Religion: Inspirational Books in America*. Chicago: University of Chicago Press, 1958.

Schuller, Robert, interviewed by G. A. Pritchard in *Willow Creek Seeker Services*. Grand Rapids, MI: Baker Books, 1996: 50.

—*Your Church Has Real Possibilities!* Glendale, Calif: Regal, 1974.

Schultze, Quentin J., ed. *American Evangelicals and the Mass Media: Perspectives on the Relationship between American Evangelicals and the Mass Media*. Grand Rapids, MI: Zondervan, 1990.

—"The Invisible Medium: Evangelical Radio," in Quentin J. Schultze, ed., *American Evangelicals and the Mass Media: Perspectives on the Relationship between American Evangelicals and the Mass Media*. Grand Rapids, MI: Zondervan, 1990.

—*Winning Your Kids Back From the Media*. Westmount, IL: InterVarsity Press, 1994.

Scott, James C. *Domination and the Arts of Resistance: Hidden Transcripts*. New Haven: Yale University Press, 1990.

Sean, Jay, Jared Cotter and J-Remy. "2012 (It Ain't the End)." Jay Sean. OFM. August 3, 2010.

Simanton, Keith. "Terry Gilliam, La Jetée, and the Omega Man," 1996 Review.

Slaven, Julie. "Lights! Cameras! Religion!" *The Charlotte Observer* (Saturday, June 1, 1996) G1 and G4.

Smart, Ninian. *Beyond Ideology: Religion and the Future of Western Civilization*. San Francisco: Harper and Row, 1981.

Smith, Huston. *The World's Religions*. San Francisco: Harper, 1991.

Smith, Lee. *Black Mountain Breakdown*. New York: Ballantine Books, 1980, 1982.

—*The Christmas Letters: A Novella*. Chapel Hill: Algonquin Books, 1996.

—*The Devil's Dream*. New York: Ballantine, 1992, 1993.

—*Fair and Tender Ladies*. New York: Ballantine, 1988, 1989.

—*Oral History*. New York: Ballantine, 1983, 1984.

—*Saving Grace*. New York: G. Putnam's Sons, 1995.

—"Tongues of Fire," in *Me and My Baby View the Eclipse*. New York: Ballantine, 1990, 1991.

—in "Lee Smith: Interviewed by Nancy Parrish," *Appalachian Journal* 19 (Summer 1992): 394–401.

—interview with William Walsh in Linda Tate, Editor, *Conversations with Lee Smith*. Jackson, MI: University of Mississippi Press, 2001.

Smith, Michael. "Author LaHaye Sues 'Left Behind' Film Producers." *Christianity Today* 45 (April 23, 2001): 20.

Smith, Rebecca Godwin. "Gender Dynamics in the Fiction of Lee Smith: Examining Language and Narrative Strategies." Dissertation, University of North Carolina at Chapel Hill, 1993.

—"Writing, Singing, and Hearing a New Voice: Lee Smith's *The Devil's Dream*," *The Southern Quarterly* 32 (Winter 1994): 48–62.

Smith, Virginia A. "Between the Lines: Contemporary Southern Women Writers Gail Godwin, Bobbie Ann Mason, Lisa Alther, and Lee Smith." Dissertation, Pennsylvania State University, 1989.

—"Luminous Halos and Lawn Chairs: Lee Smith's *Me and My Baby View the Eclipse*," *The Southern Review* 27 (April 1991): 479–85.

Sommerville, C. John. *The Secularization of Early Modern England: From Religious Culture to Religious Faith*. New York: Oxford University Press, 1992.

Spadafora, David. "Secularization in British Thought, 1730–1789: Some Landmarks," in W. Warren Wagar, ed. *The Secular Mind*. New York: Oxford University Press, 1992.

Spencer, Jon Michael. American Academy of Religion, (November 25, 1996), New Orleans, Louisiana.

—*Blues and Evil*. Knoxville: The University of Tennessee Press, 1993.

Stark, Rodney, and William Sims Bainbridge, *The Future of Religion: Secularization, Revival and Cult Formation*. Berkeley: University of California Press, 1985.

Steinken, Ken. "Where No Ministry Has Gone Before: To Be More Effective Ministers, Five Iron

Frenzy Resists the Packaging of Christian Rock Bands." *Christianity Today* 43, 6 (May 24, 1999): 74–5.

Stewart, Randall. *American Literature and Christian Doctrine*. Baton Rouge: Louisiana State University Press, 1958.

Stock, Phyllis H. "Proudhon and Morale Independante: A Variation of French Secular Morality," in W. Warren Wagar, ed. *The Secular Mind: Transformations of Faith in Modern Europe*. New York: Holmes and Meier Publishers, 1982.

Storey, John. *An Introductory Guide to Cultural Theory and Popular Culture*. Athens: The University of Georgia Press, 1993.

Strick, Philip. "12 Monkeys," *Sight and Sound* 6, 4 (April 1996): 56.

Strobel, Lee. *Inside the Mind of Unchurched Harry and Mary: How to Reach Friends and Family Who Avoid God and the Church*. Grand Rapids, MI: Zondervan, 1993.

Surya Das, Lama. *Awakening to the Sacred: Creating a Spiritual Life From Scratch*. New York: Broadway Books, 1999.

Sylvan, Robin. "Burning Man and Rave Culture: A Pre-Millennial, Postmodern, Future Primitive Popular Religious Revival," American Academy of Religion Annual Meeting, November 1999, Boston, Massachusetts.

Tan, Amy. *The Hundred Secret Senses*. New York: G. P. Putnam's Sons, 1995.

—*The Kitchen God's Wife*. New York: Putnam, 1991.

Tate, Linda, ed. *Conversations with Lee Smith*. Jackson: University of Mississippi Press, 2001.

Teem, William M., IV. "Let Us Now Praise the Other: Women in Smith's Short Fiction." *Studies in the Literary Imagination* 27 (Fall 1994): 63–73.

Tennyson, G. B. and Edward E. Ericson, Jr., (eds),. *Religion and Modern Literature: Essays in Theory and Criticism*. Grand Rapids, MI: Eerdmans, 1975.

Thumma, Scott. "Exploring the Megachurch Phenomena: Their Characteristics and Cultural Context," Hartford Institute for Religion Research.

—*The Kingdom, the Power, and the Glory: Megachurches In Modern American Society*, dissertation, Emory University, 1996.

Titon, Jeff Todd. *Powerhouse for God: Speech, Chant, and Song in an Appalachian Baptist Church*. Austin: Univesity of Texas Press, 1988.

de Tocqueville, Alexis. *Democracy in America*. Chicago: University of Chicago Press, 2000.

Toynbee, Arnold. *An Historian's Approach to Religion*. New York: Oxford University Press, 1956.

Trickle, Phyllis. "Foreword," in Brian McLaren, *A Generous Orthodoxy*. Grand Rapids, MI: Zondervan, 2004.

Trueheart, Charles. "The Megachurch," *The Sunday Oregonian: Forum*, September 22, 1996: E 1.

Tschannen, Olivier. "The Secularization Paradigm: A Systematization." *Journal for the Scientific Study of Religion* 30, 4 (1991): 395–415.

Turner, Victor. *The Ritual Process: Structure and Anti-Structure*. Chicago: Aldine, 1969.

Tweed, Thomas and Stephen Prothero, *Asian Religion in America: A Documentary History*. New York: Oxford, 1999.

Underwood, Gloria Jan. "Blessings and Burdens: Memory in the Novels of Lee Smith." Dissertation, University of South Carolina, 1991.

Vahanian, Gabriel. *The Death of God: The Culture of Our Post-Christian Era*. New York: George Braziller, 1961.

Vanocur, Sander. "TV's Failed Promise." *Don't Just Do Something*. Santa Barbara: The Center for the Study of Democratic Institutions, 1972.

Vaughan, John N. *The Large Church: A Twentieth-Century Expression of the First-Century Church*. Grand Rapids, MI: Baker Book House, 1985.

Wagar, W. Warren, ed. *The Secular Mind: Transformations of Faith in Modern* Europe. New York: Holmes and Meier Publishers, 1982.

Wald, Gayle. "Just a Girl? Rock Music, Feminism, and the Cultural Construction of Female Youth." *Signs: Journal of Women in Culture and Society* 23, 3 (Spring 1998): 585–610.

Wald, Kenneth D. *Religion and Politics in the United States*. New York: St. Martin's Press, 1986.

Wall, James, quoting Steve Johnson, Chicago Tribune critic, in James Wall, "Viewing the Megachurch: Between and Gush and a Smirk." *Christian Century* 112: 10 (March 22, 1995): 315–16.

—"Viewing the Megachurch: Between a Gush and a Smirk." *Christian Century* 112, 10 (March 22, 1995): 315–16.

Wallis, Roy and Steve Bruce, "Secularization: The Orthodox Model," in Steve Bruce, ed. *Religion and Modernization: Sociologists and Historians Debate the Seculariation Thesis*. Oxford: Clarendon Press, 1992.

Walsh, William. "Interview," in *Conversations with Lee Smith*, ed. Linda Tate. Jackson: University of Mississippi Press, 2001.

Warner, Steven H. "Work in Progress Toward a New Paradigm for the Sociological Study of Religion in the United States." *American Journal of Sociology* 98, 5 (1993): 1044–93.

Weaver, Jann Cather. "Discerning the Religious Dimensions of Film: Toward a Visual Method Applied to *Dead Man Walking*," unpublished paper delivered at the 1996 American Academy of Religion Annual Conference, November 24, 1996, New Orleans.

Wector, Dixon. *The Saga of American Society: A Record of Social Aspiration, 1607–1937*. New York: C. Scribner's Sons, 1937.

Weekley, Jacqulyn, quoted in Julie Slaven, "Lights! Camera! Religion!," *The Charlotte Observer*, (Saturday, June 1, 1996), Section G1 and 4.

Wells, David. *Turning to God*. Grand Rapids, MI: Baker, 1989.

Wells, H. G. *The War of the Worlds*. London: William Heinemann, 1898.

Wesley, Debbie. "A New Way of Looking at an Old Story: Lee Smith's Portrait of Female Creativity." *Southern Literary Journal* 30, 1 (Fall 1997): 88–101.

White, James Emery. "Churches, Listen to the Unchurched." *The Charlotte Observer* (March 27, 1995), 7A.

—*Opening the Front Door: Worship and Church Growth*. Nashville: Convention Press, 1992.

Whitehead, Alfred North. *Process and Reality (corrected edn)*. David Ray Griffin and Donald W. Sherburne, (eds). New York: The Free Press, 1978.

Whitelock, Edward, and David Janssen. *Apocalypse Jukebox: The End of the World in American Popular Music*. Berkeley: Soft Skull Press, 2009.

Wieland, Lisa Cade. "Old Times Not Forgotten: Family and Storytelling in Twentieth-Century Southern Literature." Ph.D. dissertation, Marquette University, 1998.

Wiesel, Elie. *Night*. New York: Bantam, 1982.

Williams, David. "Worlds at War," *American Cinematographer* 77, 7 (July 1996): 32–42.

Williams, Donald E. "An Oceanic Odyssey," *American Cinematographer* 76, 8 (August 1995): 40–51.

Williams, Peter. *Popular Religion in America: Symbolic Change and the Modernization Process in Historical Perspective*. Englewood Cliffs, NJ: Prentice-Hall, 1980, 1989.

Willow Creek Association staff interview. August 13, 1996.

Wilson, Bryan, "Aspects of Secularization in the West." *Japanese Journal of Religious Studies* 3, 4 (December 1976): 259–76.

—"New Images of Christian Community," in *The Oxford History of Christianity*, ed. John McManners. Oxford: Oxford University Press, 1993.

Wilson, Bryan. "Secularization: The Inherited Model," in Phillip E. Hammond, ed. *The Sacred in a Secular Age: Toward Revision in the Scientific Study of Religion*. Berkeley: University of California Press, 1985.

Wojcik, Daniel. *The End of the World as We Know It: Faith, Fatalism, and Apocalypse in America*. New York: New York University Press, 1997.

Wolfe, Gregory, ed. *The New Religious Humanists: A Reader*. New York: Free Press, 1997.

Wright, Richard. *The Outsider*. New York: Harper and Row, 1953.

Yamane, David. "Secularization on Trial: In Defense of a Neosecularization Paradigm." *Journal for the Scientific Study of Religion* 36, 1 (1997): 109–22.

Yancey, Philip. *The Jesus I Never Knew*. Grand Rapids, MI: Zondervan Publishing House, 1995.

Ziolkowski, Eric. "History of Religions and the Study of Religion and Literature: Grounds for Alliance." *Literature and Theology: An International Journal of Religion, Theory and Culture* 12, 3 (September 1998): 305–25.

Zizek, Slavoj. *Interrogating the Real*. Rex Butler and Scott Stephens, (eds). London: Continuum, 2005.

Index

Page reference numbers in italics indicate a figure; an "n." indicates an endnote.